STANFIELD

Geoffrey Stevens

STANFIELD

Geoffrey Stevens

McClelland and Stewart Limited

For my wife, Dannie.

0-7710-8358-0

The Canadian Publishers
McClelland and Stewart Limited
25 Hollinger Road, Toronto

PRINTED AND BOUND IN CANADA

Contents

Preface

This book was born of frustration. On October 30, 1972, the voters very nearly elected Robert Lorne Stanfield as Prime Minister of Canada. As a reporter in Ottawa, I had covered Mr. Stanfield ever since he became a candidate for the national leadership of the Progressive Conservative Party in the summer of 1967. I assumed, without having given the question much thought, that I knew a fair amount about this engaging, yet somehow remote politician. It was only when I began to try to picture him in the context of Prime Minister that I realized how very little I knew about him. Although Mr. Stanfield had been playing on the public stage for nearly a quarter of a century, very little of substance had ever been written about him. It struck me then that others might share my curiosity. This book is simply one reporter's view of a man who today stands within reach of the most important office in the land.

Any political reporter who sets out to write a book about an active politician leaves himself open to a charge of bias, and I should declare mine at the outset. I am not a Conservative and feel in no peril of ever becoming one. I do, however, like and respect Mr. Stanfield. I suspect he might make an exceptionally capable Prime Minister, although I have some reservations about the depth and ability of a number of the people who would inevitably be ministers in a Stanfield administration.

I am deeply grateful to many people without whose assistance this book could not have been written. I thank my former employers at *Time* who gave me access to their files, and particularly John Scott, the former Editor of *Time Canada,* for his encouragement, and Murray J. Gart, Chief of Correspondents, who arranged a leave of absence from my duties in the Ottawa Bureau to write the manuscript. Dozens of others – friends, acquaintances, and enemies of Robert Stanfiled – gave generously of their time to answer my questions, including Rod Black, Dick Donahoe, Joe Clarke, Innis MacLeod, J.W.E. Mingo, Bob Manuge, Senator Henry Hicks, Peter Nicholson, and Premier Gerald Regan, in Halifax; Ken Matthews, G.I. Smith, and Charles Stanfield, in Truro, N.S.; Frank Sobey, in Stellarton, N.S.; Russell Maxwell, in Wolfville, N.S.; Lowell Murray and Brian Mulroney, in Montreal; Philip Elman, in Washington; Dalton Camp and Norman Atkins, in Toronto; Flora MacDonald, in Kingston; Mary Stanfield, Finlay MacDonald, Senators Fred Blois and Grattan O'Leary, Gordon Fairweather, Heath Macquarrie, and Claude Wagner, in Ottawa. I owe a special vote of thanks to four people: Eric Dennis, in Halifax, who kindly permitted me to use notes and clippings that he had amassed over the years as a reporter covering Mr. Stanfield's career; Peter Scargall, of Markham, Ontario, without whose advice and editing skill this book would not have been possible; Graham Scott, executive assistant to Mr. Stanfield, who opened doors that would otherwise have remained closed to me; and, above all, Robert Stanfield who patiently answered hundreds of questions without once asking what I proposed to write about him.

All judgments in this book are mine alone. And so, of course, are all omissions and errors.

G.S.

1

The Anti-Hero

Question: *"Mr Stanfield, I want to ask you this: why is a fine man like yourself, who is wealthy with a lovely family and now a grandchild, bothering his head running for a thankless job like Prime Minister of Canada?"*

Robert L. Stanfield: *"Well, I guess you have to be a little crazy, ma'am. It helps a little anyway."*

– from a Toronto open-line radio show, March, 1972.

Had it been the Liberal Party, there would have been a brass band, a fleet of black limousines, a phalanx of plain-clothes Mounties, and a few thousand exhuberant supporters on hand to pay appropriate homage to the returning hero. The Liberals are accustomed to success. They know how to celebrate it. Canada's Progressive Conservatives so rarely have a hero to cheer, however, that no one could seriously fault them for not staging a more spectacular reception. And although few of the travellers hurrying through Uplands Airport in Ottawa on Halloween, 1972 even noticed the ragged little demonstration down by the baggage carrousels at the far end of the terminal, it was a victory celebration all the same.

Robert Lorne Stanfield, the national leader of the Conservative Party, was returning to the capital just twenty-four hours after he had humbled the mighty Liberals in the country's twenty-ninth general election. It appeared at that moment as though Stanfield was destined to replace Pierre Elliott Trudeau as Prime Minister of Canada. Not for several days would Stanfield and his party, like everyone else in the country, realize that although the Liberals had lost the election the Tories had not won it.

Because it was busy that evening at Uplands, Stanfield's chartered Air Canada DC-9 jetliner from Halifax was ordered to a parking place far away from the main concourse of the terminal. Stanfield came down the front ramp and, like a man whose fate it was to be forever landing at strange airports in widely-scattered parts of the country, he peered about in momentary confusion. Then he walked slowly and wearily into the airport through a baggage door.

It was an incongruous yet fitting arrival for the most unassuming man in Canadian public life, a politician who had weathered with grace, if not enjoyment, the frenzied hoopla of the just-completed election campaign. For the first time in seven weeks, there was – to his relief – no band to herald his arrival. There were no flags and no banners. There were no pretty "Stanfield Girls" in their eye-catching red and blue uniforms to lead the cheers, no local dignitaries to seize his hand and to invite him to make a speech to the waiting throng.

There were only about fifty people milling about in the baggage room, many of them workers from the party's national headquarters; their faces betrayed the fatigue of the long, hard campaign. They broke into a tentative, self-conscious cheer as he came through the door. A few carried crudely-lettered placards, obviously made in great haste. "Welcome Home, Mr. P.M.," read one. "You're Top Banana, Bob," proclaimed a second. A third optimistically predicted: "It's Our Future." Peter Reilly and Walter Baker, two Tories who had unseated Liberals in Ottawa constituencies the day before, rushed forward carrying a large cardboard skeleton key, meant to symbolize the keys to 24 Sussex Drive, the official residence of the Prime Minister. Mustering a thin smile, Stanfield accepted the key, shook a few hands, then wandered toward his waiting car, pausing for a few seconds to talk to a knot of newsmen. "I hope the election will produce good results for the people of Canada," he said. He sounded doubtful.

There was good reason for his doubt. The election of October 30, 1972 had been the most perplexing in Canadian history. Despite the most strenuous, most expensive, and best publicized campaign ever, the voters had been unable to reach a verdict. Pierre Trudeau had led a strong majority Liberal government into the campaign, convinced that the election was nothing more than a formality that he had to observe before he could embark on another four years of majority Liberal rule. He came out of the election with his proud party in tatters, still awesomely powerful in French Canada but repudiated across English Canada. Robert Stanfield had led the disorganized dregs of the party that had been raised to power and destroyed by John Diefenbaker into an election that virtually no one, including the Tories, gave him any chance of winning. He emerged triumphant in English Canada and denied once again in French Canada.

Liberals would argue later that they had failed to carry the election because they had tried to do too much too quickly under Trudeau's leadership. They would contend that English Canada had turned against them because the Prime Minister and his administration were too French and had been too diligent in their efforts to assure French Canadians of their rightful place in Confederation. Those arguments would be more self-serving than accurate. The Liberals had swept Quebec partly because of the woeful inadequacy of the Conservatives in that province. They had lost in the other nine provinces because the voters wanted to register a protest, and because they decided the Tories were an acceptable alternative. In the minds of these voters, Trudeau had failed to live up to the bold expectations he had created in 1968. They did not like his attitude or his style. They did not like what they considered to be his arrogance and his indifference to their problems. They felt he had lost contact with the people. They concluded that the Trudeau years had been wasted years.

Although the country had voted *against* Trudeau, it had not voted *for* Stanfield. As had happened on other pivotal occasions in his career, Stanfield had succeeded in large measure through the default of his opposition. That was what had happened in Southern Ontario, on the Prairies, and in British Columbia. In Quebec, the protest vote had gone not to the Conservatives, but to Réal Caouette's Social Credit Party. The Tories managed to win only two of Quebec's seventy-four seats; there were some who said they were lucky to have done even that well.

Still, when Canadians went to bed on election night, amazed and confused by what they had done, it seemed as though Robert Stanfield had won the election. The voters had apparently elected one hundred and eight Conservatives to one hundred and seven Liberals in the two hundred and sixty-four seat House of Commons. But the results were desperately close in many constituencies; until the official counts and recounts were completed, no one would know for certain which party had elected the most Members. When all the tabulations were finally and officially completed a few weeks later, the Liberals stood on top with one hundred and nine Members to the Conservatives' one hundred and seven.

By that time, however, the precise distribution of seats had become almost irrelevant. Trudeau had decided to remain in office. He would meet Parliament and, if he could secure the confidence of the Commons, he would govern until defeated or until he judged the moment propitious to call another election. His fate was not in Stanfield's hands. The New Democratic Party's thirty-one Members of Parliament held the balance of power, and they chose to use their power to hold the Liberals in office rather than to turn the country over to the Conservatives. They realized that they could more readily win acceptance of their policy objectives from a seriously weakened Liberal administration than they could from a renascent Conservative party. The Liberal-N.D.P. marriage of convenience was consummated within a week of the opening of the Twenty-Ninth Parliament.

All that – Trudeau's decision to remain in office, the N.D.P.'s decision to keep him there for the time being, and the first confidence votes in the Twenty-Ninth Parliament – was in the future as Robert Stanfield flew back to Ottawa and headed downtown for a nationally-televised press conference. There he staked out the basic strategy he would follow in the coming weeks. He called on the Government to resign on the ground that it had lost the confidence of the people. He declared himself ready to form a government if the Governor General were to call on him to do so. He pledged himself to the defeat of the Government if it tried to continue in office, but he also promised to support any useful legislation advanced by the Government to deal with fundamental Canadian problems. It was one of the most impressive performances of his long political career.

In the weeks and months that followed, he attempted, with mixed success, to balance the demands of his impatient caucus that he exploit every opportunity to bring down the Liberal Government against the growing desire of the public to make the minority Parliament work. He tried to keep pressure on the Government without appearing to be an obstructionist, a course that could not fully satisfy either his supporters or his opponents. Mostly, he waited – biding his time for an opportunity to move against the Government.

Although the election had shed more confusion than enlightenment on the political landscape, a few facts stood out with striking clarity, like snow-clad peaks against a darkening sky. Robert Stanfield had been the beneficiary, if not the engineer, of an electoral upset of near epic proportions. Another election could not be long postponed if the country were to have a government that could give leadership without having to barter for opposition support on every measure it submitted to Parliament. The political momentum was in Stanfield's direction and, if he could channel it to his purposes, he would follow three earlier Nova Scotia Conservatives (Sir John Sparrow Thompson, Sir Charles Tupper, and Sir Robert Borden) into office as Prime Minister of Canada.

The thought of Robert Stanfield becoming Prime Minister took a little getting used to. Few Canadians had ever seriously thought of him in that role. They did not think of him as a Prime Minister in his first federal election in 1968 because they knew he would not win; that was the year in which Canadians had abandoned the traumatic, exhausting political era of John Diefenbaker and Lester Pearson for the dramatic, exhilarating age of Pierre Trudeau. They did not think of Stanfield as Prime Minister in 1972 because they assumed – without giving the matter more than passing thought – that he could not win.

4

Suddenly, as they watched the election results flash onto their television screens on October 30, Canadians realized that they were on the verge of electing to the highest office in the land a man whom they did not understand and about whom they knew very little.

Who is Robert Stanfield? Who is this quiet, self-contained Nova Scotian whom one of his most ardent admirers, Senator Grattan O'Leary, calls "the most liberal, humane, and civilized mind on our political landscape"? It's a question that should not have to be asked about any leader who has spent a quarter-century in public life. But in Stanfield's case, the question is not only relevant but necessary. He is the man nobody really knows. He is as baffling to his friends as he is to the general public. What does he stand for? What drives him? What are the ingredients in his public and private personalities that have made him one of the country's most successful politicians? Why does he want to be the Prime Minister of Canada?

There are no quick, facile answers to anything about Stanfield. At first glance, he is an open book, seemingly the most uncomplicated and straightforward of political men; on closer reading, he is a man of considerable depth who defies superficial analysis. He is a complex political animal, pushed and pulled by forces that fluctuate wildly in both intensity and direction. He is, for example, a man who longs to lead a quiet, unostentatious life – and his private lifestyle mirrors that desire – yet he chose to live his life in politics, which he knew could be neither quiet nor unostentatious. He recoils at the suggestion that he is an ambitious man; as he puts it, "I've never been aware of any craving for power or authority." But his whole career shows him to be a man of suppressed ambition, an over-achiever who willingly accepts challenges that are seemingly far beyond his capabilities, then confounds the sceptics by overcoming them. Most of his friends insist that he is a man of great personal loyalty, a man to whom ruthlessness is a totally alien attribute. Yet, on occasion, he has been ruthless, sometimes at the expense of friends whom he has left to fend for themselves when a word from him would have rescued them. Although he is often accused of being indecisive, he has pursued his objectives with unwavering determination throughout his career. He is said to be an inept politician, yet his successes have been large, and most of his setbacks small.

He is the most improbable of politicians. In 1969, shortly after stepping down as Prime Minister of Northern Ireland, Terence O'Neill met Robert Stanfield for the first time. This is his impression, as he wrote it in his autobiography: "If ever one of nature's gentlemen strayed into politics, the name of that man is Stanfield."

The Stanfield enigma was succinctly stated by John Aitken in an article in *Maclean's Magazine* in May of 1972:

"Stanfield . . . is in many ways a more interesting politician than Trudeau. He bristles with paradox. He invokes trust in an age that prefers excitement and acceleration. He is humble and we consider humility to be embarrassing. He is diffident and that quality, in this political decade, is catastrophic. . . . Stanfield has failed the public, simply by being what he is – an insuperably reticent man who holds an office in which reticence is no virtue."

Stanfield is not the sort of man to spend much time in self-analysis and he becomes inarticulate when he tries to unravel his own motivation. Usually, when someone asks him why he wants to be Prime Minister, he shrugs the question aside by laughing that he is probably a trifle crazy. He does not deny, however, that he wants to be Prime Minister and that he wants the job badly. Although he says he wants the job only on his own terms, he is far from clear what his terms are or what he desires to accomplish as Prime Minister.

Relaxing in his shirtsleeves in his House of Commons office four months after the 1972 election, the weak winter sun filtering through the windows to glance off his bald head, he tried to put into words his reasons for pursuing political power. "My priorities are basically the same as they were when I came up here in 1967," he said slowly. "There's the problem of national unity and strengthening the country and making progress toward just living together a little more satisfactorily. When I first came to Ottawa, I thought of it mainly in terms of a French-speaking, English-speaking problem, but obviously regional differences are important. The West, as I discovered, has its own axe to grind, as I had one to grind when I came here from Nova Scotia. Cutting down at least on regional disparity was an important consideration with me then, and still is. I think I would put national unity and regional disparity at the top of my list, plus the general matter of getting rid of poverty so that people have something like equality of opportunity. . . . This may sound corny, but I want to encourage people to sort of fulfil themselves; in other words, we not only need to have a country that is diverse in terms of space and regions and also cultures, but we need also to have more tolerance and respect for people who are different. Perhaps I could put it in terms of more enlightenment."

If that bit of thinking aloud fails to clarify the Stanfield approach to national leadership, it is because Stanfield has tremendous difficulty in articulating – although not in understanding – the elusive specifics of power. Anyone who has ever listened while Stanfield attempted to explain something as prosaic as a Conservative program or policy will attest that he frequently spreads more mystery than revelation. Examination of his life and his career may reveal the sort of man he is, but it can answer only partially the persistent question: What makes Stanfield run? No one, not even those who have known him longest and best, professes to have a complete answer. That's scarcely surprising, because Stanfield himself does not know either.

Had he been born into other, less fortunate circumstances, he would have escaped a life in politics – a loss he would not have mourned. The third son of the second son of the founder of a prosperous family textile business in Truro, Robert Stanfield was, like Pierre Trudeau, spared the necessity of ever having to work merely to make a living. His father died when he was seventeen, leaving Robert $350,000, which he inherited on his twenty-fifth birthday. As prudent in personal finances as he is in politics, Stanfield salted his inheritance away, much of it in blue-chip stocks, and it grew steadily, if not spectacularly. He has given a great deal of money away over the years, on occasion writing a cheque to one of his favourite causes, such as Dalhousie University in Halifax, that exceeds his annual salary as a Member of Parliament. Today, after settling generous amounts on his four children, he is worth a little less than one million dollars. A man with little interest in the possessions and power that money can buy, he is ambivalent about his wealth. He is happy to have it, but would not be particularly distressed if it disappeared tomorrow. "Inherited money is not necessarily a good thing for a person," he says. "But I won't pretend to be anything but grateful, particularly because of the independence it has given me. It has meant doing things I wanted to do, rather than what I had to do to stay alive." He pauses for a moment, then a grin splits his doleful features: "And therein lies happiness."

It was his money that got him into politics in the first place. Because he had a private income more than adequate to support his family, he chose not to practise law or work in one of the Stanfield family enterprises. He felt he could afford, instead, to devote his full time and energies to the restoration of the two-party system in Nova Scotia. He took over the provincial Conservative Party at a time when it had no seats at all in the Legislature and, or so it seemed, precious little chance of winning any. He dedicated eight years to the rebuilding of his party before he finally became Premier of Nova Scotia. In his eleven years as premier, he established a political hold on his people that few provincial leaders could rival. Concluding that he had exhausted the challenges of provincial politics, he sought and won the federal Conservative leadership in 1967. He set about reviving the dissension-wracked national party with the same patient, unswerving determination that he had displayed in breathing life into the Nova Scotia party two decades earlier. He began to turn the federal party into a respectable, mildly progressive political organization that could appeal not only to traditional Conservative voters – the elderly and the rural – but also to the young and to the city-dwellers who had been turning in ever increasing numbers to the Liberal Party. That work was far from finished when the election of 1972 intervened, but it was far enough advanced to carry Stanfield to the threshold of victory.

His friends delight in speculating on the sort of Prime Minister he would make. In the opinion of Dalton Camp, the Toronto commentator and political adviser who understands him better than almost anyone else, Stanfield's unusual qualities would make him an intriguing head of government. "I don't think he would be socialized or proselytized," says Camp. "I think he'd look the job square in the eye. I think he'd have a very uncluttered approach to public business. It would be marvellous to see what would happen if you had someone as Prime Minister who didn't have any vanity. I'm not saying he doesn't have ego, but he has no small vanities. He reads favourable press and negative press with exactly the same expression on his face, because what he wants to do is to learn from reading it. He's not a blood-letter or vengeance-seeker or somebody trying to even a score. There's nobody to get even with; nobody to elevate. He just wants to do the job."

As Prime Minister, Stanfield would be the same as he has been as leader of the Opposition. He would be calm, reflective, intelligent, and humane. He would not be given to brilliant insights or eloquent visions of Canada's future; neither, however, would he be given to outbursts of temperament or flights of empty fancy. He would be patient, tenacious, serious, and, above all, stable. He would bring calm good sense to the never-ending search for solutions to the two most urgent problems of Confederation – national unity and regional disparity.

Those problems may well be beyond the ability of any politician to solve, but Stanfield is better equipped than most to meet the challenges they pose. Despite his party's failure to establish any sort of a political base in the province of Quebec, no politician in the country harbours greater goodwill toward French Canada than Robert Stanfield. Throughout his years as Premier of Nova Scotia, he acted as his own minister of education; in that capacity, he made a sincere (and at least partly successful) attempt to improve the quality of education available to French-speaking Nova Scotians. While Premier, Stanfield spoke out frequently and earnestly of the need for English Canadians to support French-speaking Canadians in their struggle to preserve and advance their language and culture. It is one of the sad ironies of Canadian politics that, although Stanfield has been absolutely consistent throughout his career in his support for French Canada, he has been unable to convince French Canada that the Conservative Party is no longer antithetical to the aspirations of her people.

Stanfield blames himself more than anyone or anything else for his party's inability to persuade French Canadians of its goodwill. Following the election of 1972, he set about to build the Conservative Party in Quebec in the only way he knows how – slowly and painstakingly, from the ground up.

As Prime Minister, Stanfield would not differ significantly from Trudeau on the question of the formal constitutional ties that bind Quebec to the rest of Canada. Both are dedicated federalists and Stanfield is committed to the main tenets of the constitutional reform process begun under Lester Pearson and carried forward by Trudeau until the collapse of the Victoria Charter in 1971. Where Stanfield and Trudeau differ most markedly is in their approach to the administrative or working arrangements that ought to be adopted under the Constitution to govern dealings between Ottawa and the provinces. When it comes to giving the provinces greater autonomy Stanfield is flexible. Where Trudeau takes the view that concessions to Quebec would whet the appetite of Quebec nationalists, Stanfield argues that there can be no lasting harmony in the country as long as the federal government insists on concentrating political and economic power in Ottawa. He would allow all ten provinces – not just Quebec – to opt out of federal programs in fields equally or better suited to provincial administration; he would transfer federal tax points to the provinces to enable them to finance these programs. "While I think there is a role for the federal government in, for example, the field of health,"says Stanfield, "I would say that if the federal government is not prepared to be an equal partner in the costs, it makes much more sense to let the provinces out and turn over tax points with full equalization. I really find it very difficult to understand the reluctance of the Trudeau government to go along with that. I think it must be based upon what Mr. Trudeau has said so often about how a Member of Parliament from Quebec coming to Ottawa has to appear back home to be important. He has to be involved in social welfare programs; otherwise, the people of Quebec would look to Quebec City for leadership. I think there are so many reasons why they have to look to Ottawa for a variety of things that there doesn't seem to me to be any excuse for the federal government to try to maintain this degree of centralization, particularly when the provinces want to get out of it."

If for no other reason than because he spent nineteen years of his life in provincial politics, Stanfield is an advocate of provincial rights in such areas of federal-provincial concern as social welfare and the elimination of regional disparity. The federal government, in his view, has an obligation to assist the provinces to solve their problems, but not to impose solutions from Ottawa. He makes almost a fetish of the need for ample prior consultation with the provinces before the commencement of any new federal policy.

"I believe," he says, "that the Trudeau government has made formidable use of the federal spending power, and I think this is developing more and more reaction in the provinces, particularly in Quebec. I would exercise much more restraint in the use of constitutional powers and would not be quite so hipped on centralization."

Paradoxically, the attributes that would be most appealing in Stanfield as Prime Minister are not his political attributes but his personal qualities. He is unassertive, unassuming, and totally without pretension. Every morning, the driver-messenger from his House of Commons office picks him up at his home and drives him halfway to Parliament Hill. Stanfield hops out on Sussex Drive and walks alone for the last mile or so, simply because he likes walking and because all his life he has walked to work. Sometimes he drives his aides to distraction. They have learned that if they rent a limousine to transport him to an official function, he will probably refuse to ride in it, preferring to walk if the distance is not too great. They know he will refuse to move into a suite in a hotel if, as happened in Montreal in late 1972, the hotel inadvertently books him into a single room with an uncomfortable bed that folds into the wall. ("I had this horrible premonition," says a Stanfield assistant, "that I would come in in the morning and find no Stanfield – just a tangle of arms and legs sticking out of the wall. But he wouldn't let me get him a room with a proper bed. He's like that.")

Stanfield is also a genuinely funny man, but his humour is so wry and so self-deprecating that it is lost on large public gatherings. He would far rather laugh at himself than at others. He is fond, for example, of talking about his struggle to learn to speak French and the immersion courses he has taken. He often ends these accounts with the observation that what he really needs is an immersion course in English. He also has a highly developed sense of the absurd. Finlay MacDonald, Stanfield's chief of staff, likes to tell the story of a dinner party in Halifax where the host left the liquor out on a table so that his guests could help themselves before dinner. Stanfield finished his first drink and wandered up to the table to help himself to a second Scotch and water. He poured three fingers of Scotch, then filled his glass from a pitcher of clear liquid. Returning to the sofa, he sipped the drink thoughtfully. When MacDonald went to pour himself another drink a few minutes later, he was startled by the reduced level of the gin in the pitcher. He looked suspiciously at Stanfield's nearly-empty glass. "Did you just drink a Scotch and gin?" MacDonald spluttered. Stanfield looked amused. "You know," he said, "I thought it was rather strange, but I was just getting to like it."

Conservatives despair of ever being able to convey to the country the *real* Robert Stanfield – or, at least, the Robert Stanfield they see at the office and at home. They concede that the public has no perception of what he would be like as Prime Minister. Stanfield seems to have no clear public image at all. He is a remarkably self-sufficient man, but his self-sufficiency is not projected as firmness or aggressiveness. At times, he seems almost defence-less. He also has a sense of fatalism that is often mistaken for a lack of ambition. Probably no other political leader who aspired to high office would have made the admission that Stanfield made to his Quebec lieuten-ant, Claude Wagner, in 1972. "I'm fifty-eight years old," Stanfield said. "I've got money in the bank. I've been Premier of Nova Scotia for eleven years. I've been the leader of Her Majesty's Loyal Opposition. I'm not going to cry if that's the way I go out."

Anyone who knows Stanfield well insists that it is true: Stanfield is prepared to work as hard as is necessary to become Prime Minister, but he would not be devastated if he did not make it. He will listen to advice on ways to improve his chances, but he will not change the man that he is. He insists on being himself, regardless of the opinion of his party or the public. But his personality is so unabrasive and so uncompelling that it is difficult for the public, which sees him only through the mass media or at a distance in election campaigns, to form any firm opinion of him. He is like a rock that has been worn smooth by the waves. There are no sharp corners or jagged edges for the public to seize hold of. Just when someone thinks he has grasped the essential Stanfield, the man slips away.

Even the members of his caucus in Ottawa who think they know him well find him elusive. They know him to be a man of considerable dignity, a man who never decends to vulgar language, a man whose words and actions are so utterly predictable as to preclude any element of surprise. Yet every now and again, Stanfield surprises them. He did at a caucus meeting following the 1972 election. He was busy that day and, impatiently brushing aside further discussion by his M.P.s, he said he had to leave to tend to other business. As he left, he turned and fired a parting shot: "As C.D. Howe once said, 'Today I'm busier'n a whore working two beds.'"

He left them with their mouths hanging open.

2

The Stanfields (1855-)

Stanfield's Creed:

To build a business that will never know completion;
to satisfactorily serve every person with whom we have relations;
to create a personality that will always be known for its fairness,
honesty, strength, and friendliness.

– Frank Stanfield, Sr., 1922.

Supposedly, one of the necessary attributes of any successful politician is the ability to make a favourable and unforgettable first impression on the people he meets on the street, in the meeting hall or, today, in the living-room through television. If that were really so, however, Robert Stanfield would still be back in Halifax, half-heartedly practising law on Hollis Street or perhaps teaching Economics at Dalhousie University. Few of the people who became his closest advisers and most ardent supporters in politics – men such as Rod Black, Ike Smith, Dick Donahoe, and Finlay MacDonald – can recall the first time that they met Bob Stanfield. Even Mary Stanfield, who might reasonably be expected to remember and cherish such an auspicious moment, has no clear recollection of the occasion on which she was first introduced to her future husband. She does recall, though, that when she eventually did become aware of his existence, she tried to avoid him. He was shy, ill at ease, and clearly unable to make the sort of engaging small talk that would have interested a lively young woman such as Mary Hall.

This does not mean that Nova Scotians did not know *who* Bob Stanfield was, but it does suggest that he was the most forgetable member of an unforgetable family. "Stanfield" was a household name in Nova Scotia in the early decades of the twentieth century. In their own, quite different way, the Stanfields were to their province what the Kennedys would later become to Massachusetts. The Stanfields dominated the commercial and community life of Truro and Colchester County; they were known across the province for their business enterprise and their good works. And, of course, they were very political and very faithful Conservatives. People around Truro were fond of claiming that the Stanfields had held every office in the province from dog catcher to lieutenant-governor (although there is no evidence to confirm that any Stanfield ever attained or sought the first-mentioned office!). In any event, by the time Bob Stanfield finally began to show a glimmer of interest in politics, the Stanfields were well on their way to becoming the first family of the Progressive Conservative Party in a province that seemed destined to be ruled until Eternity, and quite possibly beyond, by the Liberal Party.

Stanfield's paternal grandfather was Charles Edward Stanfield, a York-shireman who founded the family textile business in Truro; his maternal grandfather was D. J. Thomas, a Welshman and prosperous coal merchant in Truro. Charles Stanfield's second son, Frank, Sr., married D.J. Thomas' eldest daughter, Sarah Emma, and they produced five children. The fourth of those children was Robert Lorne Stanfield.

D.J. Thomas established himself in Truro in the nineteenth century. He displayed many of the same traits as his friends, the Stanfields: he was shrewd in business, active in the affairs of his community, an ardent Tory, and stubborn to the point of intransigence on matters of principle. By the last decade of the century, he was mayor of Truro, and, by all accounts, he was an intensely partisan politician, given to strong opinions and not at all reluctant to express them openly and forcefully. That's why he got into the trouble he did.

A man by the name of Frederick Andrew Laurence was recorder of the town of Truro at the time. Laurence was also, to D.J. Thomas' annoyance, a Liberal and a member of the Legislative Assembly in Halifax. In 1892, the Assembly passed a bill to increase Laurence's salary as recorder of Truro, an action that infuriated Mayor Thomas and his council. The council charged Laurence with misbehaviour for having promoted the increase of his own salary. Mayor Thomas signed and published a petition containing this allegation. Laurence retaliated by introducing in the Assembly a resolution that accused Thomas of violating the privileges of the Assembly by libelling one of its members – namely himself. The Assembly, under the firm control of Premier W.S. Fielding's Liberals, quickly approved the resolution and Thomas was summoned to the Bar of the Assembly where he argued that his actions had not been libellous and had been taken in good faith in his capacity as Mayor. Ordered to withdraw from the chamber while the Members debated his punishment, Thomas refused to wait in Province House (the seat of the provincial government). He left Halifax and travelled to Debert, a village about eight miles west of Truro, to visit his wife's family. The Assembly sent the sergeant-at-arms after him; Thomas was led back to Halifax where the Assembly sentenced him to forty-eight hours in the "common gaol of Halifax." His wife, who must have shared his political convictions, loyally joined him in his cell where they remained until Thomas secured a writ of habeas corpus from the Supreme Court of Nova Scotia.

Had he been less partisan or less stubborn, Thomas might have let the matter drop. But two days after his release from jail, he sued Premier Fielding, and the other Liberals who had voted to imprison him, for unlawful assault and imprisonment. The Assembly hastily passed a special act of indemnity retroactively protecting its members against lawsuits. When the suit came to court, the judge dismissed Thomas' action against those Members of the Assembly who had pleaded the protection of the special act. But he awarded Thomas two hundred dollars damages from the rest of the defendants who had argued simply that the Assembly had the constitutional authority to punish for libel against its members. The Liberal government carried the case all the way to the Imperial Privy Council in London, and Thomas, not about to be intimidated, hired one of the most famous Liberals in Canada to prepare his case, Edward Blake, the former premier of Ontario and former national leader of the Liberal Party. The seven distinguished jurists who heard the appeal must have been amused by the tenacity of the little coal dealer from an obscure corner of Victoria's realm. Sternly, they put an end to the dispute. They ruled that, although the British North America Act of 1867 had not specifically given the Nova Scotia Assembly the powers it had exercised against Thomas, the Assembly possessed those powers because it had been in existence before Confederation. Its prerogatives and privileges flowed from Westminster, not from Ottawa. The Privy Council overturned the two hundred dollar damage award to Thomas and ordered him to pay the provincial government's legal costs.

The story of Mayor Thomas' political woes is more than merely a revealing footnote on the determined character of Bob Stanfield's maternal grandfather – a determination inherited by the grandson. *Fielding vs. Thomas* became a landmark case in establishing the powers and privileges of provincial legislatures. It is still studied by law students in some universities.

The unhappy outcome of the lawsuit did not discourage the Thomas family nor adversely affect its standing in Truro. "I have an uncle by marriage," says Bob Stanfield, "who told people the only reason my grandfather lost the case was because the Privy Council couldn't read Blake's handwriting." One of D.J. Thomas' sons, George, went on to become Mayor of Truro and a Member of the Nova Scotia Legislature. D.J. Thomas' eldest daughter landed the most eligible bachelor in town, Frank Stanfield, Sr., the second son of Charles Edward Stanfield.

Charles Edward Stanfield, the patriarch of the Stanfield family (and Bob Stanfield's other grandfather), had immigrated to North America in 1855 from Bradford in England where he had learned the wool business as an apprentice in an uncle's mill. Charles Stanfield's first stop was Philadelphia where, soon after his arrival, he met a shipowner from Prince Edward Island who told the young Englishman that there were no woollen mills on the island. Intrigued, Charles Stanfield sailed to P.E.I. to explore the business opportunities there. He settled in the tiny community of Tryon where, with a small stake from his uncle in England, he established the Tryon Woollen Mills. Although he stayed in Tryon only ten years, he demonstrated the initiative and business acumen that were to become characteristic of all the Stanfields. He soon owned, in addition to the woollen mill, a tannery, a general store, a hat factory, and a farm. He also found time to woo and wed Lydia Dawson, the grand-daughter of a colonel in the Irish Guards.

In 1866, Charles sold out his business interests to Samuel Dawson, his partner and brother-in-law, and, after paying his outstanding debts, he had eleven thousand dollars in cash with which to establish new businesses elsewhere. He chose Truro, a small but attractive town on the Salmon River in central Nova Scotia, about sixty miles north of Halifax. Truro's most appealing feature to Charles Stanfield was probably its location on the Intercolonial Railway that linked the Maritimes with the expanding markets of central Canada.

Charles Stanfield was clearly a man who knew how to stretch a dollar. With his eleven thousand dollars, he built a large house for his family on Dominion Street in Truro, the Truro Felt Hat Works, the St. Croix Woollen Mills in St. Croix, and the Union Woollen Mills in Farnham.

Of all the Stanfields, Robert Stanfield probably resembles his grandfather Charles more than any of the others. Charles built up his businesses with the same slow determination and unswerving attention to detail that his grandson was to exhibit eighty years later in rebuilding the shattered Conservative Party of Nova Scotia. Like Bob, Charles Stanfield was not a man to spend money rashly. When he was building his house on Dominion Street, he noticed with interest that large quantities of steam generated by a laundry two blocks away were simply going to waste. So he made a deal with the owner of the laundry; he rigged up an underground pipeline and heated his new home with the excess steam. Everything was fine until the laundry owner, much impressed with this innovation, decided to cut his own home into the steam line. The boiler could not produce enough steam for two houses and Charles Stanfield was forced, reluctantly, to install a furnace in his basement.

A lonely man with few close friends, Charles Stanfield also passed on to his grandson a love of long walks (although some of Bob Stanfield's friends wish that when he invites them to go walking he would choose some place for his strolls other than Ottawa's Beechwood Cemetery). Like his grandson, Charles Stanfield had a highly developed sense of privacy, but no politician, not even a Stanfield, could carry privacy to the extreme he did. Charles Stanfield even refused to be photographed and no picture of him exists.

One of Charles Stanfield's greatest assets was his genius with machinery. He spent much of his time puttering in the workshop behind his house, designing new machinery, modifying the old or turning out hard-to-get replacement parts. In those days, his principal product was heavy woollen cloth for suits; he also produced the first cardigans and the first heavy-rib underwear in Canada. Local legend has it that it was Charles Stanfield who invented the "trap door" in men's long underwear. If he did, he neglected to patent his invention. If he did not, he was certainly the first manufacturer in Canada to produce woollies with "drop-seats." In either case, he earned the gratitude of the millions of Canadian males who have had to wrestle with long underwear.

He did invent a product called stockinet. Stockinet was simply a continuous roll of woollen cloth produced as a tube. All the shopkeeper had to do was to cut off the desired length. The lady of the house then either sewed up the toe to make an instant sock or, if she were more ambitious, knitted a foot to be attached to the stockinet. Not very stylish or comfortable perhaps, but warm and inexpensive. By all accounts, it wore like iron.

Charles and Lydia Stanfield produced eleven children, some of whom did not survive infancy. They created such a clamour around the house that Charles Stanfield was frequently driven to seek the peace of his workshop or walk in the open countryside. "It's the only time I get to think with that houseful of children," he once complained. Three times every Sunday, Charles and Lydia Stanfield led their entire brood to services in St. John's Anglican Church.

Charles sent the two oldest boys, John and Frank, Sr., off to apprentice in woollen mills in Canada and the United States with the thought that they would return not only with a sound knowledge of the business but, equally importantly, with knowledge of the advances in technology made by other manufacturers. In 1896, he sold his business to the two boys. It was a healthy enough operation, but it was by no means large. That year there were just seventeen employees. Sales were $24,000 and the profit was $2,250. John and Frank paid their father $27,000 for the business, giving him notes for that amount at 5 per cent interest.

It was John and Frank Stanfield, Sr., who turned the small family business into the largest woollen producer in Atlantic Canada. On taking over, they renamed the business the Truro Knitting Mills Ltd.; in 1906, they changed it again to Stanfield's Ltd., the name by which it is still known. The company trademark – the figures of two men hand-wrestling in their underwear – has also survived the years although the style of underwear on the figures has changed in keeping with evolving public preferences in undergarments. John and Frank, Sr., discarded some of their father's lesser lines and concentrated on knitted products – a change that did not sit well with Charles Stanfield. "I'll be buying it back in a couple of years when you find your newfangled notions don't work," he warned them.

He might have had to, too, but for two developments, one deliberate and the other unforeseen. The first was his sons' discovery of a revolutionary process for making underwear shrink proof. The other was the Klondike Gold Rush of 1897-1898. Many of the eager adventurers who rushed west to find their fortunes in the Yukon were Maritimers and they carried the fame of the Stanfield name with them to the gold fields on the other side of the continent. Overnight, the heavy, warm longjohns, known as Stanfield's Unshrinkable Underwear, were in great demand.

World War I gave added impetus to the Stanfield fortunes. At one stage, a satellite plant in Amherst turned out fifteen hundred yards of cloth a day for military use. By 1917, the Truro and Amherst plants employed a total of four hundred workers. By 1920, annual sales reached three million dollars: John and Frank Stanfield's twenty-seven thousand dollar investment was worth one and a quarter million dollars.

More impressive than the steady upward trend of the sales charts was the reputation that the company was establishing for producing quality merchandise at reasonable prices. In this age of discount houses and shoddy clothing, *Stanfield's Creed* of 1922 may seem more suited to the pulpit than to the market place. The idealism that it expressed, however, fairly represented the Stanfield approach to business. The Stanfields preached it and their customers evidently believed it.

That is not to say that the Stanfields were not aggressive promoters and imaginative salesmen; they were not above a little gentle huckstering. Witness a 1914 advertisement: "The youth who, in springtime allows his fancy to turn to thoughts of love, cannot pour his whole soul into the sweet nothings which he whispers passionately into the ear of his lady love, while a big splinter in his cheap or shoddy combinations is prodding him in the back. . . ."

Always determined to keep up with the times – in products as well as in advertising – Stanfield's Ltd. abandoned its line of woollen drawers for

17

women in the 1920s and plunged into the newfangled world of ladies' lingerie – a change that caused the older workers to shake their heads in amusement at the vanity of females. There was a ready market across Canada and in the eastern United States. Soon a major outlet such as B. Altman & Co. in New York was selling Stanfield's lingerie. From wool and a wool-cotton combination, Stanfield's moved into rayon, then nylon. By the late 1930s, the Truro plant was producing nylon pyjamas for ladies that retailed for as much as twenty-five dollars, making them luxury garments in those late Depression years.

The Depression hit Stanfield's Ltd. as it hit other manufacturers, but the company had enough reserves to weather the slump better than most, although it had to skip dividends for a few years. Always the paternalistic employers, the Stanfields treated their workers with a compassion that was consistent with the company's approach to business. When it finally had to lay off workers, it kept them on part salary, married women receiving the same amount as married men. Single workers received enough to cover their room and board with a little extra for pocket money. Stanfield's Ltd. takes considerable pride in having been one of the first employers in Canada to pay the same wage to women as to men. Also, its generally enlightened employee relations account for another company boast: in more than one hundred years of operation, there has never been a work stoppage, and no union has ever succeeded (though several have tried) to organize its workers.

John and Frank, Sr., ran the company together until 1907 when John discovered a new career, one that soon became almost as important to the family as making unshrinkable underwear – politics. Leaving Frank, Sr., to tend to the business, John ran in a federal by-election and was elected with a slender majority of 223 votes. His victory broke the Liberal monopoly on Nova Scotia's federal seats – "the solid eighteen," as they had been known. Re-elected in 1908 and in 1911, "Honest John" Stanfield, or so they called him in Ottawa, was appointed government whip in the Conservative administration headed by another Nova Scotian, Sir Robert Borden. In 1915, John Stanfield undertook to raise a brigade to fight the Germans; officially the 193rd Highlanders, this unit was inevitably known as "Stanfield's Unshrinkables." Following the war, Borden appointed John Stanfield to the Senate.

Frank, Sr. followed his older brother into politics, though he continued to run Stanfield's Ltd., representing Colchester in the Nova Scotia Legislature from 1911 to 1929. Named lieutenant-governor in 1930, he died at Government House in Halifax in the fall of the following year at age fifty-nine.

Frank, Sr., and Sarah Emma Thomas Stanfield had five children in the space of thirteen years. Frank, Jr., the oldest, succeeded his father as president of Stanfield's Ltd. in 1931 and was a federal Member of Parliament for Colchester-Hants from 1945 to 1953. Kathryn, called Kit, married Fred Davies, a son of Senator Rupert Davies, making her a sister-in-law of Robertson Davies, the author and Master of Massey College at the University of Toronto. Now widowed, Kit Stanfield Davies lives in Toronto. The next eldest, Charles, who is three and a half years older than Bob, went to work for the Royal Bank; he returned after his father's death to become Vice-President of Stanfield's Ltd., a post he still holds. Charles' public service included a period as deputy mayor of Truro. The fourth child, Robert Lorne, was born on April 11, 1914, and was named after Sir Robert Borden, the then Prime Minister and after the Marquess of Lorne, governor general from 1878 to 1883. Bob, ironically, was known in his early years as the "non-political Stanfield." The fifth child, Gordon, who is always called Pete, is an engineer and is President of Starr Manufacturing Limited, a metal-products firm in Dartmouth.

It was a warm, close family dominated by the personalities of Sarah Emma, ever concerned and compassionate, and Frank, Sr., who as a father, businessman, and politician, brooked no nonsense and did not suffer fools gladly. Conservative Senator Fred Blois, who worked for Stanfield's Ltd. for forty years – until his retirement as mill manager in 1957 – remembers Frank Stanfield, Sr., as a fair but firm employer. "He was the type of man that if you made a mistake, and I made many, you were told about it in very firm terms. But it was never brought up again. Once you were told about it, it was ended. He said what he had to say, he said it with a vengeance, and it ended." He could be as stern at home as at the plant. Senator Blois went to the Stanfield country home outside Truro for dinner one night, when Bob was a small boy. Bob, as small boys will, was jumping about the living room and making altogether too much noise for his father's liking. "Behave yourself or get out," snapped Frank Stanfield. Bob behaved himself.

"We used to rough-house in the living room on Sundays when we were little," recalls Bob's brother, Charles. "Two or three of us would sit on Dad's toes while another one would try to push him down in his chair." But Frank Stanfield, Sr., would tolerate only so much of that nonsense. "He liked to carry on a bit," says Charles, "but things had to be on the line. If you crossed the line, he'd damned soon tell you."

Frank Stanfield, Sr., was a big, square-faced man with a full head of white hair (in his later years) who carried 215 pounds on his five-foot-eleven-inch frame. He had chronic trouble with his weight, the result of a form of diabetes that kept him constantly thirsty. He could not drive from Truro to Halifax – about a two-hour trip in those days – without stopping for a drink of water along the way. Says Charles: "He knew every damn spring in the country and he always carried with him one of those little collapsible metal cups."

Ill health forced Frank Stanfield, Sr., to leave school early; he went to work at the mill as an office boy, tackling the wool business with energy and determination. When he married Sarah Emma Thomas, he told her he had two ambitions: to become a millionaire and to be appointed to the Senate. He made his first objective without difficulty, but the Senate seat went to his brother, John. Frank had to settle for lieutenant-governor of Nova Scotia.

By the time the two brothers bought out their father in 1896, Frank Stanfield, Sr., was well on the way to becoming an expert on wool. Buyers from the United States rated him as one of the most knowledgeable wool men on the continent. For many years, he personally handled all the wool blending at the Truro plant. He also had a knack for making the business pay, dropping many of the unprofitable lines and ploughing profits back into the business. He founded the Acadia Trust Company to manage the family's money, and that of anyone else who cared to trust the Stanfields with their money. Many did. Workers at the mill deposited their pay cheques at Acadia Trust, and Acadia Trust loaned the money back to them in the form of mortgages on their homes. In 1925, Frank Stanfield, Sr., and three associates each deposited ten dollars in the trust company with the instructions that it be left to accumulate, with compound interest, until the fund reached four million dollars, at which time it is to be distributed to charity. By Frank, Sr.'s reckoning, that would take a mere 365 years. There was no doubt in his mind that there would still be Stanfields around to witness the distribution.

For Frank Stanfield, Sr., it was as natural to be a Conservative as it was to assume the continuance of his family. The Stanfields were manufacturers and the Conservative Party stood for protective tariffs for Canadian manufacturing industries, whereas Liberals of those days stood four-square for free trade. It remains a matter of some regret to members of the Stanfield clan that those neat distinctions have disappeared. "Now both parties are the same," says Charles Stanfield, shaking his head sadly.

Known locally as "The Governor," Frank Stanfield, Sr., continued as President of Stanfield's Ltd. after he entered the Legislature in 1911. But politics was very much a family affair. His mother, the former Lydia Dawson, continued canvassing in elections well into her old age. His elder sons, Frank, Jr., and Charles, worked in campaigns from the time they were youngsters. As soon as they were old enough to get a driver's licence, they drove voters to the polls on election day. Strangely, though, the third son, Bob, displayed no interest in electioneering and ignored campaigns. For this aberrant conduct he earned that dubious designation of being "non-political." There was no way, however, that Bob or any of the other Stanfield youngsters could avoid the discussion of politics around the house. The dining-room table was the centre of debates, and the voices of the argumentative Stanfields – battling over politics during the main course and over sports during dessert – carried clearly to the ears of passing fellow townspeople out for a breath of air on a warm spring or summer night. "We had some awfully heated arguments," says Charles Stanfield. "The five of us got around the dining-room table with mother at one end and Dad at the other. Dad was the biggest tease of all. He'd start the argument off, then pick up his *Montreal Star* and hide behind that and laugh and listen to the argument." When the debate grew too noisy, Mrs. Stanfield would stand up at her end of the table and try to restore order, usually with little result. Then she and Kit would flee to the quiet of the sewing room.

From his father, Bob eventually acquired an interest in partisan politics and an understanding of the importance of treating others well. Senator Blois points to one incident that he considers to be typical of the Stanfield family. The wife of one of the workers at Stanfield's Ltd. had died and Blois was summoned by Frank, Sr., who wanted to know what kind of casket she was to be buried in. "Just a plain black casket, Sir," said Blois. "I want you to go to the undertaker," ordered his employer, "and tell him you want her to have a first-class funeral. First class. And you are to tell him you will pay the bill." Blois objected: "Mr. Stanfield, the undertaker will know I won't be paying the bill myself, that you will be." Frank Stanfield, Sr., cut him off, explaining that his desire for anonymity was not entirely altruistic. If the undertaker were told to bill the Stanfields, he might pad his account. "I don't care what he knows," said Frank, Sr. "You will see the bill is paid. Furthermore, I want a nice wreath of flowers sent. And another thing: if anyone dies in the family of any of the people working here, flowers must be sent to them."

"That was typical of the man," says Senator Blois. "Another thing about him was that if someone would get sick in the plant – or someone in the family – they received money in various ways. He didn't want anyone to know he was doing it. A great many things went on that he didn't want to take credit for." One year, Blois suggested that, instead of giving Christmas presents to the workers, the company distribute cheques and that Frank Stanfield, Sr., sign them. He refused. "It took me over a year to convince him that to make it really worthwhile he should sign the cheques," says

Senator Blois. "He didn't want praise for anything. The good that that man did for the town was immense and then after he passed away his wife carried on the same."

Sarah Emma Thomas Stanfield likely had a greater influence on Bob than had his father. Em (as she was called) was a small, dark-haired woman who was considered attractive without being classed as one of the great beauties of the region. It was her warmth, her genuine interest in the well-being of others, her instinctive ability to put others at ease for which she is best remembered around Truro. Her husband was admired and respected, but he was probably too outspoken, too sure of his own mind, and too much the aggressive businessman-politician to be genuinely loved by the people. But Em Stanfield *was* loved. Even local Liberals, who were only too happy to pick a fight with her wealthy husband, had nothing but good to say of his wife. Quietly and, if possible, anonymously she made substantial donations to the church still favoured by the family, St. John's Anglican, to the Red Cross, and to the Salvation Army. But she was most respected for her work among the "under-privileged" – a Truro euphemism for the Negroes who lived in the community. One of the beneficiaries of her charity was the Zion Baptist Church to which the family's Negro chauffeur belonged. Families that had fallen on hard times could usually count on a little something from Bob's mother to see them through. Fred Blois is her witness: "Mrs. Stanfield did a lot of work, but she did it so quietly that few people would know except some of the actual poor people, the people who were sick or hard up. It was done very, very quietly. She was a very, very wonderful lady."

Bob's mother was also a natural politician, perhaps the only one in the family. On Sundays, she loved to drive with her husband to visit local farmers and to pay her respects to people she had not seen for some time. This combination of compassion at the plant, discreet charity in the town, and easy friendliness with neighbours helps to explain why the Stanfield name became one of the most respected in Nova Scotia. It also helps to explain why no Stanfield has ever lost an election in the province.

Like their father, Frank, Jr., and Charles found it good business to combine business and politics, Charles at the municipal level and Frank, Jr., at the federal. In the federal election of 1945, the Conservative candidate in Colchester-Hants withdrew just before the deadline for nominations and Frank, Jr., agreed to step into the breech. The Tories won only three seats in the province that year and one of them was Frank, Jr.'s. But it was a close thing. The Liberals had won Colchester-Hants by 2,284 votes in the previous election, and the chances of taking the seat away from them seemed remote. When the ballots were counted on election night, Frank, Jr., had a fifteen-vote lead. The Liberals demanded a judicial recount, and when it concluded Frank, Jr., was declared the winner by the slenderest of margins – eight votes. That was the closest a Stanfield ever came to defeat at the polls. Frank, Jr., served two terms in Ottawa, nudging his majority up to 410 votes in 1949, before retiring from political life in 1953.

Frank, Jr., and Charles ran Stanfield's Ltd. in much the way their father had, lopping off unprofitable product lines (including, eventually, that expensive ladies' lingerie) and moving the company briskly into new fields as fashions changed. In the late 1930s, they began to produce athletic shirts and shorts – packaged in cellophane bags, a radical departure at that time. In the early 1940s, they went into work shirts. The 1950s saw them become the first Canadian company to offer circular-knit, thermal underwear. They introduced what they called the "grand-slam golf shirt," followed in the early 1960s by the "interlock, roll-neck ski-shirt." By 1967, nine out of every ten major league baseball players were sporting woollen undershirts by Stanfield's next to their athletic hides. Although it follows fashion's dictates, Stanfield's Ltd. has never entirely lost touch with the good old simple products, such as the long underwear with "trap doors" that had given it its start. Heavy woollen socks are another example. During World War II, the Truro plant was kept running around the clock to supply the armed forces with, among other things, army socks. Fred Blois went to Toronto during the war for a sales presentation to a retired British General who had come to Canada in search of socks for the British Army. A competitor was trying to convince the British to buy socks made of a blend of wool and nylon, arguing that they were cheaper than pure wool and would last longer. "I took the stand that that was true, but that a soldier gets his feet wet," says Blois. "Wet wool sticks to his feet, but his feet would slip in a nylon sock. The British General said, 'They say an army travels on its belly. That's not right. I commanded troops in Africa, in the desert. A soldier travels on his feet. I've had blistered feet and I know. I will take the socks from the gentleman who has just spoken. They are to be all wool, and I know exactly what he means!' "

Though the ageing red-brick mill in Truro looks today more like a decaying fertilizer plant than the seat of a prosperous and contemporary business, there is nothing old-fashioned about the operation inside. The 380,000 square-foot plant employs eight hundred workers with nearly two hundred more at a newer, secondary plant in Oxford. The sales network of Stanfield's stretches across the country with warehouses in major centres. Though Charles Edward Stanfield, the man who started it all, would be horrified, Stanfield's Ltd. counts among its two hundred and fifty products a line of gaily coloured undershorts for men.

Robert's eldest brother, Frank Stanfield, Jr., died in 1967. Frank was succeeded as president of Stanfield's Ltd. by his son, Tom, with Frank's brother Charles staying on as vice-president. In 1961, the Stanfields sold the Acadia Trust Company to Montreal Trust Company and Charles continued as Acadia Trust's president under the new ownership.

Today, Stanfield's Ltd. is a relative rarity in Canadian business – a successful firm that has been able to withstand bids by larger corporations, both Canadian-owned and foreign, to take it over, and that remains in the firm control of the fourth generation of the family that founded it. Although Robert Stanfield has no direct connection with Stanfield's Ltd., slightly over 50 per cent of the stock is held by other members of the family. Much of the rest is in the hands of long-time employees. Both Fred Blois, the retired mill manager, and Lou Christie, a retired sales manager, hold blocks of stock. "I remember after I came to the Senate in 1960," says Senator Blois, "a brokerage firm got in touch with me to see if there was any way they could pick up enough shares to get control of Stanfield's Ltd. I told them that is impossible. The late lieutenant-governor and his son, Frank, Jr., always said this firm will never be sold. And I don't think it ever will be."

3
Growing Up (1914-1939)

Stanfield is a humanitarian. He's compassionate. He has had to overcome his upbringing. He deliberately set out to understand the people who were disadvantaged because he was advantaged all his life.

> – Dalton Camp, guru to Conservative
> Politicians, interview, December, 1972.

Truro, when Bob Stanfield was born there on April 11, 1914, was a town of about seven thousand people. It had grown into a bustling railway centre with thirty-six freight trains and thirty-four passenger trains rolling in and out every day. It was also becoming known on a modest scale as a centre of industry, with Stanfield's Ltd. well on its way to becoming the most famous. Residents proudly – although none too accurately – called their town "The Hub of the Province" and to most of them it was just about the finest little place of its size in all of the Maritimes.

If they were put on the spot about it, the people of Truro would admit that not everyone in town was a solid citizen. There was some housing that outsiders would uncharitably describe as slums and some poor people – the usual assortment of deserted wives and able-bodied males who preferred living on the charity of others to the trauma of doing an honest day's work. There were the Negro families who might be poor, but, as the good burghers of the town assured one another, "the blacks are real fine folk." Most people in Truro liked to look at the brighter side of things: the spreading maples and elms that shaded the quiet streets, the gardeners who laboured lovingly over the lawns of the well-to-do, the housekeepers who strolled to market to buy the necessities for the dinners of their masters and mistresses. It was a town of gracious mansions and a certain smug complacency. It was a town that, as Harry Bruce was to describe it in an article in *Maclean's Magazine,* "made a statement about the people who lived there and the statement was that if men will only apply hard work, hard heads, horse sense, and thrifty business practices they can arrange their corner of the world to suit themselves."

No family had arranged its corner of the world more comfortably than the Stanfield family. Their big wooden mansion is gone now, torn down to make way for a motel, Keddy's Motor Inn. The people will, however, still tell of what it was like in the days when the Stanfield home graced the site. The house was set on a manicured lawn and surrounded by beds of flowers. There was a turret on the fourth floor, a circular driveway out front, and a tennis court. Inside, there was dark panelling downstairs, which included an extensive private library where Bob Stanfield grew to love the works of Jane Austen and that housed a collection of classical records. If young Bob tired of skating on the marsh with the other kids, he had only to come home and skate on the Stanfields' private rink – the tennis court being flooded for that purpose in winter.

One of the hoariest myths of politics is that there is an advantage in being born poor. Adversity is alleged to build character; the politician of humble origins will develop, or so it is said, initiative, determination, guts, a love for his fellow man, and an appreciation of the value of a dollar, among other thoroughly laudable virtues. Subscribers to this point of view will argue that David Lewis, the leader of the New Democratic Party, is a better politician than Pierre Trudeau or Robert Stanfield because Lewis, the son of poor Polish immigrants, had to struggle out of Montreal's Jewish ghetto by his own efforts, teaching himself English by reading Charles Dickens and working his way through school. Because Stanfield and Trudeau were born into wealthy families and, as Lewis once put it, "never had to scramble to pay the rent," they were denied the advantage of being disadvantaged. But are they poorer politicans for their good fortune? Although adversity may instill in an aspiring politician the quality of self-reliance and the ability to fend for himself in a competitive world, there is no evidence that it makes him more thoughtful, more articulate, more responsive to the needs of others or a more skilled conciliator in the delicate business of balancing his own objectives against the realities of day-to-day politics.

Being born wealthy eased Bob Stanfield's entry into politics: the Conservatives of Nova Scotia would probably not have chosen him to lead them if he hadn't had an independent income that enabled him to devote his full time to the party. But once he became a politician, he succeeded because he possessed qualities that were common to the Stanfield family: common sense, patience, the determination to see a difficult job through to completion. These qualities were bred into him, nurtured by his parents, and refined by his education.

Three dominant characteristics of all the Stanfields were compassion for the less fortunate, responsibility toward others, and a conviction that they owed a duty to their community, their province, and their political party. And although they were well off, no Stanfield ever flaunted his wealth or broadcast his good deeds. If he assisted some worthy cause, the amount of his donation and, if possible, the fact that he had made it, were kept secret.

The qualities most often ascribed to Robert Stanfield in politics are honesty and personal integrity, and they are attributes he has exhibited since childhood. The Liberals of Nova Scotia had many criticisms of his eleven years as premier; they had grave reservations about the capacities and the actions of some of his ministers; and they deplored Stanfield's inability or unwillingness to discipline his caucus. But they did not challenge the Premier's personal integrity. He sailed through public life in Nova Scotia curiously isolated from personal criticism – a politician who gave the illusion (and it was no more than an illusion) of being above politics. Inevitably his lieutenants had to bear criticisms that would have been directed at the person of a more "political" premier. It is significant that none of his lieutenants ever complained.

If, as Dalton Camp maintains, Stanfield had to overcome the advantages of his wealth and social status, young Bob Stanfield was not aware that he was much different from other youngsters in Truro. "There was nothing particularly unusual about my life in Truro," he says. "I lived in a big house, but – maybe it was because of the nature of the town where I grew up – I wasn't really aware that my people had a lot more money than other people. I had a very interesting life – games, hockey and football, and baseball, and tennis in particular. And I always enjoyed school."

"Loved" might be a better word to describe his feelings about school. He wanted to start school long before he was old enough, and once started he immersed himself in it, always leading his class and earning himself a reputation as the town bookworm. At home, the family dubbed him "The Professor." Mrs. Florence Peel, who taught him history and English, years later recalled him as a brilliant student. She pored over his examination papers, looking for an excuse to reduce his marks: "No boy of that age could possibly write an absolutely perfect paper." While others in his class were still struggling to memorize the dates of historical happenings, Bob had a sense of history that enabled him to understand the meaning of the events he studied.

If he inherited his interest in world affairs from his father, it was his lively, involved mother who gave him his love of good music and books. Particularly books. "I think one feature of Bob," says his brother Charles, "was that if he wasn't doing something in sports or studying, he didn't waste his time. He was a great reader. We had a good library. Most young fellows just waste hour after hour doing nothing. They walk the streets or something silly. Bob never did that." A librarian who knew him uncharitably described him as "a Jane Eyre type." And no one can recall Bob Stanfield paying much attention to the young girls of Truro. Any reporter poking into his background eventually comes across a middle-aged matron who was raised in Truro and who professes to have had a crush on Bob Stanfield. Real or imagined, such crushes went unrecognized by the shy, serious blond-haired boy.

It was a serene and secure life for a youngster with sober interests. The family spent the summers at the Stanfield country place outside Truro, an old farmhouse with a crank telephone, no electricity, and no running water. The boys wandered down the hill to watch a neighbouring farmer go about his chores. It was a simple life, in keeping with the lifestyle favoured by Bob's parents: the Stanfields were not the sort of people to waste their money on yachts or round-the-world cruises. For Bob, growing up was an orderly process. The closest anyone can recall him ever coming to rebelliousness was the odd occasion when he would join a few cronies in pushing a neighbour's car down a hill, then jumping in for a short joy-ride. He seemed no more cut out for a life of crime than he did for a life of politics.

His life seemed to be mapped out. After elementary school in Truro, he would, as was the custom among well-to-do Nova Scotia families, be sent away to a boarding school. Then he would go to Dalhousie University in Halifax to pick up a degree in something (it didn't much matter what) before returning to take his appointed place in one of the family businesses.

By the time he reached Grade IX in Truro, Bob's mother noticed his marks were slipping slightly and decided it was time he had a change. "My mother began to feel," he says, "that I was going a bit stale during Grade IX, and she thought it would be a good idea for me to get out of Nova Scotia for two or three years. She put it in terms of broadening me out."

Bob therefore followed his brother Charles to Ashbury College, a private school for boys in the affluent Ottawa suburb of Rockcliffe Park. Ashbury turned out to be a mixed experience. He was able to give free rein to his love of sports, playing hockey and tennis, doing gymnastics, and learning a game he had not encountered before – cricket. He excelled academically, too, and on graduation was awarded the Southam Cup for combined academic standing and athletic prowess. But Bob found the calibre of teaching uneven and left Ashbury wondering whether he had gotten as much out of his years there as he should have.

He also left Ashbury feeling the first stirrings of social conscience. His fellow students came from another – and to Stanfield – rather unreal world.

They were the sons of diplomats, deputy ministers, and rich English-speaking Montrealers from Westmount. "I had a pretty strong feeling that most of the kids at Ashbury at that time didn't know much about the real world as it existed. Poverty and that sort of thing was pretty remote from their existence. We did have poverty in Truro with very substantial pockets in two or three areas where Negroes lived, and there were quite a few others like that in many of the Nova Scotia towns – in any of the Maritime towns. I didn't think of it[poverty] in those terms particularly because I went to school with these kids, played hockey with these kids, played games with them. You know, you'd go in and out of their homes in Truro and you may not know very much about poverty, but you certainly notice it. The world of Westmount for example, in 1929 or 1930, was a very different world than that. I don't mean I had a great social conscience at that period, because I don't think I did." Bob did know, though, that he was somehow different from the usual sort of boy who attended Ashbury, and he quickly lost contacts with his classmates after graduation. None of them remained close friends in later years.

His growing awareness of the gap between the rich and the poor left young Bob arguing unpopular causes in those political debates around the dining-room table in Truro. To the staunch Tories of the family, he was a "parlour pink" or, worse, a "Mackenzie King Liberal." His brother Frank, Jr., was satisfied that Bob was a "damned Grit." Although Stanfield himself does not recall the incident, other members of the family tell of the night when Bob, then sixteen, lectured his sister, Kit, on the solutions to the world's problems, as he saw them. Removing his shoes to avoid awakening the sleeping family, he marched about the living room, banging his shoes on a table to emphasize his points. Soon the entire house was awake, and that became known as "the night Bob was noisy."

By this time he was starting to have a set of political heroes: Sir Charles Tupper, the Nova Scotia doctor who introduced free education in the province, became one of the fathers of Confederation, and later was Prime Minister; Sir John A. Macdonald; and Sir Wilfrid Laurier. As he grew older, he came to admire some statesmen outside Canada. "Sir Winston Churchill is, of course, in a class by himself," he told Peter Newman, then of the *Toronto Daily Star*, in 1967. "Among American statesmen, Abraham Lincoln was a very attractive man. I also admire [Franklin] Roosevelt's gifts, some of the qualities of Adlai Stevenson, and Harry Truman's simple courage."

Summers were spent back in the Truro area. As a teen-ager, Stanfield worked as a counsellor at a Y.M.C.A. summer camp. Later, he and a group of friends put up a little money for a cabin on Folly Lake, about twenty-five miles out of Truro, where they swam, read, and played a little poker. Bob was the one who insisted that his friends pay their gambling debts promptly.

He headed off to Dalhousie University in the fall of 1932 with no clear idea of what he wanted to do with his life or even what he wanted to study at university. He thought he would take a course in Commerce because it had always been assumed in the family, without his having considered it particularly, that he would do what all the other Stanfields had done – go into business. It was not until he went to register at Dalhousie that he was forced to think about his future. "The registrar asked me why I was going to take Commerce," Stanfield recalls. "I said I thought it was interesting with Economics and so on. Within half an hour he persuaded me to take a general arts course." The registrar told him he could transfer later into Commerce or some other specialized course, but that, if he had no career decided upon, a general education would be more valuable. "He convinced me very quickly. Perhaps I was easy to convince."

His first year at Dalhousie was an acute disappointment. He took a course in Mathematics that didn't interest him because he had no intention of pursuing the subject. French was no challenge because the French taught at Dalhousie was not up to the level at Ashbury. He whistled through Latin without opening a book. That first year at Dalhousie, however, brought Bob Stanfield into contact with the one person who, aside from his parents, exerted a profound influence on his life. He was Professor W. Russell Maxwell, head of the Economics Department, whom Stanfield describes as "by all odds the best teacher I ever had". The admiration was mutual. Maxwell steered Stanfield through an Honours Economics and Political Science course at Dalhousie, and took him to Europe when he graduated. "I've never invited any other student, so this is an indication of how much I liked him," says Maxwell. He talked Bob Stanfield into going to the Harvard Law School instead of the London School of Economics, and later recommended him for a job on the Wartime Prices and Trade Board. At each turning in Stanfield's life before he entered politics, the little, gnome-like Maxwell was there to lean on, to give advice and guidance and to provide a gentle nudge in the right direction. They have remained good friends in the years since, though Maxwell is unimpressed with the sort of economic policy Stanfield has preached as a federal politician.

In the classroom, Maxwell practised the same sort of Socratic technique that Pierre Trudeau was to develop much later into a highly effective form of political theatre. "For a long while Maxwell drove me up the wall," Stanfield confesses. "He used the Socratic method. He never expressed an opinion of his own. It was years before I found he had any. His technique was to develop one side of an argument with one fellow and develop the other side with another; when he got both sides developed, he'd leave it and go on with something else."

Maxwell was Stanfield's professor for Economics One in the freshman year. It was Bob's poorest subject that year and, perhaps for this reason, Maxwell has no recollection of Stanfield as having been among his one-hundred-and-fifty-odd students in that course. "My first clear recollection of Bob is when he came to my office at Dalhousie at the end of his first year and said he would like to apply for admission to the honours course." Maxwell told Stanfield he would not be eligible for entry to Honours Economics and Political Science until he had completed two years of General Arts, and he warned him that admission to the honours program would not be easily won. Dalhousie's honours courses at that time were tightly restricted to exceptional students; Stanfield, in fact, became Maxwell's only honours student in his third and fourth years at university.

Still at loose ends, dissatisfied with his first year at Dalhousie, and unhappy about not being able to enter the honours course for another year, Stanfield went to Europe with his sister and newly-widowed mother in the summer of 1933. In England, they stopped at Cambridge; Bob thought he would transfer there to study Economics. His mother, who wanted him closer to home, talked him out of it. The trip became more than a sightseeing venture. As they travelled, Bob began to look at ways in which European countries were trying to cope with the Depression. He tried to apply his new interest in economic theory to his emerging concern about poverty and other social problems. "I started reading people like G.D.H. Cole [the Fabian Socialist] and others, and became much more aware of social problems. I had been living among those problems, but I guess I had been taking them for granted. It was out of that that I became much more concerned and started to question the assumptions I'd taken for granted. I suppose I came back to Dalhousie in the fall – I was going into second year – as a Socialist. Not a militant one, but a Socialist in terms of attitude, in terms of questioning the system. It wasn't very easy, once you looked at it, not to question what was going on in the world in the 1930s."

There was nothing unusual about a university student of the 1930s becoming fascinated with Socialism, but it was extremely unusual when that student was a Stanfield. It appeared for a time as though that devoutly Tory family – a family that was satisfied that the initials C.C.F. stood not for Co-operative Commonwealth Federation but for "Cancel Canada's Freedom" – had produced its first renegade. Stanfield thinks he neglected to inform his mother of his conversion. "It was something of mine," he says with a laugh. "We didn't discuss this kind of thing." It was probably just as well.

His Socialism was naive and undefined. "I thought all that was necessary was to adopt a Socialist approach, that it was the right one, that the disorganized nature of capitalism and the disorganized nature of international competition was causing the trouble. I thought the solution lay more in the direction of a rational world organization and rational organization of the economy." Stanfield has never entirely gotten over this first flirtation with Socialism, though his thinking became clearer and more sophisticated the deeper he delved into economic theory. He has always stood well to the left of the mainstream of the Progressive Conservative Party, much more in the tradition of the Progressives than of the Conservatives. Some federal Conservatives still privately regard him as a Socialist. After becoming premier of Nova Scotia, he alarmed the more hidebound Tories by introducing a form of economic planning in the Province, though he took the sting out of it by inserting the word "voluntary." He created the Voluntary Economic Planning Board, a twenty-seven member body to prepare an economic blueprint for the Province and advise the government on economic policy. The membership was almost entirely drawn from outside the ranks of government, with experts from processing, manufacturing, utilities, farming, fishing, labour, and so on. Though Stanfield was proud of his creation and considered the Board to be a revolutionary innovation, there is little evidence that this idea, borrowed and diluted from his early fascination with Socialism, ever had much effect on his handling of the provincial economy. In truth, it was better politics than economics because it succeeded in identifying the leaders of every sector of the Nova Scotia economy with the Stanfield government. "I missed the point of it at first," admits Liberal Peter Nicholson, who later became Minister of Finance for Nova Scotia. "It was a brilliant piece of political strategy. I don't know what the hell the Board ever did for the Province, but it helped the Conservatives."

In his final two years at Dalhousie, Stanfield fell completely under the influence of Russell Maxwell. One evening a week, Stanfield dropped by Maxwell's rooms in King's College for long talks that strayed far beyond the realm of economic theory. They talked politics, international affairs, about the Depression, and about the urgent social problems facing the world in those Depression years. Stanfield stuck religiously to his books, taking no part in student government or in the activities of the political clubs on campus. He became a drudge, the epitome of a determined student. At Maxwell's suggestion, Stanfield wrote his undergraduate thesis on Walter Bagehot, the English economist and journalist, and editor of the *Economist,* who in 1873 had written *Lombard Street,* a classic study of the London money market. "He read an awful lot of stuff for that thesis," says Maxwell. "I remember him telling me one time that he was rewriting the history of the nineteenth century. One thing does lead to another. He produced a very substantial thesis of maybe a couple of hundred pages; it was pretty good stuff. In fact, I used to keep a copy in my desk."

Stanfield graduated from Dalhousie in the spring of 1936 with his Bachelor of Arts degree and was awarded the Governor General's Gold Medal for having the highest academic standing of any graduating student. He did not, however, accept the money that normally went with the award, allowing the university to present the money to a student with a less brilliant record but with a greater need of the cash.

That summer, Maxwell and his star student headed for Europe. While in New York waiting for their ship to sail, Maxwell picked up a copy of a book that had just come off the printer's presses. It was *The General Theory of Employment, Interest and Money* by John Maynard Keynes, an economist whose theories were to influence Stanfield every bit as much as his earlier readings of G.D.H. Cole and other Socialists. Stanfield and Maxwell headed for Hanover where they bought a pair of second-hand bicycles and set off to pedal through central Germany. In retrospect it seems an incongruous scene: the little Economics professor and the lanky, future leader of the Conservative party of Canada cycling through Nazi Germany with a Keynesian treatise for bedtime reading. Maxwell found Stanfield much influenced by Keynes, whose ideas were then very much in vogue. A classical economist who had believed in a free economy, Keynes was profoundly influenced by the Depression and swung around to advocate large-scale economic planning by governments and massive government spending to create employment. Maxwell eventually outgrew Keynes, but Stanfield remains a Keynesian in many ways. "I suppose the cardinal thesis in it [*The General Theory of Employment, Interest and Money*]," says Maxwell, "is that unemployment is not necessary, that it exists because of certain features of the capitalist economy and that all this can be corrected. Bob seems to believe this very much still. And every time I read what he is saying – and unemployment seems to be the big thing – I think, well, it's not quite as simple as that. . . . In many ways it was a tract for the times. Nineteen thirty-six was the Depression and unemployment was world-wide on a large scale. The problem of unemployment as it exists today is very different, I think. A lot different. Economists are very much influenced by the conditions of the time. There isn't perhaps a great deal of final truth in economics."

The two cyclists spent several weeks riding through the towns and villages of Hitler's Germany, stopping to investigate historic sites; Stanfield, with much greater ardour than Maxwell, also explored art galleries and museums. They generally stopped overnight at small inexpensive hotels.

That trip brought out another inherited Stanfield trait – a thrift that bordered on parsimony. It was one thing for a Stanfield to contribute generously to worthy causes, it was quite another thing to waste good money on expensive hotels or meals. Maxwell paid the bills with Bob carefully reimbursing him for his half of the daily expenses. Says Maxwell: "It was always a very small sum, overnight and breakfast and dinner, and I could almost see the satisfaction on his face each time he paid me his dollar and a half or so."

In those days, Stanfield disliked beer – even German beer – and he insisted on drinking milk. The Hitler government was promoting the sale of milk, and there were small kiosks selling milk and cheese in most cities and towns. "If Bob couldn't get milk to drink at the restaurant at which we had our dinner – and that was often the case – he would eat his dinner and then go off looking for a milk bar," recalls Maxwell. "There were very slight variations in the price of milk. It was very cheap drink anyway, but the milk bars didn't all charge the same number of pfennigs for a glass of milk. He would go around and track down the cheapest place and come back and tell me: 'I got a glass of milk for so many pfennigs. That's five pfennigs less than the place last night.' That's the kind of fellow he was. I'd far rather have a fellow like that than a fellow who was splurging on himself all the time. It's not that he needed to economize. It was just that that was the way he was."

Maxwell and Stanfield eventually reached Jena – now in East Germany – where Maxwell had arranged for them to use the university library. Stanfield had taken a course in German at Dalhousie and could read the language a little, though he could not speak it. They went to the library every day as Maxwell tried to get to the bottom of Nazi economic theories. He is not sure what Bob was reading, but he suspects it may have been something racier than Economics.

Stanfield had planned to go to the London School of Economics after Dalhousie, but Maxwell argued against it. Did Bob want to be a teacher, he asked? No, Bob replied. Was he prepared to wait his chance to land a job as an economist in the federal civil service? No. Well, suggested Maxwell, who had studied economics at Harvard, why not "go across the street to the Harvard Law school, just for a year, before committing yourself to a lifetime in economics?" Maxwell had an ulterior motive. He reasoned that Harvard Law School was about as competitive a school as any in the world, and he felt that his protege, after sailing through Dalhousie with no real competition, would profit from a good stiff dose of it. "I thought it would be good for him to compete with the best there was. I thought he had it in him to meet this competition. I thought it would develop him better than anything else."

So in the fall of 1936, armed with the works of J.M. Keynes, Bob Stanfield settled into a spartan twenty-one-dollar-a-month room on the third floor of a rooming house at 37 Langdon Street in Cambridge, Massachusetts, prepared to compete with some of the brightest students in North America. "I went down to Harvard Law School for one year," Stanfield says, "and I stayed for three years. I never intended to practise law. I probably shouldn't have stayed the three years. . . . The competition was very keen and I did well and I guess that's why I went back."

It was a tough grind. The law school weeded students out in a hurry, flunking about one third of Bob Stanfield's freshman class. Bob was never in any danger of being failed. He responded to the fierce competition just as Russell Maxwell had hoped he would, running up an academic record that was just short of brilliant. At the end of his first year, he made the *Harvard Law Review*. An invitation to become an associate editor of the *Review* was the ultimate accolade at the school and was prized by the students as highly as, say, a practising lawyer would value an appointment to the Supreme Court. The review staff was selected strictly on the basis of academic standing and only the top seventeen or eighteen students of the six hundred odd in Bob's class were invited. The editor that year was Philip Graham, later the publisher of *The Washington Post* and *Newsweek Magazine,* who became a great admirer of Bob Stanfield. Stanfield, however, was the first student in memory to decline an invitation to join the Review staff – an action that created much the same disbelief among his classmates as one would expect in Ottawa if a political hack declined an appointment to the Senate.

Experience on the Harvard Law Review was regarded as a nearly certain stepping stone to membership in one of the prestigious law firms on Wall Street or in Washington. However, the fact that Stanfield had no desire to practise law, on Wall Street or anywhere else, put him in a category apart from other students. Says he: "There was all the tremendous amount of work those guys did in their second and third years because they had to edit the Review as well as do their ordinary work, and I just took the attitude I wasn't going to kill myself that way because the law was not going to be my future. Looking back on it, I realize I should either have thrown myself fully into it [school and the Review] or gotten out of the law school." Back in Nova Scotia, later, he talked to Russell Maxwell about his decision and about his future plans. "He wanted to come back to Canada," says Maxwell. "This was his plan for his life."

Declining to work on the Review was the only dramatic thing Bob did at Harvard. He lived a monastic existence in the same room of the rooming house for the full three years. When he was not in class, he was usually found sitting by the window, reading and making notes on a writing platform attached to his armchair while his portable Magnavox phonograph played his favourite Mozart, Beethoven, and Tchaikovsky records.

Philip Elman, a lawyer in Washington, who lived in the same rooming house, recalls Bob Stanfield as very much an egghead who buried himself in his law texts, books on history, and economics tomes – a diet spiced only by the occasional dry biography. He did not waste his time on novels. "He was an intellectual person," says Elman. "He was quiet and reserved. He liked law school. The competitiveness did not concern him and I don't think he would have been disappointed if he flunked out. . . . He was different from the rest of us because he didn't intend to become a lawyer. . . . He was there for the 'fun' of it, the excitement, and the intellectual profit of it." Another classmate, Bennett Bosky, also a lawyer in Washington, sums up the Bob Stanfield he knew in three words: "Pleasant, bright, laconic."

A half-dozen other law students lived in the same rooming house, and they held frequent bull-sessions. As befitted the conversation of young men intent on making it to the top of the legal profession, the talk was mostly about the law. But they talked, too, about American politics, Franklin Roosevelt's court-packing plan, and the affairs of the world. The talk often turned to Hitler and the Nazi brushfire that was sweeping Europe. Like most of the others, Bob Stanfield was reluctant to see the British and the French take a tough stand against Hitler. They all thought Neville Chamberlain had acquitted himself well at Munich. These discussions could become heated and the others always knew when Bob was getting angry: his forehead turned bright red. He seldom showed much interest in the sort of gossip that intrigues even the most serious of students. "I never heard him say an unkind or mean thing about anyone," says Philip Elman. If the arguments grew too hot, Bob would get up and leave. Elman again: "He was always the kind of fellow who would walk away from an angry, bitter confrontation."

In his second year, Stanfield joined the Chancery Club, an eating club. He also met the staff of the Law Review for dinner from time to time to talk about the law. He and his best friend, Elman, often went for long walks. On Sundays, they would walk along the banks of the Charles River from Cambridge to Boston, stopping along the way for a good dinner. When they reached Boston, they would take in a play or concert or movie before returning to Cambridge.

By today's standards, Stanfield lived an improbably unromantic life at Harvard. "He was never one for drinking, boozing or whoring with the other students," says another classmate. Even if he had wanted to pursue girls, he would have had trouble because the no-nonsense Italian lady who ran the boarding house had strict rules about what went on in *her* place. "There were no women at all," says Elman. "I don't think a woman ever entered that house."

Stanfield's friends were vaguely aware that he had a girl friend somewhere, but he never talked about her. There was then – as there is today – a private inner core to Stanfield that even those who think they know him best cannot fully penetrate. His Harvard friends were also aware that his family were "the B.V.D. people of Canada," but he never talked about them, either. Because many rich Americans sent their offspring to Harvard, the Stanfield money did not make Bob exceptional. But, like all the Stanfields, he wore his wealth exceedingly well. He had no car and, while others stayed in the inexpensive rooming house out of necessity, he stayed by choice. Some of his friends suspected he had more money than they did, however, because he would return to his room every week or so with a new album of seventy-eight r.p.m. classical records, worth around ten dollars.

His political views were not much different from those of most of the other law students, and he would have been broadly categorized as a liberal intellectual and sceptic. He was impressed by the writings of Oliver Wendell Holmes, a judge of the U.S. Supreme Court from 1902 to 1932, whose political and social views had made him something of the darling of American liberals.

But Bob clearly had no interest or intention of going into politics himself in those days. Philip Elman expected that his friend would wind up teaching at some quiet university in Canada. "It was a great surprise to me when I learned that Bob was going into politics, because he was so much the ivory-tower type. I couldn't see him in active politics. . . . He had none of the politician's arts. He was not a flatterer. He never gave us the impression that it was important to him that he be liked."

In later years, in fact, Elman often wondered whether the Bob Stanfield he had known so well at Harvard could possibly be the same Robert L. Stanfield, the politician whom the newspapers invariably described as dour, taciturn, craggy-faced, inarticulate, and humourless, among other unflattering adjectives. Says Elman: "During the last [1972] election, I wrote him a note saying I could not recognize him from his description in the press. He was good-looking then. He had blond hair. He was tall – a very handsome man. A very handsome man. He may stammer on the hustings, but in private discussions at Harvard he was very articulate with a dry wit. I would reject the characterization of him as humourless. He was not a fellow, though, to tell dirty stories. He was not clever in a fashionable sort of way, but neither was he heavy-handed."

Bob Stanfield graduated Magna Cum Laude from Harvard in the spring of 1939, handsome and brimming over with dry wit. He had his law diploma in his hand, Europe was teetering on the brink of war, and he still had no idea of what he wanted to do with the rest of his life.

4
Becoming a Politician
(1939-1948)

While the Liberal leadership is automatically equivalent to the premiership and therefore attracts men of the highest capabilities, the rival party can offer no such alluring prospects. An individual of moderate means may be persuaded to neglect his own affairs for a time in the slim hope of capitalizing on a change in public opinion, but eventually he has no choice but to lay down the burden.

– The Government of Nova Scotia (1957)
J. Murray Beck, political scientist

The Bob Stanfield who came home from Harvard in the summer of 1939 was outwardly the same unassuming, reserved young man he had been when he left to "go across the street" three years earlier. But inwardly he had changed. He was no longer the youth who three summers before had hunted through the cities and towns of Germany for the cheapest glass of milk. He had just turned twenty-five. He was mature. His mind had been honed in competition and in conversation with some of the continent's brightest young men of his age. He had developed a political philosophy that, while it was not yet directed to partisan politics, combined American liberalism with British democratic socialism. He was convinced of the need for government intervention in the economy to correct what were, to him, the only too evident flaws in the capitalist system. He had developed an appreciation of the rights of the individual. No nationalist, he regarded the United States, as did many people in the Maritimes, as the logical market for the region's goods and as a source of inspiration for political and social ideas that might be adapted to Canadian use.

He was also, in that summer of 1939, ambitious in an as yet unfocussed sort of way. It is one of the anomalies of Stanfield's political career that he has succeeded without ever appearing to be ambitious. He does not consider himself to be an ambitious man and neither do many of the people who know him well. But others do see the ambition that has motivated him throughout his career. It is not the sort of ambition that can only be satisfied through self-aggrandizement. It is an ambition that causes him to seek competition, that induces him to accept exceptionally difficult challenges, and that drives him to see them through to a successful conclusion. It was ambition, not pure altruism (or a death wish), that was to compel him to take over the shattered remains of the Nova Scotia Conservative Party and build it into the toughest provincial political machine in the country. It was ambition plus a desire to prove himself that pushed him to provide if not the best government the Province had ever had, at least one of the best. It was ambition plus a sense of duty to party that persuaded him to seek the federal leadership in 1967. And it was ambition, plus a need to redeem himself and his party, that forced him, with infinite patience and tact, to pick up the pieces following the Trudeau landslide of 1968 and to rebuild the Conservative Party to the point where it could capitalize on the public's disenchantment with Pierre Trudeau to bring the Liberals to their knees just four years later.

"I think he is an ambitious man in terms of his private self," says Dalton Camp. "He's very very aware of the possibility of letting someone else down. . . . The trouble with Stanfield is that he's not a multi-faceted guy. He is resolute. He sets objectives and he makes them. He's like the British prime ministers Stanley Baldwin, Anthony Eden, and Ted Heath. If you put aside the aberrations like Trudeau and Kennedy, these are the guys that make it. . . . He has the dedication, the steel resolve."

The fact that Bob Stanfield has no burning desire to stand on the spotlit stage while the bands play, the crowds roar, and the television cameras zoom in does not mean he lacks ambition, pride, dedication, and resolve. He may not be consumed with lust to be Prime Minister, but he wants the job badly. The prime ministership is what Stanfield's politics is all about. His ambition is woven into the fabric of his character, and, not being a particularly introspective man, he does not waste much time worrying about it.

Attributes such as ambition, a trained and thoughtful mind, and a set of philosophical convictions are found in most successful politicians, but Bob Stanfield in that summer of 1939 was still searching for a vocation.

He knew he wanted to continue his research in Economics in the hope of understanding the causes of the Depression. But he did not see those studies consuming his full attention. He could have returned to Dalhousie to teach Economics or Law, but a teaching career held little appeal for him. Law fascinated him as an intellectual discipline, but he could not see himself devoting his life to writing wills, arranging divorces, and defending purse-snatchers. Although he suspected a career in business was inevitable, it was not a prospect he embraced with any enthusiasm. War was on the horizon and soon young men his age would be talking of enlisting. That avenue, however, was closed to him because of a curvature of the spine, which made him medically unfit for military service. What about politics? After all, the Stanfields might be businessmen first, but politics ran a close second in their affections. "I was intensely interested in political questions, social reform, and so on," says Stanfield, "but not partisan politics. My wife told me a few years later that she didn't know how she put up with my patronizing attitude toward her when she discussed any of these questions. I had quite a patronizing attitude toward politicians, practical politicians. I had no intention of getting mixed up with them." He was by no means certain that summer that he was even a Conservative.

Stanfield was sure of only one thing – that he wanted to get married and the sooner the better. He had had the girl picked out for five years. His only problem was to get her back from Europe and into the church for the ceremony.

As a politician, Stanfield displays so little public passion that it is sometimes hard to imagine him harbouring the same depths of emotion – the same capacity to love and to hate – as other, less private, less self-disciplined men. But his love for Joyce Frazee was a great love and it dwarfed any emotion he had felt to that time. She was the only important thing in his life.

He had met Joyce Frazee in the summer of 1934, following his second year at Dalhousie, and it happened, as many things seemed over the years to happen to Bob Stanfield, quite by accident. He had been idling the summer away with his friends at their cabin on Folly Lake when he decided he had better go into Truro to spend the weekend with his mother. "You're a fine brother," Mrs. Stanfield chastised him. "You haven't been over to see your sister." Kit Stanfield Davies had taken a cottage for the summer near Pictou, and Bob's mother finally badgered him into going over there to visit Kit. There were three cottages close together. Kit and her family had the one at the top of the hill and C.W. Frazee, a manager with the Royal Bank of Canada in Montreal, had the one down by the water. Frazee also had a nineteen-year-old daughter, as the twenty-year-old Bob Stanfield soon discovered. He wound up staying for the rest of the summer. The Frazees were in the habit of summering in the area because Mrs. Frazee came from a prominent Pictou County family. Her father – Joyce's maternal grandfather – was Simon Holmes, Conservative Premier of Nova Scotia from 1878 to 1882. Simon Holmes was by no means the greatest politician of his day. Two months after he resigned as premier, his disorganized Tories were defeated by the Liberals who proceeded to rule the Province without interruption for the next forty-three years. Joyce Frazee thought it distinctly ungallant when Bob Stanfield cheerfully reminded her of those facts.

Joyce was studying painting in Montreal and Bob (in his third year at Dalhousie) went there the following Christmas to see her, and again in the spring. Then the Royal Bank moved the Frazees to Vancouver, and when Joyce's father retired a year later he elected to remain in British Columbia. Geography complicated what had been a promising courtship. Joyce and Bob wrote to each other faithfully for most of the two years after she went to Vancouver. Gradually, however, her letters became less frequent and, though Bob kept writing, she stopped answering. She was busy with her art studies in Vancouver and going out with other men; as nearly as a worried Bob Stanfield could figure it out, she saw little point in trying to keep a long-distance love alive. "I had really become a bookworm at this point," Stanfield admits. "There was no question during my last two years at Dalhousie my main preoccupations were my life at Dalhousie and Joyce Frazee."

Then at Christmas, during his first year at Harvard, he heard from Joyce again. She wrote to say that her father was going to accompany her to Europe where she planned to stay on by herself for a year. They were sailing from Vancouver through the Panama Canal to New York before embarking for Europe. Could Bob come down to New York to see her for the weekend? He went down from Harvard; by the end of the weekend he and Joyce had reached an "understanding." The understanding was by no means a formal engagement. An independent-minded girl who was in no hurry to marry and not at all reluctant to try activities that were unorthodox for girls of her age, she stretched her one year in Europe to three. After the first year in London, she moved on to Florence for two years. With two girl friends, one English and the other Canadian, she hitch-hiked through Europe, getting as far as Greece. The Greek government refused to let them enter the country. Young Bob must have recognized in Joyce Frazee a girl after his own thrifty heart. "They spent very little money and prided themselves on how little they spent," says Stanfield. "They slept out at night except occasionally when it was raining very hard."

In the summer of 1937, following his first year at Harvard, he went to Europe again and eventually caught up to Joyce in France. They spent two weeks together in late summer and he persuaded her to become engaged. He went back to Harvard and she to Florence and they did not see each other again until she returned to Canada just before the outbreak of World War II in September, 1939. They were married on June 5, 1940.

Stanfield was still not settled in a career. He decided that, having spent three years in law school, he might as well be admitted to the Nova Scotia

Bar in case he ever decided he wanted to practise law. After articling for nine months, he passed his bar admission. In 1940, he went to work in Truro as assistant secretary of the Acadia Trust Company, the firm his father had established. He joined the trust company, not with any enthusiasm for a career in business, but rather, as he put it, "on the basis that it wouldn't be a very exacting job and would give me enough leisure to do the things in economic theory I wanted to do, because I still thought really of being able to find the secret of the business cycle. I was really quite committed in the sense of doing something in the area of economic theory."

The understanding was that Bob, after a suitable apprenticeship, would take over the little trust company. He soon found, however, that he had no interest in the business and no wish to spend his life managing other people's money. Early in 1942, he and the management of Acadia Trust agreed it would be in everyone's interest if he went elsewhere.

Stanfield was preparing to settle into a career with the law firm of Patterson and Smith in Truro when his old friend and mentor Russell Maxwell once again changed the direction of his life. Maxwell had made a habit of dropping in on Bob and Joyce Stanfield whenever he was in the Truro area, and he was well aware of Bob's unhappiness.

At that time the federal government had established the Wartime Prices and Trade Board with an office in Halifax to oversee enforcement of the Cabinet's wartime regulations in the economic field. Another of Maxwell's former students, Bill Jost, had been hired as enforcement counsel in Halifax. One Sunday, as Jost and Maxwell were strolling in a park in Halifax, Jost mentioned his problems in finding staff. Maxwell recommended Bob Stanfield. Jost's offer of a job with the Wartime Prices and Trade Board was quickly accepted by Stanfield. It offered the promise of work that was both challenging and useful. For Joyce Stanfield, it meant escape from Truro. After three years in Europe, Joyce was finding small-town Nova Scotian life confining. Bob thought the bright lights of Halifax would be much more to her liking. In the spring of 1942, Joyce and their baby daughter, Sarah, moved to Halifax to join Bob who had gone on ahead to start work with the Board.

He remained at the Wartime Prices and Trade Board until the end of the war, starting as a rent control officer and later succeeding Bill Jost as enforcement counsel. The work was a revelation to Stanfield – quite unlike any experience he had ever had. For the first time, he was brought into direct personal contact with the seamier side of life as it existed in the brawling port city of Halifax. It was his job to investigate complaints and track down and prosecute gouging landlords and other war profiteers. He soon won a reputation as a mild and gentle-mannered man to meet on the street but a tough and dangerous administrator to run afoul of. Those years also gave Stanfield his first insight into how government regulations work, or fail to work, and what a profound effect they have on business. "It probably had a fair effect on my attitude toward price control and regulations ever since," he says. "I came away from the Wartime Prices and Trade Board experience with the strong feeling that regulations have quite a limited role to play except in case of emergency. It is extremely difficult to keep them in touch with reality."

Stanfield's opinion of economic controls has not changed materially since those days. During the 1972 election campaign he reluctantly embraced wage and price control, doing so partly because he felt that inflation had become such a serious problem that it could be curbed only by government controls and, perhaps more importantly, because he knew advocating wage and price control was good politics. He religiously qualified his advocacy, however, by insisting that controls would be effective only if they were temporary, and that he would implement them only if absolutely necessary. If he is still something of a Keynesian, his acceptance of government intervention in the economy is tempered by his personal, wartime experience of the practical difficulties that such intervention creates.

His years on the Wartime Prices and Trade Board also gave Stanfield an insight into the injustices that government regulations can produce. He says: "The justice was rough. The regulations were set up to prevent injustice; I appreciated that and I certainly felt the work I was involved in was worthwhile. In the circumstances that existed in the war they did less injustice than they prevented. I was sure of that. But I became more and more impressed by the difficulty of controlling the economy. Each time you made a mistake, it became cumulative. You lived with it. You couldn't get rid of the darned thing." He also developed a healthy scepticism about the so-called science of economic forecasting. "The Commissars from Ottawa came to Halifax whenever they saw an emergency developing. But that emergency never developed. Others did." Stanfield was learning that managing the economy was not as simple as it had seemed to him in his student days.

At the end of the war, Bob and Joyce Stanfield bought a new home, a century-old gabled and turreted house called "The Oaks" on Gorsebrook Road in an affluent district of Halifax. Life at "The Oaks" was warm and happy as the Stanfield family grew through the late 1940s and early 1950s with the arrival of the next three children: Max (named after Russell Maxwell) in 1947, Judy in 1950, and Mimi in 1953. Never a man with a large circle of intimate friends, Stanfield preferred to spend his time with his children. He played Snakes-and-Ladders with them in the evening, took

44

them skating in winter, and went swimming and picnicking with them in summer. Each morning he walked the younger children to school. Stanfield spent hours buried in his books on Economics, still seeking an understanding of the business cycle. He and Joyce also passed many evenings listening to their favourite classical records; friends who drove past the darkened house at night suspected that the Stanfields often turned off the lights so that visitors would not interrupt them while they were listening to Beethoven or Brahms.

His job on the Wartime Prices and Trade Board ended following the war, and Bob looked around for something else to do. He did not need a job. He was financially independent and had no desire to get a job just for the sake of having something to do. He was still looking for a career that would engage his intellect and his energies. "I wasn't interested in working just to make money," he says. "I wanted to do something that interested me and that I thought was worth doing." For lack of a more compelling alternative, he decided to practise law in Halifax, entering into partnership with Russell MacInnes, an older lawyer.

From there, Stanfield, as he puts it, just "slipped" slowly but inevitably into Conservative politics. Most promising young barristers in Halifax would have slit their throats before they allowed themselves to "slip" into the Conservative Party of Nova Scotia in the mid - 1940s. It was less a party than a memory. By 1945, the Tories had held power in the province for only twelve of the seventy-eight years since Confederation. They had been out of office for the past twelve years – since 1933 when the Liberals under Angus L. Macdonald had swept to power. The Conservatives were in a seemingly irreversible decline. They won eight of the thirty seats in 1933, five in 1937, four in 1941, and then hit rock bottom in the provincial election of 1945 when they failed to win a single seat. Macdonald's Liberals took twenty-eight seats in that election with the C.C.F. picking up two Cape Breton seats. Worse, the Conservatives' share of the popular vote had been declining by about six percentage points in each election till it reached 33.5 per cent in 1945. The Tories that year polled only 97, 774 votes, barely a third as many as they had polled twenty years earlier.

The future appeared as bleak as the past. Angus L. Macdonald, a dour, hollow-cheeked Scotsman, was one of the great orators of the time, and was held in near-reverence by a majority of Nova Scotians. "All's Well With Angus L." was the Liberal rallying cry, and the people believed it. Macdonald grew stronger with each election. He took temporary leave of provincial politics to go to Ottawa to serve as Minister of Defence for Naval Services in the wartime cabinet of Mackenzie King. He returned in 1945, and his landslide victory in the election of that year showed how pleased the people were to have him home again. Even history, as the Tories were well aware, was on the side of Angus L. From Confederation to the present, no premier of Nova Scotia who has led his party to victory in an election has ever been voted out of office. It is when premiers try to pass their mantle on to a successor that changes of government occur. Angus L. Macdonald was in distressingly good health in 1945 and seemed destined to run Province House for many years to come.

For the Conservatives, the dilemma was not to decide *how* to proceed, but whether to bother proceeding at all. Some Conservatives argued openly that their party might as well admit it was extinct. Leonard Fraser, an engaging and eloquent man who had led the party to the debacle of 1945, said it all when he told his followers he was resigning as leader in 1946: "A leader, if he is properly to lead, must lead both usefully and hopefully. You are the judges as to whether I have or can lead usefully, but I alone must be the judge as to whether I can lead hopefully. In view of the results in the [last] two elections . . . I am forced to the conclusion that I can no longer lead this party hopefully and that leaves me only one course to follow."

Bob Stanfield by now was almost thirty-two years old; it seemed probable that, not having succumbed to the family's weakness for public life by then, he was immune to politics. The chances are he might never have "slipped" into political life at all if he had chosen anyone other than Russell MacInnes for a law partner. MacInnes was a friend of George Nowlan, a Wolfville lawyer in his late forties who had served two terms in the provincial Legislature before losing his seat in 1933. Nowlan, who later became a minister in the Diefenbaker government in Ottawa, was the moving spirit behind the handful of provincial Conservatives who were prepared to fight to save the party. He was in the habit of dropping in at the offices of MacInnes and Stanfield to talk politics with his friend, Russell MacInnes. Bob Stanfield got to know Nowlan on these visits, liked him, and when Nowlan suggested one day in 1946 that Bob might like to come along to a weekend meeting of Conservatives at Hackmatack Inn in Chester, a village forty-three miles west of Halifax, Stanfield could think of no excuse to decline.

It was the sort of meeting that today would be puffed up, billed as a "thinkers' conference," and presented to the public, through the press, as having some cataclysmic significance in the life of the party. Nova Scotia Conservatives of 1946 would have laughed at such pretentiousness. For them, the weekend at the Hackmatack Inn was simply a chance to get together with their fellow wounded warriors, kill a few bottles of rum, and, divided up into small groups (workshops is the fashionable description today), talk about what they were going to do about their poor, sick, leaderless party. So insignificant was most of the discussion that people who were there can no longer recall a single specific item on the agenda. Rod Black, later the party's leading organizer, got bored and walked out. Bob Stanfield stayed, though as he recalls "nothing very much happened there." Frank Stanfield, Jr., walked in, spotted his younger brother, and said with a grin, "Well, I'm glad at least to find out that you're a Conservative." Bob was not so sure: "I hadn't thought of myself as a Conservative, not with a big *C* anyway. . . . I didn't really identify myself with the party at that meeting. I went there and I suppose people like my brother thought that was an identification. I didn't see myself in terms of active party politics at all at this point."

It would be a gross exaggeration to claim that Stanfield took the Conservatives by storm that weekend. Ike Smith, who succeeded Stanfield as Premier in 1967, remembers seeing Bob at the meeting: "I don't remember him taking any great part in the general discussion. He did say something, but what it was, I don't remember." Richard Donahoe, who became Attorney General in the Stanfield cabinet, thinks he recalls seeing Stanfield at Hackmatack Inn – "but I wouldn't swear to it." Others who attended the meeting have no recollection of Stanfield's having been there. Stanfield, however, need not feel slighted. No one at all remembers that John Bracken, then the party's national leader, was also there.

Although no one could know it at the time, least of all Bob Stanfield, the insignificant little meeting at Hackmatack Inn was the beginning of the rebirth of the Conservative Party in the Province, if only because it was the start of Stanfield's political career.

His interest whetted by the Hackmatack Inn gathering, Stanfield began to devote more and more of his time to thinking and talking about the problems of Nova Scotia. Without yet regarding himself as an active Conservative, he nonetheless worried about the Liberals' virtual monopoly in the Legislature. He wondered how to restore the two-party system in the province and how to pull Nova Scotia out of the economic doldrums. Nova Scotia at that time was often described as a province of "genteel poverty." The Macdonald government was good at building roads (all Nova Scotia governments had to be good at building roads if they wanted to remain the government), but it was lethargic when it came to bringing industry to the province. Without the jobs that industry would bring, young Nova Scotians were flocking out of the province at, according to some estimates, the rate of ten thousand a year. It was said there were more Nova Scotians living in Massachusetts and Western Canada than there were in Nova Scotia – and it was probably true. More seriously, those who remained had come to accept the status quo. They were a have-not province; they accepted that they were destined to remain one. And, although they might not be happy about it, they told one another it was futile to try to change their lot.

This aura of defeatism did not seem to alarm the Macdonald government, but it troubled Robert Stanfield. In the winter of 1946-1947, he organized a study group of young lawyers and businessmen in Halifax to meet at intervals to discuss the economic problems of the province. They invited experts to join them in examination of specific areas of the economy. For example, the Deputy Minister of Lands and Forests came one evening to talk about the situation in Nova Scotia's forest industry. Most of the members of the study group were Conservatives, though that fact did not strike Stanfield as being particularly significant at the time.

Meanwhile, George Nowlan, as president of what remained of the provincial party, was following up on the Hackmatack Inn meeting and scouring the Province in search for a successor to Leonard Fraser as leader. He was having no luck. None of the people who he felt were equipped for the leadership were willing to devote the time, effort, and money that it would obviously require to rebuild the party, assuming the party could be rebuilt at all. Nowlan hosted a series of informal dinner meetings at the Lord Nelson Hotel in Halifax to discuss the state of the party and the prospect of finding a leader. Sometimes as few as five or six people attended; other times there were as many as fifteen. Stanfield attended some of these meetings, but no one, in the beginning at least, saw him as a potential leader.

Attention was focussed on others: Roland Ritchie, an Oxford University graduate and lawyer in Halifax who was later appointed to the Supreme Court of Canada; R.J. (Bob) Rankin, the managing editor of the Halifax *Herald;* Henry P. MacKeen, the party's chief fund-raiser, who became lieutenant-governor of Nova Scotia; Richard Donahoe, the most prominent practising Conservative politician in Halifax (which meant, inevitably, that he had lost every election he had run in); George Isaac (Ike) Smith, a Truro lawyer and future premier, who had come back from the war with a brilliant record as a colonel in the Canadian Army; Donald Grant, another ex-army officer; and George Nowlan himself. Nowlan could have had the leadership for the asking, but he was nearly fifty years old; he took the sensible view that, with a long period in the wilderness facing the party, the job should go to a younger man.

At one of the meetings at the Lord Nelson, the name of Bob Stanfield was raised as a leadership possibility. Stanfield demurred, saying not only was he not interested in being leader, but he was not interested in getting involved in politics in any serious way. "But," he recalls, "I told them I was interested in seeing a more aggressive attitude developed toward the problems of the province and that I'd been working with this [study] group. I said I was prepared to spend a certain amount of time doing some organizing with a view to getting the party to a position where it could attract a leader. That's really what I set out to do in that period."

With the help of Ike Smith, Dick Donahoe, Tom Coffin (later a judge), and others, Stanfield set out about the province getting to know the people in the party and to restore their flagging spirits. A meeting of the party's provincial executive was convened shortly thereafter, and Stanfield reported that he felt he was making reasonable headway in rekindling interest in the party. Then he went a step further. Says he: "I was tactless enough to say to them that the party had to get some new faces, that these people associated with defeat had to step aside a bit and that some of us would be prepared to do some work in organization if they'd give us the authority. They did and I took over [the organizational side]."

Nowlan was still president of the party at this stage; Stanfield held no official position, and the search for a leader seemed far from ended. If Stanfield harboured a secret longing to be leader then, it was not apparent to any of the others, nor even to himself. He continued his organizational work for another six months, and it began to dawn, imperceptibly, on others that the man they needed as their leader might be right under their noses. As they cold-bloodedly assessed the situation, charisma and eloquence on the platform were not the most essential qualities in a new leader. Their leader needed to be a man who had enough money of his own that he could afford to devote his time fully to building the party without the distraction of having to worry about feeding his family. Ike Smith saw it in just those terms: "We felt that the person who took it had to be in a position to do a full-time job at it, that it was not a part-time affair. If we couldn't find a person who could do it full-time and support him financially, then it wasn't worthwhile. So when we began thinking along those lines, we didn't take too long to conclude that if we could find a person who was interested and who was in a position not to worry too much about whether he worked or not, probably that would be the kind of person to have. I don't know if it was ever put to Bob that way, but I suspect it was."

It was. And Stanfield saw the logic of it. There was absolutely no way the Conservatives could hope to afford a salary for a leader – or even pay his expenses – while he worked to revive the party. With Stanfield, it would not have to. He was wealthy, unenthusiastic about the practice of law, and he had the time to devote to the party. Besides, he was becoming intrigued by the challenge and he had begun to demonstrate that he had a talent for grass-roots political organization.

It was also growing clear to others in the party that Stanfield possessed a sense of duty that, as Ike Smith puts it, "would make it difficult for him to resist, if he really thought that people were of a mind that he could do it."

Stanfield, however, has never been a man who can be hurried into important decisions. A more dynamic person would have jumped in with both feet, but he hung back, arguing that with a little more effort the party might well find someone better qualified, more experienced, and more attractive for the leadership. He did agree, however, largely at the urging of Ike Smith, to stand for the presidency of the Nova Scotia Progressive Conservative Party. While holding serious reservations about Stanfield's leadership capabilities, George Nowlan was sufficiently impressed by his organizational talents that he agreed to step aside as party president. At the annual meeting in the fall of 1947, Bob Stanfield was acclaimed as President of the Progressive Conservative Association of Nova Scotia.

"I don't want to just jump out of the cold and take on the leadership," Stanfield told Ike Smith. "I want to see whether I can do it or not, and whether people are prepared to accept the kind of fellow I am, because I'm not a very flamboyant person." He made it clear to that annual meeting he regarded the office of president not as an automatic stepping stone to the leadership, but primarily as a means to help attract someone else to become leader. "A dynamic leader would be a great help," he told the delegates to the meeting. "A poor choice would finish us. It is surely better to drive ahead without a leader until we see the man we want." As he stepped off the stage at the end of his speech, he confessed he felt utterly inadequate to do battle with the eloquent and beloved Angus L. Macdonald: "I just haven't got what it takes."

As president, Stanfield redoubled his efforts to resurrect the party. He adopted a formula and a style that were to become his trademarks. He spent a year travelling into every constituency and every town in the province, hunting up people who had been supporters of the Conservatives in the past. He talked to them about the party, its problems and its prospects; he argued the importance of re-establishing the Conservatives as the opposition party in Nova Scotia. Gently, he laboured the point that the economy was languishing under the benign neglect of the Macdonald government. When he finished, he would ask: "Well, let me see, who else around here should I go and see?" Then on to the next person to repeat the message. Once he had identified Conservatives, he revived dormant constituency associations and organized meetings at which local Tories elected new officers. It was exhausting, often discouraging work, but it paid dividends. Gradually he developed a network of contacts across the province – people who, if they believed the party could be revived, would go to work for it and perhaps stand as candidates. When he returned to a constituency for the second,

50

third or fourth time, he found that people knew him, liked him, and were coming to respect his dedication, determination, and skill as a political organizer. "He demonstrated a very considerable degree of organizational ability and inspiration in the course of that year," says Dick Donahoe, the Halifax Tory. Ken Matthews, a Truro lawyer who became one of Stanfield's most dedicated workers, says that that year as president gave Stanfield the organizational tools with which he fashioned his later successes: "A great number of elected people don't know very much about organization. They think they do because they get elected, but Bob Stanfield is one of the fellows who really does know a lot about good organization." The people he met and persuaded to work with him that year were to become the heart and the sinew of the Stanfield political machine in Nova Scotia.

By the time the party's leadership convention assembled in November, 1948, Stanfield had established himself as the obvious choice for leader. Obvious, that is, to almost everyone but George Nowlan. Though Nowlan was proud of boasting (perfectly accurately) in later years that he was the one who had brought Stanfield into politics, he did not support him for the leadership in 1948. Not only that, but for reasons known only to himself, Nowlan went out and recruited another candidate for leader: C. Fred Fraser, one-time editor of the old Halifax *Chronicle*. Though this new Fraser came from a well known Nova Scotia family, he had no background in politics and was an utter non-entity in the Conservative Party.

Four theories are advanced to account for Nowlan's mysterious action and the truth may well be a combination of the four. Stanfield attributes it to his own inability to make up his mind whether or not to seek the leadership; perhaps this led Nowlan to conclude that Stanfield would not be a candidate.

To Ike Smith, Nowlan's support for Fred Fraser did not mean he had cooled on Stanfield. "George told me he thought it would be better for Bob's confidence if there were a contest and that if he couldn't win a contest then perhaps it was just as well to cut if off then. I'm sure he hoped Bob would win." However, Dick Donahoe, who nominated Stanfield for leader, saw darker motives: "I think that Nowlan was not at all convinced that Stanfield was the right person to be elected, and I think that he wanted somebody that he thought would have a little more colour and a little more appeal perhaps than Stanfield had. I do not think they were political enemies, but, at that time, he certainly wasn't a Stanfield man or a Stanfield supporter. He still had to be convinced." Others advance a fourth theory: that although Nowlan liked Bob personally, he did not want to see any Stanfield as leader of the party. That, they say, was the result of bad blood between the two families going back to the days when George Nowlan was a young member of the Legislature and Bob's father, Frank, Sr., as party whip, had had to restrain Nowlan when he grew too lavish in his election promises of new highway construction in his riding. But if there was bad blood, it was not evident to Bob Stanfield. In later years, Nowlan, as the voice of Nova Scotia in the Diefenbaker cabinet, and Stanfield, as premier, worked together closely and in harmony to bring more federal favours to the province.

Whatever Nowlan's reasons, his candidate, Fred Fraser, got nowhere. Stanfield defeated him solidly, but not overwhelmingly, for the leadership. For better or for worse, thirty-four-year-old Bob Stanfield was the leader of the battered corpse that called itself the Progressive Conservative Party of Nova Scotia. Many Conservatives, even those who liked Stanfield best, feared it would prove to be for the worse. "It was a very tepid beginning," Rod Black recalls. "There was no enthusiasm for him at all. . . . The mood of the party was very apathetic."

Stanfield himself was not at all certain that he had made a wise decision, and he refused to look on the leadership as anything more than a short-term proposition: "I never thought of it as a lifetime career. I didn't think I could take the party very far. I thought we could get some people in the house in opposition, then somebody else could take over." His sister, Kit, knew exactly what she thought of her brother becoming leader of the poor sick party. "My God," she said. "Bob's out of his mind."

It would be several years before they all realized how wrong they had been.

5

The Maritime Mafia

Question: *"Can you define how you feel about Bob Stanfield?"*
Answer: *"Can you define with exactitude why you fell in love with your wife?"*

> – G.I. Smith, ex-premier of Nova Scotia, interview, December, 1972.

They tell a story in Nova Scotia about the new Roman Catholic priest who arrived in town shortly before a provincial election back in the age when TV was still a novelty. The priest, as everyone knew, had the only TV set in town. One Sunday after mass, several men of his parish, staunch Liberals all, inquired of the priest whether they might drop by to watch the results on election night. The priest readily agreed. On election night, his guests watched impatiently until the announcer read the results for the poll in their small community: eighty-seven votes for the Liberal candidate and forty-six for the Conservative. Instead of being elated, as the priest expected his new friends to be, they sat in stunned silence. "But Alec," said one finally to the man next to him, "how can this be? There are eighty-seven Liberals in town, but everyone knows there are only forty-five Tories." Then, as a man, they turned and stared stonily at the priest.

The story is surely apocryphal, but Nova Scotians like to tell it because it illustrates the seriousness and intensity with which they used to take their politics. There were – and still are a few – ridings where a switch of fifty votes meant the difference between landslide victory and overwhelming defeat, places where the wise poll captain checked the death notices in the newspaper for the names of supporters and opponents just as avidly as the horse player checked the race results. In places such as these, a man would have had a better chance of taking a mistress and keeping it a secret than he would have had in changing his political allegiance without his neighbours knowing. It was in this sort of political climate that the practice of "treating" (as it was euphemistically known) was born and flourished in the struggle between the parties to convert the uncertain voter. "Treating" was simply an extension of the normal process of persuading the reluctant voter by introducing into the political equation a pint of rum or a banknote of small denomination. Not all organizers, of course, found it necessary to employ such unsubtle tools, but it was a foolish poll captain or ward chairman who did not at least have a little refreshment on hand in case some of his friends stopped by to slake their thirst after the trek to the polls.

Dalton Camp, who has a rare ability to capture the feel of politics, described a typical early 1950s election day in Nova Scotia in his book, *Gentlemen, Players and Politicians:*

"Rural poll organizers knew their neighbours; they knew who was poor and what their politics and their price were. On election day clouds of dust hung over the country roads as the cars of competing political parties hustled from house to house, hauling out their vote, bargaining, bartering, and buying the poor and recalcitrant. These men, consumed by their partisan pride and fervour, compulsively rendered meaningless the fundamental purpose of their restless energy, which was to maintain a party system by allowing the free choice of free men as to who should govern them."

Robert Stanfield was raised in this political climate, but he was one of the first of a new breed of politician in Nova Scotia. He brought to provincial politics a quality of detachment, independence of mind, and freedom from partisan fervour. He was a man with an extraordinarily clear intellect, uncluttered by trivia and unsullied by emotion. He was a man who always preferred an honest, even if critical, assessment to the mindless flattery of a sycophant. He would listen to any opinion – that he was wrong, that his speeches were hopeless, that his party was doomed – as long as he was satisfied the opinion was based on fact, not fancy. Dalton Camp likes to compare Stanfield to Sergeant Friday, the protagonist in the old TV series, *Dragnet,* who had a stock approach to every problem – "just give me the facts, ma'am." "That's all Stanfield wanted," Camp recalls, "just the facts. He didn't want unsubstantiated opinion or superstition or prejudice or anything else. If he thought you knew what you were talking about, he'd agree to listen. You know the old business of the King's messenger? If it's bad news, shoot him. Well, Stanfield was the first one who ever let the King's messenger live."

Although he was an early representative of the modern Nova Scotia politician, Stanfield knew and understood the older style of politics in the province. He appreciated the importance of politics as it was still being practised along those dusty back roads, and he had a firm grasp of poll-by-poll organization and door-to-door campaigning. In a sense he straddled two political generations.

He would never have achieved the success he did, however, had it not been for a cadre of exceptionally talented, determined, and contemporary people who served him. Like Stanfield, they were people who had the background to understand the uses of the old politics and the wit to be excited by the opportunities of the new. They became his apprentices in the "Chinese Water Torture" school of politics: drop-by-drop wearing away of the awesome façade of the Nova Scotia Liberal Party until there was almost nothing left. They were Stanfield's Maritime Mafia.

Five men and one woman, they are Dalton Kingsley Camp, George Isaac (Ike) Smith, Richard Alphonsus Donahoe, Rod MacDonald Black, Ernest Finlay MacDonald, and Flora Isabel MacDonald. They are six very different people, but they are joined by a shared loyalty to Robert Stanfield.

DALTON CAMP

Dalton Camp was not the first member of the Maritime Mafia, but he became its unofficial leader. He was the epitome of the "new politician" – a brilliant play-maker who, although he had little love for the exhausting, door-knocking side of politics, had an instinctive feel for election campaigns. A complete master of political strategy, he knew how to isolate and exploit election issues. He was also a man of considerable political courage as he demonstrated in 1966 when, as national president of the Conservatives, he led the crusade to exorcise John Diefenbaker from the leadership of his party.

Camp's roots are in Atlantic Canada, as are the roots of all the members of the Maritime Mafia. He was born in Woodstock, New Brunswick in 1920; although he has lived his adult years in Upper Canada, he still does his best political thinking and manoeuvring from his cottage at Robertson's Point, N.B. In his student days at the University of New Brunswick, he was a Liberal. He was in the Chateau Laurier Hotel in Ottawa on the day that Mackenzie King announced his retirement from politics. He was back in Ottawa in 1948 to cast a forlorn ballot for Chubby Power at the leadership convention that chose Louis St. Laurent to succeed King. Soon Camp was frustrated, however, by the lack of opportunity for bright young men in the Liberal Party; by the time he returned from post-graduate studies at the London School of Economics, he was a Tory.

He went into the advertising business in Toronto with the firm of Locke, Johnson, later opening his own agency. Ever since the invention of advertising (or perhaps it is since the invention of politics) there has been a close, warm, and mutually-rewarding relationship between politicians and advertising men. And few advertising men who have assisted winning politicians have ever been known to starve for the lack of government accounts. In any event, Locke, Johnson was only too happy to allow Camp to roam the country managing publicity campaigns for Conservatives – as long as he returned with the occasional worthwhile account. His first major campaign (and his first success) came in New Brunswick in 1952 when the Tories under Hugh John Flemming ended seventeen years of Liberal administration.

On the strength of his performance in New Brunswick, Camp was asked the following year by George Nowlan to go down to Halifax to see if there was anything he could do to help Bob Stanfield in the forthcoming provincial election there. Camp had no illusions about Stanfield, knowing him by reputation to be a dull, dour man. Camp relates his first impression of Stanfield in *Gentlemen, Players and Politicians:* "Well, I thought, at least he's not pretty. Long-headed with shrewd, heavily-lidded eyes (a slight cast in one, like all the Shaws on my mother's side), a long nose and a full mouth. All else was elbows and knees. He invited me to sit down and for a while there was an uneasy silence."

It was a conversation designed to turn off even the most self-confident young advertising man. Camp had never met a politician who was so dispassionate about his party's chances in an election. Stanfield said he did not expect to win but did expect to improve on the eight seats his party had held for the past four years. That was typical of Stanfield, though it baffled Camp. He was highly unimpressed with Stanfield's marketability.

"On the other hand," Camp says, "you got the feeling you were dealing with somebody who was relentlessly honest and with a remarkable self-awareness. And for openers, that's pretty helpful. Most people tend to snow you, to tell you how great their prospects are, and how super they are going to be. He was very direct, very honest, candid, very self-effacing, realistic." As they talked, Camp became aware that he was in the presence of a man who was at least as intelligent as he was – perhaps more intelligent. Stanfield had thought his prospects through and had come to a realistic appraisal of his chances. He was interested in what Camp thought about the political situation in Nova Scotia, but only to the extent that Camp's opinions were based on facts that Stanfield himself knew to be true. Says Camp: "He operates on the basis of 'I want him to tell me whatever intelligence he can present on the basis of what I know.' . . . He knew I was from Toronto, the fast gun in the Maritimes, but he wasn't satisfied with my hallucinations about Nova Scotia. You couldn't come away from a meeting like that without a grudging respect." In Camp's view, Stanfield has not changed a bit since that spring day in 1953.

56

That strained, first meeting in Stanfield's office in Halifax was the start of one of the closest relationships in Canadian politics. The two men complement each other perfectly, despite their dramatically different styles. Stanfield's greatest shortcoming as a public figure is his inability to invest his politics with the vital dimension of emotion: feeling, passion, and excitement. He distrusts the sort of language that would elevate his speeches above the pedestrian; if he had his own way, he would seldom use an adjective or an adverb. Camp understands that politics is an art as well as a science, that good politics must also be good theatre. He knows that the public votes with its emotions as much as with its mind. It was Camp who brought Stanfield out of himself, taught him this extra dimension, and helped turn him from a plodding provincial politician into the most consistently successful Conservative of his day.

Stanfield, in turn, taught Camp the value of self-discipline, restraint, and responsibility in politics. Their finest hour as collaborators came in 1956 when Stanfield, in a campaign plotted and executed by Camp, was elected Premier of Nova Scotia. Stanfield was no longer just an awkward, inarticulate politician and Camp was no longer just another bright advertising man dabbling in politics. Both had become, in their very different ways, thoroughly professional politicians. Although in recent years they have not seen as much of each other as they used to, their relationship remains close – and private. They talk often on the telephone with Stanfield frequently seeking Camp's advice on matters before Parliament or issues facing the country. Stanfield does not always follow Camp's advice, but he respects it.

It is a relationship that developed slowly. Following their first meeting in 1953, Stanfield was as unsure of Camp as Camp was of him; the chances are that if Camp had not come with George Nowlan's recommendation, Stanfield would never have agreed to put the impetuous young advertising man in charge of his publicity and speech-writing. As it was, Stanfield cautiously appointed a publicity committee to keep a rein on Camp, and the committee laid down one absolute injunction: under no circumstances was Camp to attack Angus L. Macdonald, nor was he even to mention him by name. It was one of the anomalies of politics in Nova Scotia that, although the Tories despised the Grits and all their works, they held the Premier to be above partisan attack. It was a courtesy that the Liberals were to reciprocate in later years when Stanfield was premier.

Camp chafed under the publicity committee's injunction, and his advertising copy therefore carried more bark than bite. A sample: "There is a time when Governments who have held power for long periods – like twenty years – collapse of their own weight. They are voted into office, in the beginning, to breath a little fresh air into public offices, to clean out the dusty corners, empty the waste baskets and give strict attention to the people's business. This is Bob Stanfield's chore at this time. . . . " Much to Camp's discomfiture, that bit of uninspired prose brought the predictable and telling response from the Liberals that Stanfield only wanted to be premier so that he could empty the waste baskets in Province House!

The 1953 election results proved to Camp that Stanfield was a better political prognosticator than he had suspected. As he had forecast, Stanfield did not win, but he did improve his party's position, increasing its seats from eight to twelve.

Camp got back to Ottawa in time for the federal election that year. The next year he was appointed the national party's part-time director of publicity, dividing his time between his advertising job in Toronto and party headquarters in Ottawa. That year, 1954, also saw him back in Nova Scotia. Angus L. Macdonald had died and the Conservatives were desperately anxious to win his seat, Halifax South, in the by-election. They did, and the election of the Conservative candidate, Dick Donahoe, marked a turning point in Stanfield's fortunes. After the by-election, Stanfield accorded to Camp what in the Stanfield lexicon amounted to a ringing declaration of confidence. "Well," said Stanfield, "I'd just as soon not go into a campaign without him." Camp was back again in 1956, by now the acknowledged master of strategy, to direct the campaign that made Stanfield premier. He returned for each of Stanfield's three successful defences – in 1960, 1963, and 1967.

In the months and years in between, Camp was wherever Conservatives were fighting election campaigns: losing in Prince Edward Island in 1955, winning again in New Brunswick in 1956, winning federally with Diefenbaker in 1957, winning with Duff Roblin in Manitoba in 1958, winning with Walter Shaw in Prince Edward Island in 1959, losing in New Brunswick in 1960. The list stretches on: an election nearly every year, and in some years more than one. Camp took his share of beatings, but his victories always loomed larger than his defeats.

His toughest battle was his leadership-review campaign in 1966, which concluded with the federal party voting to convene a leadership convention to choose a successor to Diefenbaker. The following year, Camp put aside his own leadership aspirations to mastermind the campaign that brought his friend, Robert Stanfield, to the leadership of the Progressive Conservative Party of Canada.

Sadly, Camp himself seems destined to remain half hidden in the shadowy wings of the political stage. He has run for Parliament twice: in 1965 he was defeated by Mitchell Sharp, then Trade and Commerce Minister, in Eglinton riding in Toronto; three years later he was swept under in adjacent Don Valley riding by the tide of Trudeaumania.

Today, Camp lives in a comfortable, modern house in the northern part of Toronto, writes a newspaper column, and performs various services for another political ally, Ontario's Premier William Davis, whom Camp helped to win the provincial election of 1971. He writes occasional policy pronouncements for Davis; he served as a member of an Ontario Royal Commission on book publishing and as chairman of an inquiry into the status and perquisites of members of the Ontario Legislature.

It is all worthwhile labour, but Camp's real place is in the federal theatre. That place is in Ottawa as "guru-in-residence" to Robert Stanfield.

IKE SMITH

Ike Smith is a small, pear-shaped man who looks as though his chest had started to slip south but was caught in the nick of time by his belt. He bears the grey pallor of a man who has spent his life in politics and who has survived a severe heart attack. Robert Stanfield was the unquestioned leader in Nova Scotia, and Ike Smith was, without question, his righthand man. He was the absolutely indispensible number two man in the party, the loyal lieutenant who abandoned his own desires and subjugated his own ambitions to those of his leader. The two made an effective fighting machine: Stanfield slow, deliberate, thoughtful, patient; Smith fiery and articulate, a ferocious debater in the Legislature with a trial lawyer's talent for demolishing an opponent's argument. To Smith (and later, to Dick Donahoe) goes much of the credit for the steady improvement in the Conservatives' fortunes in Nova Scotia. Each day in the Legislature, Smith mounted the attack that gradually forced the aging Liberal government to fall back, to regroup, and to attempt, without much success, to counterattack. Without Smith, Stanfield could not have provided an effective Opposition in the House, and, without the reputation of having been the leader of a solid, responsible, hard-hitting Opposition, Stanfield could not have become Premier.

Smith's complete willingness to play second fiddle in the Stanfield orchestra disguised one of the best political brains in the province. His was the voice that Stanfield listened to first and last on matters of party policy, and he relied on Smith's sense of political timing to determine the moment to move against the Liberals on any issue. It was said in Nova Scotia that Ike Smith was the one man who could make Stanfield change his mind after he had made a decision.

Five years older than Stanfield, Smith was born in 1909 in Stewiacke, near Truro. After World War II, in which he served overseas as a colonel in the Canadian Army, he returned to Truro, determined to make a career in law. "I liked criminal practice," he says. "There's more human interest and excitement in it. And when you oppose all the forces of the state and win, there's a certain amount of satisfaction." But Smith was not to have long to devote to the law. Like Robert Stanfield, he was drawn into the rebuilding of the Nova Scotia Progressive Conservative Party. Long an active Conservative, Smith was one of the names on George Nowlan's short list of prospective leaders, and in most ways he would have been a more logical choice than Stanfield. "It didn't seem very logical to me," says Smith. "I didn't take it very seriously." Instead, he persuaded his friend Stanfield to become a candidate.

Stanfield and Smith entered the Legislature together in 1949; Smith carried most of the debating load until Dick Donahoe joined them in 1954. When the Conservatives came to power in 1956, Stanfield offered Smith and Donahoe their choice of portfolios. Both chose Attorney General, the prize of the cabinet posts. Donahoe would not budge, so Smith dutifully agreed to accept a lesser assignment. Donahoe became Attorney General and Smith Minister of Highways, Provincial Secretary, and minister responsible for the Nova Scotia Liquor Commission. The highways department and the liquor commission were in these days the two great patronage arms of the government, making Smith the minister in charge of the pork barrel. When Stanfield refused to clean out all the known Liberals and replace them with Conservatives, as was the tradition, it was Smith who bore the brunt of the party's anger. Stanfield and Smith used to go to political meetings together and Stanfield would have no trouble making it out of the hall afterward. But Smith would find himself surrounded by angry favour-seekers jabbing their fingers into his chest and demanding that Smith justify his failure to dismiss some Liberal and to replace him with a particular Conservative (usually the one behind the jabbing finger).

Unlike many skilled opposition politicians who wilt when they are thrust into positions of power, Smith made the transition from being Stanfield's best debater in Opposition to being his best minister in Government, without losing any of his capacity for the rough and tumble debates on the floor of the Legislature. He was known, both in Opposition and in Government, as Stanfield's "hatchet man" – an accusation that was as true as it was unkind. He was also Stanfield's running mate in Colchester, and, while his leader stumped the province, Smith diligently canvassed this constituency.

In 1962, Stanfield asked Smith to become Provincial Treasurer, a portfolio Stanfield had retained for himself in his first six years as premier. Smith's job was to convert the provincial treasurer's department into a new department of finance and economics and to implement Stanfield's program of Voluntary Economic Planning for the province. Although Smith quickly

60

agreed, he was already a very reluctant cabinet minister. Some of Smith's friends recall that as early as 1956 he was talking of leaving politics to return to his real love, the law. Smith himself dates his desire to 1959, but, every time he tried to get out, he allowed himself to be talked into staying on the ground that Stanfield needed him. By 1967, however, Smith was determined to leave. Stanfield called an election for May 30 that year, and Smith says: "I made up my mind as soon as a decent time had elapsed after the election, I was going to ask Bob to let me ease out."

But Stanfield had no sooner won that election than pressure, tentative to that point, began in earnest to persuade him to run for the federal leadership at the party's convention in September, 1967. Before making up his mind, Stanfield asked Smith for two commitments: that Smith support him for the leadership and that, if Stanfield won, Smith agree to serve as interim premier until the provincial party could hold its own leadership convention. Smith refused. "I thought," says Smith, "in a public spirited yet selfish way that he could do more for Nova Scotia by remaining in Nova Scotia than he could even if he became Prime Minister of Canada, which I didn't expect him to do, or think anybody else was likely to do, very quickly." Smith also knew that, if Stanfield left, the party would regard him as the natural successor and that he would have difficulty avoiding being a candidate for the leadership.

So, partly because he feared what might happen to Stanfield in federal politics and partly because he feared Stanfield's departure would compel him to remain in provincial politics, Smith led the fight to keep Stanfield in Nova Scotia. So effective were his arguments and such was Stanfield's debt to Smith for support over the years that Stanfield, having at one stage decided to run for the national leadership, changed his mind back again. It was only after Smith, under unrelenting pressure from others, reluctantly withdrew his objections that Stanfield announced his candidacy. "I think," says Smith, "that I did say to Bob at one stage. 'It would be a hell of a thing if you were to go up there and were to win this convention and lose the federal election and whoever succeeds you down here also loses the election, so you've got the worst of both worlds.' He just laughed."

They were not laughing later, however, because that is exactly what happened. Stanfield lost the federal election of 1968. Smith had succeeded Stanfield as leader in Nova Scotia, and in 1970 his government was thrown out of office.

The 1970 provincial election was one the Conservatives should never have lost. In 1967, Stanfield left Smith the strongest provincial government in Canada, holding forty of the Legislature's forty-six seats. At first, Smith, seemed to be in no trouble. He even picked up a Liberal seat in a by-election to raise the Conservatives' total to forty-one seats. The Dominion Steel and Coal Company steel mill in Sydney, vital to the economy of Cape Breton, was on the brink of folding when Smith moved in, quickly and decisively, creating a crown corporation that took over the plant and ran it successfully. But, as with any party that has been in power for years, there were problems lurking just below the surface. There were disciplinary problems in the party, including members with drinking problems whom Stanfield had not gotten around to firing. The potent political machine that Stanfield had built had grown complacent after too many easy elections. The Liberals were having great fun, and scoring political points, with the Tories' strawberry farm – an experimental project in Digby County where an American entrepreneur was supposed to be demonstrating that Nova Scotia farmers could successfully convert to strawberries for the Boston market. The experiment ended in chaos and a loss of a half-million dollars. Finally, there were the twin albatrosses of the Clairtone plant in Stellarton and the heavy water plant at Glace Bay. They were projects that, in the excited vision of the Stanfield government, were to usher Nova Scotia into the glamorous new age of electronic and nuclear technology. The Stanfield administration had invested rashly and heavily in the two schemes, and when both proved disasters Ike Smith reaped the whirlwind.

Smith struggled mightily, but he was unable to make the transition from lieutenant to leader. He lacked two of Stanfield's abilities: to delegate responsibility to others, and to leave his problems at the office when he left for the day. Smith laboured all day and all evening in the Premier's office in Province House, personally attending to the most minute details. When he finally got home, exhausted, he lay awake worrying. "Ike couldn't delegate," says Gerry Regan, the Liberal who succeeded Smith as premier. "I think he was a much better number two man. He worked at his desk long and late and he worried over things." Had he been less preoccupied with the problems of being premier, Smith would have noticed that the organizers and workers whom Stanfield had always relied upon for objective appraisals of the party's position were starting to hedge their advice to Smith. They began talking about losing "just a few seats" – a sure danger sign.

When the votes were counted on October 13, 1970, Smith had only twenty seats. Regan's Liberals had twenty-four seats, and two went to the New Democratic Party. Even Liberals concede that if Stanfield had stayed on, his administrative abilities and personal popularity would have carried the Conservatives to victory in the 1970 election. The machine that Stanfield had built in nineteen years as Conservative leader in Nova Scotia had fallen apart just three years after he left.

Upon turning the province over to the Liberals, Smith and his wife slipped away to Bermuda to recover and to forget. After a pleasant, envigorating day on the beach, they started to walk back to their hotel when Smith discovered he could not walk and sat down on a stone fence to rest. His wife flagged down a taxi to take them to the hotel where the house doctor took one look at Smith and rushed him to the hospital. Because the hospital's only heart specialist was in the United States that day, Smith was kept in hospital overnight until his return. Next day, the specialist was in the process of checking Smith's blood pressure when the major heart attack came.

Luckier than many, Smith lived to joke about the experience. Although he continued as a Member of the Legislature, he devoted most of his time to his law practice in Truro, doing what he had wanted to do most during his long years as Stanfield's lieutenant.

He is a man without bitterness, and he regards his loss in 1970 as entirely his own responsibility. He remains what he has always been, Robert Stanfield's most loyal supporter and there is something akin to love in his voice when he talks of his leader. "The man is innately honest all the way through the piece, in all the various things he does. There's nothing fake. He's no different today than he will be tomorrow, than he was yesterday."

DICK DONAHOE

When Stanfield became leader of the Nova Scotia Conservative Party in 1948, the Liberals had a stranglehold on both the Roman Catholic vote and the Halifax vote, and Richard Alphonsus Donahoe stood alone as *the* Roman Catholic Conservative in the capital. His later success would be the wedge that eventually split the Liberals from their traditional power base.

The O'Donoghues (as the family then called itself) were Liberals when they arrived in Canada from Ireland in the mid-nineteenth century. Most of them remained Liberals; one of the early O'Donoghues, however, was much impressed by Sir Charles Tupper's advocacy of free education, and became a Conservative. His descendants kept the faith. As a student, young Dick Donahoe earned pocket money by working as a driver and handyman around Conservative headquarters in Halifax. He went to Dalhousie University Law School where he and his classmate Ike Smith had a tall, gaunt, strangely compelling professor by the name of Angus L. Macdonald. A few years later, when Donahoe, then twenty-seven years old, ran as the Conservative candidate in Halifax South, he had the misfortune to run against the same Angus L. Macdonald, by now premier of the province. Naturally, Donahoe lost, but he escaped with his pride intact, determined to keep trying. Defeated again in the riding of Halifax in the 1940 federal election, he turned his attention to municipal politics. In 1946, he ran for mayor of Halifax and lost.

Nineteen forty-six was also the year of the Conservative conference at Hackmatack Inn in Chester and the beginning of the rebirth of the Tory party in Nova Scotia. Donahoe's was one of the names most frequently discussed for the party leadership. (He had nominated the unfortunate Leonard Fraser for leader in 1940.) Donahoe, however, did not want the job, knowing he lacked the personal financial resources a new leader would need if he were to devote his time to the rebuilding of the nearly extinct party. Instead, he pushed for Bob Stanfield and nominated him at the leadership convention of 1948. "By this time I had come to recognize Bob's qualities, and to have great confidence in him," says Donahoe. "I wasn't at all impressed by his oratorical prowess or with his personal magnetism because these things seemed to me at the time to leave a great deal to be desired. But I was satisfied of his intellectual capacity. I was satisfied with what I conceived to be his political principles, and I was convinced of his durability or long-lastedness, that he would tackle the job and stay with it. I also thought he was fortunate in his personal financial situation and that he could weather a long, tedious trial period."

Donahoe ran again in the provincial election of 1949 – Stanfield's first as leader – this time in Halifax North against the redoubtable Harold Connolly, a member of the Macdonald cabinet who later served briefly as caretaker premier following Macdonald's death.

Donahoe had had no intention of running in 1949, but he was the chairman of a party committee charged with finding candidates. The committee could find no one willing to tackle Connolly, who was generally reckoned to be the Liberals' most potent vote-getter. "The people in the constituency were about ready to throw in the towel and allow the Liberals to get an acclamation." recalls Donahoe, "when I incautiously made the remark that for two cents I would run myself rather than see him get an acclamation. I never got the two cents, but I got the nomination." Donahoe registered his fourth straight defeat, although Stanfield and Smith and a handful of others did manage to win seats in the Assembly.

Though provincial politics was his real love, Donahoe lowered his sights, and in 1951 finally managed to win an election – as alderman on Halifax City Council. In the following year, 1952, he was elected mayor, and he was re-elected by acclamation in 1953 and in 1954. At long last he was on his way.

In November, 1954, a crucial by-election was held in Halifax South to fill the seat left vacant by the death of Premier Macdonald the previous

April. As the sitting mayor, Donahoe was the logical choice for the Conservative nomination. It was the most ferociously contested by-election the province had seen in years, but Donahoe won handily and entered the Legislature, joining Stanfield, Smith, and ten other Conservatives who had been elected in the provincial general election the year before. His arrival strengthened that caucus immensely. A small man with a rich Irish baritone, he was a fearless debater with a ready wit and a passion for skewering Liberal cabinet ministers. Above all, his mere presence on the opposition benches helped to establish the credibility of the Conservatives as a prospective government of the province. Says Donahoe: "Breaking the Liberal hold on Halifax, showing that Conservatives could be elected in the metropolitan area really was an asset when the general election of 1956 was called. It was possible to go out and overcome what had been a deadly handicap for the Tories for years. As long as the people in the rest of the province thought the Tories couldn't elect anybody in Halifax, they could never create the impression that they could carry a government." On the strength of Donahoe's by-election victory, marginal seats in other parts of the province tipped into the Conservative column in 1956.

After winning in 1956, Stanfield had only two automatic choices for his cabinet: Ike Smith and Dick Donahoe, his two strongmen. Though both wanted to be Attorney General, Donahoe, being more stubborn and less disposed to submit his will to Stanfield's, got the job. "Since I was the Halifax Member," says Donahoe, "since I was a Catholic, since Ike Smith was Stanfield's running mate and so on, I felt I had a superior claim on the portfolio. So I finally told Stanfield and later told Ike Smith that having been asked what my preference was, I had expressed it and I didn't intend to change my view." Donahoe told Stanfield if he could not have Attorney General, he would accept a lesser portfolio, "but they were never going to be in the position of saying that I said go ahead and give that one to Ike Smith with my blessing, because I wasn't ever going to give that blessing."

Donahoe (who was also Minister of Health and Minister of Welfare), Smith, and Stanfield constituted what today would be called an inner cabinet. Stanfield discussed all important matters with his two lieutenants before putting them before the full cabinet, and other ministers sometimes had the uneasy feeling that the real policy decisions were taken before most of the cabinet had had a chance to offer views.

Donahoe's greatest contributions were in the health portfolio where he introduced both hospital insurance and medicare to the province. In later years, however, he came under increasingly heavy Opposition attack for his outdated views, particularly for his resistance to law reform. "Donahoe," says a Conservative who knows him well, "was a troglodyte on questions involving the law. He not only allowed harsh laws to remain on the books all those years when he was Attorney General, but he actually defended them as being a positive good." Liberal Premier Gerry Regan, who effectively exploited the law reform issue when he was in Opposition, makes the same point: "There was no provision for night courts when we came in in 1970. We had to do away with legislation in a variety of statutes that provided imprisonment, mandatory imprisonment, for breach of a statute – like it's the second or third time you're caught selling booze or shooting deer out of season. The Judge had no discretion to decide whether it should be imprisonment or not. He couldn't give you a fine."

Friendly rivals over the years, Donahoe and Ike Smith had nothing important to compete for as long as Stanfield was the provincial leader. Both argued with Stanfield that he should stay in Nova Scotia rather than run for the federal leadership when the opportunity arose in 1967, but Donahoe dropped his objections when he discovered that Stanfield had decided he had been Premier long enough: "Stanfield was of the opinion that it was desirable that he move on anyway, whether in fact he moved on to the national leadership, or out of the provincial field, or out of politics altogether. . . . He felt that too long a tenure by himself or by any one person would be bad for the party in the long run and that he might have been here too long anyway."

Both Donahoe and Smith would have been content to serve out their careers under Stanfield, but once he left, his two lieutenants were thrust into competition for his old job. Donahoe's hopes, however, suffered a mortal blow when Stanfield named Smith to act as interim premier pending a provincial leadership convention. Donahoe is still bitter: "Ike Smith, it was perfectly clear, had been elected by Stanfield to succeed him. Now, it is true that Stanfield made a statement that this was just on a temporary basis, but temporary basis be damned." When Donahoe set about rounding up support for the leadership convention, he found that other cabinet ministers, in the process of persuading Smith to drop his opposition to Stanfield's entry into federal politics, had assured Smith they would support him for the premiership. "By virtue of the position he took on the Stanfield thing he got support that if it had just been an even shake between him and me, I don't think he would have gotten," complains Donahoe.

Donahoe found little support for his own candidacy and withdrew from the race before the leadership convention, letting the job go to Smith unopposed. Says Donahoe: "I saw no reason why I should make myself a living sacrifice. But I was loyal to Smith and supported him and disagreed with him on many of the things he did." When the election of 1970 came, Donahoe became what he had been determined he would not be – a living sacrifice. He was soundly defeated in the riding he had held for sixteen years.

Today, embittered by the experience, he sits in his walk-up law office on Granville Street in Halifax, opposite the back door of Province House. Occasionally he peers across the street into the windows of the Red Room, watching workmen renovate the room where the Stanfield cabinet used to meet. Although he once turned down a Senate appointment, he dreams of one day becoming a judge. Says a friend: "That's all Dick has ever wanted."

ROD BLACK

Rod MacDonald Black was the best political organizer Nova Scotia had ever seen. While Robert Stanfield made speeches and Dalton Camp devised grand strategy, Black was out digging up candidates and teaching them how to fight elections where elections were won – in the apartment blocks, crowded tenements, and narrow frame houses that line the sloping streets of central Halifax. He was the man who transformed the dispirited Conservative organization of the late 1940s into the potent fighting machine of the 1950s and 1960s. No detail was too insignificant for his attention, from the number of coffee parties his candidates attended to the smallest irregularities perpetrated by his opponents on election day. "In Halifax," wrote Camp in *Gentlemen, Players and Politicians*, "genteel Tories remained aloof from the lower wards, where the poor lived and where the enormous Liberal majorities were produced. Black knew about false enumeration, impersonation, telegraphing, bribery, and intimidation, and all the arts and practices of party machines; but unlike his Tory contemporaries, he was not afraid to meet the practices of machine politics head on."

Rod Black came honestly by his passion for politics. His father, Percy Black, had been a federal Member of Parliament for Cumberland as well as Minister of Highways in the last Conservative government of Nova Scotia before Angus L. Macdonald swept the Tories into limbo in 1933. When Rod came back from the war, he, like other members of Stanfield's Maritime Mafia, went to the Dalhousie Law School. In later years, he practised law and was owner of a newspaper, *The Amherst News,* in his hometown of Amherst.

He was already involved in Conservative politics when he graduated from law school, and by the mid-1950s he was chairman of organization for both the federal and provincial Conservative parties in Nova Scotia. He was one of the small group that gathered around Stanfield after he became leader and set about rebuilding the party. Black enlisted key people in different counties to revive dormant constituency organizations and to scout for promising younger candidates.

It was not an easy undertaking as Black vividly remembers: "We set out deliberately to find people who had taken part in successful campaigns and there weren't too damned many of those in the Conservative Party. You had an aura of defeat throughout the whole party." Men such as Black, Tom Coffin (later a judge), and two of George Nowlan's principal campaign workers, Frank Welch (later a senator) and Ralph Shaw (another future judge), tried to shore up Stanfield's sometimes flagging spirits during those early, hard years. "Stanfield," says Black, "was doing this job single-handedly. He was trying to revive interest, talking to anyone he'd ever heard of who had any interest at any time in the Conservative Party across the province. He did a great deal, but he was scarcely dynamic in those days. Our job was to give him a lift, and once a month we'd go to some part of the province and hold meetings."

Those trips were often boisterous affairs. No one was paid for his work, nor even reimbursed for his transportation and hotel expenses, so they all felt that they might as well enjoy themselves. On one occasion they took Stanfield to Amherst. Their train was delayed by snow and there was little else for the small band of Tories to do but to sit around the hotel and to try conscientiously to diminish their impressive supply of rum. The festivities spilled over into the train on the way back as Black and his boys commandeered a smoking car to sing and, in violation of everything that was sacred in the Nova Scotia liquor laws, to polish off their remaining refreshments. Finally, an aggrieved passenger went to Stanfield (who was sitting discreetly in another part of the train trying to pretend he did not know the rowdy bunch in the smoker) and informed him that there was a group of drunken Conservatives on the train, and suggested that perhaps he would like to do something about it. He eventually went back. "He came down," says Black, "and he pulled open those green curtains they used to have on the doors of trains. There were bottles of rum and beer and a lot of singing. He looked around and said 'My men,' shrugged his shoulders, turned on his heel, and got the hell out of there." Black still chuckles at the memory: "He didn't say anything else to us. Just 'My men' and got out of there."

As they got to know Stanfield, the others discovered that he was a congenial companion to drink with in a hotel room, but he would not let himself, as a party leader, be seen carousing with the boys in public. Though he was usually tolerant of the conduct of his travelling band of supporters, he could lay down the law when he felt it was needed. Black and Finlay MacDonald were on a trip to Sydney on Cape Breton with Stanfield when the boys got a little out of hand. Someone threw a telephone out a window of the Isle Royale Hotel; someone else smashed a chair, and there was some

68

other miscellaneous damage. Just before they boarded their train for Halifax, the manager of the hotel approached Stanfield to inquire who was to pay for the damage. "I remember the way all the guys were living it up in the railway car coming back," says MacDonald, "and I can remember the silence when Stanfield said, 'This is not going to ever happen again, gentlemen.' I can remember these thugs, all of us, sitting there like kids looking at the floor while he very quietly lectured us. He didn't want ever, ever again to see a repetition of that performance in that hotel."

As campaign chairman, Black had a fetish for getting candidates out campaigning during elections; on occasion he had to enlist Stanfield to read the riot act to reluctant candidates. During one campaign, reports reached Black that the Tory candidate in Hants East, Ernest Ettinger, an undertaker from Stewiacke, was spending too much time with his corpses and not enough time canvassing. So Stanfield and Black set off to investigate. Hants County was one of the weirdest political units in the country. Election after election ended in a near saw-off and usually in a cloud of voting irregularities. In 1953, for example, Ettinger appeared to win Hants East by one vote on election night – until an additional ballot box appeared mysteriously in the shed of a Liberal poll chairman, its seal already broken. There were enough Liberal ballots inside to deny Ettinger the seat. Not surprisingly, the courts voided the election. But in the by-election, incredibly, Ettinger and the Liberal candidate wound up in a tie. The returning officer broke it by voting for the Liberal. That was typical of politics in Hants County; thus Black was understandably determined to get Ettinger campaigning. Stanfield, however, was amused by the situation. It is not clear why a politician whose family manufactured long underwear should think it amusing to have an undertaker for a candidate, but Stanfield found it funny. He thought it even funnier that the undertaker-candidate was more interested in dead voters than in live ones. "Bob and I went up to see him," Black remembers, "and Ettinger was sheepish that he hadn't been going out. Bob was taking him to task, not ungently, and Ettinger claimed one of the reasons was because he had a terrible cold, and he was making a great show of snuffling and making a very obvious gesture of wiping his eyes and blowing his nose. He said his eyes were watering so much he couldn't see through his glasses. Bob turned on his heel and said curtly: 'Ernest, we'll send you up windshield wipers for those glasses. Get going.' " It was all Stanfield could do to get back to the car without laughing. Then he threw back his head and roared at the look of amazement on the undertaker's face.

Like others who know Stanfield well, Black finds his humour fragile. Stanfield could be, and often was, extremely witty in his dry way, but his humour does not travel well. Take it out of the context of time and place and it falls flat. "It was all in the way he said things and the look," says Black. "He had a good laugh at things that amused him and certain people amused him highly. Sitting around a motel room on those trips, he would put his head back and laugh hilariously." His humour tended to the macabre. Once Stanfield went to visit a man in the Lord Nelson Hotel who was in his final illness. The man prided himself on being something of a comedian and when Stanfield asked him how he was getting on, he replied: "Pretty well, but my doctor tells me not to read any instalment stories." Stanfield loved that line and repeated it often.

As the little band of Conservatives worked its way around the province, they discovered Stanfield's warmth and his appreciation of easy, undemanding companionship. But he lacked the natural political instincts of his oldest brother, Frank, Jr., then a Member of Parliament, "Frank," recalls Black, "would have constituents from Colchester County come to his office in the House of Commons. He'd open the file cabinet and give them a couple of drinks of rum out of a paper cup and they'd all be as at ease as if they were back on the farm in Nova Scotia. Bob changed and improved a great deal, but in his early days it didn't come naturally to him at all."

Bob Stanfield's shyness and reserve often made him awkward in personal relationships and insensitive to the feelings of others. He used to drop around to talk politics in Black's tiny apartment in Halifax, an apartment so small that it was impossible for a third person to remain invisible. Yet Stanfield would act as though Black's wife was not there as he chatted with her husband. "She felt she was the hostess and it used to make her livid," Black remembers. "This was an example of his lack of perception, or shyness, or whatever, in his human relations." In those days, Stanfield seemed unable to communicate on any but the most formal basis, and he was either unable, or it never occurred to him, to express his gratitude to others for work on his behalf. "Ike Smith," says Black, "felt he was rejected and unappreciated by Stanfield, which was not the case. But Stanfield couldn't communicate that to him." One day Smith told Stanfield he was not going to be a candidate in the next election. That would have been a blow to Stanfield, but rather than appeal directly to Smith and tell him how highly he valued him, Stanfield went instead to Black and others in the organization and asked them to intercede with Smith. They took Smith out to the Sword and Anchor Restaurant in Halifax, filled him with Scotch and lobster, and talked him out of quitting. Says Black: "We convinced him it wasn't as it appeared, that Stanfield did value him very highly and that he had a duty [to stay] and Ike agreed then and there to run again. We were Stanfield's John Aldens with Priscilla, I never felt that Bob was an insensitive man. He had a shyness, a reluctance to indicate any involvement on an emotional plane. The normal man in thirty seconds would have given this indication."

Some of Stanfield's advisers also worried about his inability to be tough at times when toughness was called for. He would not discipline members of his caucus or, later, his cabinet with the ruthlessness others felt was required, nor would he dump weak candidates in favour of strong ones. He went to great lengths to avoid creating strife in the party. But he won the admiration of his workers by refusing to submit to improper pressures. A Conservative who had retired from the Legislature came to the party to demand that it settle some of his personal debts, with the implied threat that if his difficulties became public it would damage the party. "Stanfield," says Black, "was most incensed and hostile and dismissed that out of hand, as he should have. . . . He could be absolutely ruthless if he thought anything was unethical or improper."

Black watched as the party that had been so apathetic to Stanfield in the beginning grew to understand and value him. "By the early 1950s he had quite a loyal following," says Black, "just a few people, but they were all over the province, people who did admire and respect him for the qualities they saw in him. It wasn't an easy process."

Rod Black was central and indispensible to that process with his ability to extract the last ounce of effort from his candidates and his skill in managing a province-wide political organization. Stanfield made use of that skill in government. After he became premier, he chose Black to lead a special committee to oversee the introduction of hospital insurance. Before he left Nova Scotia, Stanfield put Black in charge of negotiations with the medical profession to ensure the smooth establishment of a medical care insurance program in the province.

Like other members of the group that had worked with Stanfield in the lean years in Opposition, Black got his reward. Stanfield appointed him as the province's chief liquor commissioner. When the Liberals returned to power in 1970 they left him there, realizing that they too, could make use of the talents that had served Stanfield well for two decades.

FINLAY MACDONALD

Ernest ("My first name is a secret I'll take to the grave with me") Finlay MacDonald is the old friend Robert Stanfield chose to run the Conservative election campaign in 1972 and, afterward, hired to be the chief of his personal staff. MacDonald is also the closest thing to a crony that Stanfield has in politics. Theirs is a mutual affection. Stanfield calls MacDonald his alter ego. For his part, MacDonald is the only person in the country who has every claimed that Robert Stanfield is a sex symbol. "He's a hell of a masculine guy," insists MacDonald. "Ask broads. He's got that Gary Cooper thing. I know any number of girls who are immensely taken with him, and furthermore I think Stanfield likes women better than men."

It would be hard to imagine two more dissimilar men than Stanfield and MacDonald. Stanfield, the strait-laced Anglican from Truro with the doleful features and serious mien; MacDonald, the hard-drinking Highland Catholic from Cape Breton with the looks and style of a movie star, prematurely white hair setting off his ever-present Florida tan. Stanfield, the thoughtful, reflective Harvard Law School man who shunned a career in business; MacDonald, the smooth operator who flunked out of law school in Halifax, became a radio announcer, and ended up owning the radio station and a television station to boot. Stanfield, whose reticence makes him the most improbable of political leaders; MacDonald, whose outgoing personality and love of life would seem to make him an ideal politician. Stanfield, who could not lose an election in Nova Scotia; MacDonald, who, as he puts it, "couldn't get elected dog-catcher in Nova Scotia".

Finlay MacDonald's father was a lawyer in Sydney who succumbed to politics and became Member of Parliament from Cape Breton South from 1925 to 1935. Raised partly in Cape Breton and partly in Ottawa, Finlay attended St. Francis Xavier University in Antigonish until World War II. Overseas with the Canadian Army, he served as a lieutenant without coming close enough to action to see a shot fired. He entered the Dalhousie Law School where he was a classmate of Rod Black's. Moonlighting as an announcer for radio station CJCH, he flunked out of school. Faced with the choice of repeating his year or going to work full time at the radio station, he opted for the job and the $275 a month that it paid: "I never thought I would see so much money in my life."

Despite his father's involvement in the Conservative Party, Finlay was no Conservative. In 1945, he cast his first federal vote for the C.C.F. M.P. in Cape Breton South. Four years later, he was a Liberal – one of the people who signed Angus L. Macdonald's nomination papers in Halifax South. If MacDonald was anything, he was still a Liberal in 1953 when he met Dalton Camp and became an instant Tory. Camp at that time was frustrated by the policies of the Halifax *Chronicle-Herald* and its radio station CHNS, which both required that political advertising be submitted forty-eight hours in advance of publication or broadcast for screening, and, if the management saw fit, censoring. Desperate to find an ally in the Halifax media, Camp stumbled on MacDonald, who by this time was manager of CJCH. Hearing Camp's tale of woe, MacDonald got up from his desk, marched down the hall to the studio, flipped open the microphone and announced to the world (or at least to that portion of the world within receiving distance of the CJCH signal) that henceforth the air at CJCH was open to any and all politicians – without censorship. It was the start of a long friendship between the two men. MacDonald laughs at the recollection: "That was the first time I was ever angered, inspired or motivated. It was Dalton who put up the 'death to tyrants' thing. It was a fact that there was no way you could express yourself in Nova Scotia if you were in the Opposition. There was no means. It was transparently clear there was a definite injustice."

Although it was Camp who first attracted MacDonald into the Conservative party, it was Stanfield who kept him there. "Stanfield has a strange pull," says MacDonald. "One day there would be two of us. Next day there were four. Next day eight. Next day sixteen. But there was never any sand drifting out from below. We weren't losing anybody."

MacDonald is at a loss to explain Stanfield's attraction: "The incredible thing with Bob is that he has the type of qualities people look for in a politician and are surprised when they find them. They figure he is too good to be true. There has to be something behind it. And then they realize there isn't, that he is exactly as he stands, and they have to see more of it. . . . There is nothing mercurial, or nothing quick or instant or fast about him, and because of that his appeal doesn't fall apart. After three months maybe you're still shaking your head. After six, or eight or nine months, you're hooked."

Even though Stanfield considers MacDonald to be indispensable, the combination of the two men still seems implausible. Stanfield is a man with little patience for wisecracks, let alone practical jokes. MacDonald has a passion for practical jokes, usually bad ones. Boarding a plane one day, MacDonald spotted Rod Black sitting nearby and could not resist taking advantage of Black's penchant for whittling small pieces of wood to pass the time. MacDonald summoned the stewardess and told her in tones of exaggerated concern that the man sitting over there looked exactly like a maniac who had just escaped from a mental institution. He warned her to keep a close eye on the man to make sure he was not carrying a weapon. Sure enough, when the plane took off, Black produced a knife and a block of wood and started whittling. MacDonald nearly drowned in his Air Canada drink laughing as he watched the crew put the bewildered Black through the third degree. Not even Stanfield is immune from MacDonald's pranks. Shortly after Stanfield won the national Conservative leadership in 1967, MacDonald noticed him coming off a plane in Montreal. MacDonald knew Stanfield well enough to know that he would never pay the difference to fly first class if there was an economy-class seat available. But as Stanfield came off the plane, a ground hostess recognized him and invited him to go to the Maple Leaf Lounge, to enjoy the quiet, comfort, and free drinks that the airline reserves for its first-class passengers. MacDonald waited until Stanfield was comfortably settled before he entered the lounge and, posing as an American tourist, raised a fuss about the presence of lowly economy-class passengers in the first-class lounge. "I saw that man over there riding in the economy section," he insisted, gesturing at Stanfield. The woman in charge of the lounge demanded to see Stanfield's ticket and ordered him to leave. Not the sort of man who would ever identify himself under such circumstances, Stanfield quietly gathered up his belongings and was preparing to depart when he spotted Finlay MacDonald shaking with laughter by the door.

MacDonald worked with both Rod Black and Dalton Camp in Nova Scotia elections, and, although both considered him to be a great asset, he was best working on his own. Given a project, he liked to see it through to completion in his own way. He was far too much the maverick to appeal to the average Nova Scotian. In 1963, he ran for Parliament in Halifax riding and was defeated, probably for the best: "I'm too brash to be an M.P. I like to reserve the right to tell people to go to hell." The same year, however, he was elected president of the Nova Scotia Conservative Party and organized the party's triumphant 1963 provincial election campaign. MacDonald also served three terms as a vice-president of the national Tory party, and was one of Camp's first supporters in the 1966 campaign to force a leadership convention. This act alienated him from the majority of Nova Scotia Conservatives who steadfastly supported John Diefenbaker.

Finlay MacDonald brought to the Stanfield organization a touch of class ("too much for Halifax," says a friend), a sophisticated approach to politics, the enthusiasm of a high-school cheerleader, and a quick and restless mind. Substantial though his contributions were, he was much too much his own man ever to be regarded with great affection by many other Conservatives. There was, however, no doubting Stanfield's affection. There was a time in 1967 when Stanfield might have disowned MacDonald publicly and permanently. And had it been anyone other than MacDonald, he probably would have. It happened in the dying days of the 1967 provincial election when MacDonald, who was again running Stanfield's campaign, was interviewed by two Toronto newspapermen. Asked whether liquor and other forms of "treating" still played a part in election campaigns in Nova Scotia, Mac-Donald incautiously replied that they did. But he added that such practices were on the wane, and he described Stanfield's efforts to stamp out abuses. He should have stopped at that but, warming to his subject, he went on to describe how alcohol flowed like water on election day and how some voters still took the day off work to get drunk on the free liquor distributed by political parties. Then he told the newspapermen of attending a Conservative meeting at which one worker had warned the others: "Incidentally, don't buy those niggers too soon or they won't stay bought." When the *Toronto Daily Star* hit the street with the headline, DOLLARS AND BOOZE STILL BUY VOTES IN NOVA SCOTIA, consternation gripped the Conservative Party. The New Democrats reprinted the article and distributed copies on street corners, and at least one member of the Stanfield cabinet demanded MacDonald's head. MacDonald was in a motel in Port Hawkesbury when the call came from Stanfield, who was about to go on TV to respond to the story. "He asked me if I'd seen it [the story] and I said yes," says MacDonald. "He said he was disappointed. He asked me 'Why?'" Excusing himself, MacDonald put down the phone and went to the bathroom and threw up. "I told Bob I could go into a long harangue about what I had intended to say, but that I had said what I was quoted as saying and there was nothing, nothing I could say to explain it." He asked Stanfield to accept his resignation from the campaign organization. Stanfield refused. "I begged him, but he just backed me up. He announced [on TV] that the Attorney General would see there were Mounties at every poll [to watch for drinking and other illegal practices]. I was just ready to die. I just laid down on the bed and said 'I hope I die. I hope I die.'" As it turned out, MacDonald's indiscretion had no effect on the election results. Afterward, he received a tongue-in-cheek note from Stanfield saying he hoped MacDonald had managed to live through the experience.

Within a month of that election, MacDonald was leading the behind-the-scenes efforts to persuade Stanfield to seek the federal leadership. When Stanfield finally agreed to run, MacDonald travelled with him on his leadership tour, but only as far west as the Ontario-Manitoba border – Diefenbaker loyalists having declared open season on Camp followers on the Prairies. He wrote speeches for Stanfield at the convention in Toronto and worked with Camp on overall strategy.

By this time, MacDonald had become one of the most influential men in the communications industry in Nova Scotia as owner of CJCH radio and CJCH-TV in Halifax. In 1968, he sold control to the CTV network, but continued to manage the stations. He organized the Canada Games in Halifax and early in 1970 Stanfield's successor, Ike Smith, appointed him President of Industrial Estates Limited, a crown corporation responsible for bringing industry to Nova Scotia.

Stanfield tried hard during 1971 to lure MacDonald to Ottawa to take over preparations for the election expected the following year. MacDonald, however, was reluctant to leave his comfortable life in Halifax and his beautiful shingled house overlooking the North West Arm of Halifax Harbour. Finally, MacDonald's wife, sensing her husband could not bear to remain politically inactive for much longer, phoned Stanfield and told him: "I think you had better try Finlay again."

"Finlay was a perfect choice," says Dalton Camp. "You couldn't find anybody who could do it any better. He was the guy who could come on strong with Stanfield and tell Stanfield what he thought. Finlay does that; he does it superbly well. Finlay's been around Stanfield so long he knows what he can say to him. And he knows what the answers mean when he gets them. It was a beautiful campaign."

On January 1, 1973, MacDonald joined Stanfield's personal retinue as chief of staff. The picture on the window sill of MacDonald's big stone house in Ottawa is of Bob Stanfield, and it bears this inscription: "To my dear friend and supporter Finlay MacDonald, whom I can never adequately thank." "I've always felt," says Stanfield, "that Finlay was exceedingly capable. He can serve very well as an alter ego to me. People will call up looking for me; if they can't find me or if I'm busy, they'll talk to him and be quite satisfied to have talked to him. He can play that role. He always seemed to get a good response from people."

FLORA MACDONALD

To confused strangers, it sometimes seems as though everyone in Nova Scotia is a MacDonald, Macdonald or McDonald. Red-headed Flora MacDonald comes from the same part of Cape Breton as Finlay MacDonald, and both are members of the Clanranald MacDonald, though not related. He's a Roman Catholic and she's a Presbyterian – a major distinction among the MacDonalds of Cape Breton.

Flora MacDonald is a woman with a remarkable memory, so remarkable that she, unlike most others, remembers clearly the precise moment when she first laid eyes on Robert Stanfield. It was just before her twenty-third birthday and she was walking down the street in North Sydney with her father when they bumped into John Michael Macdonald, the Conservative candidate in Cape Breton South. Macdonald was in the company of a thin, unprepossessing stranger from Colchester County – his leader, Robert Stanfield. It was during the election campaign of 1949 and Flora was not much impressed with the looks or prospects of the new leader of the Conservative party of Nova Scotia: "Mr. Stanfield was doing then what he did for the next seven years, day in and day out: going around and meeting the people of Nova Scotia in a slow, methodical, quiet way to let them get to know him. . . . I was just a young person not really attuned to the political situation and somewhat bemused by this strange man." That was the last she saw of Stanfield for some years.

Flora MacDonald was by no means a typical Cape Breton girl. With a lively interest in people and an intense curiosity about the outside world, she went to Europe in 1950, lived in Britain for a while, returned to Canada, and travelled across the country, stopping in each province and finding a job there for a few months before moving on. By the time the 1956 provincial election was called, she was back in Cape Breton, working at a college. She became acquainted with a man who had been nominated as the Conservative candidate in the riding of Victoria. When the college closed for the summer, she moved in with the candidate and his wife and went to work on his election campaign. Her candidate lost, but the Tories won the election, much to Flora's surprise: "Everybody expected the Government to do a little bit worse and the Opposition a little bit better, but we didn't expect to win."

Seeing a way in which her new love, politics, might advance her first love, travel, she set off for Halifax to apply for a job with the Nova Scotia Government's Travel Bureau, whose advertising account Stanfield had just bestowed on Dalton Camp. She did not get the job (and the man who refused to hire her did not keep his for long). She headed for Ottawa to try for a job with the Department of External Affairs on the theory that people in the diplomatic service get to do a lot of travelling. Checking her bag at Ottawa's old Union Station, she set off in search of the Y.W.C.A. and a bed for the night. She happened to pass Bracken House, which then housed the national headquarters of the Conservative Party. (It was probably better known in local legend as having been a brothel favoured by Members of Parliament in an earlier age.) She wandered in "just to tell them there was another Conservative in town." She stayed for nine years. She was ordered to take off her coat, assigned a desk, and put to work preparing for the then looming federal election of 1957. It was a fortuitous coincidence both for Flora MacDonald and for the party. Had "regional desks" been invented in those days, she would have been the Maritime region desk officer for the 1957 election. When it was over, she became secretary-cum-assistant to Allister Grosart, then the national director of the party. Later, she was office manager at headquarters. Although most Conservatives were only vaguely aware of her actual duties, she, in effect, became *the* Conservative Party for all the rank-and-file Tories who read party newsletters and who wrote to headquarters with their suggestions and problems.

Federal and provincial elections came in rapid-fire succession and Flora worked in all of them. Following the national election of 1957, she had a long talk with Dalton Camp and out of that conversation came a lasting political alliance. They were a team in Manitoba in 1958 in the provincial election that saw the Conservatives under Duff Roblin come to power. They were back in Winnipeg again in May, 1959 for a snap election and another Roblin victory, then over to Newfoundland in August to be defeated at the hands of Joey Smallwood's Liberals. But they had better luck the next month in Prince Edward Island as Conservative Walter Shaw ousted the Liberals.

When Stanfield called an election in Nova Scotia in 1960, Flora was dispatched from national headquarters to work with Rod Black on organization and with Camp on strategy and speech-writing, and to run the provincial headquarters for the duration of the campaign. She remembers all too clearly being summoned to a meeting with Stanfield, his cabinet, and his key organizers: "I think the whole thing was put on for my benefit, though I was too naive to know it at the time. They were discussing candidates and campaign managers, and as they talked they were drawing up a calendar of dates. They were going to allow John Jones that week for his drunk and that would mean the rest of the campaign would be on solid ground because so-and-so would fix it up. The next week would be allowed for someone else's drunk. These were all crucial people, some of them sitting at that very table, and I sat there thinking, 'Oh, my God.'" Stanfield was delighted with her reaction and chuckled later: "You know it was worth that meeting just to see the startled look on Flora's face." And, as Flora quickly discovered, Nova Scotia politics being what they were, some of the drunks planned in jest occurred right on schedule.

That 1960 election was an exhausting one for Flora. Stanfield was – and is – a man who believed the day begins when the sun comes up and, to make it worse, he insisted on punctuality. Dalton Camp on the other hand, considered that mornings were for sleeping; his creative juices rarely started flowing before midnight. Camp would finish writing a speech for Stanfield in the early hours of the morning and turn it over to Flora. She would take it back to her room at the Lord Nelson, pull out a dresser drawer, set her typewriter on it, and type the final version. Sharp at 8:30 a.m., the Premier would be at her door to collect his text.

Although strains and friction were soon to develop among members of the Maritime Mafia, they were still a happy group in the early years of the Stanfield government, united by an easy camaraderie. Rod Black tells of taking Flora MacDonald out door-to-door canvassing just before election day. They knocked on the door of an old Halifax man who looked as though he would not live long enough to cast his ballot. All the old fellow wanted to talk about was his health, but Black was more interested in talking about his vote. To gain the man's confidence, he introduced Flora as a nurse. The old man was delighted. He led Flora into his bedroom, reached under the bed, pulled out a bedpan, and asked Flora to analyze the contents for him. "Poor Flora turned green," Black recalls with a laugh. "Oh, God, I thought she was going to lose her biscuit right there in the poor old fellow's room. She lost all interest in his vote."

Following the 1960 election, Black tried to persuade Flora to return to Halifax as the Nova Scotia party's full-time provincial organizer. She returned to Ottawa instead, working in the federal elections of 1962, when John Diefenbaker slipped from a majority government into a minority, and 1963, when he slipped out of power altogether. She was also back in Nova Scotia for the 1963 provincial election, but this time she worked exclusively with Camp on strategy and speeches. It was Stanfield's best election as the Conservatives ran away with thirty-nine of the Legislature's forty-three seats. He was at the peak of his powers.

Back in Ottawa, however, trouble was brewing that would eventually cost Flora her job and, indirectly, Diefenbaker his. Flora was among a growing number of Tories who believed the time had come for Diefenbaker to retire. The divided party papered over its differences and lurched into the federal campaign in the fall of 1965 with some of its most important members in nearly-open revolt against the leader and with no party policy worthy of the name. Such policy as there was was written by the campaign chairman, Eddie Goodman, a Toronto lawyer, on the coffee table of his suite at the Chateau Laurier Hotel or pirated from other sources. The Tories' entire science policy, for example, was lifted holus-bolus from a speech Harold Wilson, the British Labour Party leader, had made in Scarborough two years earlier. Duff Roblin, the premier of Manitoba, rejected entreaties that he run for the federal house. In Ontario, Premier John Robarts turned out for a major Diefenbaker rally in Toronto, then did his best to ignore the rest of the campaign. Only in Nova Scotia did a Conservative premier campaign strenuously for Diefenbaker. Stanfield took three weeks out of his schedule to work for the federal party, a gesture that revealed another side of Stanfield the politician. Although he resisted any federal interference in the affairs of his provincial party, he knew the federal and provincial parties were interdependent at election time. He was always the first man at the barricades when a federal election was called. Thanks largely to Stanfield's efforts, the Conservatives carried ten of Nova Scotia's twelve federal seats in 1965. Later, Keith Davey, the Liberal national organizer, blamed Stanfield for Lester Pearson's failure to win a majority of the Commons seats: "The Stanfield machine creamed us."

Stanfield was altogether too effective for the liking of some Tories. Early in the campaign, Flora, Goodman, and Lowell Murray, another Cape

Bretoner who had worked for Conservative Justice Minister Davie Fulton, calculated that Diefenbaker would win only sixty or seventy seats. That was the ideal range. If Diefenbaker won many more seats than that he might conclude that he had a mandate to remain as leader. If he came back with many fewer, the party would not be viable for his successor, whoever he might be. But Diefenbaker was waging an amazingly strong personal campaign on the hustings. Reports flowing into Tory headquarters in Ottawa were disturbingly optimistic: Diefenbaker was gaining ground everywhere except in Ontario. Suspecting Diefenbaker just might manage to return with a minority government, Goodman, Flora, and Murray made a none-too-solemn pact. "If Diefenbaker got a minority," remembers Flora, "Eddie was to go on national television as the architect of the victory and announce that this was the greatest practical joke ever perpetrated and that jointly he, Lowell and I would climb to the top of the Peace Tower and jump off." On election night, Lowell Murray went to the studios of CJOH-TV in Ottawa to monitor the returns from the Atlantic Provinces while Flora and Goodman waited nervously downtown. The early returns showed Diefenbaker sweeping almost everything in the East, particularly in Nova Scotia. Murray phoned with a cryptic message: "Flora, Eddie, you had better get ready to jump."

The results from Ontario saved them from that fate, but Diefenbaker did better than anyone had expected, winning ninety-seven seats, two more than he had in 1963.

Diefenbaker, however, was not amused by disloyalty, real or imagined, and after the election he cleaned house at headquarters, installing as national director James Johnston, an economist and smalltown newspaper owner, whose loyalty to Diefenbaker was as boundless as his political talents were slight. On Diefenbaker's instructions, "Doctor Jim" (the title being in recognition of his Ph.D. in Economics) fired Flora MacDonald. It was a grave error on Diefenbaker's part. Instead of seeking to reconcile the warring factions of the party, he had escalated the conflict, uniting his opponents in a single cause. Flora's dismissal served to polarize the party. At a meeting of the party's national executive somebody paid tribute to Flora's years of service; the meeting immediately split down the middle. The firing hurt Diefenbaker among rank and file Conservatives across the country who still supported his leadership. To them, Flora MacDonald had been a friend who answered their letters, attended their annual meetings, and came out to help them in election campaigns; they were bewildered and angered by Diefenbaker's high-handedness. By firing her for disloyalty, Diefenbaker handed his enemies an experienced political operative who not only knew personally every important Conservative in the country but, more important, had instant access to them.

After leaving headquarters, Flora went to Prince Edward Island with Lowell Murray to campaign for the aging Conservative Premier, Walter Shaw, as he lost the 1966 provincial election. Flora then moved to Kingston and a job in the Political Science Department at Queen's University.

In May of 1966, in a speech to a closed meeting of Conservatives at Toronto's Albany Club, Dalton Camp had fired the first shot in what was to be the successful campaign to force a national leadership convention. Encouraged by the response to that speech, he went to Kingston late that summer to lay plans for making his campaign public. The plotters – Camp, Flora MacDonald, Lowell Murray, David MacDonald (a young M.P. from Prince Edward Island), and Camp's brother-in-law, Norman Atkins – met in a motel in Kingston where they planned the speech Camp was to make in September to the Junior Board of Trade in Toronto. They also divided up the work to be done before the Conservative annual meeting in Ottawa in November. Flora's assignment was to maintain contact with key Conservatives across the country who would be involved in the selection of delegates to the meeting. She was to find out who was sympathetic to the Camp cause and to use her contacts to see that as many Camp supporters as possible were named delegates. She became the clearing house for delegate information for the Camp forces, and long before the annual meeting began she had a full list of all delegates and where their sympathies lay.

Her efforts, however, were nearly nipped in the bud by Bell Canada. The Bell was alarmed about this unmarried woman who had arrived in Kingston, taken an apartment, and promptly run up a bill of between five hundred and six hundred dollars on long-distance calls all across the country. After investigation, the Bell concluded she could only be engaged in some sort of fraudulent stock promotion. Flora finally persuaded the Bell that the stock market was the furthest thing from her mind.

Once the annual meeting began, her job was to keep track of delegates and to make sure that none of Camp's supporters were wavering. Her room at the Chateau Laurier Hotel was so crammed with communications equipment, including a direct phone line to the ballroom where the principal sessions were held, that she could barely slip into bed at night. "We had a huge amount of electrical equipment," she says, "and I slept with all of it."

The annual meeting was a complete victory for Camp. He was re-elected national president, defeating the Diefenbaker candidate, Arthur Maloney, a Toronto lawyer and ex-M.P. Flora MacDonald completed Diefenbaker's humiliation when she was elected national secretary of the party. The die thus cast, delegates voted to hold a leadership convention before the end of 1967.

As the new national secretary, Flora was one of the organizers of the leadership convention. Eddie Goodman was named co-chairman of the convention committee and he proposed to nominate Flora for executive secretary of the convention, a position that would have made her responsible for the detailed arrangements and would have precluded her from working for any of the candidates. "Dalton found this out," Flora recalls, "and came up to me at the head table and said, 'Don't allow your name to go forward. What if Stanfield should run? What sort of position would you be in then?' " She quickly backed out, and Gene Rheaume, a former M.P., was named executive secretary.

From then on, the only question in Flora's mind was whether her candidate would be Bob Stanfield or Dalton Camp. She helped map strategy for Camp's campaign for the leadership, only to have that campaign abandoned when Stanfield entered the race. She became the lynchpin between the Stanfield organization in Nova Scotia and the Camp organization in Toronto. She also did for Stanfield what she had done for Camp prior to the 1966 annual meeting: used her influence to see that as many Stanfield supporters as possible were chosen delegates, building a master file of all delegates and coding them according to the candidate they were supporting or leaning toward. A month before the convention opened, she moved into a suite at the Westbury Hotel in Toronto to set up the Stanfield command post.

After Stanfield won the leadership, she toyed with the idea of running for Parliament, but when Stanfield asked her to travel with him in the 1968 election campaign she immediately agreed and acted as liaison between the leader and the candidates and party officials in the ridings they visited.

She returned to Kingston after the election and turned her considerable energies to rehabilitation work among inmates at the women's prison. She was one of the founders of the Committee for an Independent Canada, and she became the first woman ever admitted to a course at the National Defence College. In the election of 1972, she was the only woman among the one hundred and seven Conservatives elected to Parliament. A few months later, she was introduced to a meeting as "possibly Canada's first woman prime minister." Flora blushed: "That's a lot of responsibility – one I'm not prepared to consider yet." Yet!

6
Up by the Bootstraps (1948-1956)

When he got the leadership, he plodded around the countryside like an old pedlar. He was like a travelling salesman, convinced that the harder he worked the more he would sell. We underrated him seriously.

> – Peter Nicholson, Liberal, Minister of Finance for Nova Scotia, interview, January, 1973

George Nowlan was fond of telling later how he had spent the evening of the 1956 Nova Scotia election at his home in the Annapolis Valley, fiddling with his short-wave radio in an attempt to pull in election returns from Cape Breton. Suddenly through the static, he heard a voice reporting that the Conservatives had carried five seats on Cape Breton Island. He impatiently snapped the radio to a Halifax station, telling his wife: "Oh, my God. Isn't that awful. This early in the evening and they are already drunk in Cape Breton."

The Cape Bretoners, as Nowlan soon learned, were not drunk at all, although the Conservatives among them soon would be. For the first time in political memory, the Conservative Party, dominated by the Protestant establishment of the Halifax area, had knifed deeply into the traditional Scottish-Irish Catholic power base of the Liberal Party. It was a base that had been cultivated and solidified by Angus L. Macdonald, himself a Scots-Catholic from Cape Breton who had been transplanted to Halifax. That base had not only held the Liberals in power for twenty-three years, it had rendered them invulnerable to any political assault – or so it seemed. Cape Breton was the weathervane in 1956, and when it swung to the Tories, the Government fell. The long-accepted equations of Nova Scotia politics were rendered obsolete. The province had entered a new political era – the Stanfield era. The transformation that Stanfield had wrought had been achieved neither easily nor quickly. It was the result of eight years of singularly unglamourous, unspectacular politics, the sort of politics Stanfield plays best – the politics of hard work, endless travel, attention to minute detail, and sheer determination.

Nova Scotians were a straightforward and friendly people; although TV may have refined their tastes in recent years, in those days they liked their politics plain. As their support for Angus L. Macdonald had shown, they were not adverse to a touch of mysticism in their politicians, but they distrusted the politician who was too glib or who tried to overwhelm them intellectually or emotionally. The politician who won in Nova Scotia and who stayed in power the longest was the politician who could win the confidence of the voters by demonstrating virtues they understood and trusted: honesty, directness, and integrity. Such a politician was Angus L. Macdonald. Bob Stanfield was another.

It became fashionable later to compare Stanfield to Macdonald and to conclude that Stanfield had succeeded because he came from the same mould as Angus L. There was just enough truth in that myth to make it seem believable. There were certain obvious similarities. Both were men of acknowledged intellectual capacity: Macdonald, the law professor; Stanfield, the Harvard Law School graduate. Both harboured a streak of elitism, and both tended to be paternalistic in their approach to politics. But the differences outweighed the similarities. Background was the prominent difference: Macdonald, the Gaelic-speaking Highland Scot and Catholic from Cape Breton had little in common with Stanfield, the stolid, upper-middle class English Anglican from Truro, which, as Cape Bretoners would have it, was just as bad as being from Halifax. Angus L. was capable of great eloquence on the platform, though his audiences could not have known that he often turned out as many as ten drafts of a speech before settling on one that satisfied him. Stanfield was barely a public speaker at all. Straightforward, logical, and full of common sense, his speeches made better reading than listening. He delivered them with all the passion of an accountant reading the Halifax phone book. Political philosophy was another difference. Party labels did not mean much: in the context of the day, Macdonald was a traditionalist and Stanfield a reformer.

Although Stanfield and Macdonald were political rivals, they were friends on a personal level and each admired the other's abilities. It was one of the anomalies of politics in Nova Scotia that while the troops in the trenches took their politics more personally than their fellows in most other provinces, their leaders co-existed in a state of amicability that bordered on equanimity. Stanfield once distressed his more partisan followers with the comment: "None of us needs to apologize for spending twenty years in opposition while the government was led by Angus L. Macdonald." Angus

L. must have produced a similar mixture of horror and disbelief among his Liberals when he observed: "Stanfield will never do wrong by Nova Scotia." It is no wonder Nova Scotians used to say people could sleep nights knowing Macdonald and Stanfield were leading the two major parties.

The love-in lasted only until Macdonald's death in 1954; Stanfield and Macdonald's successor, Henry Hicks, did not pretend to feel the same high regard for each other. But even Hicks, who detested almost everything Standfield's party did and stood for, still finds it difficult to transfer his contempt to Stanfield himself. "Let's face it," says Hicks, "Stanfield did have an image of popularity in Nova Scotia that no other Conservative has ever had on the provincial level, certainly that none has had in this century." Gerry Regan, the Liberal who became premier in 1970, is an unabashed Stanfield admirer: "He is a gentleman, a man for whom I have considerable respect. I think he has his limitations, but so do most people."

Stanfield's success in Nova Scotia was built on two levels. On the first, more visible level, he was able to do what Angus L. Macdonald had done: to build a personal following in the province that cut across party lines, putting him perhaps ahead of even the revered Macdonald as the most popular premier Nova Scotia ever had. On the second level, Stanfield was a complete politician, quite possibly the best the province ever produced. Finlay MacDonald is by no means an unbiased observer, but his assessment is not far wide of the mark. "They refer to the political side of John F. Kennedy," says MacDonald. "There's a very definite similarity there. Stanfield recognized early on that statesmen were dead politicians, and that the only way you could accomplish anything was if you were a politician in the total sense of that word. The name of the game was to attract people to your concept and you had to do this in both a painstaking way and the most persuasive way possible."

Stanfield's concept was clear enough. In his view, the development of the province had been allowed to languish so seriously under an almost unbroken succession of uninspired Liberal administrations that Nova Scotians had come to accept that they were a deprived people, economically, socially, and politically. The psychology had taken hold: Nova Scotia was a province with fewer opportunities than other parts of Canada, fewer decent jobs, lower incomes, and inferior education for the young. Accepting their lot as second-class Canadians, Nova Scotians saw little reason to try to fight the inevitable. As R. MacGregor Dawson, one of the country's most esteemed political scientists, perceived it, his fellow Nova Scotians "are apt to spend too much time bewailing their handicaps and too little time bestirring themselves."

Stanfield could not have agreed more. "We do our province a disservice," he said on one occasion, "if we create the impression abroad and in the rest of Canada that we are a depressed area. We do ourselves a disservice if we convince ourselves that our province is poor and down-trodden. . . . Are we too ready to assume that something cannot be done here?"

From village to village and political rally to political rally, wherever he could get a handful of people to listen to him, Stanfield preached a message that was a mixture of old-fashioned optimism and traditional Conservative reliance on hard work to change men's lives. A new government would attract new industry to Nova Scotia. New industry would create new jobs and new opportunities for the people and more revenues for the government to finance improvements in education and social services. With better jobs, better education, and expanded opportunities, Nova Scotians would no longer need to leave their homes for other parts of Canada and the United States. When that day came, it would be a mark of distinction, not inferiority, to be a Nova Scotian.

It was not the sort of concept calculated to register a quick political knockout. Stanfield could plant the thought, but the people had to examine themselves and their outlook on life and convince themselves that, with effort, they could accomplish more for themselves in the future than they had attempted in the past. Stanfield was under no illusion that the process would be short. He did not expect to be around long enough to lead the Conservatives into office. "I didn't think of myself as staying on in politics for any great length of time," he says. "I guess I sort of worked from year to year in that respect."

Stanfield was realistic enough to know he started with some major liabilities as a politician. But he had one great quality: believability. They used to say in Nova Scotia that Stanfield had so much money of his own that he could not be in politics for what he could steal; therefore, he must be honest. Not very flattering perhaps, but the sentiment did Stanfield no harm. His quiet, halting manner and his evident sincerity slowly made an impression on the people he met. The apathy that had greeted his election as leader gradually changed, if not to enthusiasm, at least to a conviction that the party had a leader with whom it could build, and, perhaps, one day win. As he won the party's confidence, Stanfield's own confidence increased and he stopped thinking about leaving politics. "There was nothing drawing me in another direction particularly," he recalls. "To use a hackneyed term, I found it challenging and interesting."

Often though, the work seemed more discouraging than challenging. The crowds were often disappointingly small as Stanfield travelled about the province with Rod Black, Ralph Shaw, Tom Coffin, Ike Smith, and others.

Another in that group was Graham Murray, a professor of Law at Dalhousie, who later recalled helping to organize a meeting for Stanfield in the Eastern Shore area. Many telephone calls were made to party adherents in the hopes of attracting a respectable audience. Murray's pitch: "We're bringing a guy down to meet you. He can't speak, but we think he's good." It did not always work. One unforgetable night only two people turned out to hear Stanfield at a rally in Dartmouth. The two? Graham Murray and Murray McPhail, the secretary of the Conservative organization in Dartmouth. On the ferry on the way back to Dartmouth, Graham Murray apologized profusely for the disaster. "Oh, that's all right," said Stanfield. "Things like that happen."

Where possible, Stanfield preferred not to make a speech at all. He was happier sitting around listening as farmers and fishermen told him their problems. By the time he entered the Legislature in 1949, he knew more about many aspects of life in Nova Scotia than most other politicians, simply because he had had the patience to listen to people, people who were as deprived economically as his party was politically. "The great thing about Stanfield," says Dalton Camp, "is that he had been through the bottom rung of politics. He had been the leader of a party that had no seats and he'd risen all the way to premier, winning almost every seat there was. He always understood what it was like to be at the bottom of things."

His advisers despaired at times of what they considered to be his indecisiveness, but Stanfield insisted on building carefully. "If you'd hooked onto Stanfield in 2,000 B.C.," says Camp, "and said 'Look, Bob, I've got a great idea here. It's a circle and you put it on a cart and it's a wheel,' he would say in that slow voice of his, 'Well, I'm not going to make a speech about it until I see it. And until I see it, I'm not going to buy it.' That's the way he was."

This quality of thinking a proposition through before committing himself is what Camp and others describe as Stanfield's intellectual honesty. Stanfield has always been uncomfortable with that sort of description. He still winces when he hears himself praised for his integrity or honesty. He considers himself no different from other politicians.

Others, however, consider Stanfield to be very different from most political leaders, both in substance and in style. Dick Donahoe, the Halifax Tory who nominated Stanfield for the leadership in 1948, quickly spotted Stanfield's unusual attributes. When he returned home after that leadership convention, Donahoe made a shrewd prediction to his wife: "We have chosen the man to lead our party who will be the hardest possible man to defeat." A similar prophecy was attributed to the late Ralph Shaw, and historians can take their pick. Said Shaw: "This guy has the makings of another Abe Lincoln. He's going to be hard to elect, but if we ever get him elected, they'll never get him out." Peter Nicholson, the Liberal, watched Stanfield closely in those early years and was amazed by his patience and determination. His description of Stanfield as an itinerant pedlar captures perfectly the essence of Stanfield's political style. "Nova Scotians," says Nicholson, "have to get used to a fellow. Once they do, God knows how long he may stay in."

Stanfield was no sooner chosen leader than he had to take his political wares on the road. In November, 1948, the same month as Stanfield became leader, James Lorimer Ilsley, who had been Minister of Finance and Minister of Justice in the Mackenzie King cabinet, resigned to return to private legal practice and the government called a federal by-election for December 13 in Annapolis-Kings. The Conservatives nominated George Nowlan, and Stanfield threw himself energetically into his first electoral contest. It was a good way to start because Nowlan won with a majority of 1,588 votes. "I think Bob really enjoyed it," says Ike Smith. "He worked hard and the result was satisfactory. When it was all over, he was really pleased that he had taken such an active part and that it had been such a useful effort. He found that getting to know people in the context of an election campaign was quite a satisfying and interesting experience."

The following spring, Angus L. Macdonald called a provincial general election for June 8 and Stanfield led his party into the war. He travelled more than fifteen thousand miles in that campaign, poking into every forgotten corner of his small province. As the leader of a party with no seats, Stanfield knew it would be more than presumptuous of him to pretend he had any chance of knocking off the Liberal government, but he appealed for the election of enough Conservatives to give the province an effective opposition. His campaign betrayed a certain lack of consistency, but consistency has never been a value much prized among opposition politicians. He criticized the government for having increased taxes. He attacked it for having allowed the province's per-capita debt to rise from $82.70 when they took office in 1933 to $120 by 1948 (a state of affairs one might think could only have been avoided by still higher taxes). Then Stanfield turned around and attacked the government for having fattened the provincial treasury to the tune of $60 million in profits from the sale of liquor. How the government was supposed to finance improvements in roads and social services and at the same time reduce taxes, borrow less, and cut liquor prices was not made clear in the Conservative campaign. It was also clearly not an ecology-conscious age. The Conservatives damned the government for having refused to allow the Shell Oil Company to build a bunkering plant in Halifax. The government wanted the site for a hospital instead.

Unconcerned about the scatter-shot Conservative campaign, the Liberals took the high road, campaigning under the slogan, "All's Well With Angus L." The Conservatives replied with a slogan of their own: "The Tide Has Turned."

Neither slogan, as it turned out, was accurate. The tide had not turned yet, but all was not too well with the Angus L. Liberals either. His Liberals won twenty-seven seats, only one fewer than they had in 1945, but the electoral map had been redrawn in the meantime and there were thirty-seven seats up for grabs in 1949, an increase of seven. Stanfield's Conservatives won eight seats while the C.C.F. held its two seats. Although Dick Donahoe was swamped in Halifax North by the popular Harold Connolly, Stanfield and Ike Smith won easily in their dual riding of Colchester. Equally as impressive as the eight seats they won was the increase in the Conservatives' popular vote; it climbed by six percentage points to 39.2 per cent.

At least, the Conservatives went to bed on election night thinking they had won eight seats, but irregularities clouded the result in Hants West. After a round of legal challenges so typical of Nova Scotia politics, the Conservative, George Wilson, was unseated and a by-election ordered. Wilson, however, won the by-election in 1950, giving the Conservatives an eight-man opposition.

Three weeks after the 1949 provincial election came a federal general election, and although Stanfield stumped the province for his party the results were disappointing. The Conservatives won only two of the province's thirteen seats. Frank Stanfield, Jr., managed to hold Colchester-Hants, but George Nowlan, whose by-election victory had buoyed the Conservatives the year before, lost by four votes in Annapolis-Kings.

Stanfield, meanwhile, was preoccupied with moulding his eight-man caucus into a hard-hitting Opposition. He and Ike Smith carried the load in the House, constantly attacking the government for its failure to bring forward a program of industrial development for the province and exposing the operation of the government's sophisticated system of political patronage. Liquor agents were Stanfield's and Smith's favorite target. These liquor agents were Liberals or friends of the Liberal Party who were paid a commission by brewers and distillers on sales that the breweries and distilleries made to the provincially operated liquor commission. It was strictly illegal for the liquor agents to do anything to earn their commissions, though it was generally accepted that they did open doors in government for the liquor companies, and used their influence to increase the liquor commission's purchases of their patrons' products. It was also taken for granted that liquor agents kicked back a portion of their commissions to the

Liberal Party. The liquor agents had been on the scene in Nova Scotia for so long that their activities had become an accepted public scandal. People seldom gave them a second thought until Stanfield and Smith started to close in on them. "It was known pretty well," says Stanfield, "as these things are known, as to who quite a few of these liquor agents were. We made quite a bit of mileage out of this, although in a sense they'd been around so long that it was sort of old hat." Most of the mileage was made by Ike Smith, the acknowledged star of the Conservative opposition in the House. Stanfield's flat, at times bland, speaking style suffered in comparison to the inquisitorial, trial-lawyer approach of his lieutenant, Smith. "Stanfield was so soporific," says Peter Nicholson, "he could be scathing without even appearing to be so!" "He was a lousy leader of the Opposition," recalls Finlay MacDonald. " . . . He'd support the damn government whenever it had a policy he thought was worth supporting. He wouldn't say anything for political advantage when he thought it would hurt someone personally. For God's sake, what sort of a leader of the opposition was that?" So uninspired was Stanfield's performance in the Legislature that rumours began to circulate within the Liberal Party that the Conservatives planned to dump Stanfield before another election. "He was awfully low-key," Nicholson remembers. "If he'd turned sideways, you'd have marked him absent."

Stanfield, however, was still very much preoccupied with rebuilding his party and he continued to go about it in the same slow and patient way as he had before the election of 1949. He built better than he or anyone else realized at the time. Ike Smith says: "He knew the province by now and he knew how to do it. He knew what was effective and what wasn't effective." When the Legislature was not sitting, he was over in the tiny cubbyhole office in downtown Halifax that the Conservatives called their provincial headquarters. Or he was travelling around the province by car and train selling the party to anyone who would listen. The party did not yet have the effective organization that would emerge during the 1953 provincial election campaign and, aside from the weekend trips with his little band of supporters, he had to do much of the work himself. Conservatives would have laughed if anyone had suggested in those days that there was such a thing as a Tory machine.

By the spring of 1953, Bob Stanfield concluded that the Twenty-First Legislature had about run its course and that the inevitable election would soon be called. But he was in a minor personal quandary. Joyce Stanfield was not at all enamoured of her husband's political activities and she particularly disliked the nights and weekends he spent on the road, leaving her alone with the children. She longed for a quieter, more normal life, with her husband free to spend his evenings at home at "The Oaks." Bob decided it would be a good idea to take her away for a week or ten days to Virginia or the Carolinas after the Legislature finished at Easter. He was concerned, however, that the Government might decide to go straight into an election campaign when the House rose. Governments traditionally guard their election plans as though they have some strategic military value, but Stanfield decided to call Angus L. Macdonald anyway and ask him what he was up to. The Premier's secretary advised Stanfield that Macdonald was tied up with a delegation from Inverness County that was importuning him about highway improvements for their area. "Well, don't bother him then," said Stanfield. "Oh, I think he might like to be bothered," replied the secretary. She brought Macdonald to the phone. Says Stanfield: "I told him what my problem was and he said, 'When were you thinking of going, Bob?' and I told him. And he said, 'How long were you thinking of being away?' and I told him. He said, 'If I were you, Bob, I don't think I'd do that, but you and I are the only ones that know that.' " Sure enough, Macdonald called the election. The incident only served to reinforce Stanfield's admiration for Macdonald: "That was an indication of the way Angus was, but he fought hard. He was very effective in that Legislature. He was a formidable opponent."

Although some observers later claimed to have detected that Angus L.'s powers were failing during the 1953 election, he remained a formidable opponent. Stanfield went into the campaign privately predicting fifteen or sixteen Conservative seats (or double his 1949 total) and was disappointed when he came out of it with only twelve seats. The Liberals, continuing to slip, elected twenty-three members, and the C.C.F. again elected two. Though the Liberals ran advertisements headed "Wrong Way Stanfield Again," it was apparent from the results that Stanfield was headed in the right direction. The Conservatives' share of the popular vote climbed another 4.2 points, to 43.4 per cent while the Liberals' slid to 49.1 per cent, the first time in two decades they had dropped below 50 per cent. It was the sort of argument that losing politicians console themselves with, but it was true nonetheless: if the Conservatives had won just six hundred more votes in the right ridings, Stanfield would have been premier. As it was, he defeated one cabinet minister, the speaker of the Legislature, and the chief government whip. The Conservative Party was not only alive, but challenging.

Equally as important as the election result was the fact that the 1953 campaign brought Bob Stanfield and Dalton Camp together for the first time. Camp gave Stanfield confidence, an appreciation of the importance of effective language and an awarness of the potency of radio as a political tool. Although the best advisers money could rent could not in later years turn Stanfield into a sparkling performer on television, his deep voice and clear, deliberate speech made him shine on radio. From his base in the Lord Nelson Hotel, Camp also honed a new edge on Stanfield's political style, sharpening his attack on the issues of the day: liquor agents, pensions voted by the government for cabinet ministers, conflicts of interest in the Macdonald administration, and the failure of the government to attract new industry to the province. Even Rod Black, who clashed frequently with Camp over the emphasis to be given to organization as opposed to strategy, has a grudging admiration for Camp's influence on Stanfield. "Camp was extremely articulate," says Black, "and he has an excellent brain, and a great deal of clarity in seeing an issue. But indirectly, I used to feel his greatest asset was the sense of confidence he gave Stanfield. After collaborating with Camp, Stanfield's delivery always appeared far superior and far more confident, and he was a far more forceful speaker than when he prepared it only on his own or when he didn't have Camp's judgment. . . . They reacted well in developing policy and so on together, in the interchange between them. But this caused some resentment because some people felt Stanfield depended too much on Camp and that his advice was of paramount importance to Stanfield and they felt belittled."

The 1953 election produced another far-reaching development – the emergence of the Stanfield machine, the organization put together by Rod Black to beat the Liberals at their own game. Black's boys showed in 1953 that they could at least hold their own with the Liberals, and sometimes go them one better – in city streets and back concessions alike. The Marquess of Queensberry might not have liked the rules of their game, but he probably would have admired the spunk of the Tory organization.

The following year, 1954, was the pivotal year in Stanfield's political life. Four things happened. Angus L. Macdonald, Stanfield's friend and rival for the previous six years, died in the spring. Joyce Stanfield died tragically in the summer when her car skidded off the road as she was returning from a day at the beach with their three oldest children. In the fall, the Liberal Party split along religious lines as it rejected the interim premier, Harold Connolly, a Roman Catholic, and elected a Protestant, Henry Hicks, as its new leader. Finally, before the snow flew, Dick Donahoe won Angus L. Macdonald's seat in a by-election.

Bob Stanfield was attending a political rally with George Hees, then national president of the Conservative Party, the day that Joyce was killed. Like many deeply private men, he did not have a large number of close personal friends. He lived for his family. His anguish when Joyce died was intense and long lasting. His supporters felt helpless, wanting to commiserate with him in his loneliness, but not daring to invade his grief. Rod Black recalls going to "The Oaks" the day after Joyce's death. Bob's brothers were there. "We must have stayed about three quarters of an hour and we never talked about politics," says Black. "We talked about baseball or whatever was relevant at that season. I don't think I ever actively said to him, you have to stay on. You have a duty to stay on. I think it would have been the wrong tactics."

Suddenly faced with the prospect of raising four motherless children (the youngest, Mimi, being less than a year old), Stanfield made up his mind to get out of politics. "I made up my mind that I'd have to," he remembers. Although they thought it all but inevitable that he would leave, the Conservatives urged him to postpone a decision for a while. As subtly as they could, they tried to interest him in things that were happening in his own and in the Liberal Party. They made cautiously oblique references to the problems that the Conservative Party, now restored to moderately good health, would have in maintaining its momentum if he left. Stanfield credits old Dr. George H. Murphy, a respected surgeon and one-time Minister of Health in Nova Scotia, for persuading him not to resign. George Nowlan sent Dr. Murphy to see Stanfield. "We sat out on the lawn and we talked about things," Stanfield recalls, "and he said 'Just take your time about these things. You may find you can do both, that you can look after your children and still carry on as leader of the party.' That was the technique they used, sort of 'Don't make any decision. Don't make up your mind at the moment and just see what's possible.' Well, I guess I just sort of drifted back into it again."

Joyce's mother arrived from British Columbia to care for the children, and after she left Stanfield hired a full-time nurse. Many of Joyce's friends pitched in as well and Stanfield concluded that perhaps he could manage both the youngsters and the leadership. But he laid down one condition: on no account would he go away overnight on political business. For many months, he drove home to Halifax in the middle of the night following political meetings in other parts of the province. Gradually, however, he eased that condition and resumed a more normal politician's life.

The vicious infighting in the Liberal Party could only have encouraged him to remain in politics. As long as Angus L. was alive, his party enjoyed an aura of invincibility. When he was gone, the Liberal Party looked strangely vulnerable. It was rumoured that on his deathbed Angus L. had named Harold Connolly as his political heir. Like all such rumours it was unverifiable, but it had the not inconsiderable virtue of also being irrefutable. By all normal yardsticks, Connolly was the logical successor if the party were to make a smooth transition. Like Macdonald, Connolly was born in

Cape Breton and, also like Macdonald, he had established his political base in Halifax. They ran in adjoining ridings and there was only one Liberal in the province who rolled up larger majorities than Angus L. Macdonald did in Halifax South, and that was Harold Connolly in Halifax North. Connolly had the seniority to claim the leadership; he had been a member of the Legislature since 1936 and of the Cabinet since 1941. Most significant of all, Harold Connolly, like his late leader, was a Roman Catholic.

When the Cabinet met after Macdonald's funeral it voted to install the experienced and politically wise Connolly as interim leader, pending a leadership convention. This was done following an undertaking – if not a firm commitment – from Connolly that he would not be a candidate at the convention. Several other ministers carried leadership ambitions in their briefcases and they were not about to allow any potential candidate to enjoy the great advantage that would accrue to the man who was sitting in the Premier's office in Province House at convention time. Although Connolly felt his years of service entitled him to sit at Angus L.'s desk for a few months, his interest lay in another direction. Just as old stallions reach an age when they grow more interested in the pasture than in the brood mares who frequent it, so Connolly, though only fifty-three, was ready for a less vigorous life. He had already sounded out Robert Winters, the cabinet minister responsible for doling out federal patronage in Nova Scotia, about the possibility of an appointment to political Valhalla, the Senate. Winters had indicated he felt this reward could be arranged without undue difficulty. Winters, however, was not about to be rushed; Connolly's concern mounted as spring turned to summer and the leadership convention grew near with no word from Ottawa. At one point, Connolly reportedly warned Winters that if the appointment were not soon made, he would go to the leadership convention and win on the first ballot. Apparently annoyed by Connolly's persistence, Winters is said to have replied that if that was the way Connolly felt about it, then perphaps he could do just that.

In early summer, Henry Hicks, then Minister of Education, went to see Connolly and demanded to know whether he intended to be a candidate. Connolly replied he would call a group of ministers together the next day and announce his intentions. Next day, recalls Hicks, "Connolly announced that having regard to the whole Liberal Party he had decided it would not be in the best interests of the party for him to run. He referred to the fact that he felt one Catholic shouldn't succeed another one. There was such a sigh of relief passed round the Cabinet when he said this that two members, my best friend, Wilfred Dauphinee, and Geoffrey Stevens (a minister without portfolio), thought they had better make Mr. Connolly feel better. They assured him most solemnly there was no truth to this, that Catholicism had nothing to do with it, and so on. He'd said he wasn't going to run and, as it turned out, they talked him back into it."

Other ministers began to assess their own prospects. Hicks, who had been M.L.A. for Annapolis since 1945 and Education Minister since 1949, did not think he had much chance of winning, but, after talking to a few of his constituents, he agreed to think about running. He went off salmon fishing in New Brunswick and Newfoundland. When he returned in August, Hicks met his supporters again and they agreed he had no chance. So he wrote a statement announcing he would not be a candidate and left it with a sister-in-law in Halifax to be delivered to the press at ten o'clock that night. But when he got back to the Annapolis Valley, another group of constituents bearded him, telling him a strong anti-Connolly sentiment was developing in the Valley and that if Hicks did not run people would conclude he was afraid of the interim premier and he might have trouble winning re-election in the Valley. No argument is more persuasive to a politician than the argument that if he does not do something he may lose his seat. Hicks immediately saw the logic of the appeal. "If you put it to me like that," he said, "I won't mind going to the convention." At five minutes before ten, he telephoned his sister-in-law in Halifax and told her not to release the statement.

By the time the convention met in September, Connolly was the odds-on favourite to win. So confident was he that he announced to Dick Donahoe, the mayor of Halifax, two days before the convention that he was going to win on the first or second ballot. Six candidates were nominated: Connolly, Hicks, Ronald Fielding (the nephew of W.S. Fielding, the premier whom Bob Stanfield's maternal grandfather had fought so stubbornly), Arthur MacKenzie, Malcolm Patterson, and Hector Hill. Significantly, all but Connolly were Protestants.

The convention was a classic example of the way weaker candidates can join forces to deny the strongest candidate. It was also a classic example of the way religious bigotry, real or imagined, can destroy a political party. Connolly's fate was probably sealed – and the interpretation that would be placed on the outcome was made inevitable – when the woman seconding Connolly's nomination ended her speech with an appeal to all devout Catholics to support her candidate. Connolly was far ahead on the first ballot with 216 votes while Hicks languished back in the pack with only 83 votes. The candidate with the fewest votes dropped off after each ballot and, ballot after ballot, virtually all their votes went straight to Hicks. On the second ballot, Connolly moved to 232 votes while Hicks climbed to 108. But Connolly was at his peak and Hicks was still gathering strength. On the next three ballots, Connolly polled 229 votes, 224 votes, and 229 votes. Hicks, meanwhile climbed to 178 votes on the third ballot, went ahead with 263 on the fourth and won with 312 votes on the fifth ballot.

Although Hicks' victory was widely attributed to Protestants having ganged up on a Catholic, that interpretation was not entirely accurate. Connolly's supporters included a number of Protestants, just as Hicks' included a number of Catholics. If anything, Connolly's defeat was due less to religion than to resentment in the party at his decision to run for the leadership after he had at least tacitly disavowed any intention of doing so. His supporters, however, put out the story that Connolly had been the victim of a Protestant conspiracy; not even a public statement from Angus L. Macdonald's widow denying the truth of that could convince many Catholic Liberals that they had not been done in by a band of vengeful Protestants led by Henry Hicks. Their conviction was reinforced when Connolly refused to serve in Hicks' cabinet. "If Mr. Connolly," says Hicks, "had been able to do for me what Paul Martin did for Mike Pearson after the [federal] convention, then I would have won the election in 1956." But Connolly would not make that gesture of party solidarity, and Catholics who had voted Liberal all their lives started to look at Stanfield with a new interest.

Religious problems in the Liberal Party aside, Stanfield, had he been a sorcerer, could scarcely have conjured up a more ideal Liberal leader – ideal, that is, for the Conservatives' purposes. As long as Angus L. Macdonald was alive, the voters were choosing between two men who, however different in most ways, both had a political appeal that was more personal than partisan. Like Macdonald, Stanfield built his success on the trust and affection that he was able to establish with the electorate. But when Hicks became leader of the Liberal Party, the contrast between the leaders was heightened dramatically. The divergent political images of Stanfield and Hicks could be likened – unfairly perhaps, but not entirely inaccurately – to the difference between a family doctor and a patent medicine salesman.

Conservatives are fond of denigrating Hicks, but in many ways he was an attractive politician. He was born and raised in Bridgetown, a town on the Annapolis River in northern Nova Scotia where his pre-Loyalist ancestors had settled after leaving the United States. One of his forebears was the first member of the pre-Confederation Legislative Assembly of Nova Scotia for the Township of Granville. A brilliant student, Henry Hicks earned his Bachelor of Arts degree at Mount Allison University in Sackville, and a Bachelor of Science degree at Dalhousie where he won a Rhodes Scholarship. He returned from Oxford with Bachelor of Civil Laws and Master of Arts degrees. He was a captain in the Canadian Army in World War II; established a law practice in Bridgetown; and entered the Legislature in

1945. He was, by general consensus, Angus L.'s best minister, and he had one advantage over Harold Connolly: Hicks was Macdonald's personal choice for Minister of Education in 1945, whereas Connolly had been appointed to the cabinet by A.S. MacMillan, the interim premier who ran the government during the years when Macdonald was in Ottawa serving in Mackenzie King's wartime cabinet. Conservatives used to claim that Macdonald was furious when he learned MacMillan had put Connolly in the cabinet. After losing the election of 1956, Hicks stayed in politics and lost again to Stanfield in 1960. His subsequent appointment as President of Dalhousie University was recognition of his considerable administrative talents. His enshrinement in the Senate in 1972 merely confirmed that the surest path to the Upper Chamber was to have been Liberal leader in Nova Soctia when Robert Stanfield was leading the Conservatives. (Hicks' predecessor, Connolly, finally made it to the Senate in 1955; his successor, Earl Urquhart, was appointed in 1966.)

For all his intelligence and ministerial ability, Hicks lacked two vital political qualities that Stanfield possessed: judgment and patience. His acerbic tongue darted ahead of his agile brain. He was too outspoken and often too sarcastic, at times offending even his friends by telling them exactly what he thought of them when, if the truth were known, he likely had not thought of them at all. As a politician, he was a passionate partisan who loved the battle and could not restrain himself from dashing into the breach at the slightest provocation. So compelling was his desire to attack his enemies that he repeatedly made the worst political error of all – that of fighting his opponents on their own ground. As a kamikaze pilot he would have been a spectacular success; as an air marshall he proved a disaster.

Perphaps it was typical of Hicks' impetuosity that rather than direct his energies to consolidating his position and reconciling the alienated Catholics in the party after he won the leadership, he decided to prove his leadership with an immediate test at the polls. Three Legislature seats were vacant. The election in Hants East in the 1953 provincial election had been overturned by the courts. In Inverness, one of the two sitting Liberal members, Alexander McKinnon, had been appointed to the bench. Halifax South had been vacant since the death of Angus L. Macdonald. Hicks called the three by-elections for November 16, 1954. They were to be his vote of public confidence.

All three were marvellous by-elections, full of the drama, significance, and total irrelevance of Nova Scotia politics at its best. Inverness was obviously going to be retained by the Liberals who nominated Clyde Nunn, a one-time Conservative. To oppose him, the Conservatives resurrected Isaac Duncan Macdougall, who had served three terms in parliament in the late 1920s and early 1930s, and who in 1930 had actually defeated the immortal Angus L. Macdonald when Macdonald first tried for a federal seat. (The defeat so angered Macdonald, or so they said, that he refused even to be buried in Cape Breton.) Ike Macdougall was one of the legendary characters of Cape Breton with a gift for oratory and a sobering capacity for intoxicating beverage. The Conservatives got him more or less on the wagon, found someone to keep an eye on him and set him loose to run against Clyde Nunn. The candidates traded insult for insult. Macdougall gibed that the Liberals had no horse-sense or they would not attempt to race a "Clyde." Nunn replied that if Macdougall were a race-horse, he was certainly a winded and broken one. Macdougall had fun with a petty scandal involving the Liberal Government's purchase of snow-blowing machines. As he pointed out to the electors, Inverness County had no need of snow-blowers as long as it had Rod MacLean, the Liberal who held the other seat in the dual constituency of Inverness. Predictably, when the last insult wafted away, Nunn retained the seat for the Liberals by a comfortable 1,620-vote majority.

Hants East was where the Liberals concentrated their horsepower and, had Stanfield invested a little more effort, the Conservatives could have won the seat. The Liberals nominated Alfred Reid, a merchant, and the Conservatives renominated Ernest Ettinger, the Stewiacke undertaker, who had seemingly won the seat by a single vote the year before, only to see his victory vanish when an additional ballot box turned up; the courts had voided the election. The by-election campaign produced the sort of charges and counter charges of vote-buying and corrupt practices that were to be expected in Hants County and the result, as usual, was close. This time Ettinger and his Liberal opponent each polled 2,256 votes and the Liberal, Reid, was declared elected on the tie-breaking ballot of the returning officer. All of which prompted Ettinger to make the memorable observation: "We're pretty evenly divided down here." (Poor Ettinger was not long denied a seat in the Legislature. He won in 1956 in a veritable landslide – a majority of 49 votes.) The Conservatives chastised themselves after the by-election for not having put more work into Hants East, but Stanfield's attention was on Halifax South.

Inverness and Hants East were just by-elections. Halifax South was, for the Tories, a crusade. The stakes were high for two reasons. First, for the first time in a generation, the Conservatives knew they had a real chance of winning a seat in the provincial capital. Psychologically, Halifax, in the provincial scheme of things, was rather like Quebec is in the national context. To demonstrate its ability to form a government, a party had to be able to show the rest of the province that it could win in Halifax.

Secondly, and just as importantly, a victory in Halifax South would give the Conservatives a toe-hold among the Catholic voters of the province. The provincial ridings in Halifax were informally divided along religious lines. Halifax South and Halifax North were the "Catholic ridings."

There were two candidates for the Liberal nomination in Halifax South, Dr. Henry Reardon, a physician, and Alban Murphy, the head of a family clothing business, one-time chairman of the local school board, and president of the board of trade. The nominating convention chose Murphy and he, in the opinion of Premier Hicks, was the wrong choice. "The Murphys," says Hicks, "belonged to the category of people whom Angus L. had thought had been his life-long friends. They had had a lot from the Liberal government. Murphy was a Catholic but there was a great deal of jealousy directed against the Murphys, and Alban himself was an opinionated fellow, not very popular, but he manipulated the workers enough to get the nomination."

Three men were eyeing the Conservative nomination: Dick Donahoe, by now mayor of Halifax and a man who had proved his worth to the party; Finlay MacDonald, the manager of CJCH, who was one of the rising figures in party councils; and John Milledge, the Tory whom Angus L. Macdonald had defeated in the provincial election the year before. Everyone, however, acknowledged that Donahoe was by far the strongest candidate and neither of the other two contested the nomination.

The Donahoe-Murphy struggle was a textbook battle between two Irish Catholics, with no quarter given and none asked. With Dalton Camp handling Donahoe's radio speeches and Rod Black running the organization, the Conservatives fought as though control of the province rested on the outcome – which, as it transpired, it did. "The winning of that by-election was the bell-wether," says Finlay MacDonald, "because while we had a good organization and a growing organization, it lacked depth, province-wide. So what we did was we brought in all the fastest guns we had from Cape Breton North right down to Yarmouth. Rod Black had a superb organization for a by-election and with those two armies – the best the Liberals had to offer, and they were superbly organized, and the best we had to offer – you could hear the clank of armour in the middle of the battlefield."

As Stanfield and Camp had hoped, Henry Hicks played into their hands, charging into the by-election campaign with reckless abandon. The Conservatives were still flogging the liquor-agent issue and over the previous three years they had made some headway. Hearings were held in Cape Breton, and out of them came the disclosure that some liquor store employees had accepted gifts from liquor agents for pushing sales of certain brands. Though the Conservatives did not give him the credit he deserved,

Hicks was genuinely concerned to clean up the liquor-agent problem and had introduced reforms after taking office. But his political timing was bad. Early in the campaign, he went on radio to announce the names of seven individuals against whom charges had been laid as a result of the Cape Breton hearings. Not satisfied to let it go at that, Hicks challenged Stanfield either to reveal the names of other liquor agents or shut up about them. For a week, Stanfield and Camp plotted their next move. They realized they would be playing Hicks' game if they published the names. Instead, Stanfield went on CJCH, Finlay MacDonald's station, to announce he had written a letter to Premier Hicks giving him a list of the names of people Stanfield believed to be liquor agents. Most of the names, he noted, were already public knowledge. And, he continued, he had sent Hicks a second list containing the names of people whom the Conservatives believed would be valuable witnesses on the subject. That list included the names of the chief liquor commissioner of the province, a Liberal appointee. Stanfield then called for a Royal Commission inquiry into the whole question of liquor agents. "We still remain of the opinion," he wrote to Hicks, "that the proper course of action is not solely a series of charges against individuals, however proper that may be at this time, but the course of action most consistent with the public interest is a complete and exhaustive inquiry into the entire matter."

In tactical terms, Stanfield had painted Hicks into a corner. By laying charges against the seven individuals in the first instance, the Hicks government had, in effect, repudiated the position taken by the Macdonald government over the years that there was no such animal as a liquor agent. The charges amounted to an acknowledgment by Hicks that Stanfield had been right in his attacks on the activities of liquor agents. Now, if he wanted to wring any political advantage out of the situation, Hicks would either have to release the names that Stanfield had sent him, or order an inquiry, or both. Either would be an admission that the charges laid so far were but the tip of the iceberg. And, as Stanfield well knew, if Hicks named more names or ordered an inquiry, he would risk further antagonizing members of the Liberal Party who already felt that he was too willing to sacrifice his own supporters to gain political advantage against the Conservatives. Stanfield was free to continue his attack on the liquor agents; Hicks was left without an effective reply.

The art of politics relies as much on illusion as on reality. The liquor agent episode created the illusion that Stanfield was a leader who put the pursuit of justice and the interests of the province above narrow partisan considerations. Hicks, in contrast, appeared to be a premier who was prepared to stoop to unsavory partisanship to embarrass an opponent. Lest anyone miss the point, the Conservatives skilfully exploited the differences between Henry Hicks and Angus L. Macdonald. They eulogized the late Angus L. while belittling Hicks. As Dick Donahoe assured the voters of Halifax South: " . . . the old government and the new are one and the same, different only by the absence of that great Nova Scotian, Angus L. Macdonald."

The reality of the situation was quite different from the illusion served up to the voters by Stanfield and Camp. Hicks was honest, well-meaning, and capable. He was premier for only two years, but in that brief span he showed himself to be something of a reformer. He made major improvements in the province's educational system and he made a start on cleaning out the patronage-ridden government that Angus L. Macdonald had presided over. It is still a matter of dispute between Liberals and Conservatives as to which party actually abolished the liquor agents. Conservatives claim Stanfield did it. Liberals say it was Hicks who stopped the practice and that when Stanfield came to power he allowed the practice to grow up again. The subject is murky, but there is probably an element of truth on both sides. Neither man would tolerate corruption, but both accepted that a certain amount of political patronage was not only inevitable but perphaps even desirable in the political system as it then existed. Both were prepared to live with the pork barrel, as long as it was not on public display.

Hicks traces the appearance of Liberal liquor agents to the period following the selection of Angus L. Macdonald as Liberal leader, when it became apparent to everyone that Macdonald was going to lead the Liberals back into power in the next election [held in 1933]. "It was quite clear that people who supported Angus L. after he became leader in 1930 were just getting on the band wagon," says Hicks. "But Angus couldn't see this and he maintained a loyalty to them even to the point where he almost lied to the Nova Scotia Legislature. He had a quibble. He said we had no liquor agents in Nova Scotia. The saving fact was that they were agents of the companies that sold to the government [not agents of the government itself] and with this quibble he denied the existence of agents when everyone knew they did exist. When I took over from Angus in 1954, I stopped this system, everywhere, at once. But the liquor companies made contributions to the Liberal Party and to the Conservative Party. One thing I would never allow in my time was for them to make contributions in exact proportion to the sales they made. I told my collectors, 'You will make no deals with anyone that they pay fifty cents a case, or something like that.' It is my belief that Mr. Stanfield returned to a so-much-per-case basis."

Although the Conservatives diligently exploited every hint of corruption and patronage in the Liberal administration, it was not patronage or corruption that cost the Liberals the Halifax South by-election in 1954 or the general election that followed two years later. Hicks lost office because of the Protestant-Catholic split in the Liberal Party, and because Stanfield more closely represented the type of premier Nova Scotians had grown used to in the past and wanted to have govern them in the future. Above all, Hicks lost because Stanfield was the better politician. "Mr. Stanfield," says Hicks, "is tough and cold-blooded in his political ambition. . . . I know how hard Mr. Stanfield worked. He really is an excellent political organizer. . . . He worked very hard to become Premier of Nova Scotia."

The Halifax South by-election carried Stanfield a big step closer to becoming premier. Dick Donahoe ground Alban Murphy underfoot and won going away with 5,876 votes to Murphy's 4,585. With that victory, the Conservatives proved they could win the Catholic vote and that they could win in Halifax. The fact that Halifax South had been Angus L. Macdonald's seat was icing on the Tory cake.

The election of Donahoe gave the Conservatives thirteen members in the Legislature and, more importantly, it made available another aggressive, articulate debater to join Ike Smith in the daily hammering at the Liberal Government. They chipped away at the Government so successfully that eight months before the 1956 election Stanfield confided to Smith that he felt confident of winning. It was the first time he had ever predicted victory and he made his prediction public in the autumn, just before the election was announced. "The Hicks Government," Stanfield forecast, "will be removed on whatever day it choses to be defeated at the polls."

By this time, Stanfield had attained a place in the affection of Nova Scotians that was somewhat like the place Angus L. Macdonald had occupied for so many years. The people admired his dignity, courtesy, simple lifestyle, honesty, and perhaps his fatalism. Though it was not an entirely accurate picture of the man, Stanfield had the image of being a politician who was not consumed with ambition. If the people wanted him to be premier, they would make him premier. If they did not, Stanfield would accept this verdict. Inwardly he cared very much, but outwardly he gave the impression of a man who would accept with grace and understanding whatever fate the voters chose to assign him.

Like any good politician, however, Stanfield did his utmost to influence that fate. The Conservative machine was ready with almost all its candidates nominated before the election was announced. Had he been a more patient man, Hicks would have waited. In Nova Scotia, Governments are elected to five-year terms, although elections are usually held every four years. There were still two years to run in the mandate he had inherited from Macdonald, but Hicks was determined to prove he was his own man and that he could win on his own merits. He judged, very wrongly, that the time was propitious and called a general election for October 30, 1956.

Hicks confidently predicted he would win thirty seats in the enlarged forty-three seat Assembly. Hicks also warned the Conservatives that they would not win a single seat on Cape Breton Island, a prediction that seemed safe enough at the time. The Liberals opened a basket of election goodies designed to guarantee their return to power. The main goodies were a hundred million dollar highway-construction program over the next four years, a thirty million dollar expansion of the province's hydro-electric system, increased provincial grants to municipalities to ease the burden of rising education costs, cancellation of the highway tax paid by municipalities, and grants for new hospital and nursing-home construction.

Stanfield unveiled a nine-point program for the industrial development of Nova Scotia, the first point of which called for "hard surfacing without delay all roads in the province that are now ready or near-ready for paving." He promised to improve other secondary roads, to re-examine the financial arrangements under which education costs were divided between the province and the municipality on the basis of the municipality's ability to pay, and to establish greater co-operation with the other three Atlantic Provinces, particularly with a view to persuading Ottawa to do something about high shipping costs to and from the markets of central Canada. Claiming that Nova Scotia was "riding along on the coattails of the rest of Canada," Stanfield proposed the establishment of a "Maritime House" in Europe to attract industry to Atlantic Canada. He also dropped into the election hopper an idea that Ike Smith had advanced at a meeting of Conservative candidates. The idea was that the province create a "Nova Scotia Industrial Development Corporation," capitalized at ten million dollars (half from the provincial treasury and half from public subscription) to assist industry to locate in the province. It would be operated, not by government, but rather by an independent board of prominent Nova Scotia business leaders. Though Smith was credited with first broaching the idea in public, the concept of an industrial development agency had been on Stanfield's mind since those days a decade earlier when he and his study group had pondered ways to stimulate the chronically sluggish Nova Scotia economy and to create new jobs for Nova Scotians. The Industrial Development Corporation never came to pass, but it was the forerunner of Industrial Estates Limited, which Stanfield formed shortly after he took office. It became the crowning achievement of his provincial career and the albatross that destroyed his successor.

Oddly, although the Industrial Development Corporation was the most daring of Stanfield's election planks, it had little influence on the outcome of the election. Roads were the issue in 1956 as they had been in virtually every election in the province. Voters could always tell an election was imminent when work crews materialized to drive mysterious stakes alongside country roads all over the province. Once the election writ was issued, heavy equipment was rolled out by the government of the day to lumber back and forth along the dusty roads, ostensibly preparing the base for paving. Once the ballots were safely counted, the machines lurched away, not to be seen again until the next campaign. Between elections, the government boasted of the number of miles of road it had made ready or near-ready for paving. It had been thus in Nova Scotia since the invention of the road grader and it seemed destined to continue in the same way for ever after.

The quadrennial exchange of road-building promises by the Liberals and Conservatives was the most futile exercise in Nova Scotia politics and it seemed even more ridiculous than normal in 1956. Stanfield's meaningless promise to pave every road "ready or near-ready for paving" sparked a thoroughly silly dispute with Hicks. Stanfield had chosen the expression "ready or near-ready for paving" in an attempt to illustrate the absurdity of the Liberals' ritualistic frenzy of road-improvement activity in election campaigns. "What good is it," the Conservatives asked, "having roads ready or nearly ready for paving, if you don't do anything about it?"

But the Conservatives' promise to pave every road ready or near-ready for paving was so vague that not even Stanfield knew how many miles of roads might be involved. Had Hicks been a man of more considered political judgment, he might have contented himself with mocking the meaninglessness of Stanfield's plank while trumpeting his own hundred million dollar highway-construction program. But Hicks decided to challenge Stanfield on the Conservative leader's ground. He accused Stanfield of irresponsibility. According to an estimate that Hicks produced from somewhere (possibly from out of thin air), it would cost the province two hundred million dollars to pave every road ready or near-ready for paving. With Camp pulling the strings behind the curtain, Stanfield pounced. At the generally accepted paving cost of thirteen thousand dollars per mile, he said, Hicks must mean that 15,000 miles of roads were ready or nearly ready for paving. Was Hicks admitting the Liberals had improved 15,000 miles of roads almost to the point of paving, then not troubled to pave them? (The 15,000 mile figure was as absurd as the argument itself because there were at the time only 7,786 miles of improved gravel roads in all of Nova Scotia.) Hicks' weak reply was that paving costs were up a bit that year. It was a silly dispute, unworthy of both Stanfield and Hicks, but it redounded to the credit of Stanfield and the discredit of Hicks. Hicks was made to appear to be (a) opposed to paved roads, (b) unsure of his facts, and (c) prepared to juggle the truth for political advantage. It was a bum rap, but Hicks had to live with it. Stanfield, on the other hand, came out of the dispute as the man who (a) was genuinely concerned to get rural Nova Scotians out of the mud and dust, (b) knew what he was talking about, and (c) was unwilling to play fancy games with the facts. That was not an entirely accurate picture either, but the Conservatives exploited it to the hilt. There was a ring of self-righteousness in Stanfield's voice as he read the words Camp had written for him to a rally in Yarmouth. The speech was broadcast across the province. "Let me say this," Stanfield concluded his speech. "I don't propose to campaign for votes in Nova Scotia by being cute with the truth. We are going to talk sense and talk straight, and if we can't then we shouldn't say anything at all. There is, after all, a clear distinction between a fact, a false impression, and a falsehood. And no one can tell the difference any quicker than the people of Nova Scotia."

That was a lofty, if not particularly precise, assessment of the astuteness of the province's voters. The people of Nova Scotia never did figure out where the facts lay in the paving dispute. But they went to the polls with the impression that Stanfield had somehow managed to keep one jump ahead of Hicks throughout the campaign. They knew they trusted Stanfield and were not sure whether they could trust Hicks. Still, as they went to cast their ballots on October 30 in church basements and Legion Halls across Nova Scotia, their mood was unclear.

Henry Hicks was preoccupied as he walked with Peter Nicholson, who was running in the next riding, to his final campaign rally in his hometown of Bridgetown. "I've got a queer uneasy feeling," he told Nicholson. "You don't think those buggers could slip in under us, do you?"

Bob Stanfield was in his hometown, too, in Truro, and his earlier confidence was waning. "Well," he told Ike Smith on election-day afternoon, "I guess I'd better get two statements ready, one in case I lose and one in case I win."

7

The Stanfield Years (1956-1967)

TWO VIEWS

Robert Stanfield is perhaps the world's most well-rounded chief executive, exhibiting all the behaviour characteristics leading to excellence in management. Mr. Stanfield has the intellectual flexibility of an Adlai Stevenson, the human warmth of a John F. Kennedy, and the organized preciseness and skill of a Herbert Hoover.

> — Jerome Barnum, New York
> Management Consultant, 1967

Bob's every inch a political animal and that's why he never gives up. He understands that success and failure are equal imposters, that you may win when you should have lost, that you may lose when you should have won. . . . In this province he had and has a magic in relation to the people.

> — Gerald Regan, Liberal, Premier of
> Nova Scotia, interview, December,
> 1972

Bob Stanfield spent election night 1956 at Ike Smith's house in Truro listening to the results on the radio. When the outcome became clear, he stuffed one of his statements into his pocket, and, with Smith, headed downtown to the Conservative committee rooms for Colchester County. Something extraordinary was clearly happening. The normally quiet streets were so jammed with people that Ken Matthews, a Stanfield worker who was headed for the same place, had to park his car on Prince Street and let the crowd carry him the rest of the way. The reason for the excitement soon became clear: after twenty-three years of uninterrupted Liberal rule, Nova

Scotia had rejected the party of Angus L. Macdonald and Henry Hicks. They had elected twenty-four Conservatives, to eighteen Liberals and one C.C.F.'er. A Truro boy was the sixteenth Premier of Nova Scotia.

It was a great victory and no one could accuse the staid Halifax *Chronicle-Herald* of overstatement when it observed editorially: "The victory of the Progressive Conservatives at the polls in Nova Scotia . . . must be regarded as the climax of a party revival that has been little short of spectacular." Stanfield's eight years of unremitting labour in the political wilderness had finally paid off.

The exuberant Conservatives, some of them openly amazed by their triumph, promptly set about organizing a victory celebration to end all celebrations at the Lord Nelson Hotel on the following night. Conservatives from all over the province poured into Halifax to savour their hour of victory. But Bob Stanfield made it clear on election night that he could not throw himself into the festivities. "Tomorrow night," he said, "is Hallowe'en. I have a date with some children. We're having a Hallowe'en party."

Cape Breton was the key to the Tory election. Just three years earlier, the Conservatives had been unable to win a single seat there. But on October 30, 1956, they walked off with five of Cape Breton's ten seats and it was apparent that the Catholic vote had made the difference. "That Highland Scottish Catholic group," says Flora MacDonald, "was really responsible for electing Stanfield. . . . The cleavage in Nova Scotia politics had always been between the Halifax-Truro coalition and the Scottish Catholics, because the Catholic element had always been very weak in the Conservative Party and very strong in the Liberal Party. Now it forms the base of the Conservative Party." Stanfield also saw the Cape Breton vote as the cornerstone of his victory, telling a post-election interviewer: "From the results of previous elections it was apparent that more Cape Bretoners voted against the government than for it. But it was always a split between the C.C.F. and the Conservatives. The Liberals held the majority, however, except in the C.C.F. ridings. I honestly believe that Cape Bretoners realized two things: that the great Angus L. Macdonald was gone, and that if they wanted to change governments they would have to vote for the Conservatives."

As Stanfield pondered the election results, however, he saw that although Cape Bretoners and other Nova Scotians might have wanted to change the government, their support for the Conservatives was short of awesome. The bare election results were deceptive. Stanfield had a five-seat majority in the Legislature and the Conservatives had pulled ahead of the Liberals in the popular vote – 48.6 per cent to 48.2 per cent. But the Conservatives were still in trouble in Halifax. Dick Donahoe's victory in the Halifax South by-election two years earlier had helped convince voters in other parts of the province that the Conservatives could form a government, but it had not convinced the doubting Haligonians themselves. Donahoe managed to retain Halifax South, though with a reduced majority, but six other Tories had gone down to defeat in the capital. Outside of Halifax, Conservative candidates in nine ridings had won with majorities of under 200 votes. In fact, had Henry Hicks' Liberals been able to poll just 598 votes more in those nine ridings, they would have won twenty-seven seats, just one fewer than Angus L. Macdonald won in his great landslide of 1945. The four tightest Conservative victories were in Kings West (six votes), Pictou East (eight votes), Lunenburg West (seventeen votes), and Hants East (forty-nine votes). If as few as forty-three people who voted Conservative in those four ridings had voted Liberal instead, Hicks would have won all four seats and held a bare majority of twenty-two seats in the Legislature.

So Stanfield's elation was tempered by concern. He knew better than to start talking, as some of his supporters were, of a Conservative dynasty in Nova Scotia. Having won the province, he was realist enough to know it was not yet his to keep. A month after assuming office he went to Ottawa to be the keynote speaker at the federal Conservative leadership convention that elected a compelling Prairie lawyer-M.P. John Diefenbaker. Stanfield spoke plain sense to that convention and his words were addressed as much to his party back home as they were to the delegates assembled in Ottawa. "Elections are not settled by public opinion polls, by prophecy or by political pundits," he said. "The Canadian people are, I believe, neither influenced nor moved much by any of these. Those who have studied the Canadian political scene for the past quarter of a century are impressed by the increasing number of independent voters. These are the voters who create majorities in elections. There are not enough Grits and Tories, or followers of any other party, left to elect any man of any party to any office. . . . If I might paraphrase the remark of a distinguished Canadian politician: the age of the supermen is fast coming to a close."

It was a message that Stanfield took to heart in Nova Scotia. A reformer as much as he was a Conservative, Stanfield was determined to give Nova Scotia the best government it had ever had. He set out to create new opportunities for Nova Scotians by improving the education system and by attracting new development to his province. At the same time, he settled down to strengthen his party and to build a political following that would ensure its re-election. His search for the balance between the idealism of the reformer and the realism of the politician is what politics, at its best, is all about.

Province House, in the heart of Halifax, fairly reeks of history. It is guarded by a statue of the greatest Nova Scotian of them all, Joseph Howe, and by a cannon that was taken from the decks of H.M.S. *Shannon,* the British ship that captured the American frigate, *The Chesapeake,* in an historic naval duel off Halifax in 1813. On November 20, 1956, Robert Stanfield walked up the curved drive and probably glanced with a new proprietory interest at the statue and the cannon before passing through the main doors, framed by lamps that had lighted London's old Waterloo Bridge in the early nineteenth century. He had walked the same route hundreds of times before, but there was a difference that day: it was his first day as premier of the province. He crossed the tiled foyer, turned left, and entered his new office. There he found a woman busily cleaning out her desk. After introducing himself, Stanfield asked her where she was going. "Well, I figured you would want to bring your own secretary in," she replied. "Oh," said Stanfield, taken aback, "I am counting on you to help me out a good deal." Mary MacKinnon, secretary to Angus L. Macdonald and Henry Hicks, stayed on in the premier's office and, if the truth were known, Stanfield needed every bit of help she and anyone else could give him.

Bob Stanfield was forty-two. He was, as the newspapers liked to point out, the youngest premier in Canada. That statement was no less true for the convenient omission of the fact that he was eleven months older than his immediate predecessor, Henry Hicks. Stanfield's first cabinet was no better and no worse than Hicks'. It was notable chiefly for its leanness, a characteristic of Stanfield's method of operating – then as now. There were only eight ministers, including Stanfield, and the new premier had to scratch to find seven able men; with only twenty-four M.L.A.'s, many of them elected for the first time, he was not overblessed with cabinet material. Stanfield gave himself four jobs. Besides premier, he was Provincial Treasurer, Minister of Education, and chairman of the Nova Scotia Power Commission (the provincially-owned utility). His chief lieutenant, Ike Smith, became Minister of Highways, Provincial Secretary, and minister in charge of the Liquor Control Act. Dick Donahoe, Stanfield's second lieutenant, was Attorney General, Minister of Health, and Minister of Welfare. Clifford Levy, a fifty-one-year-old lawyer from Bridgewater, took two portfolios: municipal affairs, and lands and forests. Stephen Pyke, a payroll clerk from Springhill, also had two jobs: labour and public works. Edward A. (Ned) Manson, a druggist from Sydney on Cape Breton, took on the ministries of trade and industry (a vital assignment in the Stanfield scheme of things), and mines. Only Edward Haliburton, a journalist-turned-fruit grower, escaped double or triple duty. He became Minister of Agriculture.

That left one Minister Without Portfolio, Layton Fergusson, a lawyer from Glace Bay. Five of the eight were lawyers, one a druggest, one a clerk, and one a farmer. As a cabinet, they were very green. Their average legislative experience was only three years.

Stanfield was the unquestioned boss of that first cabinet, running it almost as though it were a board of directors. Without sacrificing his own control, he gave his ministers considerable latitude in running their departments. "He has a frightening capacity for decentralizing," says Rod Black, the head of Stanfield's political organization, "and if he believed in someone he would give them responsibility and suddenly it would scare the ass off them." Ministers went to cabinet meetings with a certain trepidation, suspecting that Stanfield knew almost as much as they did about what was going on in their departments; they knew that if they made fools of themselves they could expect to be cut down with a caustic, "Now that's a lot of nonsense," from Stanfield.

"Cabinet meetings were orderly and firm," recalls Dick Donahoe. "Everyone got his chance to speak up. The routine business was brought forward on an agenda, and we began every meeting by dealing with the agenda items." When the cabinet finished the agenda, it turned to other matters, often matters with sensitive political overtones, and Stanfield kept a record of the decisions taken in a little book he carried with him. That practice distressed the Liberals when they returned to office and could not find Stanfield's little book. "We could never be certain what had been decided in cabinet before," complains Premier Gerry Regan.

Stanfield took his ministers into his confidence whenever he was considering a policy or an action that might be contentious. He would invite their views and listen carefully to their opinions, and although he polled the table informally he did not make motions or take votes. If one of his ideas ran into opposition, he would let the matter drop, but the cabinet soon learned that if Stanfield was determined to have his way he would get it eventually. He would wait a few weeks and try again, disguising the idea by presenting it in slightly different form. The ploy did not fool the other ministers, but they knew there was little point in arguing indefinitely once Stanfield had indicated he intended to keep on trying. "He never jammed anything down our throats," says Donahoe. "But he persisted. The uniform result was he always got his way, but he got it without riding roughshod over the feelings and opinions of the people who at first blush were not prepared to go along with him."

According to Ike Smith, Stanfield led by example and argument. Having introduced a topic, he would let the others exhaust their arguments without intervening himself. Once a consensus emerged, he would cut the discussion off and move on to the next subject. "He is a very patient man," says Smith, "and you can have the most vigorous debates with him. You can say anything that's as rough as you want or as frank as you want about anything. There's no rancour about it. Whatever result the debate may have, when it's over, it's over."

Ed Haliburton, the Minister of Agriculture, found Stanfield had an ability to wring a consensus from the cabinet and a knack for reducing the most complex issues to easily grasped fundamentals. Though every minister except one was older than Stanfield, it struck Haliburton (who was sixteen years older than Stanfield) as though the ages had been reversed: "Stanfield had a sort of parental control over us. He could transfix us with a level look that made one feel like a naughty boy."

Dick Donahoe can remember only one occasion when Stanfield failed to get his way in cabinet. That was when the Union of Nova Scotia Municipalities came to make its annual submission to the Cabinet and Stanfield broached the idea of developing housing and welfare policies that would give preferential treatment to the sorely impoverished Negroes of the province. "He was shot down in flames by a lot of people from the municipalities who said it would be discriminatory," says Donahoe.

Stanfield's patience and painstaking search for a consensus extended beyond the cabinet chamber. He liked to condition the public to new programs, rather than to take the people by surprise. That was why he created an advisory committee headed by Rod Black to prepare the public for hospital insurance (and, coincidentally, for the sales tax that would have to be imposed to finance it). He did the same thing later as the Government prepared to introduce medicare. "Everything," says Donahoe, "had two or three runs at it in a tentative sort of way, so that the people could get familiar with the idea and accept it before it became a *fait accompli.*"

That sort of government-by-consultation worked reasonably well as long as Stanfield was running a provincial government with a budget not much over sixty million dollars a year. Today, with a provincial budget ten times that size, problems seem ten times as numerous and ten times as large. Special interest groups are ten times as vocal and participatory democracy, although perhaps more meaningful, seems ten times more difficult. The personalized democracy that Stanfield practised in Nova Scotia has all but disappeared in the increasing complexity of modern government. Indeed, it was on its way out before he left Nova Scotia.

Stanfield's approach to government organization seems equally old-fashioned by contemporary yardsticks. He operated without the advantage (or hinderance) of flow charts, super-ministers, and planning and priorities subcommittees to funnel business through the cabinet. He had no permanent cabinet committees of any sort, not even a treasury board to vet departmental spending plans. If a matter were important enough to warrant the cabinet's attention, it would be placed before the full cabinet. The full cabinet met once a week (usually on Thursday) all year, and meetings often lasted all day. If Stanfield felt some question required a closer look, he would strike an *ad hoc* committee and, when it finished, the *ad hoc* committee evaporated.

The same lack of frills and unnecessary appendages characterized the administration of the Premier's office. For all of his eleven years as Premier, Stanfield doubled as Minister of Education, and for the first six years he was Provincial Treasurer as well. He was running almost half the government of the province, and he ran it with an office staff of just three people – an administrative assistant, Innis MacLeod, who had been a senior solicitor in the department of the attorney general when Stanfield asked him to head his staff; a private secretary, Mary MacKinnon; and a stenographer. After 1960, he also had an executive assistant, Joe Clarke, who worked out of Conservative headquarters and took care of the political side of the Premier's duties. Today, some middle-echelon civil servants have larger staffs to help them run their tiny corner of an insignificant government department than Robert Stanfield needed to run half a province. Amazingly, everything got done. Stanfield is an immensely well-organized and self-disciplined man; one of the small things he insisted on was that all the mail coming in to the Premier's office be answered within twenty-four hours, if possible, and certainly within forty-eight hours. Anyone corresponding with any government in the 1970s is delighted if the bureaucracy can produce an answer in less than forty-eight days!

The meagerness of Stanfield's personal staff reflected the man's utter lack of pretension. Although a government limousine went with the job, Stanfield usually preferred to drive his own car if he had to travel farther than he could conveniently walk. If he had to fly to Ottawa or any place else on government business, he travelled in the back of the plane with the other economy-class passengers, and he insisted his ministers do the same. For all the years he was premier, his home telephone was listed in the Halifax phone book. Anyone could dial 422-3130 and in all probability the phone would be answered by Stanfield himself with his deep, tentative "Hullo." Once a reporter called in the middle of the night and woke Stanfield up with an unnecessary question. Stanfield hung up on him, but called back in the morning to apologize for having been rude. It was the same at the office. If Mary MacKinnon were out, it was often the Premier who answered the telephone or the door. In almost any other man, such unpretentiousness would have seemed studied at best and phony at worse, but with Stanfield it was – and is – genuine. He does not refuse to cloak himself in the trappings of office; he simply ignores the sort of trappings that other men work all their lives to achieve. His unassuming mien is one of the attributes Stanfield's supporters most admire. Some of them, however, wish that occasionally Stanfield would accept a few of the perks available to him, so that he would look the way they think the public wants a leader to look.

Every morning in Halifax, Stanfield left "The Oaks" on Gorsebrook Avenue, walked his younger daughters to school, kissed them at the door, and walked on downtown to Province House, a distance of over a mile. Occasionally, he would pause to talk to someone. The smiles of workers on their way to the office showed that they rather liked having a premier who walked to work, as though he were just an ordinary man with an ordinary job. But most people were embarrassed to stop him for a chat. They did not seem to know what to call him – "Bob" or "Mr. Stanfield" or "Mr. Premier" or what? Unless he seemed inclined to pause, they let him pass undisturbed.

"Bob's father was the same way," says Senator Fred Blois, the long-time manager of the Stanfield mill in Truro. "His father always walked to the office, in fine or wet weather. He knew everybody. You would be amazed the people around town who called his father by his first name. . . . The man who was sweeping the street, or anyone, they would stop and talk to him and that has gone right through the family."

The first fifteen minutes of Bob Stanfield's day at the office were spent with Innis MacLeod. By the time Stanfield arrived, MacLeod had scrutinized all the incoming mail and divided it into three piles: letters with dreaded (for MacLeod, a civil servant) political connotations; letters MacLeod judged he could handle himself; and letters that required instructions from Stanfield. Stanfield flipped through the "political" correspondence, handing back to MacLeod any letters he felt the civil service could handle without reference to the Conservative Party. The rest of the political mail he either kept to answer himself or farmed out to Joe Clarke at party headquarters. MacLeod quickly briefed Stanfield on the routine government mail in the second pile, advising Stanfield as to how he proposed to answer. The third pile – that requiring Stanfield's attention – took slightly longer, but Stanfield wasted little time. His instructions to MacLeod were terse. If he was not ready to make a decision on a matter raised in a letter, he did not spend time discussing it with MacLeod. "Maybe I'd better think about this," he would say and go on to the next letter.

At noon, Stanfield avoided the Halifax Club, the watering spot much favoured by other lawyers and politicians. Instead, he walked home, ate a light lunch, and walked back to the office again. Though all that walking took a chunk out of his day, the time was not wasted. By the time he returned after lunch he had thought through the problems of the office and had a new batch of instructions ready for MacLeod. He always tried to finish at a reasonable hour in the afternoon so that he could walk back home in time to have dinner with his children, and, if it was a fine evening, to tend to his prized rose garden.

As premier, Stanfield budgeted his time carefully, yet he was always accessible on short notice if someone had to see him. "One of the things you admire about him is that he can organize his day in such a way that he has time for everything," says a Halifax lawyer who had frequent need of access to Stanfield in those years. "He was the kind of person who, if you had to see him and you were prepared to discipline yourself in seeing him, you could see him any time. I would call his secretary and say I had a small problem I would like to discuss with him and it will take me five or six minutes. Can he fit me in? They might say come over in an hour and a half, or tomorrow at ten o'clock. You would get in there and you would get ten minutes. Provided he could trust you not to screw up his day, he would give you the time. It was beautiful from your point of view, and from his point of view he got first-hand information or feedback on whatever the situation was. I have seen a lot of governments operate where this doesn't happen at all. Everybody is so bloody busy that if you ask for an appointment you could wait for two months."

In Dalton Camp's not unbiased view, Stanfield's self-discipline enabled him to overcome the exceedingly slender resources available to the Premier of Nova Scotia. "He was the most self-disciplined man in that office," says Camp. "I suppose that's the essence of Stanfield. He goes to the office every day and does what has to be done. He never leaves anything undone. There are hardly any politicians in Canada who can make that statement. . . . He may be too good for public office."

The chief criticism of Stanfield's methods as premier is that he made do with too little assistance. He had a true Conservative's distrust of big government and fat bureaucracy, and, because his own personal style was simple and uncluttered, he was under-staffed all the years he was premier. Smallness is not necessarily an unalloyed virtue in an age when government is growing increasingly complex. Premier Gerry Regan's point is partisan but well taken: "The most disturbing thing about Bob has been the fact that over the years he never surrounded himself with bright young men. While he was an academic himself, I'd almost suspect him of being an anti-academic." Stanfield would have better-served had he recruited a small corps of advisers to do for him in government what the Maritime Mafia did for him in elections – advisers with the intellectual ability to grasp the ramifications of the policies the government was following, plus the political sense to know when the government was headed for trouble. Had there been a corps of such experts in the premier's office when Ike Smith took over, Smith might have been able to weather the seas that submerged him after Stanfield left.

Stanfield's passion for efficiency and economy of operation extended beyond his own office to encompass the entire civil service of Nova Scotia. Shortly after taking office, he hired a firm of New York efficiency experts, Jerome Barnum and Associates, to examine the entire operation of the provincial bureaucracy and to recommend improvements. It was natural after being out of office for twenty-three years that the Tories would want to put the civil service under a microscope, although the bureaucrats, who dubbed it the "Barnum and Stanfield Circus," were unimpressed. They found it disconcerting suddenly to find a platoon of bright young men from New York peering over their shoulders and demanding to know what they were doing and why they were doing it the way they had been doing it all their working lives. Eventually the consultants brought in a report claiming that, if all the recommendations were implemented, the government could save a million and a half dollars a year. Many of the recommendations were adopted, most notably a reallignment of government departments; Stanfield could not, however, go all the way with the consultants. He had tied his hands to a degree in the beginning by promising that no civil servant would lose his job as a result of the study. Although the civil service remained highly sceptical, the study did have two worthwhile results: it slowed the growth of the provincial bureaucracy for a while, and it caused the mandarins to re-examine procedures they had long taken for granted. Stanfield and the cabinet were well pleased, claiming the consultants had saved the government far more than they had cost. The assertion was unprovable, but may have been true. For their part, the consultants were obviously much taken with Robert Stanfield, to the extent that Jerome Barnum years later felt inspired to invest him with the virtues of Stevenson, Kennedy, and Hoover (Herbert, not J. Edgar). One hesitates to think what American personalities Barnum might have summoned up to stand as a testament to the qualities of a Mackenzie King or a John Diefenbaker!

Although he ran a disciplined office in Province House, Premier Stanfield was by no means a difficult man to work for. He liked to tease the staff and especially Innis MacLeod, who was a Cape Bretoner by birth. Somewhere Stanfield had picked up a book written by an American who had toured Nova Scotia in the nineteenth century, getting as far as Cape Breton. The author had a number of pungent observations to make about the characteristics of the Highland Scots of that region, and every so often Stanfield would wander out of his office, his finger marking a page, and accost MacLeod: "Say look, here's another story about you Scots. What do you have to say about this?" He would shove the book under MacLeod's nose and return to his office, laughing.

Stanfield also kept up a running, light-hearted battle of wits with Jack Wheatley, the man whose job it was to drive the big black car that Stanfield preferred not to use. Wheatley was a baseball buff and although Stanfield was not much of a baseball fan he made a point of checking the scores so that he could rib Wheatley when his favourite team lost. "Stanfield," says Finlay MacDonald, "would never let Wheatley forget whenever his favourite team lost a game. Never. There was a note that went to Wheatley, or Bob would tell someone to give a message to Wheatley, 'When are those old bums going to win a game?' or something like that. He was constantly ragging Wheatley." MacDonald was with Stanfield on a trip to Antigonish when Wheatley got back at his boss. On this occasion they were using the office limousine and Stanfield and MacDonald were sitting in the back seat. It started to grow cold as they neared Antigonish a little after five o'clock in the afternoon. "Do we have to freeze back here, Jack?" Stanfield demanded of his driver. "Sorry, Mr. Premier," Wheatley shot back, "the engineer went off duty at five o'clock." They all roared.

To his cabinet, Stanfield was an object of admiration and, at times, dismay. The ministers did not object when he made them fly economy class, but some of them were unhappy when he cut off their pensions. Under legislation adopted by the Angus L. Macdonald government, a retired cabinet minister on reaching the age of sixty-five could draw a pension of up to seven thousand dollars a year. In the election campaigns of 1953 and 1956 Stanfield had campaigned against the pension scheme and had promised that, if elected, he would abolish it. He did just that in 1957. Haliburton, his agriculture minister, felt that Stanfield – the only wealthy man in the cabinet – had too little appreciation for the problems of less affluent politicians.

When Volvo (Canada) Ltd., with the financial backing of the Stanfield government, opened its automobile assembly plant in Dartmouth, the first car to roll off the assembly line was presented to Stanfield. He turned that car over to the government, but bought another for his own use and suggested gently to his ministers that they, too, might like to set an example for the province by driving the Swedish-designed cars. Some of them did buy Volvos. Stanfield still drives one, as does Ike Smith, but Dick Donahoe decided enough was enough. Finding it too hard to get service for his Volvo, he turned it in on a car built in Ontario.

116

As the years passed, Stanfield changed in subtle ways. He had been an uncertain performer in the Legislature in his years as leader of the Opposition, but as premier he gained confidence commensurate with his new status. In the opinion of Liberal M.L.A. Peter Nicholson, he became the master of the House. "His wit started to come through," says Nicholson. "He became an able debater and he had a memory like an elephant. His style was getting more easy and his stature was growing to beat hell. . . . His disarming appearance belied the fact he was a political animal. He lives, breathes, and sleeps politics." Nicholson, a great admirer of Stanfield, was impressed with his forebearance. "He had tremendous patience and he would listen to all sides. He always tries to do the right thing and when he makes a decision he never doubts that it is the right decision." Only once did Nicholson see Stanfield lose his patience. The session was drawing to a close and Stanfield was waiting for the Law Amendments Committee to process a batch of motor vehicle amendments before he adjourned the Legislature. The committee, under the chairmanship of Attorney General Donahoe, was wrestling at great length with the amendments. "Stanfield came into the room where we were meeting several times to inquire how we were getting along," Nicholson remembers. "He finally got exasperated and said, 'This committee will sit here until it finishes.'" The committee sat long after midnight and finally passed the amendments. But the amendments were so badly drafted that they had to be rewritten at the next session of the Legislature.

Official business took Stanfield away periodically, though infrequently by today's standards. In 1958, he went to England where he met the Queen. But the trip was less memorable for this introduction to the monarchy than it was for a horse race. Stanfield went to the Epsom Derby and decided to place a small wager on a dark-horse, Hard Ridden. But before he could get his bet down he was paged to take a telephone call. It proved to be a crank call, but by the time Stanfield got back it was too late. Hard Ridden had won the Derby, at odds of eighteen to one.

Government became a more complex and time-consuming vocation as the years went on and Stanfield was forced to change his routine. To save time he stopped walking home for lunch and drove instead. He had less time for old friends, including Russell Maxwell, his Economics professor and mentor from his days at Dalhousie. "Prior to his becoming Premier," says Maxwell, "I used to go over to his home almost as a matter of routine every Sunday evening. I'd call him up and go over. After he became Premier, the understanding was he would call me when he was free and when he wanted to see me. That happened occasionally, but that was all."

Stanfield had never been a gregarious man and being Premier was a lonely job. Unlike the ordinary man who works from nine to five in an ordinary office, he had little opportunity to socialize at the office or after work. It was one thing for a Premier to walk to work, it was quite a different thing for him to stop in at the pub for a pint with the boys on the way home. In addition, Stanfield has always had a tendency to draw away from close personal involvement with other people. He is lonely without being a real loner. His classmates at Harvard had noticed it in the way he never discussed his home, his family or his girl. His colleagues at Province House noticed it, too. "I sometimes wonder what the reason for that is," says Ike Smith. "Sometimes I think it's just because people don't get a chance to know him well. Other times I think he's perhaps a believer in this theory that some people hold that if you have too many close friends you've really not got the ability to be sufficiently dispassionate in public decisions."

The greatest change in Stanfield's life occurred just six months after he became premier. On May 10, 1957, with just two friends in attendance, Bob Stanfield remarried. His bride was Mary Hall, daughter of Mr. Justice W. L. Hall of the Supreme Court of Nova Scotia. She had been one of Joyce Stanfield's best friends, and had often helped to look after the four Stanfield children in the three years following Joyce's death. So secret were their wedding preparations that they set off for a honeymoon in Bermuda and got as far as Boston before the press caught up to them.

One of the fondest boasts of the Conservatives of Nova Scotia is that Robert Stanfield abolished political patronage. The boast is nonsense. As long as there are politicians who must get elected and governments that have favours to dispense, patronage will flourish. The differences in the practice of political patronage from one politician to the next and from one government to the next are mostly differences in degree. The politician who distributes patronage carelessly may enhance his power in the short run, but in the end he will destroy himself. The sensible politician looks after his friends, but he takes care to look after the public interest, too. Bob Stanfield belonged in the latter category. He was an honest leader and the administration he ran was as honest as any in the country. His government was untouched by corruption – a claim that could not have been made for earlier governments in Nova Scotia. He outlawed the worst abuses of the pork barrel. He refused to let the people who contributed to his party dictate policy to his government. He forebade the party to accept kickbacks from companies awarded government business. He refused to purge the civil service of everyone who was known or suspected to be a Liberal. By today's standards Stanfield's restraint is unremarkable; in the type of politics practised in Nova Scotia in the 1950s, it was quite radical. "The old Nova Scotia or Atlantic history was that there be a complete blood-bath after every election," says Rod Black. "Stanfield was the first who didn't do that. When the Liberals came in in 1933, there were major dismissals in the civil service. But the concept of security in the civil service had developed. You can't make a valid comparison between 1956 and 1933. The times were changing."

The fact that Stanfield broke with tradition did not, however, mean that he was unaware of the uses of patronage. "Stanfield is an elitist," says Dalton Camp, "but he's also a democrat in that he respects the system. . . . His definition of patronage was that it's fine as long as the public interest is protected." Loyal Conservatives could always count on government sinecures during the years Stanfield was in office – whether it was the chairmanship of the Workmen's Compensation Board or the Nova Scotia Liquor Commission, or a minor judgeship, or (with an assist from a Tory government in Ottawa) a seat on the provincial Supreme Court or in the Senate of Canada.

No Conservative who wanted to do business with the Stanfield government ever starved. Although it was never proved, it used to be said that "nothing moved in Nova Scotia" unless it passed through the hands of a firm operated by the treasurer of the provincial Conservative Party. Judicious use of the pork barrel ensured that the party never had any difficulty putting the touch on grateful suppliers when the time came to raise the $150,000 to $200,000 that it cost in those days to run a provincial election campaign. To the Stanfield government, political patronage, as long as it was quietly spread and carefully supervised, was good business and good politics.

"Any politician," says Ike Smith, "would rather do business with a friend than with an enemy. . . . But the fundamental rule that was laid down was that if you did buy something from a friend, you had to be satisfied that you were not costing the public any more, either in money or in terms of quality."

Premier Gerry Regan offers a realistic appraisal: "Stanfield is honest, but in my view he totally accepted the fact that in Nova Scotia patronage was a way of life." Stanfield's predecessor, Henry Hicks, endorses that view: "It is commonly known in the trade that Stanfield was far more efficient at collecting campaign money than his Liberal predecessors had been. . . . I am not suggesting for one minute that Mr. Stanfield allowed the supporters of his party to wrongly influence him in decision making. Indeed, I don't think he did. But at the same time, I won't have him state that he abolished the system that still thrives in Nova Scotia very much the same way it has throughout the whole of our history."

If Stanfield did not abolish the pork barrel, he at least brought it under control. Having done that, he proceeded to pretend to the public that it did not exist. He sought to walk the narrow line between the public interest and the party interest. That he succeeded was evidenced by the fact that he satisfied neither his enemies nor his friends.

On election night, 1956, many Conservatives could scarcely conceal their glee. After being frozen out for twenty-three years, they were at last to have their chance to wallow in the pork barrel. There would be comfortable jobs for old-time Tories on government boards and commissions, and suitable little jobs in the civil service for their relatives. There would be fat government contracts to supply the government with everything from snowploughs for the highways to pills for the province's mental institutions. It was great to be back in power again, and who could blame them if they drooled just a little?

Stanfield, however, quickly pricked their balloon. Two weeks after the election – before he had even been sworn in as premier – he went before six hundred excited delegates at the annual meeting of the Nova Scotia Conservative Party and laid down the law: "I do not intend to allow the claims of any individual seeking reward to jeopardize the future of the Conservative Government or the Conservative Party of Nova Scotia." That was bad enough, but it got worse as Stanfield went on to play the refrain he was soon to play as keynote speaker at the national leadership convention in Ottawa. "Some," said Stanfield, "may say to me: 'The important thing is to keep the Conservatives happy, so that we will have an energetic party when the next election comes.' Some will say: 'Don't forget friends.' Now, let's face the future frankly. If you want to consider this subject in terms of party advantage only, there are not enough Conservatives in Nova Scotia to elect a Conservative Government. We will be re-elected next time with the support of the independent voter, just as we were elected October 30. . . . We Conservatives should not forget that for a moment. . . . Without the support of these people, we are lost. We will not retain that support if we are vindictive or self-seeking. . . . I have some friends who say the only way to build up a party is to sweep every Grit out of office and put a friend in his place. . . . I am told that the Liberals in 1933 even replaced the charwoman."

Stanfield's Conservatives did not like that one bit. After waiting so long, their hands were being slapped away from the trough. For many months afterward, rank and file Conservatives at political rallies across Nova Scotia complained bitterly that Liberals who had campaigned strenuously for the old government were left untouched in their government jobs, whereas Conservatives who had struggled mightily for their party were denied the rewards that compassion, tradition, and simple political good sense would seem to dictate that they receive. They wondered bleakly what sort of a premier they had. Their anguish was genuine and their frustration was, in a way, understandable. "After all," says Flora MacDonald, "when jobs are scarce as they always are in Nova Scotia, it means your bread and butter. I can feel some sympathy with these people." Dick Donahoe, the new attorney general, was appalled. Stanfield owed Donahoe favours for all the years Donahoe had laboured for the party and Donahoe owed favours to all the people who had worked for him and had contributed to his losing campaigns in Halifax. "I don't mind saying that as a minister I used to feel frustrated," says Donahoe. "I couldn't do anything for my political supporters who came to me and asked for business to be awarded to them in return for their support. . . . It was frustrating to be charged with patronage when you knew in your heart and soul you couldn't work patronage. If there was any minister who could have worked it, I would have been one of them."

While Conservatives fumed that Stanfield was too parsimonious with patronage, the labour movement worried that Stanfield was going to be too generous. One of the first delegations to wait on him in the Premier's office was from the 50,000-member Nova Scotia Federation of Labour, which asked that Stanfield protect the' jobs of all civil servants. The Cabinet debated its course and announced that some civil servants would be fired. The rule laid down was that any government employee who had engaged in partisan election work or who was considered by the new government to be incompetent would be dismissed. In practice, however, there were almost no dismissals, largely because the government required sworn affidavits to support allegations of political activity. The only important civil servant to be fired outright was the province's director of tourism, the man who had refused to hire Flora MacDonald; he was dismissed for incompetence, not political activity. There were few firings in the Nova Scotia Liquor Commission, which had for years served as the great reservoir of Liberal poll workers. Liquor stores were required by law to close on election days and they released a small army of employees to hustle out the vote for local Liberal candidates.

Only in Ike Smith's highways department was there anything approaching a blood bath, and that was restricted to part-time employees. The chief victims were the road foremen. These men were a breed peculiar to Nova Scotia. Active Liberals all, they were local people who were assigned responsibility for the maintenance of a set number of miles of county roads in their areas. Each was given a budget and allowed to hire the help he needed to run the heavy equipment; not entirely surprisingly, all the people whom the road foremen hired were also Liberals. Some of the foremen were important cogs in the rural Liberal machines and the Conservatives had warned during the 1956 election campaign that they would be fired. They were. Altogether, Smith sacked eleven hundred foremen and replaced them with about eight hundred Conservatives. Naturally, when spring came, the new foremen hired Tories to run the equipment. "We thought it only fair," says Smith delicately, "that there should be some change in the recipients of employment." If it happened today, there would be a public outcry, but the replacement of the road foremen was taken for granted in Nova Scotia at that time – so much so that the displaced Liberals did not even bother to complain.

The Conservatives, however, were far from satisfied. There was an outcry when Smith declined to discharge 150-odd Liberals who worked part-time for the highways department as snowplough operators. There was nothing humanitarian about Smith's refusal. The Conservatives did not take office until November 20 in 1956; Smith knew he could not recruit and train new plough operators before the first snow storm. He let the Liberals work through the winter then simply did not rehire them in the fall. Their replacements were not Liberals.

One of the major reforms made by Stanfield was the abolition of what was known as the "bottle exchange." Like the liquor agents, the bottle exchange was simply a racket, a blatant but widely tolerated form of pork barrelling. Nova Scotians with a taste for beer could not in those days return their empties to their neighbourhood liquor store for a refund. Instead, they had to take them to a bottle purchaser who was the local agent for a syndicate based in Halifax. In a town the size of Truro, only one bottle purchaser had the franchise to sell empties to the syndicate in Halifax; only the syndicate could sell bottles to the breweries. It was all very much under the table. There was nothing in law to prevent the breweries from buying empties directly from the public, but brewers knew that if they wanted to remain in the good graces of the Liberal Government, which, through its appointees on the Liquor Commission, controlled the listing of beer in liquor stores, they would be wise to buy bottles only from the syndicate. The members of the syndicate were Liberals and one of them was the treasurer of the Liberal Party of Nova Scotia. No one ever knew how much the syndicate reaped from this arrangement; estimates ranged from $40,000 to $200,000 a year. The proportion that found its way back into the coffers of the Liberal Party was also unknown, but was believed to be substantial. Under Stanfield, the government took over the operation of the bottle exchange, turning a tidy profit for the taxpayers.

Stanfield's greatest reforms were in the provincial purchasing system. Although he was under considerable pressure to fire the province's purchasing agent, who was a Liberal appointee, Stanfield kept him on. He brought in legislation under which the purchasing agent reported directly to the Legislature rather than to a cabinet minister. The effect was two-fold: it reduced the amount of direct influence the government could wield in the awarding of business; and it opened the purchasing agent's books to scrutiny by all parties in the Legislature. Stanfield laid down two rules. First, no payments were to be required from any supplier to do business with the government. Second, no Conservative was to get preferred treatment in the awarding of business, *if it meant a higher price for the public to pay.* Small purchases could still be made on the open market, but major ones had to be put out to tender. The catch was this: tenders were not publicly advertised. Rather, invitations to tender were extended to companies whose names were on special government lists. The majority of companies on the lists were run by friends or supporters of the Conservative Government. It was not impossible for a Liberal to get on a list, but he knew without being told that his chances improved in direct proportion to the enthusiasm with which he supported the Tories. This arrangement permitted the Government to give business to its supporters, while at the same time enabling it to claim with great righteousness that it always accepted the lowest bid. The Government did not feel it was necessary to point out that, for the most part, Conservatives were tendering only against Conservatives. As a practical politician, Stanfield was prepared to go that far to look after his friends. "I don't think he minded that too much," says Dalton Camp.

Camp himself was the central figure in the only notable outburst about pork barrel politics during Stanfield's years as premier. The Liberals had been watching with acute interest the amount of government-advertising business that was being handed to Dalton K. Camp and Associates. "It was in the hundreds of thousands of dollars a year," recalls Peter Nicholson, the Liberal M.L.A. who became minister of finance in 1970. "Finally, one of our members, Dr. Henry Reardon from Halifax, got up and made a fiery speech. He got a little carried away and I think Henry regretted it later. He referred to Camp's involvement as 'patronage' and 'graft.' At some point Ike Smith got up and said, 'I resent being called a grafter.' Stanfield said he wasn't sure just what Henry had said and he'd have to check the transcript."

The next day, an angry Stanfield announced that a committee of the Legislature would be convened to investigate Reardon's charges. Reardon would have been on unassailable ground had he confined himself to an allegation of patronage; there was no evidence at all that graft was involved. Not surprisingly, the Tory-dominated committee declared the Government to be above reproach and censured Reardon. It was the only time many members of the Legislature ever saw Stanfield angered. "He was a man of impeccable character and Reardon's charges went right to the quick," says Nicholson.

Gerry Regan, the Liberal premier, has a certain admiration for Stanfield's judicious use of the pork barrel. He says that Stanfield managed to run the province for eleven years without ever once appointing a Liberal to any important position. "Except for those special commissions where you had to appoint two Conservatives and one Liberal, or something like that, I don't think he ever missed the opportunity to appoint Conservatives," says Regan. "I'm not saying this necessarily critically because it was a part of the era. But Bob's a political animal. He understood that these were the rules under which politics was played. He took the view that 'Subject to these rules I'll run as straight a government as I can.' That's what he sought to do and that's what he did."

One of Bob Stanfield's early callers after he became premier was the man he had defeated, Henry Hicks. Hicks came to brief Stanfield on three industrial projects that the Liberal government had been negotiating to bring to Nova Scotia. The first was a giant pulp mill for Port Hawkesbury on the Strait of Canso, the narrow body of water that divides Cape Breton Island from the mainland. The Hicks Government had tried to interest the Hearst publishing complex in the United States in building the mill; when those talks broke down, it turned its attention to a Swedish industrial combine, Stora Kopparbergs Bergslags A. B. The second project was a hydro-electric development for Cape Breton. Hicks was bewildered by Stanfield's reaction: "I told him of the first item of business and he listened to me and he didn't say 'Thank you' or 'That's interesting.' He didn't say anything. He just sat there with a enigmatic look on his face as much as to say 'If you want to go on talking, I am here.' So I moved to the second topic and got exactly the same reaction and I never mentioned the third one at all. I can't even remember the third item, the one I didn't discuss with him." Hicks was puzzled; thinking it over later, he concluded that Stanfield either had not believed him, or was simply so new to the job that he did not trust anyone.

The hydro project never came to pass, but the pulp mill was built. Although negotiations had languished, Stanfield was able to revive them and Stora Kopparbergs, through a Canadian subsidiary, Nova Scotia Pulp Ltd. (now Nova Scotia Forest Industries), built a forty million dollar bleached sulphite pulp mill three miles south of Port Hawkesbury. That mill, with its ten million dollar annual payroll, was regarded in later years as one of the great feathers in Stanfield's cap.

His caution with Hicks was understandable, however. Stanfield was just beginning to appreciate the enormity of the job that had been handed to him. Post-war developments in industry, transportation, and technology had largely by-passed Nova Scotia. The province, admittedly, had vast reserves of coal and the coal industry was still the largest employer, with about 7,500 miners. But coal was becoming obsolete as a fuel for industry, and the costs of mining it and transporting it to market were prohibitive. The mines stayed open only because of massive federal subsidies. Steel was the second largest employer, and the Dominion Steel and Coal Company (DOSCO), the largest employer east of Quebec, had about 4,000 steelworkers in Cape Breton. Coal production was already falling when Stanfield took office and, though no one knew it then, the steel industry was to turn turtle, too.

The big financial underwriters in New York, where Nova Scotia did much of its borrowing, were well aware of the province's shaky economy. Shortly after becoming premier, Stanfield made the requisite pilgrimage to New York to submit himself to the scrutiny of the underwriters. He told his old professor Russell Maxwell about it when he got back. "He told me he thought Nova Scotia was going to lose its 'A' rating," says Maxwell, "and he told me some of the questions they had asked him. They were very penetrating questions. How about your school buildings? How do you amortize your school buildings? That sort of thing. They were very, very keen questions, and they seemed just sufficiently doubtful about the way Nova Scotia was doing things that he thought they were probably going to lose their 'A' rating. But they didn't. He was able to convince them, partly on the strength of his promise that things would be mended somewhat."

Stanfield remembers the challenge clearly: "We felt we had to run very hard just to stand still. In agriculture we had a system of small farms, which people were constantly leaving. Fishing was in a state of revolution. The so-called inshore fisherman was pretty well disappearing in most parts of the province. That involved a large expansion of the trawler fishing industry and the centralization at certain points. The forest industry had to be re-organized substantially. The coal mining industry was failing rapidly."

The mayor of Stellarton came to Stanfield in a state of desperation. One of the coal mines in Pictou County had closed and a second was headed in the same direction. "What are we going to do?" he asked. Stanfield gave him some money to make a survey to determine what sorts of industry the area might be able to support; then he set to work himself trying to broaden the economic base of the county. "In Springhill," says Stanfield, "when the first disaster took place, we wondered what we would ever do with it – there were two mines there – if they both went. And they both went. But with the help of the federal government and of quite a few small industries that we put there, and by placing a hospital there and making it a bit of an educational central, the economy of the town was broadened. It was broadened considerably. These are examples of what I mean when I say we had to run pretty hard just to stand still."

No one could accuse Stanfield of not running hard enough. He faced more problems than any premier should have to face; if he did not overcome them all, he did solve more than most people could reasonably have asked. Without him, the economy of Nova Scotia might have collapsed. He turned the province over to his successor in better shape than it had been in when he received it. He gave it enough of an industrial base that Nova Scotians could look to better years ahead.

Stanfield brought to the task a true Conservative's conviction of the salutariness of hard work in overcoming almost any obstacle, and the willingness of a reformer to seek out new ways of attacking old problems. Unlike the normal Conservative, including some in his own cabinet, he did not believe that the highest purpose of government was to preserve exisiting institutions. As his agriculture minister, Ed Haliburton, once wrote: "Stanfield is the kind of leader who can adapt to changing situations. He is not doctrinaire, not dogmatic; his ideas are not rooted in the past."

Some of the changes Stanfield wrought were small, some far reaching. He introduced hospital insurance, and he prepared the ground for medicare. He increased assistance to municipalities for the relief of the poor, and pumped money into institutions for the "harmless insane." He provided pensions for older miners, and put some idled miners to work on a reforestation project and others on the restoration of the fortress at Louisbourg. He gave Nova Scotia its first provincial parks; he raised the ceiling on agricultural loans from $8,000 (barely enough to buy a heavy tractor) to $100,000. He helped livestock farmers to build a million dollar abattoir by contributing three dollars in provincial funds for every dollar the farmers raised. He appointed an independent auditor general (after the federal model) responsible to the Legislature, with the power to comb through the government accounts.

He appointed Nova Scotia's first ombudsman, made grants to keep Halifax's Neptune Theatre alive, and modernized the province's Victorian drinking laws. He poured money into hospital construction and nurses' training. And he went on a road-building spree. In the 1956 election, the Liberals had promised a four-year one hundred million dollar program of highway construction. Stanfield and Ike Smith did better than that, spending a hundred and ten million in the first four years to give Nova Scotia a modern highway system. "I suppose," Stanfield says a trifle sadly, "the thing on which our electoral support was based was the job we did in things like roads."

126

His scheme for voluntary economic planning for the province was derided by his opponents as window dressing and political gamesmanship, and it was probably both. But, if nothing else, it gave Stanfield an independent source of advice on the sort of economic policy he should pursue. Starting in 1962, Stanfield and Ike Smith carved the provincial economy into ten sectors and enlisted non-government experts in each sector. By 1965, about five hundred Nova Scotians, from fishermen to mining executives, were involved in the process, meeting periodically to discuss problems in their sectors and funnelling ideas through the twenty-seven-member Voluntary Economic Planning Board. The Board's first report in 1965 did not tell Stanfield anything that he didn't already know. It warned that the province needed to double its rate of job creation to the point where it would be creating three to four thousand new jobs a year, and it added a reminder: "It will be necessary for Nova Scotia to develop a whole new group of secondary manufacturing industries." Stanfield had been working on just that problem for the past eight years.

Although he had gone through the 1956 election promising to create a "Nova Scotia Industrial Development Corporation," Stanfield had no detailed idea of what he was going to do. "I remember him telling me this after the election," chuckled Russell Maxwell. "He'd become premier and suddenly he was saddled with this burden." He knew, of course, what had to be done. He knew the number of new jobs that could be created in the primary industries was limited and that primary industry would, if anything, become even less labour-intensive as new technology reached the province. He knew he would have to promote labour-intensive secondary manufacturing if the province were to overcome its most discouraging problem. "This is the traditional problem of Nova Scotia," says a man who worked closely with Stanfield in those years. "It has to export a very substantial percentage of its maturing population because it can't supply them with jobs, and it loses some of its best people that way. It has always been considered a depressing feature of our life down here. If you educate your family, you virtually ensure they can't live here."

In his first session as premier, Stanfield introduced legislation to create a Nova Scotia Industrial Development Corporation, to be financed equally by the provincial treasury and, through the sale of shares, by the residents of the province. The bill was passed and the Government set about establishing its new corporation. The theory was that the people would be given an opportunity to participate actively in the revival of their province. The problem was that there was no way the development corporation, if it were to be effective, could expect to pay a return on the shareholders' investment. Profits had to take second place to the creation of jobs.

Stanfield's minister of trade and industry, Ned Manson, sought the advice of a British expert, General K. C. Appleyard, who had successfully developed an industrial estates program in England. The general's advice was plain: forget about selling shares to the public because that will only create a conflict in the aims of the corporation; let the government be the sole owner and concentrate on jobs, not profits. Stanfield got the same advice from a group of the province's leading businessmen whom he called together in secret meetings at the Lord Nelson Hotel. The most important businessman there was supermarket tycoon Frank Sobey, the president of Sobey Stores Ltd. and owner or director of about twenty other major concerns. "We told Bob that for various reasons we thought he was wrong having the public involved," says Sobey. "We were going to go out and develop industry. You would have to give some incentives and after paying for the cost of the operation there would be nothing in it for the shareholders."

Ike Smith and Dick Donahoe were concerned about the political damage if, after incorporating a company in which the public would be involved, the Government changed its mind and excluded the public. Stanfield, however, saw the logic in Sobey's argument. "We will just tell the Opposition we were wrong," he said, with characteristic candour.

So in the autumn of 1957, the Government replaced its initial legislation with an act to create Industrial Estates Limited (I.E.L.), a wholly-owned Crown corporation backed by an initial twelve million dollars in government funds. The key figure in I.E.L. was Frank Sobey who became the new corporation's unsalaried president, a post he was to hold until 1969. Sobey is a true Horatio Alger figure in Atlantic Canada. His father was a carpenter who quit his dollar-a-day job, borrowed five hundred dollars, and opened a grocery store. Frank Sobey built his father's business up until it became one of the two largest supermarket chains in the Atlantic Provinces. He is convinced that everyone, with a little drive, could do every bit as well.

Sobey still runs his business out of a spartan warehouselike building in his hometown of Stellarton, one hundred miles north of Halifax. Not a man to waste time or money on unnecessary accessories, Sobey operates with one black telephone on a table beside his cluttered desk. There is no intercom – nor any secretary in evidence – and when he wants to talk to his son, Bill, who is in charge of the day-to-day activities of the supermarket chain, he simply bellows through the thin partition dividing their offices. Bill bellows back. (In this way, one day in late 1972, they worked out the details of a five million dollar investment in a Calgary shopping centre!)

Away from the office, Sobey leads a completely different life. He collects expensive art, and works by Krieghoff and the Group of Seven fill the living room, line the walls beside the stairs, and spill into the bedrooms on the second floor of his elegant home outside Stellarton. Sobey has one of the few guest bedrooms in Canada with an original A. Y. Jackson over the bed. "I don't know how many I have," he says of his Group of Seven paintings. "Maybe a dozen or twenty." For all that, Sobey remains a plain man who fought his way to the top.

Sobey and Harold Egan, a business consultant and tax expert, were the driving forces behind I.E.L. in the early years; they ran it very much along the no-nonsense lines favoured by Sobey in his own business. In the beginning, I.E.L. operated with a staff of just two people: a general manager and a secretary. By the time Sobey resigned in 1969, it still had a staff of only thirteen to manage one hundred million dollars in government money.

Though Stanfield's industry minister was a member of the I.E.L. board, the Premier did not interfere in I.E.L.'s activities, carrying non-intervention to such an extreme that a member of his cabinet once complained that Stanfield would not even allow his ministers to visit the offices of I.E.L. It was a sensible precaution. If I.E.L. got into trouble, as it eventually did, the Government could let I.E.L. take the blame. If I.E.L. succeeded – and its successes outnumbered its failures – Stanfield could claim the political credit. And he did.

Stanfield always knew what I.E.L. was up to. Sobey came to see him frequently, always giving him an opportunity to object whenever Industrial Estates started to negotiate a particularly large or potentially risky agreement with an industry. There were many problems in the formative stages. The directors of I.E.L. hired a general manager, made the mistake of giving him a contract (a practice that Sobey deplored), and then found that they could not get along with him. This was only six months after I.E.L. had started operations; Sobey told Stanfield that the directors felt that they would have to buy up the man's contract. "I said to Bob, this might be embarrassing to you." "Well," replied Stanfield "We have to face these things. You do what you think you should do." Sobey went out and hired the sales manager of Canada Packers as I.E.L.'s new general manager. When he resigned a couple of years later, Sobey went back to Stanfield to enquire whether there was anyone the Government would like to see appointed. Stanfield declined to make a nomination, saying, "You get who you think you should get." On another occasion, Sobey went to Stanfield to report some second-martini gossip among Halifax's Conservative lawyers about the fact that a prominent Liberal lawyer, Bill Mingo, was getting all of Industrial Estates' legal business. "Isn't he doing a good job?" Stanfield asked. "Yes," Sobey replied. "Well," snapped Stanfield, "as far as I am concerned when gossip on Hollis Street and in the Halifax Club starts to influence the way I run my government, I am getting out and somebody else can get in." Bill Mingo remained as I.E.L.'s general counsel.

Those experiences made Sobey a great admirer of Stanfield. "Bob Stanfield wouldn't get excited about anything," says Sobey. "He's very level headed. He would think a question out. I think he was a strong, able administrator." Sobey pays Stanfield what is, for Sobey, the ultimate compliment: "He could have run a big business very successfully."

Very much a pioneer in its field, Industrial Estates changed over the years from being essentially a lending institution to being an active partner in new industrial ventures. In the beginning, its function was to create industrial parks and it operated with lease-back arrangements. It built factories to companies' specifications and leased them to the companies at the prevailing prime interest rate, plus one per cent for depreciation. At any time, the company could buy the plant for what it cost I.E.L. to build it. I.E.L. would also advance up to 70 per cent of the cost of equipment for the plant. Many companies settling in Nova Scotia found the terms attractive: they needed to put up none of the capital for the plant and as little as 30 per cent of the cost of machinery. I.E.L. soon discovered, however, that industries were not particularly interested in locating alongside one another in industrial parks; so I.E.L. let them choose other sites around the province. A half-dozen years after I.E.L. started, changes to the federal Income Tax Act made lease-back arrangements less attractive to industry, and I.E.L. began lending money directly to industries and purchasing their mortgage bonds. Unlike the federal government and the governments of some of the other provinces in the industrial development field, I.E.L. did not make outright grants or forgivable loans. The loans it made were legally repayable and when industries that it assisted went sour – as nearly one third did to some degree – I.E.L. was left holding the bag. In theory, I.E.L. was to be self-supporting though it has never reached that stage.

Stanfield was pioneering when he established I.E.L. No other province had hazarded a provincial development corporation, and none faced more obstacles than Nova Scotia did in trying to attract industry. Until I.E.L. came along, in fact, it was almost impossible for an industry to obtain a mortgage from traditional lenders if its plant was to be anywhere in Nova Scotia other than in Halifax.

The first industry brought to Nova Scotia by I.E.L. was a small textile plant, operated by Donato, Faini, and Figli in Stellarton. It was followed by a string of other companies, some medium-sized, but most of them relatively small, at the rate of five or six new industries a year. National Sea Products built a fish-packing plant employing close to 600 workers at Lunenberg. General Instrument of Canada Ltd., with a payroll of 941, settled in Sydney. Crossley-Karastan Carpet Mills created 458 jobs in a rug-making plant in Bob Stanfield's hometown of Truro. Anil (Canada) Ltd. hired 247 workers for a hardboard plant at Chester. E.M.I.-Cossor (later taken over by Hermes Electronics Ltd.) established a plant employing close to 500 in Dartmouth. Industrial Shipping Co. Ltd. chose Mahone Bay for a small boat-building plant, got into trouble, and was rescued by I.E.L. Now a subsidiary of Atlantic Bridge Company, this firm, known as Paceship Yachts, produces pleasure craft. Canada Cement settled in Brookfield.

Two automobile manufacturers came to Nova Scotia with I.E.L. assistance. Volvo (Canada) Ltd., assembles 230 cars a week at its plant in Dartmouth; Canadian Motor Industries runs a much smaller plant at Sydney where Japanese Toyota cars are assembled. I.E.L.'s biggest catch was the French tire-maker, Michelin, which employs 1,500 workers at its plant in New Glasgow in Pictou County. The Michelin negotiations began while Stanfield was still premier although the deal was not concluded until after he had gone to Ottawa.

Stanfield knew he was taking substantial risks with a great deal of the taxpayers' money (seventy-five million dollars by the time he left in 1967), but he also knew that Nova Scotia would not win industry easily. He was prepared to let I.E.L. gamble, and many of the gambles paid off, some of them spectacularly.

By the time Stanfield left Nova Scotia, I.E.L. had assisted 53 companies to settle in Nova Scotia, and those 53 employed a total of 4,500 people. Another 7,200 jobs were created indirectly as a result of the arrival of these companies, bringing the total number of new jobs attributable to I.E.L.'s involvement to nearly 12,000 during the Stanfield years. Understandably, Industrial Estates was the favoured child of the Stanfield administration. He left it alone; given that trust, it helped to turn the economy of Nova Scotia around. It was only later that Stanfield would wonder if he had not put too many political eggs in one basket.

Next to industrial development, Stanfield's greatest contribution to his province was in education. He was his own minister of education for all eleven years, and in the opinion of many Nova Scotians he did more for education in the province than any leader since Sir Charles Tupper introduced free schooling before Confederation.

Henry Hicks, first as Angus L. Macdonald's education minister and later as premier, had pursued an ambitious program of reorganizing educational financing in Nova Scotia. Out of the recommendations of a Royal Commission, Hicks produced a new education act, known as Bill 66. Bill 66 abolished many of the small school-boards in the province and created new boards to administer larger areas. They were, inevitably, more expensive boards to operate. A "foundation program" was established under which the province assisted school boards to meet the cost of teacher salaries and other expenses. The provincial government did not dictate to boards the amount they had to spend to educate a pupil, but it provided a carrot. Boards that brought their spending up to a minimum scale were eligible for more generous provincial contributions. The aim was to encourage school boards to improve the standard of education by raising teacher salaries and related expenditures. The results were better education, and higher costs for the province and municipalities alike. Hicks' reforms were daring, though they did him little good at the polls.

Although Stanfield and the Conservatives voted against Hicks' legislation, they did not hesitate to follow his principles when they came to office. Stanfield dramatically increased the amount of money available for provincial-municipal sharing in education. "That was not for the purpose of making teachers happy," says Ike Smith, "but to ensure that we were competitive with other jurisdictions that were competing with us for good teachers."

The Stanfield government pursued a program begun by the Liberals of consolidating rural schools and broadening the high school curriculum. Although the Liberals had made a start on building vocational schools, post-secondary education in Nova Scotia remained predominantly academic in its orientation. The high schools were preparing students for university or nothing – unemployment frequently being the fate of students who could not afford to continue to university. With the province paying 75 per cent of the cost of construction and initial equipment for technical and vocational schools, Stanfield built a system of schools to prepare non-university students for the labour market. At least as importantly, his government was the first to make regular contributions to the operating budgets of Nova Scotia's universities. It was a modest enough gesture when it began in 1960 – just $250,000 for the entire province. But by the time Stanfield resigned as premier in 1967, the universities were collecting one hundred times that amount every year. In addition, he introduced a capital assistance program under which the province paid up to 90 per cent of the cost of university buildings.

French-language education was a long-standing problem in Nova Scotia. When Stanfield became premier, French-speaking students could go only as far as Grade VIII in their own language. To make matters worse, all the textbooks were in English. Stanfield managed to introduce French texts and to extend education in French through Grade XII, although he was not able to bring Nova Scotia's French-language schools up to the level of schools in Quebec. Graduates had to go out of the province for at least one year's additional education before they could qualify for admission to Laval or to the University of Montreal. Despite repeated efforts, Stanfield had less success in upgrading the standard of French taught in the province's English schools. The bureaucracy that ran the school system was set in its ways and, he admits, "I don't think I accomplished very much." But even an old enemy such as Henry Hicks was impressed with Stanfield's work in education. "Stanfield," he says, "was the last premier of Nova Scotia who was really interested in education."

One incident during Stanfield's years as premier illustrates the lengths he will go to when crossed. It started in the summer of 1966 when the giant Bell Telephone Company of Canada (assets $2.7 billion) announced an offer to acquire 51 per cent of the shares in Nova Scotia's locally-owned Maritime Telegraph and Telephone Company (assets a mere $114 million). The Bell gave as its reason "the urgent need to assure the continuing Canadian ownership of the principal telephone systems of the Maritime provinces" – although no evidence was ever produced to indicate that any foreign enterprise was casting even faintly covetous eyes at little M.T. & T.

Stanfield was concerned on three grounds. First, he did not want to see control of the province's dominant communications company go out of Nova Scotia. M.T. & T. had been incorporated by a special act of the Legislature in 1910; although Bell already held 6 per cent of the shares in M.T. & T., the bulk of M.T. & T. stock – 71 per cent – was owned by resident Nova Scotians. Second, Stanfield knew that a takeover by the Bell would mean M.T. & T. would have to purchase its equipment from Bell's subsidiary, Northern Electric. But M.T. & T. was buying cables made by Phillips Cables Ltd. in Dartmouth, across the harbour from Halifax – a company in which Industrial Estates had invested heavily. Third, there seemed to be no advantage to be gained from becoming a part of the Bell empire. It was true that M.T. & T.'s service was not quite as efficient as the Bell's; on the other hand, its rates were appreciably lower.

The Halifax *Chronicle-Herald* entered the fray with front-page editorials emblazoned with the Nova Scotia flag. The editorials urged Nova Scotians to rally against the invader. "In the public interest the control of Maritime, and by a substantial margin, must remain in Nova Scotia," declared one editorial. "Nova Scotians have controlled Maritime for more than half a century; they must continue to do so," trumpeted another.

Stanfield agreed completely. He tried to reason with the Bell, suggesting everyone would be happier if it would drop the takeover bid. "He told them what his attitude was and what the position was and they decided to go ahead and to hell with him," remembers Dick Donahoe, who was the attorney general at that time. Annoyed by the Bell's persistence, Stanfield gave the company five days to meet representatives of the Nova Scotia government to discuss alternate means of forestalling an American takeover of M.T. & T., if indeed there was any such danger. He warned that if the Bell did not cooperate he would summon a special session of the Legislature. The Bell declined to talk. "During my ten years as premier, I have never encountered men who pursue their own interests so ruthlessly while expressing patriotic sentiments," snapped Stanfield. The Legislature met in special session and approved a bill that guaranteed M.T. & T. would remain in Nova Scotian control. Bell Telephone could buy all the shares it wished, but no shareholder, however large, could exercise voting rights to more than one thousand shares.

As the years passed Stanfield became the most popular man in Nova Scotia. His opponents did not attempt to deny it. "Let's face it," said James Aitchison, a political scientist who led the New Democratic Party to oblivion in the Stanfield years, "to most Nova Scotians, Stanfield can do no wrong. They consider him the most wonderful man to come along in 2,000 years." "The real reason Stanfield won in Nova Scotia," says Dalton Camp, "was that he had a perception of what Nova Scotians really wanted from government, what their expectation was. Although he may have had his own concerns and his own interests, he never let them become hobby horses. For example, he knew that roads were important. That's a very nitty-gritty simple-minded sort of thing, but he knew people cared and he had this enormous highway program in Nova Scotia."

To Allan MacEachen, the Nova Scotian in the federal Liberal cabinet, Stanfield's popularity was more simply explained. "Stanfield," says MacEachen, "was 'made' by the *Chronicle-Herald,* just as Walter Gordon was 'made' by the *Toronto Daily Star.* The *Chronicle-Herald* gave him twenty years of unswerving devotion. They treated him as though he were a member of the Royal Family, though his talents are no greater than any of ours."

Basically, Stanfield succeeded because he was the sort of leader Nova Scotians wanted. He knew better than to encourage his people to expect more than he could deliver; as a result they listened to him and trusted what he told them. He had a rare relationship with the people of his province.

Joe Clarke, his executive assistant at provincial party headquarters, tells of accompanying Stanfield to a political meeting in Cape Breton one Friday night. "Miners can be a pretty noisy audience on a Friday night, particularly if it's a pay day, and it was. The speakers before Stanfield were constantly interrupted by interjections and shouts, and we wondered what Stanfield would do with this crowd. But when he was introduced, all of a sudden, everything went very quiet. They listened to him very carefully. That made him a pretty effective communicator. People listened and tended to believe what they heard."

134

Ian Donaldson, a Halifax journalist who had covered Stanfield for many years, was outside a meeting hall in Antigonish on a warm spring evening during the 1967 provincial election campaign when Stanfield drove up alone in his dusty Volvo. Donaldson reported the scene to *Time:* "A knot of rally-goers – fishermen, woodsworkers and farmers – is on the hall steps, dragging on a last cigaret before going in to sit on the grey metal chairs. The knot breaks, men nod, then look at their feet. The Premier smiles at them. A local party worker bounds down the steps to shake the long slender Stanfield hand. A fisherman wearing red-soled rubber boots, green-checkered windbreaker, and grease-flecked cap, a pint of Black Diamond rum sticking its neck out of his hip pocket, leans toward the newsman and, speaking through two and a half teeth, says: 'I say it don't matter nothin' what that fellow Regan [Liberal leader Gerry Regan] says. He ain't never gonna beat him.' . . .

"How does Stanfield do it? The answer is that he doesn't. At least he doesn't do it in the campaign. He doesn't do it on the platform. . . . Stanfield wins elections because he fairly oozes integrity as he walks along the street, as he sits like a pretzel on the platform, as he speaks, as he does everything. In the back of everyone's mind, of course, is his government's record. It is a good record, but it is also a clean record. You watch him and he reminds you of your father – if your father was a good man – reading to the children after dinner. And if your father was a bum, then Bob reminds you of your lucky friend's father or of how you wished your father had been. Age doesn't matter. Young men feel it. Young women, who find Stanfield about as attractive as a yak, feel it. But older people, people old enough to be Bob's parents, feel it, too. Keep Dad at home and all will be well."

They kept Dad at home as Premier for eleven years and, to make sure he did not wander, they handed him a succession of ever-greater majorities. If Stanfield's performance at the polls were translated into graph form, it would show no peaks or valleys – just a steady upward curve. The eight seats he won in his first election in 1949 became twelve in 1953, twenty-four in 1956 (the year he became premier), twenty-seven in 1960, thirty-nine in 1963, and forty in 1967. Everyone agreed that, short of Stanfield's running off with a topless dancer from wicked Toronto, there was no way the Conservatives could lose in Nova Scotia. Unless, of course, he went into federal politics.

There seemed to be no chance of that. In 1962 John Diefenbaker tried to entice Stanfield to Ottawa to no avail. The entreaties from the federal party grew more urgent in the years after Diefenbaker fell from power. The way Ottawa Conservatives put it – more in hope than in conviction – was that, if Stanfield would join Diefenbaker in Ottawa, when the time came for

Diefenbaker to pass the party on to another he would look favourably on Stanfield as his heir. These suggestions were tenuous, and Stanfield knew better than to put much faith in such uncertain proposals. "I have no plans to leave here," Stanfield told reporters following the 1963 provincial election. "The fellows in Ottawa have a hard life and I don't find it attractive at all. I certainly have no intention of getting into it."

Besides, Stanfield was enjoying himself too much in Nova Scotia. He had discovered his niche. He liked provincial politics, he liked success, and he very much liked being premier. No longer did Conservative organizers have to phone ahead to drum up a crowd. He was recognized and respected. He would never be a great stump speaker, but public appearances were no longer the chore they once were. People even laughed at his thin little jokes, though he often used the same ones twenty nights running. It was less a matter of Stanfield having changed his style than it was of the province having grown accustomed to him. The people found they liked a politician who would listen to their problems and ideas; Stanfield obliged them by often taking his cabinet on the road to meet the people.

He approached election campaigns with about the same degree of excitement as he approached, say, federal-provincial conferences on tax sharing. Although he preferred the quieter periods between elections, he was not adverse to going on the hustings. "He didn't revel in elections," says Joe Clarke. "They were a necessity. They were just another job he had to do."

His opponents wished he had not done the job so well. For some reason – and it is one of the lesser unexplained mysteries of politics – Conservatives outside Nova Scotia concluded that Stanfield was in trouble as the time approached for the election of 1960. It was Stanfield's first test since taking office, and Tories in Ottawa worried about him and wondered what they could do to help him. In Fredericton, Premier Hugh John Flemming's government went through an "after-you-Alphonse" routine with the Nova Scotia Conservatives, delaying the New Brunswick election until after the one in Nova Scotia. New Brunswick Tories were sure that they were going to be re-elected, but they felt Stanfield's slender chances would be strengthened if the Nova Scotia election were held first. Stanfield called his election for June 7 and won easily. Flemming followed on June 27 and was defeated by the Liberals under Louis Robichaud.

The 1960 Nova Scotia election finished Henry Hicks; he lost his own seat by fourteen votes. He turned to his wife and asked: "Well, Mummie, what do we do now?" If by "we" Hicks meant himself, the answer was not long in coming. He went to Dalhousie University as Dean of Arts and Science, and later became president of the university. If he meant the Liberal Party, the ending was not so happy. Earl Urquhart, a lawyer from West Bay and a veteran member of the Legislature, filled in as opposition leader in the House until the dispirited Liberals finally got around to holding a leadership convention in 1962. Flora MacDonald was with Bob and Mary Stanfield in George Nowlan's suite at the Lord Nelson Hotel the night of the Liberal convention in November. They watched on television as the Grits confirmed Urquhart as leader. "The smile on Bob Stanfield's face was from ear to ear," says Flora.

Stanfield had cause to be pleased. Poor Urquhart could do nothing right in the face of the Tory machine. For no good reason – other than the usual good political reasons – Stanfield called a general election for October, 1963, nearly two years before an election was required. The Conservatives campaigned on the banal slogan "Much has been done: more is to come." So dull was the election and so predictable the outcome that the politicians themselves seemed at times to be asleep. For the want of opposition criticism to counter, the Conservatives devoted themselves to trying to prove that Bob Stanfield was an ordinary mortal. Ned Manson, one of Stanfield's ministers, took eight minutes at the biggest rally of the campaign to establish that Stanfield was just like any other fellow. His evidence: like other husbands, Stanfield sometimes forgot to take out the garbage. Stanfield privately predicted the Conservatives would win forty of the forty-three seats. A week before election, he asked a reporter for his prediction. The reporter predicted thirty-two Conservatives, and the Premier chided him for being pessimistic.

The Tories won thirty-nine seats to the Liberals' four. The Conservative share of the popular vote soared to 56 per cent, more than three percentage points higher than Angus L. Macdonald had ever reached. Both Urquhart and the NDP leader, Mickey MacDonald, lost their seats. Politicians who like to play the "if only" game calculated that "if only" the Conservatives had polled 559 more votes in the four ridings won by the Liberals, Stanfield would have captured every seat in the Legislature. Not that he needed the extra seats. He held the strongest mandate of any politician in the country. When the election was over, the CBC made its customary offer of free time for the Premier to address his province. Stanfield declined. "I think the people are tired of politics at this point," he explained. "They would not be interested in listening to me again."

The election of 1967 followed the pattern of 1963. The Liberals, now under the leadership of Gerry Regan, a lawyer-broadcaster and former M.P., promised to reduce taxes and take over 100 per cent of the cost of education (a neat trick if it could be done). Stanfield dismissed the opposition platform as something the Liberals did not believe in themselves, and "So why should I?" He paid little attention to his own party's platform, talking instead about his record and asking the voters to give him a chance to do more. As the posters, bumper stickers, and match packages made plain, it was no longer the Conservative Party. It was the Stanfield Party. Stanfield's name and picture were everywhere; all the Tory candidates were "Stanfield candidates." As in 1963, the outcome was never in question. A scallop fisherman, his pockets bulging with cash after a good trip to the banks off Virginia, wandered into the Clipper Ship Tavern in Yarmouth and offered thirty to one odds if anyone would put money on the Liberals. There were no takers.

Redistribution before the election had increased the number of seats from forty-three to forty-six and Stanfield won forty of them. Regan's Liberals inched upward from four to six. The New Democrats were wiped out again. It was an overwhelming victory though not quite so awesome as the 1963 triumph. For a change, the Liberals managed to elect their leader and the Conservatives' share of the popular vote fell to 53 per cent. But as long as Stanfield was at the helm what difference did it really make?

After leaving politics in 1970, one of Stanfield's ministers, Ed Haliburton, sat down to write about his experiences. The result was a slim volume of memories entitled *My Years with Stanfield*. In it Haliburton wrote: "It could be said that nothing spectacular happened during the Stanfield regime. He dislikes the spectacular. The social legislation was evolutionary, but it was common across Canada. . . . Yet in essence it was revolutionary and spectacular, since it turned our socio-economic system into a new channel, for better or for worse."

That is a fair assessment of the Stanfield years. Nothing happened in those years that was of the magnitude to take men's breath away or to cause them to pause in wonder or disbelief. There was no point at which anyone could say: today Robert Stanfield has done something that will revolutionize life in Nova Scotia. Other provinces were introducing hospital insurance and medicare at much the same time. Other provinces reorganized their educational systems, many of them in advance of Nova Scotia. Stanfield built more highways than any premier of Nova Scotia had ever built, but he built them at a time when the federal government was picking up much of the bill. He gave the province a welfare system that it could be proud of, but when he left the minimum wage for unskilled workers was still disgracefully low – thirty-eight dollars for men and twenty-eight dollars for women for a forty-hour week. Per capita income doubled during his years, but it remained 25 per cent below the national average. His great achievement was in bringing industry to the province; yet when he left unemployment was nudging 10 per cent, nearly double the national figure.

Still, Stanfield left an indelible mark on Nova Scotia because he was a totally different sort of politician than the province had seen before or has seen since. He was both a Conservative and a reformer. *Time's* Richard Gwyn once caught the essence of Stanfield with this description: "An aristocratic Socialist in the style of the Oxbridge types in the [British] Labour Party, he is a staunch Conservative Party man yet heads a government that has pushed its field of action as far as any on the Continent." As a reformer, Stanfield saw what had to be done and he committed himself to doing it. As a Conservative, he accepted the fact that he had to work with the limited options open to the premier of a poor province such as Nova Scotia. "I think," says Dalton Camp, "that he accepts – and this is the Conservative in him – the limits of politics, the limits of government."

There is, however, one vast piece of political terrain where a premier can operate without limits. That is in the psychology of a province, in the mental attitude of its people. It was here that Stanfield had his greatest impact. He gradually persuaded the people of Nova Scotia (to paraphrase the words of MacGregor Dawson) to stop bewailing their handicaps and to start bestirring themselves. He convinced them they did not have to remain a backwater, retarded and depressed. He convinced them that they had a future worth working for.

Wherever he went in those years, Stanfield challenged his people to start thinking about their opportunities. "I . . . question our right to consider ourselves poor as a province although we are not as well off as the average Canadian," he told the Halifax Board of Trade in 1965. " . . . Can it be that we love our province dearly and yet feel sorry for ourselves in the sense that we feel others have kicked us around? Is someone else really responsible for our incomes being about 25 per cent below the Canadian average? Or are we partly responsible ourselves? That is a question we might profit from trying to answer honestly. . . . Have we made the most of our opportunities? Are we a resourceful and enterprising people? . . . How many of our communities are hoping that some outside person or corporation will solve their problems by locating there? . . . Are our business people perhaps too comfortable and complacent? . . . Do too many of us sell out when the going gets rough and live on our investments instead of fighting on and perhaps doing the swallowing instead of being swallowed? . . . Are we in Nova Scotia sometimes the prisoners of our past?"

Those were not questions Nova Scotians could answer overnight. But the answers started to come. The new schools, roads, and industries were only an external reflection of the changes that were occurring inside. The people began to understand that they *could* change their destiny. All they needed was patience, imagination, and a willingness to work. "Stanfield's given us the feeling that we can solve our own problems and make Nova Scotia a good place to live," said Donald LeBlanc, a Liberal and deputy mayor of Halifax, in 1965. "He's managed to get us back on the rails. We've recovered our self-respect. In his own way, he has instilled a certain esprit de corps. The old Nova Scotia attitude – that 'it won't work' – is disappearing."

Dick Donahoe agrees: "We used to be simply a place where you raised children for export to the rest of Canada and the United States. Today in this province there is a feeling that, properly handled and properly promoted, the province has a future. I think that that is Stanfield's gift to the people of this province."

8

Stanfield's Vietnam

Ah, but a man's reach should exceed his grasp,
Or what's a heaven for?

— Robert Browning

There is a simple word association test to separate the Tories from the Grits in Nova Scotia. Mention the words "Robert Stanfield." If the reply is "Prime Minister," you are talking to a Conservative. But if the reply is "Clairtone" or "Heavy Water," you have a Liberal on your hands.

Clairtone Sound Corporation and Deuterium of Canada Ltd. were the two most exciting industrial developments brought to Nova Scotia by the Stanfield government. They oozed glamour. Clairtone was to make Nova Scotia the capital of stereophonic sound systems and colour television for the carriage trade of all North America, and perhaps even the world. Deuterium of Canada Ltd. (D.C.L.) was to place Nova Scotia in the forefront of the nuclear age. The province took a twenty-million-dollar bath on Clairtone; all that remains is a bitter taste in the mouth and a watchman who makes his rounds at a vacant seven-acre factory in Stellarton, making sure the doors are still locked. D.C.L. was to build a thirty-million-dollar heavy water plant on Cape Breton Island. Ten years and one hundred and thirty million dollars later, the people of Nova Scotia wonder whether the pile of rusting junk at Glace Bay will ever produce enough heavy water for even a sponge bath. On a per capita basis, heavy water has cost Nova Scotians more than the space program has cost the citizens of the United States. And, as they say in Nova Scotia, the Americans at least got a man on the moon.

Disasters of the order of Clairtone and heavy water were probably inevitable. Stanfield knew he was gambling when he established Industrial Estates Ltd. to bring industry to Nova Scotia. He knew there would be failures, but so compelling was the need to create new jobs that he was prepared to run risks that no businessman and few politicians would nor-

141

mally dare to take. He had no way of knowing how great the gamble was. The stories of Clairtone and D.C.L. illustrate what can happen when a government, with the best intentions in the world, tries to do too much too quickly.

The founders of Clairtone, Budapest-born Peter Munk and David Gilmour, the son of a well-to-do Toronto family, met at a cocktail party in Toronto in the mid-1950s. Robert Stanfield could be excused for wishing that at least one of them had been run down by a streetcar on his way to the party. It was a fateful meeting. Munk, a 1952 graduate of the University of Toronto, had gone into business for himself producing custom hi-fi equipment for Toronto society. David Gilmour, whose father was a stockbroker and his mother a retired opera singer, was also in business for himself, designing and importing Scandinavian-style furniture. As Munk and Gilmour talked, the idea seemed irresistable. Why not pool their talents to manufacture phonographs that would not only reproduce quality sound but would be beautiful to look at as well?

Their concept was as simple as it was shrewd. The hi-fis sold in those days were ugly – vulgar square boxes that no lady wanted in her living room. If Munk and Gilmour could come up with a phonograph that would satisfy the ear of the husband while attracting the eye of the wife with the elegant lines and fine workmanship of its cabinet, they could make their fortunes.

With three thousand dollars of their own money and three thousand borrowed from a bank, Munk and Gilmour incorporated Clairtone Sound Corporation and went into production in 1958. They were on their way. They had an excellent product, one that was almost as well engineered as it was designed. They promoted it (and themselves) relentlessly and developed a marketing strategy that was nothing short of brilliant. They aimed exclusively for the upper end of the price range in the home entertainment field – four hundred dollars and up – scrupulously avoided discount houses and awarded dealerships only to the best stores.

In 1961 Munk and Gilmour did something their Canadian competitors had lacked the initiative to do – they invaded the American market. Soon Clairtone stereos were being sold by such internationally-known pillars of American consumerism as Marshall Field, Jordan Marsh, Wanamaker's, Gimbel's, Macy's, Bloomingdale's, Georg Jensen, and Abraham & Straus. Clairtone's enthusiastic press agents in New York and Toronto relayed the good news – 40 per cent of the top department stores in the United States carried Clairtone, a figure that was soon to be inflated to 80 per cent, then to 90 per cent as the bubble grew ever larger. North American sales moved up 92 per cent to $6,727,000 in 1962, and up to $8,910,000 in 1963. (Even Frank Sinatra had purchased a half dozen Clairtone units to give away for

Christmas.) With U.S. sales alone nearing three million dollars a year, Clairtone opened an American subsidiary, Clairtone Electronics Corporation, and David Gilmour moved to New York to run it.

By 1964, Peter Munk, the president, was billing Clairtone as "North America's leading stereo specialist," and the company was looking for more new worlds to conquer. He and Gilmour bought a 49 per cent interest in a new British company, Ditchburn Clairtone Ltd., to manufacture and distribute Clairtone products in England and on the Continent. They obtained exclusive rights to manufacture Wurlitzer phonographs for the American market. Moving into an alien field, they obtained, for a little over one million dollars, controlling interest in yet another new company, Canadian Motor Industries Ltd. (C.M.I.), which was to assemble Japanese cars in Cape Breton for the Canadian market. Also, in 1964, Munk and Gilmour made their first big mistake: they moved their phonograph operations from the Toronto suburb of Etobicoke to Nova Scotia.

Clairtone moved to Nova Scotia because Industrial Estates Ltd. made Clairtone, as the saying goes, a deal that was too good to refuse. Not that everyone at I.E.L. was enthusiastic about putting money into Clairtone. Rumours were already making the rounds in Toronto that Peter Munk and David Gilmour were better promoters than they were businessmen, and that the company was expanding far too rapidly in an uncertain and unpredictable industry. Then, too, not everyone was charmed by Munk and Gilmour. "I was very much against Clairtone from the beginning," says one of I.E.L.'s directors. "I didn't like the personality of What's His Name? [Munk] and Goody Two Shoes [Gilmour] who was in New York. It was just a general sense of distrust." Unfortunately, that distrust did not rub off on the other directors. Clairtone agreed to build a 250,000 square-foot plant worth $3.5 million at Stellarton (the home town of Frank Sobey, I.E.L.'s president) in Pictou County. In return, I.E.L. purchased $7,945,000 worth of Clairtone bonds. Of this total, $3.5 million was for the new plant, $2 million for working capital – $1 million to retire some old Clairtone debt, and $1 million to cover Clairtone's investment in Canadian Motor Industries. (I.E.L. did not discover until it was well into negotiations for the Stellarton plant that Clairtone was sinking money into C.M.I. Munk and Gilmour knew nothing about the automobile industry and, had I.E.L. had its wits about it, it would have broken off talks with Clairtone at that point.) The remaining $400,000-odd was taken back by I.E.L. in lieu of interest on its investment; Clairtone was excused from paying interest on the bonds during its first three years in Nova Scotia.

That was not all. There was a municipal tax deal under which local taxes were frozen at one per cent of the cost of construction for the first ten years.

143

The federal government agreed to give Clairtone a holiday from corporation taxes for the first three years, plus accelerated capital cost allowances. In addition, Clairtone qualified for a 30 per cent freight subsidy on all products it shipped out of Nova Scotia. It all added up to a most attractive proposition, and the best part of all was that Clairtone did not have to put up a nickel of its own money. "This arrangement is absolutely fantastic," enthused Peter Munk. "I can't understand why more companies don't take advantage of it." Munk dropped a hint that there might be even more exciting things ahead in Pictou County's future. Clairtone, he allowed, might just build an entirely new city near its plant and maybe, just maybe, it ought to be called "Clairtone City."

It was easy enough to understand why I.E.L. was attracted to Clairtone. It was a young and rapidly growing Canadian company in the burgeoning home entertainment field. It had a solid sales base in Canada and had successfully established itself in the American market. Its sales were rising every year and it turned a reasonable profit. It offered Nova Scotia a sophisticated type of industry with a fair quotient of technology. Above all, it was labour intensive. The Stellarton plant would, it was estimated, employ a thousand people with a possible increase to two thousand. That would soak up a lot of displaced coal miners.

Before closing the deal, I.E.L. conducted an investigation of Clairtone, examining its finances, its management, and its operating methods. But the investigation was not nearly searching enough. If it had been more thorough, I.E.L. almost certainly would have backed away from the deal. It would have discovered, for example, that, although Clairtone was strong in design and marketing, it was weak in production management. It might have come across the man from Clairtone's own underwriters in Toronto who that year confided to a reporter his opinion of Munk and Gilmour: "They're merchandisers with a good product. They're young and impetuous and they've run a little too fast." Or I.E.L. might have talked to the Canadian sales manager for one of Clairtone's competitors who described Munk and Gilmour as "two nice and bright young men who have a terrific press agent." Or, had I.E.L. talked to Dalton Camp, who had done advertising work for Clairtone, it would have received some surprising advice. "I didn't think Clairtone ought to come into Nova Scotia," says Camp, "because I had some personal knowledge of the personnel involved." None of this – and other – information was secret. It was all available, but it would have required staff and time to gather it; I.E.L. did not have the necessary resources.

Industrial Estates did not woo Clairtone with its eyes tightly closed. It knew there were risks. Frank Sobey, the I.E.L. president, made a surprising admission in a 1968 interview with *Time's* Martin Sullivan: "We knew Peter Munk was going to get into trouble the day we signed the deal, but Clairtone as a name and as a product is about the best there is. And we expect some of our deals to get into a little trouble from time to time." Stanfield, too, though he kept away from the day-to-day operation of I.E.L., knew and accepted the risks the Clairtone deal posed. "Stanfield," says Camp, "really saw it in a larger context. He decided that the reason a lot of people thought Clairtone was bad was because this was an example of a Nova Scotia company getting an Ontario firm. Therefore he would discount what you said to him in the interest of a larger principle. But that can happen to anybody. It happened to him."

Clairtone moved at first into temporary quarters in an I.E.L.-owned factory. When its own plant, covering seven acres under one roof, was ready in 1966, it laid on a special train to bring the dignitaries, including Stanfield, to Stellarton for the grand opening. Sales kept climbing – to $9,582,811 in 1964; $11,263,800 in 1965; $15,453,053 in 1966; and $17,620,706 in 1967. In 1966, an American Congressman, Seymour Halpern, made a speech in the House of Representatives in which he said of Clairtone, "It seems to me that the extraordinary success of this company should serve as an inspiration to free enterprise everywhere." That same year, Clairtone's executives bought themselves a little present – an executive aircraft.

But there were toubles very close to the surface, and they started with Clairtone's management. Peter Munk was a "doer," an engineer, and an aggressive promoter who did not hesitate to step on others to get to his goal. David Gilmour was more the dreamer; he was the designer but, like Munk, an astute promoter. Both lacked the skills to manage a large-scale integrated manufacturing operation such as the one at Stellarton where raw logs were wheeled in one door and finished stereos out the other. Their American market was vital to the company's wellbeing, but American dealers demanded a large variety of models to offer their customers. Clairtone's combined Canada-U.S. market was not big enough to permit long, efficient production runs of any one model. Production costs kept rising to the point where it was costing Clairtone more to manufacture a stereo in Nova Scotia than it could sell it for in Manhattan. There were chronic labour woes with three unions competing for the right to bargain for Clairtone's workers. "At times that place was a shambles," says a man connected with I.E.L. By now sixty per cent of Clairtone's sales were south of the border; the time when the company most needed to increase sales, however, coincided with a period when all U.S. manufacturers of phonographs, radios, and television sets were being squeezed severely by low-cost imports from Japan.

Clairtone's worst and ultimately fatal trouble came when it decided to go into colour television. Late in 1965, Clairtone asked I.E.L. for another three million dollars. Of this, one million was to be used to refinance Clairtone's unfortunate investment in Canadian Motor Industries (the entire investment was finally written off in 1966). The remaining two million was to finance Clairtone's colour television venture.

In a sense, Clairtone was forced into colour television. Dealers demanded a full line of home entertainment products and Clairtone had no television to offer. To avoid losing dealers and sales, it decided it had to go into colour television. Unfortunately, Clairtone knew absolutely nothing about the manufacture of television sets.

Even so, Clairtone might have survived had it not jumped at precisely the wrong moment. In the United States, the first flush of public excitement over colour television was abating and consumers were sitting back, waiting for the price to come down before embarking on another buying splurge. While customers were waiting for colour sets to come down to $500, Clairtone was trying to sell models ranging in price from $850 to $1,700. The market was not there.

The great Canadian success story turned sour in stages. After showing a small profit ($601,000) in 1966, Clairtone plummeted to a loss of $6,622,000 in 1967. The next year, with sales declining, the loss was $8,977,052. Production was cut back drastically in 1969 to the point where sales were barely half as much as the year before; the company still recorded a loss of $2,636,843. Gradually, the operating deficits dragged Clairtone under.

Clairtone went to I.E.L. again in the summer of 1967 for more working capital. I.E.L. agreed to provide another two million dollars, but the price was steep – Munk and Gilmour would have to give up control of their company. Only twelve shareholders bothered to show up for a stockholders meeting in Toronto at which control of Clairtone passed to I.E.L. The shareholders approved a ten-for-one split of 300,000 Clairtone preference shares held by I.E.L. That gave I.E.L. three million votes, or 84 per cent control. Having already pumped thirteen million dollars into Clairtone, I.E.L. struggled mightily to save the company and the Nova Scotia taxpayers' investment. It shunted Peter Munk aside and installed as the new chief executive officer J.W. Mangels, a corporate trouble-shooter from the United States. Mangels had once worked for the Ford Motor Company in Detroit where, as he put it, "one of my jobs was closing out the Edsel." Mangels was unable either to restore Clairtone to health or close it out. It was downhill all the way.

146

Production at Stellarton was progressively reduced and workers were laid off. The manufacture of Clairtone merchandise was halted in early 1970 and I.E.L. bailed out, dumping the company into the lap of the provincial government. The plant limped along for a little while turning out small quantities of private brand equipment for department stores. But by the end of 1970, there were only forty workers left at Stellarton, and Clairtone stock, which had once sold for $15.25 a share, was down to 41 cents on the Toronto Stock Exchange. The doors soon closed; I.E.L. foreclosed on the mortgage and the search began to find some one to buy or rent the factory.

There were points along the Clairtone road when either I.E.L. or the Stanfield Government could have bailed out. Stanfield thinks the best point might have been early or when I.E.L. discovered that Munk and Gilmour were sinking Clairtone money into C.M.I., the Japanese car plant. "They [Munk and Gilmour] were very capable people," says Stanfield. "They expanded rapidly and had a good deal of success and they were over-confident. The beginning of their trouble was getting into the car business. It turned out to be an excellent thing if you knew the car business and had enough capital to carry it through. When we found out they had made these commitments to get into the car business, perhaps at that point we should have said no dice at all." Another obvious point was when Clairtone decided to move into colour television and came to I.E.L. for the money to finance the venture.

Clearly the best time to have said No was at the very beginning, with a closer and harder look at Clairtone and its principals. Peter Nicholson, the Liberal who became Nova Scotia's finance minister, remembers approaching Stanfield at a reception in Halifax and asking him, "Tell me frankly. What sort of investigation are your people in I.E.L. making of the principals in these deals?" Stanfield replied: "Well, they make the usual sort of inquiries through the banks and so on." "Today," says Nicholson, "before we give money to a man we want to know the size of the shoes he wears and the type of coughdrops he uses."

Although Clairtone was an I.E.L. disaster, much of the blame must be laid squarely on the doorstep of the Stanfield government. "I think," says Dick Donahoe, "that the cabinet would have to admit that it had the opportunity to prevent it."

As had been the case with Clairtone's Peter Munk and David Gilmour, the sad story of the heavy water plant turned around a shrewd, smooth-talking outsider. He was Jerome S. Spevack, an American nuclear scientist turned businessman with impressive credentials. Early in World War II he had worked at Columbia University in New York with Dr. Harold Urey, the

Nobel Prize winning scientist who had discovered deuterium. From 1943 to 1947 Spevack worked for the U.S. Atomic Energy Commission in the development of the atomic bomb. Later he invented an "improved" process for producing heavy water, the essential coolant in nuclear reactors fueled by natural uranium. Though the United States was developing reactors using enriched uranium, Canada – through a federal crown corporation, Atomic Energy of Canada Ltd. (A.E.C.L.) – had chosen the natural uranium route and was in the process of investing a billion dollars in its "CANDU" reactor, the natural uranium reactor pioneered by A.E.C.L. In 1959, Spevack obtained U.S. patents for his improved heavy water process, and in Nevada he incorporated his own company, Deuterium Corporation, the following year. He appeared on the Canadian scene in 1961 to register his patents with the federal government. In June, 1962, with an eye to future business with A.E.C.L., his Deuterium Corporation established a Canadian subsidiary, Deuterium of Canada Ltd. (D.C.L.).

D.C.L. did not have to wait long for action to develop in Canada. In February, 1963, Atomic Energy of Canada called for proposals for the supply of heavy water for the reactors at nuclear generating stations planned by Ontario Hydro. The winning bidder would be expected to build a heavy water plant to fill an A.E.C.L. order for two hundred tons of heavy water annually for five years, at a price not to exceed twenty-two dollars a pound. Seven companies indicated interest before the May 31 deadline. The competition quickly narrowed to two: Spevack's D.C.L., which at that time proposed to build a thirty million dollar heavy water plant in Alberta, using Alberta natural gas as the fuel and fresh water in the process; and Western Deuterium Co. Ltd., a newly-formed subsidiary of Victoria Machinery Depot Ltd., a shipyard company that had no connection whatsoever with atomic technology until its president decided it was "a field we should get into." Like D.C.L., Western Deuterium planned to build a heavy water plant in Western Canada, and it proposed to use as fuel either natural gas from Alberta, Crow's Nest Pass bituminous coal or lignite from Saskatchewan. Each proposal had its selling point. D.C.L. had Spevack's technology; Western Deuterium was 100 per cent Canadian owned.

A.E.C.L. preferred the Western Deuterium bid and the contract would undoubtedly have gone to the British Columbia firm had it not been for a fortuitous (as it seemed then) coincidence. D.C.L.'s legal business in Canada was handled by a Toronto lawyer, Alex MacIntosh, who happened to be a native of Pictou County in Nova Scotia; and MacIntosh told Spevack about Nova Scotia's efforts to attract industry and directed him to Industrial Estates Ltd. Early in June, 1963, Spevack and his wife, Ruth, came to Halifax to talk to the people at I.E.L. and to officials of the government of

Nova Scotia. The Spevacks were a team; Ruth Spevack was the secretary-treasurer of D.C.L., and she sat in on every important negotiating session in Halifax. Some of the people who met them thought she was every bit as astute an operator as her husband. Six weeks later they had an agreement with I.E.L.

Instead of locating in Alberta, Spevack would build his thirty million dollar heavy water plant in Cape Breton, using Nova Scotia coal. D.C.L.was to raise eighteen million of the cost by selling first mortgage bonds to Canadian investors. I.E.L.would provide the remaining twelve million by purchasing second mortgage bonds from D.C.L. But – and it was an important caveat – Industrial Estates did not have to put up a cent until D.C.L. had raised its eighteen million. "Everyone was a little scared of the gamble," recalls Frank Sobey, the former I.E.L. president. "But at that time the mines were closing down in Cape Breton and this plant was going to use the steam equivalent to a good many man-days of work in the mines of Cape Breton."

I.E.L.'s negotiations with Deuterium of Canada were top secret, but word of them leaked out; the story was broken in the late summer of 1963 by the *Cape Breton Post*. The story had a galvanizing effect on Cape Bretoners. Not only were the coal mines in trouble; the steel mill in Sydney was struggling to survive, and the Point Edward Naval Base was on the verge of closing. As Linden MacIntyre, a reporter for the Halifax *Chronicle-Herald*, later wrote: "Cape Bretoners seized on the news as shipwreck victims would welcome the vision of a rescue boat."

There followed some of the most frantic lobbying and backstage politicking that Ottawa had seen in years. Both Stanfield and Allan MacEachen, the Nova Scotian who was the federal minister of labour at the time, pleaded the Nova Scotia case with Bud Drury, who, as industry minister, was responsible for A.E.C.L., and with Prime Minister Lester Pearson himself. Pearson appreciated the logic of their argument that the plant should go to Nova Scotia. He was worried about the chronically high rate of unemployment in the Atlantic Provinces. Although the heavy water plant when completed would employ a relative handful of workers, the construction stage would employ hundreds, perhaps thousands of men in an area that desperately needed jobs of any sort. The plant would also bring to Nova Scotia a new class of worker, scientists and highly trained technicians who were in critically short supply in the province. Further, the heavy water industry held the promise of becoming the cornerstone for the economic development of all of Cape Breton. Stanfield was so anxious to get the plant that his government tossed in an added inducement – a $500,000-a-year provincial subsidy on the already federally-subsidized coal that the plant would use. Spevack was thus able to submit a bid of $20.50 per pound of heavy water, undercutting Western Deuterium's bid of $22.00 a pound. That prompted Western Deuterium to go shopping for a provincial ally, too, and it found one in Saskatchewan. With help promised from the Government of Saskatchewan, Western Deuterium dropped its bid to an even $20.00.

But Spevack's D.C.L. by now was the clear favourite. The only serious stumbling block to acceptance of its proposal was the nagging question of foreign ownership. Given its huge investment in the CANDU reactor, Ottawa was extremely concerned at the prospect of having its long-range supplies of vital heavy water in foreign hands. In October of 1963, the federal cabinet quietly passed the word to Nova Scotia that the Nova Scotia bid would be accepted if D.C.L. became Canadian controlled.

The Canadian-control requirement drastically changed the rules of the game as far as the province of Nova Scotia was concerned. Instead of being merely a lender of money through I.E.L., Nova Scotia was being asked by Ottawa to become the majority partner in an admittedly risky venture and to accept the responsibility that that control implied. In later years, Nova Scotia politicians, with the notable exception of Robert Stanfield, would blame this new requirement for all the troubles that came tumbling down on the province's head. "We understood the contract was going to be awarded to Nova Scotia," says Ike Smith who, as premier, later had to live with the heavy water disaster. "Up until that time all we were thinking about was providing loan money through I.E.L. Now, when you're on the verge of getting what you think you need – and we thought we needed this keystone type of technology, applied technology – and you're suddenly told you have to meet another condition to get it, then perhaps you're more readily tempted to meet that other condition than you otherwise would be."

Stanfield and his ministers were tantalized. They knew they were being asked to take prime responsibility; but everyone knew the market for heavy water could only grow by leaps and bounds. The province stood to make a killing. "I feel myself that without that [Canadian-control] condition we would never have done any more than we first committed ourselves to do," says Ike Smith. "But we bit." Dick Donahoe, then the attorney general, agrees. Mixing his idioms a little, he says: "We couldn't just throw it down the drain. But what happened was that our whole agreement with Spevack went out of the window. The effect was to let him off the hook for the sums of money he was supposed to provide as part of the original capital."

Stanfield agrees that Ottawa had changed the rules part way through the game, but his only complant is that when Canadian General Electric came along later with plans to build a heavy water plant of its own in Cape Breton, Ottawa did not insist on Canadian control. "C.G.E. is a noble institution," says Stanfield, "but it isn't Canadian. . . . As far as we were concerned insisting on Canadian control [of D.C.L.] tended to increase our responsibility. But I don't criticize the federal government. I think Mr. Pearson stuck his neck out a long way to 'encourage' – and I use the word in quotes – A.E.C.L. to accept the bid. I think he felt it was important that something be done in Cape Breton. And we were prepared to take pretty substantial risks."

Swallowing its doubts, the Nova Scotia Cabinet decided to go ahead; it instructed I.E.L. to negotiate a new arrangement with Deuterium of Canada. Had the heavy water plant come into production more or less on schedule, and had the cost been more or less in the thirty million dollar range, the decision would have been viewed as an intelligent, far-sighted decision. But the dream turned to dust and the Cabinet's decision can only be interpreted as a terrible mistake; one of a series of horrible blunders that marked the heavy water saga.

On October 25, 1963, Industrial Estates Ltd. signed a new deal with Spevack under which I.E.L. acquired 25,001 of the 50,000 shares in Deuterium of Canada Ltd. D.C.L. was still to raise the eighteen million in first mortgage bonds before I.E.L. had to put in the remaining twelve million. The difference now was that I.E.L., as majority shareholder, would have to make good if D.C.L.'s management could not raise the initial eighteen million. The agreement called for the patents held by Spevack and his American firm, Deuterium Corporation, to be made available to Deuterium of Canada Ltd. Spevack was made president and chief executive officer of D.C.L. The U.S. consultants he favoured, Burns and Roe, were to be given the contract for the design and engineering of the heavy water plant. It was to be built at Glace Bay, near Sydney, on Cape Breton. By implication, one tiny escape hatch remained to I.E.L.; it could call the deal off at any time up to the moment a final heavy water contract was signed between D.C.L. and Atomic Energy of Canada Ltd.

In November, 1963, the final bids from D.C.L. and Western Deuterium went before the federal cabinet and a few weeks later the momentous announcement was made: heavy water was coming to Nova Scotia. Nova Scotians rejoiced and none more than Bob Stanfield who fired off a telegram of thanks to Lester Pearson, telling the Prime Minister the award "will mean much to the people of Nova Scotia."

According to estimates at the time, the contract meant two thousand jobs for the two years that the plant would be under construction. After it was finished, there would be two hundred jobs running the plant and work for five hundred miners producing the coal that the plant would devour. What did Nova Scotia have to lose? Within seven years, the province would recover its full investment from the operating profits.

No one even dreamed the plant might not get built or that it would not produce heavy water. "It is ridiculous now," says a man who was intimately involved in the negotiations, "but at the time it looked like a fairly straightforward proposition. . . . You might as well get in a little rowboat and try to sail the Atlantic in a gale."

Stanfield's government began to realize it was in a gale when it discovered that no one really had any accurate idea of how much the plant would cost. The thirty million figure proved to be, at best, a "guesstimate"; until the consulting engineers produced a final feasibility report and cost estimate, there was no way D.C.L. could sell a single dollar's worth of that eighteen million in first mortgage bonds. Harold Egan, a director of I.E.L., and Bill Mingo, I.E.L.'s general counsel, went to New York at the beginning of 1964 to demand a feasibility report from Burns and Roe. A few weeks later, the consultants produced an interim feasibility report that claimed the cost of construction would not exceed $28.5 million. Thus encouraged, Nova Scotia made another mistake. On February 7, 1964, the final contract with A.E.C.L. was signed. The escape hatch slammed shut.

Other mistakes followed in rapid succession. In March, I.E.L. signed four new contracts with Jerome Spevack. I.E.L foolishly agreed to advance its twelve million share of the construction cost without waiting for D.C.L. to raise its eighteen million. The patents and technological know-how involved in the Spevack process were assigned to D.C.L., but – and it was to prove a costly oversight – improvements or inventions made in the course of the development of the Glace Bay plant were to become the property of Spevack's American company, Deuterium Corporation. Another mistake: Spevack was given a management contract to run Deuterium of Canada for twenty years at an annual salary of $35,000, and there was no requirement that he treat it as a full-time job. In return, Deuterium Corporation guaranteed that the Glace Bay plant would, in fact, produce heavy water and that the construction cost would not exceed thirty-five million dollars or 110 per cent of the final engineering estimate. (These last-mentioned guarantees were sensible ones. Nova Scotia could have held Spevack and Deuterium Corporation legally responsible for some of the problems that subsequently developed had the greatest mistake of all not been made two years later. At that time, in the process of buying out Spevack, the province agreed to rescind the 1964 agreements. Thereafter Nova Scotia was on its own.)

Burns and Roe's interim report notwithstanding, the province still had no firm cost estimate. By June of 1964 – four months after the contract with A.E.C.L. was signed – the projected cost nudged upward to thirty-one million. The Nova Scotia appointees to the board of D.C.L. began to feel helpless. "We are not sufficiently informed on the program to evaluate what is being done and have no control over the present proceedings," Harold Egan complained to the directors. By autumn the estimated cost had risen to nearly thirty-three million dollars and was still not firm. By the end of the year, it reached thirty-seven million. Starting in late 1964, I.E.L. and the Government began shopping anxiously for someone to take the heavy water plant off their hands. They made at least seven separate attempts, but could find no takers among such corporate giants as Imperial Oil, Distillers Corporation, Cemp Investments, and Canadian General Electric.

By February, 1965, D.C.L. gave up trying to sell its first mortgage bonds and I.E.L. forked over another fifteen million to keep the heavy water dream alive. Labour troubles plagued the construction: the project was hit by twenty-four strikes in the first two years. Design changes compounded problems. In the course of 1965 and 1966 there were twenty-five hundred changes made in the mechanical drawings. Water supply was a great headache. D.C.L. had planned to use fresh water in its cooling tubes, but Burns and Roe estimated it would cost three and a half million dollars to pipe fresh water to the plant, as opposed to one and a half million to convert the plant to salt water, which was available in unlimited quantities at the plant's doorstep. D.C.L. decided to switch to salt water, only to have the conversion cost soar to five million. Not only was that a costly decision, but it was to prove to be the straw that broke the camel's back.

There was another major turning point in early 1966 when A.E.C.L. offered D.C.L. a new contract. If D.C.L. would double the capacity of its still-uncompleted plant, A.E.C.L. would double the size of its order to four hundred tons a year, a change that would enable the province to recoup its full investment – now estimated at seventy-three million for the enlarged plant – in just eight years. The Cabinet agonized over that proposition. It seriously considered rejecting it and insisting on getting the first phase into operation before committing itself to an expansion. But the province was in too deeply to back out. "We did it," says Dick Donahoe, "because we thought it was an assured thing. We thought if you were going to do well on selling so many tons of heavy water you would do twice as well selling twice as many tons. . . . I can remember being fully conscious when we reached that decision to double capacity, fully conscious that a real element of gamble was involved in that, but by that time you kept hoping you could come out of it triumphantly. None of us realized that she wasn't going to produce at all." Like a losing gambler, the province took yet another plunge, agreeing to double the stakes on what was looking like a poorer and poorer bet.

In 1966, the province finally severed its connection with Jerome Spevack – at a cost of three million dollars. It paid two and a quarter million dollars for the shares that Spevack and Deuterium Corporation held in Deuterium of Canada, plus more than seven hundred thousand dollars for patented and unpatented improvements developed at Glace Bay. The 1964 agreements under which Spevack's Deuterium Corporation had guaranteed to make the plant produce heavy water were rescinded. Spevack was off the hook and Nova Scotia was impaled.

Stanfield watched in growing despair as the costs continued to mount and as the completion date marched resolutely into the future. With an election campaign in progress, he put the best possible face on an impossible situation by going to Glace Bay in early May, 1967 to officially open the plant, the first phase of which was not even due to be finished for another eighteen months. The province's investment, originally to be no more than twelve million, had grown to eighty-three million by the time Stanfield declared the unfinished plant open.

Stanfield resigned as premier four months later and thus had the good fortune to escape the worst consequences of the fiasco. Late in 1968, the engineers started up the first phase of the plant and it worked – briefly. It actually produced a little heavy water, according to Ike Smith, the new premier. "Some heavy water actually was squeezed out, or so the man in charge told me," says Smith. "He called me late one weekend when I was at home to tell me he had just seen the first heavy water. If it had gone, it would have been a great success."

That was not to be, and the new villain was the salt water. Unlike fresh water, salt water is highly corrosive; it could only be used if it were kept moving rapidly through the stainless steel tubes. In an unthinkable display of incompetence, someone (no one was sure who) neglected to instruct the men manning the plant to keep the salt water moving. It corroded the pipes, allowing deadly hydrogen sulphide to escape into the atmosphere. By this time, Nova Scotia had already sunk a hundred and eight million dollars into the heavy water enterprise; an independent study warned it would take at least thirty million more to bring the plant into production. In desperation, Nova Scotia looked to Ottawa for help.

Atomic Energy of Canada Ltd. rode reluctantly to the rescue in 1971. A.E.C.L. still needed the heavy water and it decided that, rather than build a new heavy water plant from scratch (at an estimated cost of one hundred and thirty-five million dollars), it would be further ahead to put ninety-five million dollars into the Glace Bay plant and try to make it work. Besides, it was the only way to protect the hundred and thirty million in taxpayers' money that the province had already expended. A.E.C.L borrowed the ninety-five million dollars from the federal government, took over the plant, and by the summer of 1972 had finished pulling it apart. Barring additional snags (and snags seem endemic at Glace Bay), the plant may go into production in 1975. It will take the full proceeds from the first sixteen years of production to enable A.E.C.L. to repay its loan from the federal government. Then it will turn the plant back over to the government of Nova Scotia. Only then – twenty-eight years after it first stumbled unwittingly into the nuclear age – can Nova Scotia begin to recover some of its investment. Its chances of ever recouping it all are remote.

So great was the disaster, financially and politically, that members of the Stanfield cabinet could not understand how it could have happened. One of those ministers, Ed Haliburton, in his book *My Years With Stanfield*, put it this way: "It was a decision that came naturally at its inception; and the denouement, later, seemed incredible, unbelievable, incomprehensible as well as completely unexplainable." Stanfield's old Economics professor, Russell Maxwell, watched in concern and disbelief as the troubles gathered around his former pupil: "It was a sound idea, but it was embarked on with far too little study, a highly technical enterprise that is still going wrong, even with the best technical advice the country has. . . . It was a flop and it's cost the province a good deal of money. Stanfield wasn't responsible for it, for everything, but he was the premier of the province." A man at I.E.L. who was involved from the start is considerably blunter: "It's a big story. It's like the history of World War II. It's Nova Scotia's Vietnam. Stanfield's Vietnam, if you like."

Why did it happen? The best answer comes from Robert Stanfield. "First, we were very concerned about the economic condition of Cape Breton in terms of employment and future employment, with the mines going down one by one," he says. "Second, I guess we'd had a good run of success with industries. We'd had the Volvo people and so on and perhaps we'd become a bit over-confident about the capacity of the people running Industrial Estates. Third, we were attracted unquestionably by the idea of the new atomic age, by the glamour, that kind of thing. And we didn't conceive of it being a particularly difficult enterprise. . . . I thought myself of it being somewhat similar to an electric power plant, not much more difficult in terms of construction."

The stories of Clairtone and the heavy water project are quite different. But the two schemes had something in common: they were both so glamourous that they led the Stanfield Government and its child, Industrial Estates Ltd., to set aside their normal prudence and caution. Both illustrated a point that should have required no illustrating – that Nova Scotia, as a poor province, lacked the expertise and resources to make the sort of sophisticated judgments that must be made in a technical field, whether it is stereo and colour television or nuclear technology. Unfortunately, the

Stanfield Government did not realize it was beyond its depth until the houses of cards built by Peter Munk and David Gilmour and Jerome Spevack collapsed about its ears.

Neither experience was without its bright side. The brief presence of Clairtone helped to rejuvenate the economy of Pictou County and to attract more industry there. The fact that Deuterium of Canada was building a heavy water plant in Cape Breton was an important factor in Canadian General Electric's decision to put its more successful heavy water plant in Nova Scotia. The latter plant, on the Cape Breton side of the Strait of Canso, has helped to turn the strait into a hub of industry with a half-billion dollars worth of power plants, refineries, and other industries already there and another half-billion worth to come.

But the Clairtone and D.C.L. schemes themselves were total failures. As a premier who chose to delegate heavy responsibility to others, Stanfield had to bear the ultimate blame when the people to whom he delegated proved unequipped to discharge that responsibility. One member of the board of I.E.L. contends that the directors were too often bypassed, and that Stanfield relied too heavily on his two strong men at I.E.L., Frank Sobey and Harold Egan. Premier Gerry Regan agrees with that. "Bob desperately wanted development for the province," says Regan, "and if he had a weakness in government, he tended to be too much impressed by people in business, by the Frank Sobeys and so on and so forth, and to allow their judgment to go unchallenged, perhaps not to do enough digging into it. . . . He seemed prepared to rely on these advisers. He tended to be a relatively easy target for the fast-talking, outside operator."

When Finlay MacDonald took over as president of Industrial Estates in 1970, in time to mop up the last of the Clairtone mess, he perceived the narrowness of the organization's focus. "The old mistakes of industrial development corporations were made by people whose entire backgrounds had been financial," he says. "Just because you or I made seven million dollars because we inherited a buggy whip business does not necessarily make us the kind of adjudicators you need as to the type of industrial development a province should have. Look, who can be conned faster than a big industrialist?"

But any premier who was as anxious as Stanfield was to create new opportunities for Nova Scotians was bound to place a few bad bets. Dalton Camp's assessment is close to the mark: "I think the reach exceeded the grasp."

9

The Man with the Winning Way (1965-1967)

I have considered it [federal politics] in much the same way I have considered ski-jumping.

— Robert L. Stanfield, February, 1965.

While Robert Stanfield was building his political dynasty in Nova Scotia, the federal Conservative Party was foundering, like a derelict left to drift to sea by its disheartened crew. Her Ahab-like captain, John Diefenbaker, clung to his command, though he had lost his power. Dismissed by the public and denounced by the more enlightened members of his crew, he seemed bent on letting the ship sink before he would admit it was leaking. But, as mutineers, the rebellious crewmen were an inept lot. They knew they could never return to office as long as Diefenbaker remained at the helm, but they did not know how to get rid of him, and they seemed to lack the will to find a way. They had no plan, no leader, and no organization. They could not agree on who among them, if anyone, would make a better captain.

The "termites" – as Diefenbaker called them – vented their frustration with increasing bitterness and decreasing hope as the months and years dragged on. They pulled out the same tattered lists of possible leaders, and their despair deepened. There seemed to be no one to take over. Perhaps that was Diefenbaker's greatest disservice to his party; suspecting plots even when there were none, he refused to develop lieutenants who might one day seek to succeed him. The front benches in the House of Commons were lined with tired loyalists, men of slender talents who had been sucked dry by years of submission to the Diefenbaker ego.

If, as Peter Newman once wrote, "The history of Canada's Conservative Party . . . had been dominated by the unremitting search for a re-incarnation of Sir John A. Macdonald," the search of the 1960s was doomed to failure. Admittedly, there were a few federal Conservatives who might rival Sir John A. in his fondness for a drink, but there were none who had the other qualities that had made Macdonald the greatest Conservative of history. Not surprisingly any discussion of the leadership among intelligent Conservatives turned in the end to provincial politicians. There were four Conservative premiers in the early-to-mid 1960s. One, Walter Shaw of Prince Edward Island, was clearly out of the question because he was eight years older than Diefenbaker. Of the remaining three, one stood out – Ontario's John Robarts. Only Robarts had the national stature and the electoral base to carry the Conservatives back to power in Ottawa. But Robarts did not want the job, and he said as much to anyone who asked.

The other two premiers, Manitoba's Duff Roblin and Nova Scotia's Bob Stanfield, were acknowledged to be fine men, capable premiers and proven vote-getters. But they came from small provinces and could not claim to be more than regional politicians, unfamiliar with national issues, and largely unknown beyond their own corners of the country. It seemed academic anyway. There was no reason on earth why Stanfield or Roblin should be any more willing than Robarts was to trade the security and influence of their premierships for the doubtful distinction of leading a federal party that had a repulsive habit of devouring its leaders.

Bob Stanfield was certainly not interested. John Diefenbaker had asked him back in the 1962 federal election campaign whether he would be interested in coming to Ottawa as a member of the government. Stanfield had been flattered but had shrugged the suggestion off with scarcely a thought. He had not even troubled to ask Diefenbaker what portfolio he had in mind. Then, following the 1965 election, Alvin Hamilton telephoned Stanfield to point out the obvious – that the party needed a new leader. Would Stanfield, he wondered, be interested in federal politics? Stanfield turned the thought aside. "I didn't see any role for myself at all at that time, as a member of the official opposition here in Ottawa or even as a member of the government," Stanfield says. "To some extent my attitude was based on the fact that I was running my own show in Nova Scotia. . . . I wasn't tempted by any other role."

Though Stanfield had always been interested, in the abstract, in federal politics, it was relatively late in the day before he saw a role for himself in Ottawa. He is not sure when he first began to think seriously of switching to federal politics, but he suspects it was probably not until after the climactic national Conservative annual meeting of November, 1966 when the party voted to hold a leadership convention before the end of 1967. People began to put real pressure on him, but Stanfield is uncertain if that was when the idea first took hold: "It is pretty hard to know yourself. Pretty hard to know what your real motivation is."

Some Stanfield watchers had concluded before then that he was destined for national politics. Flora MacDonald first detected a real spark of federal interest in February, 1965 following a crucial meeting of the party's national executive at which Stanfield had voted to sustain Diefenbaker's leadership in the face of a challenge from Leon Balcer, the Chief's Quebec lieutenant. After the meeting was over, Stanfield turned to Flora and said pensively: "I wonder how my action will be interpreted by the fellows in Quebec?" Flora was struck by that remark and wondered why Stanfield, "having no connection with Quebec, other than as another provincial premier who had to deal with Quebec from time to time, should have a specific interest in the interpretation in Quebec, rather than in Ontario or any place else."

Dalton Camp was not fully alerted to Stanfield's federal ambitions until an incident arose during the provincial election campaign in Nova Scotia in May, 1967. Word of a pending patronage scandal involving the purchase of drugs for provincial hospitals had reached Camp's ears. Rumour had it that the Stanfield government, rather than buying cheaper generic drugs, was purchasing brand name drugs from a Toronto manufacturer who, it was said, was kicking back part of his profits to the Nova Scotia Conservative Party. Ordering a secret but thorough investigation, Stanfield satisfied himself that although the more expensive drugs were being purchased, it was the result of a misunderstanding, not corruption. But in the course of the investigation, Stanfield turned to Camp and said with a rueful laugh, "When this comes out, they won't want me for a national leader." "It was the first time I ever really realized he was interested," says Camp.

But perhaps the first clear inkling that Stanfield saw himself as more than just another provincial premier came in April, 1964 when he addressed the Canadian Club of Montreal. In that speech, he stepped out of the role of premier to talk forcefully and with concern about national problems. He talked about pride in Canada, trade, foreign ownership, and the problems of relations between English and French-speaking Canadians – all areas that federal politicians like to regard as their private preserve. It was a thoughtful and intelligent speech, one that would have been a credit to any national leader or prime minister.

"Surely," Stanfield told the Montreal audience, "we can readily ease the fears of French-speaking Canadians regarding their language and culture. I realize some Canadians, perhaps many Canadians, feel we should have only one culture in Canada, a Canadian culture. I suppose they really have in mind a common culture with English as the common language. Any such concept is, of course, abhorrent to a French-speaking Canadian. There is surely no reason why we cannot have two languages and two cultures existing side by side and yet have an effective nationhood.

"English-speaking Canadians should accept and welcome the French language and culture in Canada as a continuing fact. This involves no more than the acceptance of reality and the recognition that the French tradition is a great tradition that has contributed and will contribute much to our national life."

That speech established Stanfield as a politician far removed from the Diefenbaker school of Progressive Conservatism. While Diefenbaker was soon to rush storming to the barricades in defence of the British connection in the great flag debate, Stanfield told the Montreal group that Canada needed her own distinctive flag and anthem. He confirmed his apostasy by endorsing Lester Pearson's dream of a bilingual federal civil service. "English Canadians," said Stanfield, "ought surely to be prepared to accept measures that the federal government considers necessary to assure equality of opportunity for French Canadians in the federal service."

Thoughtful Conservatives could not help but be impressed by the contrast between Stanfield's calm good sense and the semi-hysterical "unhyphenated Canadianism" that Diefenbaker so ardently preached. Some Tories were listening and made a mental note of that speech. It would be one of the reasons they would cite to explain why they were so anxious to have Bob Stanfield as a leadership candidate three years later.

Viewing Stanfield's career as a whole, his move into federal politics was not only logical, but inevitable. He has always been a party man. Though he guarded jealously his prerogatives as leader and premier in Nova Scotia, he never presumed at election time to differentiate between the interests of the provincial party and those of the federal party. He saw them as being one and the same, and he worked as hard for federal Conservatives as he did for his own provincial party. A strong Conservative presence in Ottawa, he believed, strengthened the provincial party in Nova Scotia. And he knew a strong provincial base in Nova Scotia meant a stronger Conservative Party in Ottawa. "To Stanfield, if you're a Conservative, there's only one party – the Conservative Party," says Dalton Camp.

When Stanfield became premier in 1956, federal Conservatives were a vanishing breed in his province, holding only one of Nova Scotia's twelve seats. The following year saw Diefenbaker come to power with a minority government and Nova Scotia led the way, giving Diefenbaker ten of her seats. In 1958, the year of the Diefenbaker landslide, Nova Scotia elected twelve Conservatives. Stanfield's greatest contribution to the federal cause was unquestionably in 1965 when, with the federal pary torn by dissension over Diefenbaker's leadership, Stanfield took three weeks off from Province House to stump the province for his federal brethren. Every time the Chief entered Nova Scotia, Stanfield was at his elbow and he stayed there as long

160

as Diefenbaker was in the province. Keith Davey was not exaggerating when he said afterward that Stanfield had "creamed" the Liberals. Prime Minister Lester Pearson's Liberals would have won the parliamentary majority they craved had they been able to hold their five seats in Nova Scotia, but Stanfield cut them back to two seats.

As a good party man, Stanfield was loyal to Diefenbaker. Although he had grave doubts about Diefenbaker's ability to lead the party back to office after 1963, he kept his reservations scrupulously to himself. The "termites" looked wistfully to Stanfield for encouragement in their opposition to Diefenbaker and received neither support nor solace. At the national party's annual meeting in 1965, Stanfield swung the Nova Scotia delegation solidly behind Defenbaker as the party gave him an overwhelming standing vote of confidence.

Stanfield's commitment to the federal party did not end with election campaigns. He was the only premier who regularly took the trouble to attend federal party gatherings – meetings of the national executive, annual meetings, and thinkers' conferences. He never took a leading role at these meetings, preferring to sit back and listen to others. Some Conservatives wondered who the shy gaunt man with the serious manner was. Norman Atkins, Dalton Camp's brother-in-law, delights in telling a story about Stanfield at the Conservative Thinkers' Conference in Fredericton in 1964. Stanfield came into the cafeteria and sat down beside Tom Hockin, a young professor who was doing post-graduate work at Harvard. "I hear you're at Harvard, my old alma mater," said Stanfield. Hockin looked at Stanfield and asked: "What do you do now?" "Well, I'm the Premier of Nova Scotia," was the reply. There were times, particularly when the federal party was wrestling with its leadership problem, when Stanfield could have avoided controversy if he had followed the examples of John Robarts and Duff Roblin by sending one of his ministers to represent him at national meetings. But he always came. "He voted on the merits of an issue," says Camp. "He had the guts to do it. He didn't send proxies."

Even if he had wanted to, Stanfield could not have avoided taking sides as the leadership dispute came to a boil in 1965. That was the year of the second serious attempt to dump Diefenbaker. The Chief had weathered the first challenge two years earlier when his cabinet disintegrated and his government fell over the nuclear arms issue, but it was only a matter of time before his foes tried again. The second challenge had its origins in Diefenbaker's filibuster against the adoption of the Canadian Flag in 1964 and in his incomprehensible opposition to the Fulton-Favreau formula for amending the constitution. In January, 1965, Leon Balcer, on behalf of Conservatives from Quebec, wrote to Dalton Camp, the party's national president, to demand that a leadership convention be held. Balcer charged that Diefenbaker had alienated French-Canadians in the party because "on every issue touching on the taproots of Confederation, the hopes and aspirations of French Canada had been distorted, misinterpreted, and ignored."

The national executive met in a stormy session in early February to consider Balcer's letter. The device by which the Quebec lieutenant's demand was presented to the meeting was a questionnaire soliciting the views of the executive on four questions. Only the first two were of any direct significance. The first question asked whether the executive felt it would be in the best interests of the party to convene a leadership convention. The second asked members of the executive to indicate whether they gave "full and unqualified" support to Diefenbaker, or whether they believed it would be in the general interest of the party if the leader were to "consider making way for a successor." The questionnaire seemed unnecessarily byzantine, but it was elaborate for a reason. It gave everyone at the meeting a range of options. Diefenbaker's enemies would vote against Diefenbaker on the second question and for a leadership convention on the first or, if that was too harsh for their taste, they could vote confidence in Diefenbaker and still vote to let the full party render judgment at a leadership convention. Diefenbaker's supporters could vote confidence in Diefenbaker and vote against a leadership convention or, if they preferred, they could vote for a leadership convention in the expectation that Diefenbaker would be triumphantly re-elected and thereby silence his enemies once and for all. The voting was to be by secret ballot, a provision that enhanced the prospects for Diefenbaker's enemies.

Before the members of the executive could vote, however, a Diefenbaker loyalist, Erik Nielsen, the M.P. for the Yukon, moved that the second question – confidence or non-confidence in the leader – be deleted from the questionnaire. In the angry confusion that followed, three standing votes were taken. They were all close, but they all supported the Nielsen amendment: 51-49, 53-49, and 57-55. With the crucial second question thus excised, the revolt collapsed. By secret ballot the executive decisively rejected calling a leadership convention. Both Balcer and Rémi Paul, another M.P. from Quebec, left the Conservative Party with Balcer refusing to return to the fold in the federal election nine months later. "There is no place," Balcer said, "for a French Canadian in the party of Mr. Diefenbaker."

Stanfield attended that executive meeting as he attended them all. Although he stayed out of the furious debate, he voted in favour of deleting the second part of the questionnaire. The national executive was not quite ready to vote non-confidence in Diefenbaker, and neither was Stanfield; had the second question remained, he would have voted to uphold Diefenbaker's leadership. He certainly did not regard himself in early 1965 as a candidate for the Diefenbaker mantle. As he had told newsmen before leaving Halifax to fly to Ottawa for that meeting, he had about as much interest in becoming a federal politician as he had in taking up ski-jumping.

Stanfield's attitude changed with the federal general election of November 8, 1965. Despite his diligent and successful efforts on Diefenbaker's behalf and despite the fact that the Conservatives returned with ninety-seven members (two more than they had won in 1963), Stanfield knew the cause was hopeless. He knew the country would not turn again to the Conservative Party as long as Diefenbaker remained its leader. He understood why Diefenbaker was anathema in Quebec and urban Ontario. No one had to tell him it was only a matter of time before the "termites" would try again or that he himself would be forced to take a public stand. Any doubt that there would be another attempt was dispelled when Diefenbaker ordered the dismissal of Flora MacDonald from the headquarters staff. In his book *Mandate '68*, Martin Sullivan has an apt description of the torment in the Conservative Party during the lull that followed the 1965 election: "From November until May, the Conservative chieftains waited to hear his resignation, like officers in a Prussian regimental mess anticipating the shot that would tell them their disgraced colonel had taken the gentlemanly way out. It never came. And slowly, reluctantly, the dread machinery of court martial was set into motion."

But how does a political party go about organizing a court martial? What would the rules of procedure be? Who would be the prosecutor, who the jury? Who would carry out the sentence? The conspirators did not know. "As people running a coup," says New Brunswick M.P. Gordon Fairweather, "we were as hopeless as one of Woody Allen's movie scripts." The plotters waited, overcome with a sense of empty frustration. Into that vacuum stepped Stanfield's old friend and valued ally, Dalton Camp, the party's national president and a most reluctant executioner. After brooding for months, Camp went to McMaster University in Hamilton in May of 1966 to attend a Young Progressive Conservative Conference. While he was there, he huddled with Heath Macquarrie and a few others in the anti-Diefenbaker movement, telling them of his plan to bring the leadership issue to a head at the party's annual meeting in Ottawa the following November. He told them how he planned to start – with a speech to a closed meeting of prominent Tories at Toronto's Albany Club on May 19. The Albany Club was and is the bastion of old-line Toryism in Toronto. Its members are men who would create the Conservative Party in their own image, as a vehicle to preserve and enhance all that is right and proper and sacred in Canadian society – as seen from the crystal-clear perspective of Bay Street. Needless to say, the men from Bay Street have never had much use for John Diefenbaker with his funny populist ideas about the equality of men, human rights, and the worth of the little fellow. The Albany Club speech was Camp's trial run. If he was well received there, he would carry his campaign for "a reassessment of policy, a reform of party organization, and the reconfirmation – or otherwise – of the leadership" to the party at large. Knowing the Albany Club, he knew there was no way he could bomb.

In early September, Camp and Norm Atkins went to Kingston for a motel-room conference with their key collaborators – Flora MacDonald, Lowell Murray, and David MacDonald, a young clergyman and M.P. from Prince Edward Island. The others were distressed to discover that Camp had embarked on his crusade with no real plan for bringing it to a successful conclusion. He proposed simply to turn the election of the national president – which, unlike the traditional vote of confidence in the leader, was conducted by secret ballot – into a referendum on Diefenbaker's leadership. He would stand for re-election as president on a leadership reassessment platform, and, if he won, his election would constitute a demand that the leader step down. It was a courageous enough approach; if Camp lost, his influence and credibility in the party would be destroyed. But it was an approach that could easily be thwarted by the loyalists. All they had to do was ignore Camp, to run no candidate against him and let him win the presidency by acclamation. Then they could swing the delegates – and no one doubted they could do it – into a standing vote of confidence in Diefenbaker. The Camp campaign would be rendered irrelevant. Or, the Diefenbaker forces could – as they later tried to do – rig the agenda so that Diefenbaker would get his vote of confidence before the election of the national officers, including the president. Diefenbaker would be perfectly entitled to carry on as leader, even if Camp won a contested election.

The Kingston group considered these and other problems and laid their plans accordingly. They agreed on one absolutely fundamental point – Camp must stick scrupulously to the high ground; he must argue only for the principal of leadership review and never, under any circumstances, should he attack the personality, John Diefenbaker. Camp did better than that; he never once mentioned Diefenbaker by name. When, in private conversation, he could not avoid referring to the leader, he called him "Charlie." Before leaving the motel in Kingston, the conspirators also drew up the organization they would need to win delegates to their cause in November and they worked over the draft of an epic speech Camp was soon to make to the Toronto Junior Board of Trade.

Camp "went public" in that Junior Board of Trade speech on September 20. It was a brilliant speech, one that succinctly and eloquently defined the relationship that should and must exist between a party and its leader. "Leaders," Camp said, "are fond of reminding followers of their responsibilities and duties to leadership. And followers sometimes need reminding. What is seldom heard, however, is a statement on the responsibilities of the leader to those he leads. Leaders are fond of saying how arduous their labour, how complex the circumstances, and how unfair the press criticism, as though they had been called to their high office by the supreme power rather than those they are addressing. . . . It [leadership] is not, as every politician knows, a lifetime contract."

Camp told the Junior Board of Trade about the two-way loyalty that must bind a leader and his party. "The leader should give at least as much loyalty to his followers as he demands from them. This is not personal loyalty, but rather loyalty to the party, to its continuing strength, best interests, and well-being. . . . In the relationship between the leader and the led, there is a mutuality of interest and, as well, a continuing common experience of discovery, learning, and revelation. Where the leader does not know the limits of his power, he must be taught, and when he is indifferent to the interest of his party, he must be reminded."

Camp made three proposals in that speech: that the party have fresh leadership and fresh policies in time for the next federal election; that aspirants for the leadership make their views on policy known and that the party provide forums for discussion of those views so that Conservatives would not be taken by surprise by their new leader, as some felt they were by Diefenbaker in 1956; and that a leadership convention be held in any event no later than the spring of 1968. As he told his Toronto audience, Camp was well aware of the fate that awaited him if he failed: "If I am wrong, than the usual penalties of politics will apply. But it is important that we no longer perpetuate instability, indecision, and expediency."

That speech immediately polarized the party. Those who agreed with Camp praised his selflessness; they heartily endorsed the editorial view of *The Globe and Mail:* "It is a service to his party and indeed his country." Those who disagreed with Camp – and his enemies outnumbered his friends at that stage – accused him of launching a cowardly, vindictive, and self-serving attack on a leader and a party that had raised him to a position of some prominence in Canadian public life. Thus divided, the Conservative Party reeled with excitement and foreboding toward the showdown in November. Its members knew that they were destined to make history. But they very much feared that they might destroy their party in the process.

Bob Stanfield was, as he himself puts it, "tormented." He had always been loyal to Diefenbaker and, more importantly, he accepted the principle that a party owed its leader its undivided loyalty. But he could not ignore

Dalton Camp. Stanfield owed much to Camp for his advice, assistance, and friendship over the years, and he held Camp in a personal affection he could never feel for Diefenbaker. As a modern politician, Stanfield also agreed totally with an assessment that Camp made in the course of the fall of 1966: "The business of politics is nearly bankrupt, run down by obsolescence and over-run by change. No one can remember when the passions of politicians were so far removed from the consensus of their constituents. We have never had a political renaissance in this country, but it is vital that we have one now and that it be launched in the spirit and resolution of a true revolution." Stanfield did not for a moment question Camp's conclusion – "If my party is not the first to reform, it will become an artifact of history."

Stanfield only wished Camp had taken him into his confidence before launching the renaissance. There was no reason why Camp should have told Stanfield of his plans, but, if he had, the show could have gone straight to Broadway without having to open first in Albany. And Albany was Halifax.

By the time of Camp's speech to the Toronto Junior Board of Trade in September, 1966, Stanfield had already decided to call a provincial general election in 1967, and he had started to put his organization in shape for the campaign. The Stanfield cabinet met and the ministers all agreed that the first thing they needed to do was to get Finlay MacDonald re-installed as president of the Nova Scotia Conservative Party. MacDonald had been the president in 1963; in that capacity he had managed the party's overwhelmingly successful election campaign that year. At the end of his term he had stepped down, on the sensible ground that others should be given a chance to serve as president. The incumbent president in 1966 was a merchant from Shelburne, Maurice Flemming. Foolishly, Stanfield did not bother to talk to Flemming; he took it for granted that Flemming would follow MacDonald's example by stepping aside when his term expired in early November, 1966. By tradition, the choice of the president was made by the leader and the party obediently ratified his nominee. Stanfield wanted MacDonald and with the Cabinet's blessing, Stanfield approached MacDonald who quickly agreed to return as the president.

It was a tidy little arrangement and it went awry because MacDonald was also a vice-president of the national party and a supporter of Dalton Camp. After Camp's Junior Board of Trade speech, MacDonald rushed into the dispute in support of Camp and, typical of MacDonald, his support was forcefully, unequivocally, and publicly given. Significantly, one of Stanfield's ministers had not been present when the Cabinet had endorsed MacDonald. James Harding, the Minister of Welfare, was a staunch Diefenbaker man, as was Maurice Flemming. Harding watched with concern as the national party chose sides between Camp and Diefenbaker. He watched as Finlay MacDonald, the Camp man, prepared to sail unopposed to the presidency in Nova Scotia. Like Flemming, Harding came from Shelburne; he went to Flemming, urging him to seek re-election. He put Flemming in touch with Arthur Maloney, the Toronto lawyer whom the Diefenbaker forces had chosen to battle Camp for the position of national president.

Camp recalls receiving a telephone call from Flora MacDonald's brother, Ronald MacDonald, a reporter for the Halifax *Chronicle-Herald,* who told him Harding had been talking to Maloney and to James Johnston, the economist whom Diefenbaker had installed as national director of the party. Camp telephoned Stanfield. "I was all agitated," Camp remembers, "and I said 'Bob, what are you going to do? I think you should talk to What's-his-face, the absent minister – Harding – and tell him what the score is.' And he said rather curtly, 'Leave it to me.'" Camp made the mistake of leaving it with Stanfield. "That," says Camp, "was the start of it. That was the slaughter of Finlay MacDonald.

Stanfield did nothing. He did not tell Harding that MacDonald was his personal choice for provincial president. He did not try to discourage Maurice Flemming from seeking re-election. Flemming announced he would run again and Stanfield sat silent on the sidelines. Just one week before the national annual meeting was to begin in Ottawa, the Conservatives of Nova Scotia assembled at the Lord Nelson Hotel in their own annual meeting. Suddenly, the election of the provincial president, which should have been a mere formality, had become a confrontation between the forces of John Diefenbaker and Dalton Camp. "I didn't know how to get out of it," says Finlay MacDonald. "I knew I was in for a real crasher. I didn't do any campaigning at all. I knew it was hopeless."

The Diefenbaker players stole the show. If the middle-aged Conservatives of Nova Scotia who attended that meeting had any doubts about what was happening, there to remind them was the guest of honour, John Diefenbaker himself, sitting benevolently on the stage as Bob Stanfield's Tories executed Finlay MacDonald. Flemming and MacDonald were each allotted ten minutes to address the delegates. Two minutes into his speech, MacDonald had to stop, unable to hear his own voice over the shouts of "traitor" and "Judas Iscariot" from the back of the hall. "I looked to my right," says MacDonald, "and Dief was seated there with Stanfield and I could see Bob's knuckles were white. It was his party and it was a mob scene. The party was tearing itself apart. There was a loud sea of Conservatives not allowing another Conservative to speak." Somehow, MacDonald struggled through his speech, took his defeat with the best of grace possible and even managed to get off a good line afterward. "Did you see that audience?" he asked a group of young Conservatives. "It looked as though the Pied Piper had passed through." "I suppose," Stanfield concedes, "I left Finlay in an embarrassing position actually, out on a limb. . . . I'd asked him to seek the presidency, but I had no intention of putting pressure on the annual meeting in any way to ensure he would be elected, or to work against Maurice Flemming or against anyone else who might have come forward." Some Tories view the sacrificing of Finlay MacDonald as proof of Stanfield's ability to be ruthless in politics; others see it as evidence of his weakness as a leader – he will sit idle rather than take hard, unpopular action.

Dalton Camp inclines to the former view. He argues that the incident revealed a tough streak in Stanfield; he would sacrifice Finlay MacDonald rather than alienate the hard-core Diefenbaker people in the provincial party whose support Stanfield would soon need in the provincial election. "Stanfield is able to turn on people," says Camp. "He can dispatch people, not forever, not for all time. He'd rescue them later. . . . Stanfield is not the kind of guy who, if there is a submarine down underneath and survivors in the water, won't drop the depth charges. Because he will. He won't be conditioned by the facts that he's in charge of the convoy. He'll go after the submarine. He's tough that way."

The preview performance in Halifax had two important consequences when the "Dalton and Dief Show" opened in Ottawa a week later. Camp's supporters, furious with the way MacDonald had been abused in Halifax, came to Ottawa in an ugly mood. They repaid Diefenbaker in kind on the opening night of the national annual meeting, refusing to rise when he entered the hall and heckling him at intervals throughout his speech. The second consequence was that Bob Stanfield came to Ottawa, seething at the interference of Diefenbaker and James Johnston in his provincial party by promoting the candidacy of Maurice Flemming. Says Dalton Camp: "I think that meeting in Halifax was when Stanfield realized the game was a bigger game than he had thought. I suppose Stanfield, circa 1966, thought this was a pretty civilized kind of game. . . . But Dief was there in Halifax and Finlay was gored. That's the one time anyone can remember that Stanfield was angry, in public anyway. He was really outraged. He never really thought that the federal party would come down in his ball park and make trouble for him. He thought they'd leave that for him. If they'd left it to him, his role at the national meeting might have been different." Stanfield came to Ottawa and quietly cast his lot with Camp.

The delegates to the national annual meeting were just starting to trickle into Ottawa when the national executive met on Sunday, November 13, at the Chateau Laurier Hotel to deal with a crucial issue. Johnston, the national director, had mailed out an agenda for the annual meeting that was designed solely to give Diefenbaker a tactical advantage. It provided for Diefenbaker to address the convention on the first night, Monday, with the election of national officers not to take place until the final afternoon, Wednesday. Camp feared that someone would propose a "spontaneous" vote of confidence in Diefenbaker at the conclusion of his Monday speech. If it did not happen then, the traditional standing vote of confidence in the leader would have to be taken on Tuesday or Wednesday morning during the debate on resolutions. Camp's strength lay in the secret ballot. There were many Conservatives whose patience with Diefenbaker was exhausted but who lacked the nerve to knife him in broad daylight. They would vote against him on a secret ballot, but if they did not have a cloak of anonymity they would leap cynically to their feet to support him in a standing vote. Camp knew that if they gave Diefenbaker his standing vote of confidence before the secret-ballot election of the national president, the outcome of his battle with Arthur Maloney would lose its significance. He was determined that the national executive should change the agenda to place the election of officers on Tuesday before the debate on resolutions. Stanfield was, as usual, the only premier who attended that national executive meeting, and he voted with Camp to change the agenda. They won by eighty votes to forty-one.

Stanfield took no public part in the debate that quickly engulfed the annual meeting. As he had in Halifax a week earlier, he took the course of least resistance, sitting silent when he might have come publicly to Camp's aid. He had a reason, albeit a thin one. Eight of the ten Nova Scotia M.P.s were working for Arthur Maloney and they made no secret of their unhappiness with their premier's quiet support for Camp. Robert Muir, a Diefenbaker M.P. from Cape Breton, gave Stanfield a blunt warning at a meeting of the Nova Scotia delegates: "The men who today are knifing Diefenbaker may well be doing it to you tomorrow in Nova Scotia." Stanfield decided he could not risk splitting the Nova Scotia delegation any more than it already was. But everyone knew where he stood and he expressed his view to delegates who asked him. It was: disenchantment with Diefenbaker was so great that he would never again be able to unite the party, and Diefenbaker's continued leadership would drive away the young people Camp was attracting to the party.

Camp won his crusade at the annual meeting. In a close vote, 564 to 502, he defeated Maloney for the presidency. Flora MacDonald beat Diefenbaker loyalist Kenneth Binks for national secretary. It seemed a bit like an anti-climax when the delegates went on to vote 563 to 186 to hold a leadership convention before January 1, 1968.

But although Camp had attained his immediate objective, all his lofty talk of a political renaissance rang hollow. The Conservative Party had barely weathered some of the worst moments of its long history. The party had never had to endure anything like the Monday night scene when its leader was booed and hissed by people who were supposed to be his supporters. At one point Diefenbaker had stopped to demand of the hostile audience: "Is this a Conservative meeting." "Yes. Yes," came the derisive chorus.

As the dust from the annual meeting settled, leadership hopefuls began to emerge. Almost all came from the tired little list that had so discouraged the "termites." There was Davie Fulton, the former Minister of Justice; George Hees, the former Minister of Trade and Commerce; Alvin Hamilton, the former Minister of Agriculture; Mike Starr, the former Minister of Labour; Donald Fleming, the former Minister of Finance who had spent the previous four years in self-imposed political exile; Senator Wallace McCutcheon, the millionaire businessman from the Argus Corporation whom Diefenbaker had brought into his cabinet in a futile bid to reassure the business community. Conservatives scanning the list were overcome with a sense of *déjà vu*. Worse, all the candidates seemed to be running as much to prove something to themselves as to win the leadership. Fulton and Fleming sought to prove to themselves that the party had been wrong when it picked Diefenbaker instead of them in 1956; Hees to prove he was more than an amiable jock; Hamilton to prove he was more than a shadow of John Diefenbaker; Starr to prove he was somebody important; McCutcheon to prove that a man did not have to be a politician to be prime minister. "There were a lot of people who were not running for election, who were running for other reasons," observes Camp. "They were running for redemption."

Camp was distressed as he watched the race unfold. In his view, there was no one in the federal party who could complete the renaissance. He started to look at the provincial parties for a candidate to support. One name often mentioned in speculation in the first half of 1967 was that of William Davis, then Minister of Education in Ontario, and a man with a keen interest in federal politics. Camp had lunch with Davis and talked him out of running. "I told him there was no way he could get there from where he was," Camp recalls. "It would have been disaster. Disaster. The people who would have eaten him alive were the Conservatives of Ontario. He had no sort of relationship with Robarts, for God's sake. They weren't friends. Robarts was about to call an election and do you think they would have supported Davis if Davis had deserted the ship? No way. Bill was an asset to them."

170

Camp went to Robarts who had been premier of Ontario since 1961. As he expected, Robarts was totally uninterested in running for the federal leadership; he turned Camp down immediately. "He had everything he wanted," says Camp. "He knew what it was like to be Premier of Ontario. . . . He had not the slightest interest in being leader of the opposition. He was a burnt-out volcano and he knew it."

That narrowed Camp's short list to just two men – Roblin and Stanfield. He knew both well and knew both could be interested. Both played the hesitant virgin, telling Camp they were interested but would have to think about it for a while. He made an identical pitch to both: he would support the first one to enter the race and he would support him on the candidate's terms. He would support him publicly, or he would support him by not endorsing him at all. Camp knew, given the hatred with which he was regarded by many Tories, that his non-support might be more valuable than his support. It did not matter much to Camp which of the two premiers entered the race, as long as one of them did. "I always thought that temperamentally, Stanfield was the better of the two," says Camp. "He would find it easier to endure. He'd have the patience and he'd wear better. . . . But my perception of them was equally good, equally valid."

Stanfield, meanwhile, had been going through much the same mental process as Camp had – examining all the probable candidates and finding them all lacking in one vital respect or another. He had a clear perception of the problems the new leader would face and the clarity of his political thinking was evident in an off-the-record interview that he gave a few days after the annual meeting of November, 1966: "The key to it all is Diefenbaker, and I haven't got an idea what he'll do. Obviously, he can't unify the party; he ought to step down and counsel his supporters to give up the fight, but he's not the resigning type. More likely, he'll hold on till the convention and, I suspect, run again. That would present a problem. Anyone running against him would know that even if he won, he'd be taking on a badly split party." Stanfield did not at that stage see himself as a leadership candidate: "Personally, I'd be very reluctant to run. I certainly wouldn't be an active candidate. The life of Prime Minister doesn't appeal to me at all, and I'd have to be convinced that it was a matter of real urgency before I'd take it on."

In the ensuing months, however, Stanfield became increasingly convinced that it was indeed a matter of real urgency. He and his closest advisers in Halifax, men such as Ike Smith, Dick Donahoe, and Finlay MacDonald spent endless hours talking about the state of the federal party and the problem of finding someone who could heal its wounds. "My God, we talked. Constantly. Constantly," says MacDonald. The only declared candidate who, in Stanfield's mind – as those close to him read it – came close to having the necessary qualities was Davie Fulton. But Fulton seemed to be a spent force politically. The Stanfield people could not convince themselves that Fulton could lead them to victory. There was only one potential candidate whom Stanfield believed could give the party the unity and vigour it needed and that was Duff Roblin. As Stanfield repeatedly told his advisors, if Roblin would run, he would not consider running himself.

As the summer of 1967 neared, Stanfield became preoccupied with matters closer to home. He called a provincial election for May 30 and had no further time to worry about federal problems until it was over. Some of his friends concluded that he was hoping the federal dilemma would somehow evaporate during the provincial campaign, but of course it did not. He won such a towering victory – far more impressive than Roblin's the year before – that the pressure to become a leadership candidate doubled in intensity. The pressure came from several directions: from the anti-Diefenbaker M.P.s in Ottawa, people such as Ontario's Jean Wadds and Gordon Aiken, Prince Edward Island's David MacDonald and Heath Macquarrie, and Alberta's Gerald Baldwin and Doug Harkness; from Stanfield men at home, men such as Finlay MacDonald, Labour Minister Tom McKeough, and Provincial Secretary Gerry Doucet; and from Camp and his "Eglinton Mafia" which was dying for a chance to parlay its triumph at the 1966 annual meeting into a victory at the leadership convention. Camp came to Halifax to see Stanfield following the provincial election in May, and although Stanfield told him he would think about becoming a candidate, he advised Camp to go to see Roblin. Camp went to see Roblin in Winnipeg on June 20; he could not get an answer from him either. He was offended when Roblin's office leaked a story that the Premier was "uneasy" about Camp's visit. Camp's deadline for an answer from Roblin was the end of June, and when that deadline passed with no word from Winnipeg, Camp set July 10 as his new deadline.

It began to appear that if Camp wanted a candidate he could support he would have to run himself. In fact, that thought had been in Camp's mind for several months, and he had already done some preliminary planning. In the spring of 1967, Flora MacDonald attended a series of secret meetings with Camp's Eglinton Mafia in which they mapped out the strategy for a Camp campaign. They progressed to the point of discussing the timing of Camp's announcement. "One of the questions was, should he resign as president?" Flora remembers. "He was going off to England for three weeks. Should he resign before he went and then, when he came back, say he was running? I was opposed to this as I thought he should be absolutely frank about it and say he was resigning with the intention of running."

Having committed himself to support either Stanfield or Roblin, if one of them ran, Camp marked time until the premiers rendered their decisions. Flora MacDonald went to Toronto again to meet with the Eglinton group during the first week of July. They reviewed the situation. There was no word from Roblin, and, although they knew that pressure on Stanfield was mounting, they were unaware of how much effect it was having. They polled the anti-Diefenbaker M.P.s in Ottawa and found that although at least twenty were prepared to support Stanfield, only two would fully commit themselves to backing Camp if he became a candidate. The M.P.s knew that Camp's candidacy would further divide the strife-torn party. Although Camp was very close to entering the race, he, too, understood the problems that his entry would create. "Dalton always felt the only way he could win was by a very short, very dramatic campaign," says Flora. "To have it too long drawn out would allow the seeds of disunity to really grow." After that meeting in Toronto in early July, Camp left for his cottage at Robertson's Point in New Brunswick to ponder his next move.

Communications were the greatest difficulty that Conservatives not committed to any of the declared candidates had to overcome in the summer of 1967. No one was quite sure what anyone else was doing. Camp had no way of determining what Stanfield's and Roblin's decisions would be, and, equally important, when they might be made. Stanfield was sitting in Halifax hoping Roblin would run, but not really knowing whether he would or not.

A key in figure in finally persuading Stanfield to run was Senator Grattan O'Leary, editor emeritus of *The Ottawa Journal* and one of the grand old men of the Conservative Party. O'Leary had met Stanfield only once – during the 1963 federal election campaign – but he liked what he had seen. He also remembered something Mary Stanfield had told him that day – that she thought she might rather like to live in Ottawa. Like many other Conservatives in the summer of 1967, O'Leary was dissatisfied with any of the declared candidates and frustrated by his inability to find out what was happening. A group of M.P.s sat in O'Leary's office in the Senate one day in late June discussing their dilemma. They agreed Stanfield would be the best candidate. But would he run?

Not a man to pussyfoot around, O'Leary picked up his telephone, called Stanfield in Halifax and asked: "Look here, would you run? I can't get a clear answer here. Will you run?" O'Leary offered to fly to Halifax, but Stanfield said he was going to be in Toronto the next day for a meeting of provincial education ministers and suggested that they meet there. O'Leary flew to Toronto and went straight to Queen's Park to see John Robarts. Robarts told O'Leary that he would welcome Stanfield's candidacy and that he would support Stanfield. An hour later, O'Leary met Stanfield at the Westbury Hotel where the two men had tea and talked for two hours. O'Leary laid it on the line. He told Stanfield he was unquestionably the best man for the job, that he had a duty to the country to run, and that although he had done well in Nova Scotia he could not do much for Canada as long as he stayed in provincial politics. O'Leary also used the same argument that the Conservatives of Nova Scotia had used two decades earlier in persuading Stanfield to take over the provincial party; he reminded Stanfield that, as a man of independent means, he would be able to devote the time necessary to rebuild the dissension-wracked federal party. "Grattan worked me over pretty hard," says Stanfield, laughing at the memory. Stanfield promised to consider O'Leary's arguments and said he would give him an answer soon. A week later, Stanfield called from Halifax, said he was going to be in Ottawa and suggested that they meet again. O'Leary and Patrick Nowlan, who had succeeded his father, Goerge, as an M.P., met Stanfield at the Chateau Laurier Hotel where they had a long talk. They left with the distinct impression that he would be a candidate.

Stanfield's own reluctance overcome, there was only one major obstacle left – the opposition of his Minister of Finance, Ike Smith. Back at home, Stanfield called Dalton Camp at his cottage in New Brunswick and asked him to come to Halifax. Camp flew over and met Stanfield and a small group of advisors, including Smith, Dick Donahoe, and Finlay MacDonald, in the garden at "The Oaks" on Gorsebrook Avenue. They assessed Stanfield's chances of winning the leadership and concluded that although there was no great groundswell of support for him in the federal party, there was no strong sentiment for any other candidate either. He would have as good a chance as anyone else, and a better chance than most. Dick Donahoe, the Attorney General, had by this time dropped his reservations and was urging Stanfield to run, leaving Ike Smith as the lone holdout. Ever since the provincial election of May 30, Smith had been fighting to convince Stanfield to stay in Nova Scotia, arguing that there was unfinished business to be done, that Stanfield could do more for the province as premier than as leader of the opposition in Ottawa, and that he might get his throat cut by the rough boys in the federal party. Above all, Smith worried that if Stanfield left, he would have to remain in provincial politics himself and would be unable to get back to his first love, the law.

In these discussions with Smith, Stanfield had advanced two main arguments as to why he should try for the federal leadership. The first was that after eleven years, he had been premier long enough, and that it would be healthy for the party and the province if he were to give someone else a chance to be premier. His second argument was, in Smith's words, "Bob's very strong feeling that unless Roblin ran he'd not be happy to see the party in the hands of any of the declared candidates." But Stanfield told Smith he would not agree to become a candidate unless Smith gave him two undertakings: that Smith would support him for the leadership; and that he would stay in politics and take over as interim premier, pending a leadership convention. Smith steadfastly refused through June and the first half of July to give those commitments. So determined was his opposition that Stanfield at one point appeared to give in. He told Smith he had thought it all through and had decided against running. But knowing the increasing pressure on Stanfield to run, Smith resisted the impulse to celebrate his apparent victory. "I thought that would not be the last of it," he says. It wasn't. Smith's phone started to ring as Conservatives across Nova Scotia and in other parts of the country called to urge the determined little minister of finance to help talk Stanfield into running. Smith refused, but he was astute enough to know his position was being eroded by Duff Roblin's inability to make up his mind. One day Stanfield told him he had talked to Roblin on the telephone and that the Manitoba premier was still undecided. Stanfield, Smith deduced, was coming to the conclusion that Roblin would not run.

That was the situation when the group met in the garden at "The Oaks." The others were urging Stanfield to run and Smith was refusing to budge. And unless Smith budged, Stanfield would not commit himself to becoming a candidate. "Dalton was pretty gloomy," Smith remembers. "He wasn't making much headway with Bob. Dalton was saying the same thing over and over again as people do in these circumstances. I left there without saying anything that would encourage either one of them to think that I would try to persuade Bob to run." The meeting broke up without a decision one way or the other. Camp and Smith left together, pausing to talk for a few minutes on the driveway before going their separate ways.

It was one of those conversations in which the only two people involved have diametrically opposite recollections of what was said. Smith recalls leaving the garden with Camp, but he does not remember saying anything to him that would have encouraged him to conclude that he was going to drop his opposition to Stanfield's candidacy. Quite the reverse. "I remember saying to Dalton," says Smith, " 'Look, why the hell don't you do it yourself if you're so anxious to get people to run? Why don't you do it yourself?' Dalton said, 'Well, if we don't get somebody better, I may have to.' " Camp, on the other hand, remembers Smith as having been conciliatory. Recalls Camp: "Ike said 'You know I really hate to be the square oar in this thing. Really, I suppose if he wants to do it, I should do the decent thing and agree to it.' "

So convinced was Camp that Smith had finally given in, that he returned to the Lord Nelson Hotel and started telephoning his supporters with the news that Stanfield would run. Flora MacDonald was asleep in her flat in Kingston when Camp called and announced: "You should be happy, your man is going to run." Still half-asleep, Flora did not know whether he was talking about himself or Stanfield. "Then he told me who it was," Flora says, "and I was thrilled because I had always thought Stanfield wouldn't do it." Camp asked her to fly to Halifax that coming weekend to help on the text of Stanfield's announcement and to lay plans for the campaign.

As Camp remembers, he got a telephone call at the hotel the next morning from Ike Smith who told him he had spoken to Stanfield and was withdrawing his objections. Smith, however, could not have been very convincing with Stanfield because Camp – to his utter amazement – then received a call from Stanfield who told him he felt he could not run. "There were three or four reasons," recalls Camp. "He had had a report from the treasury that indicated a shortfall in revenues, which meant there would be some sort of budgetary crisis in the province that might require a tax increase. He had a minister who had been out drunk and he was going to have to fire him. . . . He said 'I don't feel I should leave the ship in this current state. I'm sorry to have wasted all your time, but it's all over.' "

Stanfield had essentially the same conversation with Finlay MacDonald who drove over to the Lord Nelson Hotel to have breakfast with Camp. It was a morose meal. "We sat there," says Camp, "and said, 'What do we do now? We don't have a candidate. We don't have anything.' " Both men were buried in their thoughts as MacDonald drove Camp to the airport in his Thunderbird. Camp flew back to his cottage and told his wife: "Stanfield's not going to go, so that's that." He telephoned Linda Camp's brother, Norm Atkins, in Toronto, and told him of Stanfield's decision. Atkins phoned Flora MacDonald in Kingston. "One minute I was sort of elevated," Flora says, "and the next I felt absolutely dejected." She told Atkins she would cancel her arrangements for going to Halifax on the weekend, but Atkins told her not to. "Just change them and go to New Brunswick," he said, "because this has cleared the way for Dalton." Flora spent the weekend at Robertson's Point with the Camps and another old friend, Richard Hatfield, the Tory M.L.A., who three years later became Premier of New Brunswick. They mapped out Camp's leadership campaign that weekend.

Back in Halifax, however, the Stanfield candidacy was not as dead as the people at Robertson's Point assumed it was. Stanfield was still tortured. One minute he thought he could not possibly run, the next minute he thought he should. His labour minister, Tom McKeough, was still urging him to run and Stanfield asked him to talk to Ike Smith. McKeough went to Smith and gave him the same sort of working over that Grattan O'Leary had given Stanfield a few weeks earlier. "One of the arguments he put to me," says Smith, "was something like this: 'Are you prepared to assume the responsibility for keeping this man from becoming Prime Minister of Canada?' In those words. That's a tough question."

Smith did not succumb immediately. He told McKeough he would not change his mind, but, at home in Truro for the weekend, he began to rethink his position. The more he thought about it the more he was impressed by McKeough's argument that he should not stand in Stanfield's way. He also began to see the logic of an argument that Camp and Finlay MacDonald had been using: if Stanfield decided to become a candidate despite Smith's objections – which Smith thought he might do – all that Smith's objections would have accomplished would have been to delay Stanfield's entry into the race, thereby diminishing his chances of winning. By pre-arrangement, Stanfield called Smith, then drove to Truro to see him. Smith packed it in. He told Stanfield that, financial crisis or no, he thought Stanfield should run and that he would stay on to look after the provincial ship.

On Monday, July 17, Stanfield told Finlay MacDonald that he had decided to be a candidate, and MacDonald, elated, tried to telephone Camp at his cottage. But the cottage was on a party line and MacDonald could not get through. By this time, the group at Robertson's Point had finished discussing Camp's plans for a short, dramatic leadership campaign. Flora MacDonald was dispatched to another cottage where there was a private telephone to call Finlay MacDonald at CJCH-TV in Halifax to find out about television times for Camp's announcement. "How the hell do you get in touch with you people over there at Robertson's Point?" Finlay demanded. "Why? What do you mean?" Flora asked. Finlay told her Ike Smith had changed his mind and Stanfield was going to run. Flora had to break the news to Camp. "There was a rather stunned silence, a pregnant pause," she recalls. Gently, she suggested, "Dalton, you had better go and have a chat with Finlay." Few of the people who knew Camp best had realized how much he wanted to be leader himself. Stanfield's decision came at almost the last possible moment. Had Stanfield agonized for a few more days, Camp would probably have entered the race. As it was, Stanfield's entry dashed Camp's hopes of becoming leader in 1967 and perhaps forever. Camp was subdued when he came back from talking to Finlay MacDonald. "Dalton is the most phlegmatic man," says Flora. "He is inscrutable. He said very little. In fact, for forty-eight hours, he said just about nothing."

It is fascinating to speculate what would have happened if Camp, not Stanfield, had been the candidate. Camp was certainly better known within the federal party, and he had a better grasp of national issues than Stanfield had. He was more articulate and more attractive to younger Conservatives. Camp, however, would not have had Stanfield's solid base of Maritime delegates, and, because he was so despised by the Diefenbaker supporters, he could not have presented himself as a unity candidate the way Stanfield did. Jean Wadds, the Tory M.P. for the Ontario riding of Grenville-Dundas, illustrated the difficulties Camp would have had in mounting a winning campaign. A few days before Stanfield's decision, Flora MacDonald told Mrs. Wadds that Camp might be a candidate instead of Stanfield. "Flora," she replied, "I am still with you all the way but instead of being able to deliver my whole constituency, I can only deliver my own vote." If Camp had run, the likely result would have been an easy victory for Manitoba's Duff Roblin.

When Stanfield decided to run, Camp sat down and drafted Stanfield's announcement; Flora MacDonald dictated it over the phone to Finlay MacDonald's secretary. The draft contained no reference to John Diefenbaker, an omission that troubled Stanfield, who pencilled in a few words about the leader and asked Camp for his opinion. "You're asking the wrong person for that," Camp replied. "I'm afraid I can't give you an objective opinion on that." But Stanfield deleted the reference after checking it with a staunch Diefenbaker man, Joe Clarke. Clarke, the Nova Scotia party's provincial director, convinced Stanfield that any tribute from a man who was seeking his job would be worse in the Chief's eyes than no mention at all. Before making his decision public, Stanfield sent a telegram to Diefenbaker who was travelling in Western Canada.

The Red Room at Province House was crowded on Wednesday evening, July 19, for Stanfield's press conference. At 8 p.m., he walked in, wearing a grey suit with a faint black pinstripe, and sat down before a battery of microphones in the high-backed red plush chair he used when he was presiding at cabinet meetings. Deciding the chair was a little ostentatious for the occasion, he started to move to a more modest chair, but was persuaded not to by the television cameramen. There was no sign of Camp or Finlay MacDonald. Stanfield had asked them to stay away, knowing their presence would only alienate Conservatives who had opposed Camp at the annual meeting the previous November.

He read the statement Camp had written in an even voice that betrayed only a little of the anxious deliberation that had filled the preceding weeks. "After much earnest discussion during the past fortnight, with my colleagues in the Nova Scotia government and with provincial and federal members of the Progressive Conservative Party of Canada, I have come to a decision to declare myself as a candidate for the leadership of the Progressive Conservative Party of Canada." He paused, then admitted: "I never thought I would reach this decision, but in my heart I feel it is what I should do." The decision had been particularly difficult, he continued, because it came so soon after the provincial election, but his cabinet colleagues had assured him they would carry out his election promises. "I appreciate very much their understanding and goodwill, without which I could not have reached the conclusion represented by this statement," he said.

Even for Stanfield, it was a low-key performance. Leadership candidates are supposed to predict victory. Stanfield would not, although he did admit to feeling a certain confidence. Leadership candidates are supposed to dazzle their listeners with revelations on matters of policy, foreign and domestic. Stanfield had no policy to announce, and he grew vague to the point of incomprehensibility when the assembled reporters tried to elicit his views on national issues. They did discover that he thought the challenge facing the new Conservative leader would be rather like the challenge he had accepted nineteen years earlier when he took charge of the tattered remnants of the Conservative Party of Nova Scotia. One reporter wanted to know whether, now that he was leaping into federal politics, Stanfield planned to take up ski-jumping, as well. He got a frank reply: "I don't think so. One bit of foolishness is enough for one time." He was less than frank, however, when asked to identify individuals or factions within the party who were supporting his candidacy: "Quite frankly, I don't propose to know who'll be supporting me." Another reporter wondered, very diplomatically, whether Stanfield might not be a wee bit dull and perhaps a shade old fashioned. "I don't want to sound presumptuous," the candidate replied, "but Mackenzie King was a little dull."

The national press, bored to distraction by the tired field of leadership candidates, embraced Stanfield enthusiastically. "Mr. Stanfield's entry," wrote *The Globe and Mail's* George Bain, "very greatly changes the complexion of the P.C. leadership race, for one thing, giving it what it didn't have – a dominant figure, one man the others must all concentrate on catching." Peter Newman waxed descriptive in the *Toronto Daily Star:* "Until Robert Stanfield became a candidate . . . the Conservative leadership race had aroused about as much excitement as a long-distance engagement between two World War I zeppelins, with the candidates floating around the country like dirigible airships, taking only the odd pot shot at each other. But the Nova Scotia premier's decision changed all that. Suddenly the race has become real. . . . "

The other leadership contenders, actual or prospective, did not attempt to scale the heights of the Newman prose. Michael Starr condemned Stanfield as an instrument of Dalton Camp and warned that his entry would increase disunity in the party. Duff Roblin would still not discuss his own plans, but he allowed: "I'm glad to see Mr. Stanfield's name in the ring." John Diefenbaker bit his tongue – "I have no observation to make on that." At home in Nova Scotia, only one man was distraught. James Aitchison, the leader of the provincial New Democrats, was incensed that Stanfield would run away to Ottawa so soon after the provincial election. "It's time the truth were known about him," snapped Aitchison. "His performance has in fact been so despicable, even scandalous, that the federal Tories ought to be on guard against him. . . . With his move into federal politics, the people of Nova Scotia find that they bought a ten dollar suit of Stanfield underwear in the May election and are left with only the label." No one paid Aitchison the slightest heed. For Nova Scotians, it was a time for champagne, not sour grapes. An elderly man spoke for just about everyone in Nova Scotia when he approached Stanfield as he left Province House following his press conference. "Let me shake the hand of Canada's next Prime Minister," the old man said. "Now, now," replied an embarrassed Stanfield, "Let's not be presumptuous."

The next day, Thursday, the Stanfield forces held their first organizational meeting at Camp's cottage in New Brunswick. In addition to Camp, those attending that council of war were Norm Atkins from Toronto; Joe Clarke, the provincial director from Halifax; Cyril Sherwood, the one-time Tory leader in New Brunswick; Gordon Fairweather, the M.P. from New Brunswick; Paul Weed, an organizer from Ontario; and the three Mac-Donalds – Flora, Finlay, and David, the M.P. from Prince Edward Island. They agreed on a fundamental point of strategy: that there were so many candidates in the field (eight by this time) that no one was going to win enough delegates to have the leadership locked up before the convention began. Although Stanfield's pre-convention travelling would be useful in exposing him to delegates who did not know him, he would win, or lose, on his performance during convention week in Toronto. The major part of the organizational effort had, therefore, to be directed to the five days of the convention.

It also became apparent at that meeting at Robertson's Point that someone would have to decide who was to be in charge of the campaign. The Stanfield organization was composed of an uneasy alliance between two groups, each jealous of its prerogatives. The provincial Conservative machine, led by Maurice Flemming, regarded Stanfield as its personal property. He had been their leader for nineteen years; if he wanted to be federal leader, they were determined to win him that prize. Their determination was tempered only slightly by the fact that they had no idea of how to go about it. The second group, the Camp organization, also regarded Stanfield as its candidate. The Camp forces had liberated the party from John Diefenbaker; now they were bent on completing the revolution by handing the leadership to Bob Stanfield. As they had demonstrated at the 1966 annual meeting, they knew how to mount a successful campaign in the national party, but that experience was also a liability. The sight of "Camp's storm troopers," as Diefenbaker Tories called them, would be enough to send hundreds of potential delegates rushing into the arms of other candidates. Dalton Camp felt he was a pariah in the eyes of Stanfield Conservatives in Nova Scotia, most of whom had been Diefenbaker supporters. Camp was moody and unpredictable, telling the others at the cottage: "I have done my bit. I have written the announcement speech. Now I am going to stay here quietly at Robertson's Point for the rest of the summer. Good luck to you all."

It fell to Flora MacDonald, the Cape Breton girl who had worked with Camp for ten years in campaigns across Canada and who was respected by both sides, to act as mediator. Leaving Camp behind, she flew to Halifax on Saturday, two days after the council of war. She spent Sunday with Stanfield, briefing him on the situation in the federal party and the strengths and weaknesses of his leadership opponents. She warned him of the difficulties he would encounter if he allowed his Nova Scotians, who did not know most of the power brokers outside of their own province, to direct his campaign. "I told him," she says, "what a big battle there was ahead of him and that he needn't necessarily count on all the people who were voting with Dalton at the national meeting to be with him."

The next night, Flora attended a meeting in Halifax of Stanfield's Nova Scotia supporters. Neither Camp nor Atkins nor Finlay MacDonald (who was still distrusted because of his part in the dump-Diefenbaker movement) had been invited. Half an hour into the meeting, Flora stopped it. "Look," she said, "I have a question that I have to bring up. This is, how do you expect to run a campaign from here and organize a convention in Toronto with people you don't even know? The first issue you really have to face is how much of this campaign is going to be run by Dalton and his associates. Really, I feel if he is not included there is no way I can really be of any assistance to you either." They debated that pronouncement and Flora got unexpected support from Dick Donahoe, the Attorney General, who convinced the others that she was absolutely right. They agreed to postpone their meeting until the following day while Flora attempted to entice Camp out of hiding at his cottage. She phoned him and, taking substantial liberties with the sentiment of the meeting, told him the Nova Scotians were waiting impatiently for him to come and give them the benefit of his expert advice and guidance.

Camp agreed to come to Halifax, and he and Atkins and Finlay Mac-Donald joined the original group. Stanfield, who had not attended the Monday meeting, came to the Tuesday gathering. The others included Maurice Flemming, Joe Clarke, Senator Frank Welch (the old George Nowlan organizer), Ken Matthews (the lawyer-organizer from Truro), and Robert Coates (the M.P. for Cumberland who just eight months earlier had been such an ardent Diefenbaker supporter that he had threatened to leave politics unless the annual meeting voted confidence in the Chief). "It was an embarrassing meeting," Camp recalls. "All the yahoos of the party were there and everybody was pretty cool to me."

The most disturbing part of the meeting, however, was Flora Mac-Donald's announcement that she had learned that Duff Roblin intended to be a candidate. She had previously made arrangements for Jim Doak, a Manitoban who was a vice-president of the national party, to organize delegates for Stanfield in Manitoba. But Doak called her with a cryptic message: "Don't ask me the reasons why. I'm not going to spell them out loud and clear. But now I can't come to Nova Scotia." Doak's meaning was distressingly obvious to everyone in the Stanfield organization. Though it would be another nine days before Roblin made his announcement, the Stanfield people knew it at that meeting on Tuesday night, July 25. Flora remembers Stanfield's reaction to the news: "Should I withdraw?" The others persuaded him not to.

That meeting established the basic organization of the Stanfield campaign. Camp would direct the campaign, but at Stanfield's insistence he was to remain invisible. He spent the rest of the summer at his cottage, orchestrating the efforts of the others by long-distance telephone. So many calls poured into Robertson's Point that the other subscribers on the party line were driven to near-distraction. Finally, the telephone company ran a four-mile-long private phone line into Camp's cottage; it was said to be the longest private line in the province. Camp remembers the summer of 1967 almost as fondly for his private phone as he does for the election of Stanfield as national leader.

Maurice Flemming was made chairman of the Stanfield campaign, a title that implied more authority and responsibility than it imparted. In fact, Flemming was a figurehead whose chief function was to reassure dubious Tories that Stanfield was not the tool of that nefarious man, Dalton Camp. The Camp people ignored Flemming and circumvented him at will. They all had a good laugh later when a local newspaper in Nova Scotia hailed Flemming as the architect of the Stanfield victory. The organization was split into three parts: a regional organization to canvass for delegate votes around the country; a pre-convention organization responsible for Stanfield's tour in the weeks leading up to Labour Day; and the crucial convention organization that master-minded the Stanfield effort during convention week. To assuage the egos of the two groups working for Stanfield, every committee and sub-committee had co-chairmen, one from the Camp team and the other from Nova Scotia. Flora MacDonald was assigned to do what she had done so successfully at the annual meeting – to build a file of all delegates and code them according to the candidate they were supporting or leaning toward. She had the only complete list in the party. She was also assigned to organize support among the "termites" in the federal caucus while Bob Coates worked on M.P.s who had remained loyal to Diefenbaker in 1966. Pat Nowlan, the young M.P. from Nova Scotia, was shipped out to British Columbia, where he had once practised law, to organize delegate support there. Finlay MacDonald travelled with Stanfield, taking care to duck out of sight when they crossed into Saskatchewan, Diefenbaker's home province. Next to Camp, the key man in the organization was Norm Atkins who ran the convention committee. Seven sub-committees reported to him on details for receptions, demonstrations, advertising, press, communications (the network that linked Stanfield workers), delegate registration, and floor management and scrutineers. It was Atkins' organization that delivered the leadership to Stanfield.

Most, but not all, of the people who had worked for Camp at the 1966 annual meeting joined the Stanfield organization. As Camp puts it, "There had to be a certain amount of breakage." Lowell Murray, the young Cape Bretoner, was already managing Davie Fulton's campaign, and working with him was Joe Clark (an Albertan who became Stanfield's speech-writer after he won the leadership and who was elected to Parliament in 1972). Also working for Fulton was Brian Mulroney, a twenty-eight-year-old Montreal lawyer of Irish descent who had known Stanfield since his days as a campus Conservative at St. Francis Xavier University in Antigonish. All three were bright and progressive and would have been assets to the Stanfield campaign. But, as it turned out later, they proved even more valuable to Stanfield working for Fulton. Another of the Camp group, Michael Meighen, a wealthy young Montrealer and grandson of former Conservative Prime Minister Arthur Meighen, went to Roblin. So, under pressure from the Union Nationale in Quebec, did Heward Grafftey, a brash and peripatetic M.P. from Brome-Missisquoi. Those were the principal defections. Otherwise the Camp machine was intact. In Toronto, men such as Paul Weed, lawyers Roy McMurtry and Donald Guthrie, and businessman Chad Bark went to work for Stanfield. Almost all the Ottawa "termites" joined the cause – M.P.s such as New Brunswick's Gordon Fairweather, Prince Edward Island's David MacDonald and Heath Macquarrie, Ontario's Gordon Aiken, Alfred Hales, and Jean Wadds, and Alberta's Gerald Baldwin and Doug Harkness. From the Senate – Grattan O'Leary, Fred Blois, and John M. Macdonald. All the eight Nova Scotia M.P.s who had battled Camp in 1966 swung behind Stanfield. On July 28, twenty M.P.s announced their support for Stanfield, giving him more caucus support than any other candidate until John Diefenbaker entered the lists. Stanfield had all of the Conservative M.L.A.s in Nova Scotia and most of the ones in the other three Atlantic Provinces.

For all the political experience available to him, however, Stanfield ran a thoroughly inept campaign in the weeks leading up to the convention. It staggered from one small setback to the next. He went into Montreal ill-prepared and performed so badly that his workers reckoned he had thrown away what little support he had in Quebec. Don Guthrie was driving him from Toronto to London for an important press conference, but no one thought to check the fuel gauge. The car ran out of gas, stranding Stanfield on the Macdonald-Cartier Freeway. They took him to Hamilton on a sweltering summer day and dropped him into a hall where the air-conditioning did not work. Half the perspiring delegates walked out before he finished his speech, and those who remained were not much impressed. "I went all the way to Hamilton to see him," groused a delegate from Welland, "and I wouldn't walk across the street to see him again." There was no one to check on such elementary things as hotel accommodations. The Stanfield party arrived late one night at the Constellation Hotel near Toronto-International Airport and found that Bob and Mary Stanfield had been booked into a room not much bigger than a cupboard with just one single bed. Ronald MacDonald, the reporter covering the tour for the Halifax *Chronicle-Herald,* discovered he was in a room with two huge double beds whereas his sister, Flora, slumbered in the hotel bridal suite – in a canopied and curtained heart-shaped bed on a raised dais.

Stanfield had trouble with the press. Accustomed to the gentle gopher balls served up by the docile Nova Scotia media, Stanfield was baffled by the low curves thrown by the national press. For their part, the newsmen found him unbelievably vague. He seemed to have no opinion on any national issue and little perception of what the issues were. It was not until the latter part of August that Stanfield developed a technique for handling loaded questions on complex issues. Borrowing perhaps from the teaching style of his former professor, Russell Maxwell, Stanfield dissected each question, listing all the pros and cons. He generally did not venture an opinion of his own, but he satisfied his interrogators that at least he understood the issue.

Delegates who met him were puzzled by his diffidence and Stanfield sensed their bewilderment. "I wonder why anybody comes to see me at all," he told a group of delegates in Montreal. On another occasion, he walked into a dining-room full of delegates in the Ottawa Valley and assured them he would understand perfectly if they wanted to leave to attend to more pressing matters. He seemed a little surprised when they stayed. But if they expected to hear a stirring message, they were sorely disappointed. Stanfield told them how much good federal Liberal policies had done for Nova Scotia, and he praised Prime Minister Lester Pearson's handling of French President Charles de Gaulle after de Gaulle's "Vive le Québec libre" outburst. "Our campaign left a lot to be desired," admits Finlay MacDonald. "The wheels fell off as we tried to roll."

Though it seemed relatively innocuous at the time, the most important event in the weeks and months prior to the leadership convention was the Conservative "Thinkers' Conference" at the Dominican Maison Montmorency on a cliff overlooking Montmorency Falls in Quebec. All the leadership candidates were invited to attend, as observers rather than participants. The part of the conference that got the most attention at the time was the closing speech made by Dalton Camp. In a reworked version of an address he had made a few months earlier to the Canadian Institute of International Affairs, Camp – though it was heresy for any Conservative to hold such views – called for Canada's defence spending to be rechanneled into foreign aid. While Camp's speech captured the headlines, it was a seemingly routine policy resolution that was destined to cause the party great grief. The "Montmorency Resolution," as it became known, dealt with relations between English and French Canada and contained this key paragraph: "That Canada is and should be a federal state. That Canada is composed of two founding peoples (*deux nations*) with historic rights who have been joined by people from many lands. That the constitution should be such as to permit and encourage their full and harmonious growth and development in equality throughout Canada."

On the face of it, that resolution was a statement of the obvious. It seemed so straightforward that no one, certainly not Bob Stanfield, could object to it. It was the translation of the English "two founding peoples" into the French *deux nations* and its mistranslation back into English as "two nations" that later divided the party. It was the "two nations" issue that John Diefenbaker seized on to justify doing what he planned to do anyway – to stand as a candidate at the leadership convention. It was the "two nations" issue that was exploited by Pierre Trudeau and the Liberals to destroy the Conservatives in the election of 1968.

For the moment, however, the Montmorency Conference was for Stanfield little more than a pleasant August interlude in a period of arduous campaigning. Though Stanfield's organizers knew they had gained little or no ground since he had entered the race, they were not unduly disturbed. They were prepared for Roblin's entry, and by the time the Manitoba premier declared on August 3, Stanfield had locked up his federal caucus support, some of which would otherwise have gone to Roblin. Roblin did not cut significantly into Stanfield's support, but he weakened some of the other candidates. With the active support of some of Premier Daniel Johnson's organizers, Roblin sliced deeply into Davie Fulton's and Donald Fleming's delegate strength in Quebec. He dashed Alvin Hamilton's slender hopes of becoming leader by making it impossible for Hamilton to put together a Prairie coalition.

Compared to Roblin, Stanfield had two great assets. The first was his solid base of delegates from the Atlantic Provinces. The four provinces sent only 452 delegates to Toronto, but 90 per cent of them were committed to Stanfield before they left. They would stay with him until he won or released them to vote for another candidate. On the other hand, Roblin could control only 70 per cent of the Manitoba delegation. Stanfield strategists knew that if their man performed respectably in his public appearances in Toronto he would pick up enough votes from Ontario and British Columbia to give him, when added to the Atlantic block, a lead on the first ballot. His other asset was his second-ballot strength. Stanfield had no enemies in the party. Many delegates were thoroughly *under*whelmed by him, but none had any urgent objection to him. He was honest; he had proved he could win elections; he had been loyal to Diefenbaker, yet he was a progressive in party matters; and he had cared enough to come to all those meetings over the years when the other provincial leaders had not deigned to put in an appearance. The party liked him and respected him. In the backs of their minds, delegates supporting other candidates knew that, if necessary, they could turn to Stanfield on later ballots with confidence that he would not lead the party astray.

Stanfield's liabilities were his weakness on the Prairies and in Quebec. With Hamilton and Roblin (and eventually Diefenbaker) thrashing the Prairie wheatfields for votes, there was nothing left for Stanfield. As far as Quebec was concerned, Stanfield knew he would have to settle for whatever scraps remained when the three French-speaking candidates – Roblin, Fulton, and Fleming – had finished. All Stanfield could do was to plod along, impassively reading his little French speeches, and hope that his obvious goodwill toward French Canada would rub off on a few Quebec delegates. Gerry Doucet, a young Acadian whom Stanfield had appointed to the

Cabinet in Nova Scotia, made the pitch much better than Stanfield ever did when he told an audience in Chicoutimi how he felt about his boss, M'sieu Stanfield. "I think," said Doucet, "it is more important to understand the aims of French Canada than it is to speak the language." Stanfield displayed his sympathy for Quebec's situation in a ghosted article that appeared under his name in the Montreal daily, *Le Devoir,* in August: "Quebeckers feel that, in order to achieve their aims and ambitions, they must be given more authority over economic and social affairs in their province. I don't think any solutions that we will find for the problems of our federation will be able to ignore this feeling in Quebec." Though *Le Devoir* approved of Stanfield's common sense, only a relative handful of the province's delegates to the leadership convention were sufficiently impressed to make Stanfield their first choice. It is doubtful whether Stanfield got even twenty votes from French-speaking Quebec delegates on the first ballot. Duff Roblin did his best to exploit Stanfield's weaknesses. His workers asked delegates to consider one question: if it came down to a choice between Roblin and Stanfield, could Stanfield in an election hold the old Diefenbaker vote in the West and win Quebec? It was a valid question and sound strategy on Roblin's part. Had the Manitoba premier entered the race sooner, he might have pulled it off.

The great leadership convention opened in Toronto on the day after Labour Day, 1967, starting first at the Royal York Hotel and moving later to Maple Leaf Gardens. After consulting their accustomed muses, the pundits concluded that Stanfield stood no better than fourth among the contenders – behind Hees, Fulton, and Roblin and ahead of Fleming, Hamilton, McCutcheon, Starr, and John Maclean (a Hertz agent from Brockville, Ontario, who vanished from the national political scene as quickly as he had appeared). John Diefenbaker had yet to be heard from, but only the blindest of the Diefenbaker fanatics seriously thought the old Chief could challenge the front four. There was an eleventh candidate, Mary Walker Sawka, a Toronto grandmother who materialized during the convention and de-materialized on the first ballot.

Bob Stanfield had spent the three nights prior to the opening of the convention at Don Guthrie's farm near Barrie in central Ontario. He had travelled 27,000 miles since July 19; he needed a rest and time to go over the final plans for the convention. On Monday, Labour Day morning, he and Dalton Camp sat for three hours on the lawn of the farm, talking about the convention and what Stanfield should say in his speech to the party's policy committee on Tuesday night. At noon, Norm Atkins drove Camp and Bob and Mary Stanfield to Toronto, stopping at a restaurant en route to telephone ahead to have the band warmed up for Stanfield's arrival at the Royal York Hotel. They dropped Camp off at the Westbury Hotel where he went to work on the text of Stanfield's speech. As an afterthought, Atkins asked the Stanfields if they would like to take a look at Maple Leaf Gardens. The arena, home of the Toronto Maple Leafs hockey team, was like a vast deserted barn that holiday afternoon, and Bob Stanfield felt very small as he looked around and studied the huge portraits of Conservative prime ministers that workmen had hung behind the specially-constructed podium. He gulped, then laughed – nervously.

The Conservative leadership convention was an extravaganza that deserved all the superlatives heaped on it. For the first time, a Canadian political party had set out to emulate in scale and style an American presidential nominating convention. It had marching bands and balloons and pretty girls by the hundreds, floor demonstrations, and lavish cocktail parties for thousands. It was a great show and it made great television. More than that, it had great drama. Would John Diefenbaker attempt one last stand? Or would he accept the inevitable and quietly receive the honours due to him, allowing the party to choose his successor? Could the Conservatives find any man with the patience, understanding, and tact needed to reverse the centrifugal forces that seemed determined to tear the party to pieces? Partly because it was the first convention of its kind and partly because of the Diefenbaker drama, the Conservative convention occupies a special place in the memories of the people who were there. It had an excitement that not even the Liberals could match seven months later when they met to elect Pierre Elliott Trudeau, the most intriguing political figure of the age. The Tory convention is the yardstick by which all other leadership conventions must be measured.

The turning point in the Stanfield campaign came early in the convention. It came, in fact, on the very first night, Tuesday, when 700 (of an eventual 2,256) delegates gathered at the Royal York to hear the leadership candidates address the policy committee. That speech turned Stanfield, everyone's number four candidate, into the front-runner. It was an excellent speech, and it appeared even better than it was because of the inadequacy of his opponents' speeches. Duff Roblin, wrongly advised by his staff that he was expected merely to say a few general words and then answer questions, arrived unprepared. He scratched a few notes as the others spoke; when his turn came his delivery was uncertain and his message unclear. Davie Fulton tried hard: his speech was intelligent but dull. George Hees, speaking on foreign trade, sounded like a coach giving his team a locker-room pep talk between periods of a college football game. Though he had been an able minister of trade and commerce in the Diefenbaker government, Hees was unable in that speech to dispel the image that the delegates had of him as an intellectual featherweight.

If anyone had asked delegates a week later what Stanfield had said on that Tuesday night, no one would have remembered. Stanfield said nothing he had not said a dozen times before, but his speech sounded fresh. It was thoughtful, almost eloquent in two or three places, and mercifully brief. He spoke with feeling of the need to improve the quality of Canadian life. "I do not believe it is our purpose to set back the clock or to stop the clock," he said. "It is our purpose, in my opinion, to hasten the day when more and more of our fellow citizens may enjoy a more satisfactory personal sense of participation in the economic growth and development of this country, in the social, cultural, and political processes of our country, and can give fuller expression to their own distinctive and unique personality. . . . There are values in being a Canadian citizen beyond those reflected in the gross national product." Though it may have rattled the crystal in the august Albany Club, Stanfield dispelled any notion that he was the usual watch-chain and waistcoat caricature of a Conservative. "The Progressive Conservative," he told the delegates, "accepts the role of government in economic development. He also accepts, in my opinion, the fact that there are no nice ideological solutions to economic problems, nor is there any original sin in economic planning."

So effective was Stanfield's speech that John Bassett, the Conservative publisher of the Conservative Toronto *Telegram,* left the meeting, dumped his initial choice for leader, his old friend George Hees, and pronounced his editorial benediction over Robert Stanfield. The *Telegram* could not be considered to be one of the important voices in moulding public opinion in Canada; it was too trite and flashy for that. But it was a Tory paper, and the delegates to the Conservative convention naturally read it, possibly more than they read any other newspaper. That editorial blessing plus a *Telegram* poll of delegates that showed a sudden upsurge in support for Stanfield gave the Stanfield campaign a new momentum. (The poll, however, was more a tool of the Stanfield campaign strategy than an accurate measurement of its effectiveness. By the simple expedient of getting all their committed Maritime delegates into Toronto at the beginning of convention week, the Stanfield organizers created an illusion of greater strength than they really had. Any newly-arrived delegate, newspaperman or pollster walking into the lobby of the Royal York Hotel found himself wading through a forest of Stanfield placards. Almost everyone he spoke to seemed to be supporting Stanfield. One wondered at times whether the Stanfield delegates were ever allowed to eat or to go to bed, or whether they were consigned to spending twenty-four hours a day on prominent display in the lobby. It was an old military trick and it worked nicely for Stanfield.)

Of less influence but greater significance than the endorsation of the Toronto *Telegram* was the assessment of Stanfield's policy speech by Claude Ryan, the editor of *Le Devoir.* "The simple, spare, and effective style of the man," wrote Ryan, "appears to us to correspond to an indistinct but real expectation of the Canadian people. The election of Mr. Stanfield would be the logical continuation of the spirit of renovation."

From Wednesday through the balloting on Saturday, the problem for the Stanfield organization was a new but pleasant one – to maintain their momentum. Stanfield advanced that cause on Wednesday when he threw a reception and luncheon for the press. The reporters who attended discovered that Stanfield might have a dry manner but he was not dull. He entertained them with a sparkling little speech written by Camp and himself in which he announced his intention to establish a new bureaucracy, to be known as the Canadian News Relations department. "This department," he said, in apparent seriousness, "will be dedicated to the principle that no news is good news, and that suppression is the better part of valour. This new C.N.R. will insure that no news will henceforth ever lack good news management." Unaccustomed to hearing levity from lips of Robert Stanfield, some newsmen did not recognize it for what it was; they took feverish notes. Finlay MacDonald watched in amusement as one of the reporters scribbled frantically. "Then he realized it was a joke and said 'Oh, shit' and went over to the bar for another drink," laughs MacDonald. That night, Stanfield took over the Canadian Room of the Royal York, hired the late Don Messer and his Islanders and served free drinks to two thousand delegates and hangers-on until 1:00 a.m. It was the biggest and wildest party of the week.

Stanfield proved to be a model candidate, following the instructions of his organizers to the letter and stoically accepting the hoopla and carefully-planned "spontaneous" demonstrations that went into convention week. Blue-jacketed Stanfield demonstrators turned up at intervals at all the major hotels where delegates were staying to march and chant and wave their diamond-shaped Stanfield placards. One side of the sign, in white letters on a blue background, read "Stanfield." The other, in white letters on red, bore the Stanfield slogan: "The Man With The Winning Way." That was also the title of the Stanfield song that assaulted the eardrums of delegates all week long. To the tune of *This Land Is Your Land,* it went like this:

Sing out for Stanfield, for Robert Stanfield,
The Nova Scotian with the winning way,
Come on, let's hear it, get in the spirit,
Stanfield's the man to lead the way.
This man is your man, this man is our man,

For party leader he's A-O-K!
There's nothing to it, come on, let's do it,
For Stanfield, the man with the winning way.

Finlay MacDonald remembers the meticulous timing that went with the supposedly impromptu exhibitions of enthusiasm for Stanfield. He watched at the Westbury Hotel as Stanfield prepared to walk down the street to Maple Leaf Gardens. Inside the hotel lobby, a man with a walkie-talkie tracked Stanfield's progress as he stepped from an elevator and moved toward the doors. On cue, an honour guard of Stanfield girls started a cheer. On a second cue, they stopped. A third cue flashed to the director of the Stanfield band, hidden just out of sight. "Out come the majorettes and the band," says MacDonald. "Stanfield looks like he's going to his funeral with all the trappings. That's what he looked like – horribly uncomfortable and completely unaware of where in God's name all this had come from. He just looked around, unbelieving." Only once in the whole week did Stanfield refuse to cooperate with his exhuberant workers. For some reason he agreed to preside at the official opening of a restaurant in the Toronto-Dominion Centre. Told that after the ceremony he was expected to march back to the Royal York behind his band, he refused. "That's all fine," he said, "but I don't want to go down Yonge Street with a band."

On Friday morning John Diefenbaker entered the race to save the party from the "two nations" heresy; that evening all the nominated candidates addressed the full convention. Although Duff Roblin chose to tackle the "two nations" dispute head on (and got high marks for his courage), Stanfield avoided it. He carefully refrained from saying anything that would add fuel to the fires of dissension already blazing in the party. His speech had the same ring as Camp's Junior Board of Trade speech a year earlier. Stanfield gave his subject a reverse twist, telling the delegates that it was customary for a leadership candidate on such an occasion to tell the party what kind of a leader he would be. But Stanfield proposed to tell them what kind of a party he wanted to lead. It was a party, he said, "that will be recognized not merely for its affluence, for its comfort, for its power – but for its humanity, for its compassion, and for its decency."

Stanfield was not surprised by Diefenbaker's decision to run, and the old Chief's candidacy hurt Stanfield less than it did other candidates who were counting on the votes of Diefenbaker's admirers, particularly in Western Canada. Dalton Camp disputes the conventional wisdom that Diefenbaker's entry damaged the party by exacerbating its divisions. "It was good for the party, for Stanfield, that Diefenbaker ran," says Camp. "If he hadn't run, the new leader would have suffered from the hypothesis that he was still wanting in proof, that he couldn't have beaten Diefenbaker. Other than that, Dief was irrelevant, except for the media. He was big for the media."

As expected, Stanfield led on the first ballot on Saturday afternoon, though his 519 votes (23 per cent of the ballots cast) were far short of the 700 he had anticipated. But Duff Roblin, too, was weaker than expected; Diefenbaker's entry had denied Roblin vital Prairie votes and his first-ballot total stood at only 347. That was just four more than Davie Fulton received. George Hees, in decline all week, managed to salvage only 295 votes, leaving him a weak fourth. Another mild surprise was Diefenbaker's poor showing. The man who had led the party for nearly eleven years and had served three terms as prime minister could muster but 271 votes. Only one Conservative in eight was still prepared to "Follow John." The rest of the field trailed, out of contention: McCutcheon 137; Hamilton 136; Fleming 126; Starr 45; John Maclean 10; Mary Walker Sawka 2. As low candidate, Mrs. Sawka dropped automatically from contention, and Maclean withdrew.

The second ballot told the story of the convention. Diefenbaker lost 99 votes – down to 172 – as even his faithful followers realized the cause was doomed. McCutcheon, Hamilton, Fleming, and Starr all lost votes. Fulton and Hees stayed almost stationary, Fulton picking up 3 votes and Hees 4. But Stanfield climbed by 94 votes to 613 and Roblin gained 83 to 430. The race was between Stanfield and Roblin. The others were still alive, but they had no chance; the best they could hope for was to play kingmaker.

Stanfield was the picture of unconcern as the afternoon wore on and turned to evening. He sat with his wife and children in the box of seats assigned to them near the floor of the Gardens. Mostly, he ate. Every time the television cameras panned to the Stanfield box, the candidate had something in his mouth – once a banana, the next time a hamburger or grapes or a glass of noxious-looking orange soda pop. While he ate, the organization masterminded by Norman Atkins moved into high gear. It was by far the most sophisticated organization at the Gardens. Two spotters with binoculars – one high above the floor in the broadcasting gondola and the other in the section of the stands reserved for the press – kept track of the whereabouts not only of the Stanfield personnel but of the major workers for the other candidates as well. If, for example, a Roblin worker headed in the direction of the Hees delegates, a spotter passed the word to the Stanfield troops on the floor in time to head him off. The spotters were linked by direct telephone lines to eight Stanfield floor managers with headsets who were posted at four strategic locations on the floor. There was a Stanfield poll captain for each of the twenty voting machines; each wore a black top hat with the number of his machine chalked on it for instant identification. The information flowing over the phone lines was monitored by Flora MacDonald and relayed as necessary by hotline to Stanfield campaign headquarters in the Westbury Hotel. Camp, meanwhile, had installed himself comfortably in front of a television set in the directors' lounge at the Gardens, to follow the action, assess trends and, as required, order negotiations with other candidates.

The third ballot established the importance of a good organization. Stanfield picked up 104 votes to give him 717, but Roblin began to narrow the gap, adding 111 votes for a total of 541. The Stanfield workers started to worry. They knew several things. They knew that Diefenbaker's and Fleming's votes would eventually go to Roblin. They knew George Hees would come personally to Stanfield, but that he would not be able to deliver his delegates. It would be up to the Stanfield agents to move swiftly to sweep up the strays. They knew Fulton would support Stanfield rather than Roblin. Earlier in the week, Finlay MacDonald and a dozen other Stanfield people had unilaterally advised Fulton that if Stanfield were knocked out of contention and if Fulton were still in the running they would switch to Fulton. They did not pretend to speak for the entire Stanfield organization; many of the M.P.s backing Stanfield would have gone to Roblin rather than Fulton. No deal was made and no return commitment was sought from Fulton. MacDonald was confident that Stanfield would run well ahead of Fulton, but, by making a no-strings offer, he helped to ensure that when the crucial moment came, Fulton would support Stanfield. MacDonald also knew that most Fulton delegates could also be swung to Stanfield because Fulton's key organizers, Lowell Murray and Brian Mulroney, had both worked in earlier years for Stanfield's Conservatives in Nova Scotia; both knew Stanfield and respected him. "Lowell Murray and Brian Mulroney were our sort of group," says MacDonald. "They're our kind of guys. They're progressives."

The full third-ballot results showed Stanfield still leading with 717, followed by Roblin with 541, Fulton 361, Hees 277, Diefenbaker down still further to 114, Hamilton 106, and Fleming 76. Fleming was eliminated and threw his support to Roblin, to no one's surprise. Diefenbaker had already walked out of the convention, sending his national director, Jim Johnston, back with his withdrawal slip. Some of Diefenbaker's votes went to Hamilton, but Roblin got most of them on the next ballot. Hees withdrew and endorsed Stanfield. That left four candidates in the running on the fourth ballot: Stanfield, Roblin, Fulton, and Hamilton. Although Davie Fulton would emerge as the kingmaker, it was to be Alvin Hamilton who would derail Duff Roblin. Stanfield was lucky. Months earlier, long before Roblin became a candidate, Hamilton had wooed the Manitoba premier and had been encouraged to feel that Roblin was favourably disposed toward his candidacy. Later, Hamilton was offended when Roblin rejected his suit. When Roblin finally entered the race himself, he dealt Hamilton's chances a mortal blow. Alvin Hamilton had not forgotten.

The fourth ballot showed Roblin suddenly breathing down Stanfield's neck. Stanfield still led with 865 votes (up 148 from the previous ballot), but Roblin had shot to within easy catching distance with 771 votes (up 230). Fulton dropped 4 votes to 357, and Hamilton picked up 61 to 167. But as low man, Hamilton was automatically eliminated.

Stanfield was still 216 votes short of a majority. Roblin was only 94 votes behind him and closing fast. The odds were against Roblin, but he still had a clear shot at the leadership, if two things happened. First, Davie Fulton, who had held his delegates amazingly well all afternoon and evening, either had to endorse Roblin or stay in the contest for one more ballot. Second, assuming Fulton stayed in, Roblin needed the support of Alvin Hamilton in order to pick up enough Hamilton votes to move ahead of Stanfield. If Roblin could move into the lead on the fifth ballot, he would have a better than ever chance of winning on a sixth ballot. But neither Fulton nor Hamilton would play Roblin's game. Hamilton retreated with his supporters to his room under the stands where they debated the merits of Stanfield and Roblin. As a fellow Westerner, Roblin would have been the natural choice for Hamilton, but Hamilton was still smarting from the way Roblin had refused to support him earlier. He emerged from the room, pipe clenched tightly between his teeth, refusing to indicate any preference whatsoever.

Meanwhile, Fulton was making his most difficult decision. After four long ballots he had only 14 more votes than he had had at the start. He could stay in for one more ballot, but he could not win. And he knew it. He yielded to the urgings of Murray, Mulroney, and others among his organizers who advised him to get out while he still had the power to swing the convention to Stanfield. Fulton went in front of the television cameras to announce his withdrawal. He was freeing his delegates to vote as they chose, but he intended to vote for Robert Stanfield.

That was exactly what the Stanfield organization wanted, but they faced a major problem. The delegates were not watching television and they had less idea of what was going on behind the scenes than the armchair politician watching the convention in the comfort of his living room. Somehow there had to be a signal to the delegates in the Gardens that Fulton was backing Stanfield. But Fulton was a proud man. He had wanted desperately to be leader and had failed twice to make it. His pride would not permit him to make the customary gesture of joining Stanfield in Stanfield's box.

The Fulton organization flashed the word to the Stanfield organization. In the most dramatic gesture of the day, Stanfield walked to Fulton's box and shook his hand. The Fulton and Stanfield organizations joined forces to round up Fulton's delegates before voting started on the fifth ballot. After that, the fifth ballot was almost an anti-climax. Stanfield won going away with 1,150 votes to Roblin's 969. With Maple Leaf Gardens in pandemonium, Lowell Murray and Flora MacDonald embraced in the middle of the floor. It seemed both natural and appropriate.

It had taken seven frantic hours of balloting, but at 10:24 p.m. on Saturday, September 9, 1967, Robert Lorne Stanfield was declared the new leader of the Progressive Conservative Party of Canada. As he looked down from the podium, all he could see bathed in the television lights was a sea of wildly excited faces disappearing under hundreds of blue and white balloons drifting down from the rafters. He was not deceived by the euphoria of the crowd. He knew the party had been through a civil war and that its survival was not yet assured. He was well aware that the process of reconciliation was beginning, not ending. He took his first tentative step toward reconciliation in his brief acceptance speech. Turning to Diefenbaker, who had returned to the Gardens, Stanfield said: "I appreciate very much the size of the shoes I am now to try to fill." Then, for the benefit of the reformers in the party, he added: "Personally, I'm determined to get along with that fellow Camp."

It was not a night to say much more than that. Even so, it was a very small step on a very long road to unity in the party – a road that would have to pass through two general elections before it ended. Had Bob Stanfield known on that warm September night in 1967 how long and arduous the journey would be, he might have abdicated on the spot.

10

Just a Dull, Dour Man?

I don't regard myself as well-known across the country, certainly not a household word.

         – Robert L. Stanfield,
         Halifax, July, 1967

I think there are a good many Canadians who don't pay too much attention to politicians except perhaps at election time to whom I'm still somewhat obscure, probably.

         – Robert L. Stanfield,
         Ottawa, August, 1972

It was mid-1971 and the Leader of Her Majesty's Loyal Opposition was making another of his incessant political pilgrimmages to British Columbia, flying this time in a small single-engined plane. Suddenly, the motor stalled and, as the plane fell earthward, the Leader's senior assistant, Tom Sloan, screwed his eyes tightly closed and entertained a fleeting wish that he had a God with whom he could make his peace. The Leader was vexed – though for quite a different reason. Glancing out the window at the ground rushing up to meet him, he commented in a stern and disapproving voice: "This is going to play hell with my schedule." An instant later, the confused pilot located the reserve-fuel switch and the motor coughed back to life, thereby saving the Leader's schedule, among other things.

That anecdote tells more than a dozen television interviews could ever hope to tell about Robert Stanfield, the man nobody really knows. In popular opinion, he is – as Dalton Camp observed him to be at their first meeting in 1953 – a dull, dour man. As the public sees him, he is about as lively as a grave-digger on the night shift and about as entertaining as a hangover on a Monday morning. He is a cardboard figure without a soul or, if indeed he has a soul, he harbours therein no joy and no poetry. He is, as popular opinion would have it, a nineteenth-century politician who had the ill-luck to be born in the twentieth.

But possibly there is another Robert Stanfield. Perhaps there is a Stanfield who is warm, and human, and even witty – in an understated, self-deprecating sort of way. Assuming there is such a Stanfield, he would be a man who regards his job with the seriousness it warrants without, refreshingly, taking himself seriously at all. He would be a man who would sooner laugh at himself than at others. He would be the Robert Stanfield who, during the bad old days when Pierre Trudeau was waltzing with Barbra Streisand, was told it would be good for his image if he, too, were seen with a movie star – to which he replied, drily: "Would you believe, with Gloria Swanson?" He would be the Stanfield who made a guest appearance at the NDP Christmas Party in 1971, roaring on the stage as a knight in shining armour to rescue the fair Guenevere from a fate worse than death, and uttering these immortal lines: "I represent help for the helpless, hope for the hopeless, and bras for the bra-less." There must be more than one Stanfield. How else can one acknowledge the validity of popular opinion and still explain the Stanfield who year after year outsparkles the Great Communicator, Pierre Trudeau, at the annual Parliamentary Press Gallery Dinner? Or, as Stanfield himself explained the phenomenon at the 1971 dinner: "Tonight is . . . a time for a summing up of my four years as Leader of the Opposition – years of remarkable development for me. Four years ago, I was certainly not a national sex symbol, and as some of you may remember, I was not *always* the witty and spontaneous master of repartee that my aides and other paid advisers now assure me that I am today. I have become eloquent in French and fluent in English."

The Conservatives who elected him as their national leader in 1967 could not be faulted for not knowing there was a private Stanfield. They barely knew the public Stanfield who stood on the high podium above their heads at Maple Leaf Gardens accepting the mantle they had given him. Oh, they knew a little about him. They knew his family made long underwear and that he had quite a lot of money. They knew he had a lively and friendly wife who, if ability to meet people easily is the hallmark of a politician, was a better politician than her husband. They knew he spoke better French than John Diefenbaker (who didn't?), but that he was far from bilingual in an age when people were saying there would never be another unilingual prime minister of Canada. They were dimly aware that he was something of a progressive as politicians go; at least, he sounded as though he meant it when he talked about the quality of life and that sort of thing.

The Conservatives had, however, no clear perception of why Stanfield had decided to seek the leadership, nor what he intended to do with it when he got it. Stanfield himself was far from certain of his own motives. "I had a feeling," he says, "that I was taking myself rather too seriously in weighing the pros and cons and the change it would make in my life if I had the leadership. It was a feeling that I had been taking myself too seriously and that I should let her go and let nature take her course. I used to jokingly say that it was my contribution to the Centennial year, but in a sense it was true, as I understood what was going on inside me. I had some concerns about the party and the country, from the point of national unity and some of the economic directions of the [federal] government, and I decided in the end to let the party decide whether it wanted me."

Given that less-than-clarion call, the next few years were destined to be years of discovery both for Stanfield and for the party he led. It took a long time, but as the Conservatives came to know him better, they found they liked him more and more. They discovered that he was not the cold, aloof man they thought he was. He was quiet, direct, unassuming, and unpretentious to a fault. They found him to be a man who just naturally holds doors open for others to pass through, who helps them on with their coats, and who, if he is arriving by plane, much prefers the airport bus to a limousine. He was a man, they discovered, who guarded his time, yet was accessible, who could listen to the prattle of fools without betraying the pain or boredom he felt inside. He was a contemporary politician, yet a gentleman of the old school. That was a rare combination.

But the Tories never reached the point where they felt they really knew him. Few outside his family do. Though he has become less reserved in recent years, there remains that inner core of personal privacy that no outsider can fully penetrate. Finlay MacDonald, who knows him better than almost anyone else in Ottawa, has the sort of relaxed relationship with his leader that entitles him to walk into the Stanfield home without knocking, to fix himself a cup of coffee in the kitchen, and to join the family at the breakfast table. But not even MacDonald can explain adequately what makes Stanfield tick.

The best place to look for clues is at "Stornoway," the official residence of the leader of the opposition at 541 Acacia Avenue in Rockcliffe Park. A big stone house set back on a handsomely treed lot, "Stornoway" can almost be described as a mansion, though it is not as ostentatious as some of its neighbours. Owned by the government, it is an old place. It was left vacant for a period between the time the Diefenbakers moved out and the Stanfields moved up from Halifax. Someone forgot to keep the furnace going and the pipes burst, causing extensive damage to the interior. The whole house had to be redecorated; the decorating reflects the Stanfield taste – conventional, with the emphasis on comfort rather than appearance. The walls, carpets, and furniture are in light colours, giving the house a sense of brightness and air. "Stornoway" has a lived-in feel. The painting over the fireplace is by an English Victorian artist, W. Clarkson Stanfield. A relative? "Bob claims him as a relative," laughs Mary Stanfield, sneaking a cigarette in her husband's absence, "but he doesn't really think he was. Mr. Stanfield [Bob's father] picked it up in London and . . . his mother left it to Bob because he always wanted it."

Mary Stanfield is very much the mistress of "Stornoway," and everyone, including her husband, does her bidding. Brian Mulroney, the lawyer-organizer from Montreal, was at "Stornoway" one Sunday morning early in the 1972 election campaign as a camera crew was shooting film for the Party's television commercials. The producer decided to move everyone to Parliament Hill to get some footage of Stanfield with the Parliament Buildings in the background. As they prepared to leave, Mary's voice came down the stairs: "Bob, don't forget to put the plant out before you go." Everyone in the room leaped in the direction of the large potted plant, but Stanfield stopped them and picked it up himself. "Mary wanted *him* to take the plant out and he was going to do it," says Mulroney.

There is a rare, gentle quality in Stanfield's voice when he talks about Joyce, his first wife. She was his first love, and he has never entirely gotten over the tragedy of her death. His relationship with Mary is special in a quite different way. She is everything he is not – vivacious, quick in her movements, alert to the emotions of others, and she has a mischievious sense of humour. Stanfield is proud of her and she amuses him immensely.

Bob and Mary Stanfield cannot agree on when they first met. Bob recalls meeting Mary Hall about 1930 at the closing ceremonies at Edgehill, a private girl's school in Windsor, Nova Scotia. Mary's older sister and Bob's sister, Kit, had been classmates at Edgehill, and Bob remembers being introduced to Mary and her sister that day. Mary concedes he could be right, but she is dubious.

The Halls and the Stanfields had known each other for years. Both families were in politics and both were Conservative. Mary's father, Laurie Hall, and Bob's father, Frank, Sr., had served together in the Legislature, and Hall was the Conservative house leader for five years. After World War I, Hall took in as his law partner a young veteran, Russell MacInnes, who had been a prisoner of war. After World War II, with Laurie Hall gone to the Supreme Court of Nova Scotia, MacInnes took as his new partner a young lawyer named Bob Stanfield. Stanfield had occasion to plead just one case before Mr. Justice Hall, but the judge was impressed and told his daughter that young Stanfield was a promising lad. So, Mary Hall had always been more or less aware of Bob Stanfield's existence, but he did not impress her much. He was too awkward and unfriendly. She remembers him sitting one time in the library of her father's house. "I was waiting for him to leave," she says with a laugh.

Mary Hall was one of Joyce Stanfield's closest friends and she got to know Bob fairly well, on a casual basis, when she dropped by to visit Joyce. One evening Mary and Joyce went to a concert in Halifax given by a German-born singer from South America. Chatting happily about the singer's magnificent voice, they arrived back at "The Oaks" and Joyce invited Mary to come in. Mary thought her friend wanted a little moral support because she knew that George Drew, then the national Conservative leader, was talking to Bob. "Anyway, we went in," says Mary, "and said 'What a wonderful concert,' and George Drew took the wind right out of our sails by saying: 'You should have heard her in her prime.' "

Mary Hall was godmother to Mimi Stanfield, the youngest of Bob's and Joyce's four children, and after Joyce was killed in 1954, Mary used to help the Stanfield nurse to look after the children. On occasion, Mary sat with the youngsters when Bob had to go out of town on the nurse's night off. "Mimi was my godchild, but Judy was very close to me and she was the one who needed me at the time," Mary remembers. "Mimi wasn't a year old when her mother died, but Judy, who is two years older, was going through a clinging stage with her mother, a shy stage. It was a very bad time for her." The other two children, Sarah and Max, were older and were a little less deeply affected by their mother's death.

A year or so after Joyce's death, Bob started to feel like going out again and he occasionally took Mary Hall to dinner or a show. He also dated a few younger girls, girls in their mid-twenties. "I was then about forty," says Stanfield, "and I found them relatively young as far as I was concerned." The Tories who worked with Stanfield suspected something was afoot between Bob and Mr. Justice Hall's daughter. Some of them used to drive past the Stanfield and Hall homes, checking to see whose car was parked in whose driveway. "There was a certain amount of gossip in a place the size of Halifax," says Stanfield. "They're always busy marrying everybody else off. Perhaps it had gone on for a sufficient length of time that people had decided nothing was going to happen."

It was in the summer of 1956 that Bob and Mary decided to marry, but they kept their decision a secret from everyone. There never seemed to be time to get married. The Liberal government called a provincial election in the fall, the Conservatives won and Bob became Premier. Mary Hall joined members of the Stanfield family to see him sworn in as premier in November and that should have tipped off the gossips in Halifax. In the next few months, Stanfield was pre-occupied with setting up his government and preparing to meet the Legislature in late February. It was not until the spring of 1957 that he again had time to think about getting married.

Mary viewed with some trepidation the question of telling the children of their plans. Bob was off on a political trip and left that chore to her. The eldest of the four children, Sarah, was home in Halifax on vacation from Havergal College, a private school in Toronto; Mary drove her out to the airport and broke the news. Sarah replied that there were two things that bothered her. "I thought 'Oh goodness, these are going to be big hurdles,' " Mary recalls. "You don't like convertibles," said Sarah, "and my family all loves a convertible." "That's easy," Mary told her, "we can always have two cars. You can drive the convertible and I won't have to." The other thing that troubled Sarah was what she should call Mary after the wedding. She did not feel she could call her "Mother," Mary told her she did not expect her to.

Another problem was the wedding ring. Mary told Bob she wanted to have a wide band. Bob, knowing they could scarcely keep their plans secret if he were seen picking over wedding rings in a jewelry store, sent his administrative assistant, Innis MacLeod, out to make a selection. Bob arrived at Mary's with a whole tray of wedding rings, all of them narrow bands. Mary rejected all of them. Bob came back with another tray; again all were narrow rings. "After two trips, he was annoyed and I was annoyed," says Mary. "And I said 'What's the cheapest one on the tray?' It was eight dollars. I said I'll take that one because I hate them all.' Then I said to my sister, 'I don't think I am going to marry him if he can't even buy me a wedding ring I want. Of course, he hadn't been passing the message on to Innis."

On the morning of May 10, 1957, Premier Stanfield met a delegation of coal miners in his office and discussed with them the possibility of going up to Westville to open a new mine. Then he slipped home, packed his suitcase, and went to Mary Hall's home to get married. Even the members of his cabinet were taken unawares. There were only two guests at the ceremony – Bill Jost, the man who had hired Stanfield for the Wartime Prices and Trade Board, and his wife. The Josts were both Liberals and *that* caused a few raised eyebrows around Halifax. "I've always said the only people at our wedding were a couple of Liberals," says Mary with a laugh. "The old-fashioned kind of politician doesn't understand Liberals and Conservatives being friends."

After the ceremony, they drove to Halifax Airport to catch a plane for Boston en route to a honeymoon in Bermuda. By sheer coincidence, they found themselves on the same plane as Stanfield's maiden aunt, Eleanor (Nell) Stanfield, going for her annual checkup at the Lahey Clinic in Boston. By the time the plane reached Boston, the press had gotten wind of what had happened and there were photographers at the airport to meet Stanfield and his bride. But the Boston press had no idea what the Premier of Nova Scotia looked like, and they snapped away at every tall man and short woman coming off the plane. The photographers were amused when they learned the fellow they wanted was the serious-looking chap who seemed bent on going on his honeymoon with his bride and his spinster aunt.

Back at "The Oaks" after the honeymoon, the Stanfield household settled into a new routine. Mary Stanfield did her inept best to lose the narrow wedding band she despised, on the theory that if she lost it she could, with a clear conscience, buy one she liked. "I used to leave it lying around in the first year and everytime it dropped off a table someone kept finding it and putting it back," says Mary. "It's been a family joke ever since. I'm still wearing the thing."

Every morning, Bob Stanfield walked Judy and Mimi to school, pausing long enough to kiss them goodbye, then continuing on downtown to his office. One spring, Mimi came to Mary to ask: "When I am in Grade IV could you think of a way that I could ask Daddy not to kiss me goodbye." "Why?" wondered Mary. "The kids tease me," Mimi confessed. "Even the teacher said something today: 'Well, did you leave your boyfriend well this morning?' I don't want to hurt Daddy's feelings and it's just automatic, but all my friends laugh. When I am in the next grade, it really has to stop." The next September, Mary told Bob to walk the girls to school but to stop kissing them. "I didn't realize I did," he replied. "It was just part of the ritual."

The four children are very different. All have independent minds, and Bob and Mary let them choose their schools and pursue their own interests. Sarah, who became a librarian, finished Havergal and went to Dalhousie for her B.A. before entering the School of Library Science at the University of Toronto. As a young girl, she made a pact with a Halifax friend that neither would marry until she was twenty-five. Neither did. Sarah was twenty-six when, a month after the disastrous (for the Tories) federal election of 1968, she married Edo Nyland, a Dutch-born physicist, in a small ceremony in the chapel at Ashbury College, her father's old school. ("A big wedding on Saturday?" a friend asked the bride's father. "No," he replied firmly, "a small wedding on Friday.") Sarah and her husband settled in Edmonton where they have one child, Benjamin, who is Stanfield's only grandchild.

Max (for Maxwell, after his father's former professor) had what Mary Stanfield calls "a very chequered academic career." He spent two disastrous years at Trinity College School, a private school in Port Hope, Ontario. He hated his first year, but went back for a second. When Mary later asked him why he had gone back, he said: "I thought it would be a waste of Daddy's money to just go one year and that I should try it for two." Mary was not amused: "Max, you've just wasted two years." Max returned to Halifax to complete high school, then went to Dalhousie to earn his B.A. After graduating, he started on a master's course, but interrupted it to go to Europe where, among other things, he spent several months at the University of Grenoble, emerging fluent in French. He returned to Dalhousie to resume work on his M.A. in Economics. Max and Sarah travelled with Bob and Mary in the 1968 election campaign, with Max attracting considerable attention from the pretty girls who are trotted out at political meetings to cheer the touring leaders. By the time the 1972 campaign rolled around, Sarah was in Edmonton, Max was locked up with his books at Dalhousie, and it was their little sisters' turn.

Judy – who is sometimes described as the far-out Stanfield – attended Mary's old school, Edgehill, in Nova Scotia, then went to Queen's University in Kingston from which she graduated in 1972 with a degree in Physiotherapy. She once told an interviewer how she used to bring home boys who tried to get her father to argue politics. "He resents it when someone tries to talk politics with him," she said. " . . . Boys around twenty or twenty-one think they know everything about politics. He gets quite annoyed." After finishing her course in Physiotherapy, Judy decided to take a year off to think, to meditate, and to find herself before doing the required internship. "She's studied hard all her life," says Mary Stanfield. "She is our best student and she says she's never had time to read. She is doing some pottery, reading, searching, and she is young enough to do this." Mary wanted her to spend the year travelling, but Judy preferred to stay in Kingston. "She didn't feel there was any point in just travelling," says Mary, "She had no goal. She has to find out more, to learn, to read. . . . But I hope she'll go back and do the internship." Joining her father and Mary for the last half of the 1972 campaign, Judy looked as though she would prefer to be anywhere in the country rather than on a political platform.

The youngest Stanfield, Mimi (for Miriam), is all gentle curves with the sort of buxom figure that makes it hard for male photographers to keep her father in focus. She is the sexy Stanfield, but she is also very much Daddy's girl, sharing his love for Jane Austen and other gentle authors. A quiet girl with a pliant personality, she is the dreamer of the family. After elementary school in Halifax, she went to Elmwood, a girls' school in Ottawa, which is situated just across the street from the back door of "Stornoway." Yet she somehow managed to be late for school eight times in her first term. "She has always been very slow," says Mary. "She would take three quarters of an hour to put on a pair of socks. Easily. She was just dreaming." Mimi learned to speak German in Ottawa from the wife of a diplomat at the West German Embassy and, for Grade XIII, she decided to go to the Canadian Junior College in Lausanne, in the French part of Switzerland. She finished there and was back home on holidays when the 1972 election campaign began. After travelling with her parents for the first part of the campaign, she had to leave to fly to France to start classes at the University of Strasbourg. Stanfield's aides and organizers decided to surprise Stanfield by smuggling Mimi back to Halifax for election night. After passing the hat, they bought her an air ticket, but Mimi refused to come without her father's permission. So eager was he to see her that Stanfield was at the airport in Halifax an hour before her plane was due to arrive. He paced back and forth impatiently. Yet when she finally alighted, he displayed no emotion, greeting her with all the formality that he might have reserved for welcoming the ambassador from Upper Volta.

Tiny, grey-haired Mary Stanfield is just about the ideal wife for a political leader. She has an advantage over most politicians' wives – she comes from a political family and loves politics. Unlike the wives of most politicians, she did not marry a young lawyer only to see him succumb to the political life. He was the premier when she married him and she knew what kind of life she was getting into. The only thing she had not counted on was that her husband would end up in federal politics. Although she was sure he would not contest the federal leadership, she kept scrupulously out of the discussions in the summer of 1967 when he was debating whether to run. "I gave absolutely no opinion whatsoever." she says. "I didn't want to influence him one way or the other because I felt it had to be his decision. I would have been quite happy if he hadn't, and yet I wasn't terribly upset because he did. I thought it was a natural step for him in a way. He had had eleven years [as premier] and if he didn't do it then, there wouldn't be another leadership convention. It would have been too late."

The only time she regrets being married to a national leader is when she has to get up at six o'clock in the morning on election campaigns. "I'm a night person and Bob is a morning person," she says. "But I know that it is absolute self-indulgence on my part, I *can* do it in the mornings; I am getting better at it." On her first federal campaign, in 1968, Mary laid down one law to the campaign organizers – she would do whatever campaigning they wanted, but, she insisted, not early in the morning. "Certainly, Mrs. Stanfield," they replied. "That didn't last two days," Mary laughs. By election-time in 1972, she did not even bother insisting.

The Stanfield's private life has changed drastically since the peaceful days at "The Oaks" in Halifax. All the children are gone and "Stornoway" does not have the magnificent garden Stanfield had in Halifax to putter in. Even if he had a big garden, he would not have time to tend to it. When they can, the Stanfields watch hockey and football games on television, and on occasion they slip down to Montreal or Toronto for a live National Hockey League game. They do not party much in Ottawa, and seldom go to the theatre or to concerts at the National Arts Centre. Bob loves to eat and he enjoys nothing more than a huge meal; he likes his meat rare and some of his friends suspect he would eat it raw if Mary would serve it that way.

If he has a completely free evening, he likes to spend it reading in a deep easy chair, his feet up on a stool and a glass of Scotch and water (no ice) close at hand. Though he still goes back to Jane Austen and Samuel Pepys, his taste in literature has broadened in recent years to encompass such diverse authors as Robertson Davies and Eldridge Cleaver. He works hard on his French, reaching the point where he can handle himself confidently on hot-line radio shows in Quebec, though he is in no danger of being mistaken for a French-Canadian. His French is slow and halting, giving the impression that he is uncertain of his vocabulary. The impression is inexact: he speaks English the same way. After being elected leader, he took an immersion course in French and he has kept it up since then, as time has permitted. Stanfield speaks French in the Commons to his Quebec lieutenant, Claude Wagner, reads the French newsmagazine *L'Express* every week, and when he goes on vacation it is usually to the French island of Guadaloupe where he lies on the beach reading detective stories by the French master Georges Simenon. Even a good thing, though, can be carried too far. For Christmas, 1972, Mimi sent her father a French translation of Russian novelist Alexander Solzhenitsyn's *August 1914*. Solzhenitsyn is heavy enough going in English, but Stanfield dutifully ploughed through the French version.

He likes to practise his French and that, too, can lead to unforeseen situations. Arriving at Montreal International Airport late one night at the end of 1972, he hopped into the mini-bus carrying passengers to the Airport Hilton, and decided to show off his French to the girl driving the bus. "Est-ce-que vous conduisez toute la nuit?" inquired the Leader of her Majesty's Loyal Opposition. Mistaking a pleasantry for a proposition, the girl turned with a willing smile. "Non, M'sieu," she replied. "Je finis à minuit."

11

And Now,
Pierre Trudeau (1967-1968)

Stale, Stagnant Stanfield Is Too Damn Conservative.

> – A sign at a Stanfield rally, Prince
> George, B.C., April, 1968.

When Robert Stanfield became national leader of the Conservative Party, there were two courses he could have adopted. He could have completed the renaissance that Dalton Camp had begun in 1966 by turning the party organization over to Camp and his reformers, by demoting the Diefenbaker loyalists in his caucus, and by promoting the M.P.s who had supported his own candidacy to positions of influence in the House of Commons. Or, he could try to restore unity in the party by working to win over the Diefenbaker wing of the party – even at the expense of denying the perfectly legitimate aspirations of his own supporters.

Stanfield has always been a man who worries more about reconciling his enemies than rewarding his friends. So it was not surprising that he chose the latter course, even though he could have established control over his caucus and his party much sooner if he had followed the advice given him by Camp.

Shortly after the leadership convention, Camp, in his capacity as national president, flew to Ottawa to tell Stanfield of his plans for reforming the party. He proposed to re-organize the entire party machine, starting with a house-cleaning at national headquarters. "It [headquarters] was the first crucial thing," says Camp. "We wanted to re-organize the headquarters in our own lifestyles and times." Stanfield looked at Camp and turned him down, saying: "Well, I'll look after that myself."

Camp and his supporters were hurt and bewildered by Stanfield's rejection, feeling that they had been denied a right that they had earned with their victories at the annual meeting of 1966 and the leadership convention of 1967. "Back in Mafialand," says Camp, "they said 'He has read us out of the party. Therefore the son of a bitch will take whatever's coming to him, because we're not going to lift a hand.' You see, he didn't carry through the revolution."

Although Stanfield did not sever his long relationship with Camp, Camp took no active part in the day-to-day activities of the party. Neither did the members of Camp's personal political organization – the group he calls his "Eglinton Mafia." They worked for Camp in his losing attempt to win a Commons seat in Don Valley in the 1968 general election, but they stayed out of the national campaign.

Stanfield, meanwhile, concentrated all his energies on making peace with the dissidents in the Tory caucus and he knew that it would not be an easy task. Following the decision of the 1966 annual meeting to hold a leadership convention, seventy-one M.P.s had signed a pledge of loyalty to John Diefenbaker, asking him to continue as their leader. By the fall of 1967, some of those M.P.s had accepted – with resignation if not enthusiasm – that the Diefenbaker era was finished and that the Stanfield years were beginning. Many others, however, would not bow to the inevitable; bitterly, though privately, they refused to accept the leadership succession. Although it was impossible to divide the Tory caucus into neat pro-Stanfield and anti-Stanfield camps, his detractors outnumbered his admirers by nearly two to one.

Immediately after the leadership convention, Stanfield had flown back to Halifax to submit his resignation as Premier and to turn the provincial government over to Ike Smith. A Conservative backbencher from Nova Scotia, C.F. Kennedy, resigned his Commons seat, Colchester-Hants (which took in Stanfield's hometown, Truro) to provide a riding for the new leader. Prime Minister Pearson obliged by calling a by-election for November 6; to facilitate Stanfield's entry into Parliament, the Liberals did not field a candidate against him.

For the two months between his election as leader and his election to the Commons, Stanfield was forced to run the Opposition at arm's length. Conscious of the sensitivities of the old guard in the caucus, he chose Michael Starr, Diefenbaker's last House Leader, to act as Interim Leader of the Opposition. Until the by-election, Stanfield was not entitled to an office on Parliament Hill and he rented office space in the Chateau Laurier Hotel down the street. Recruiting Gene Rheaume (the ex-M.P. who had organized the leadership convention) to serve temporarily as his executive secretary, Stanfield began to look around for permanent staff.

He decided on Lowell Murray, a young Nova Scotian whom he had met through the campus Conservative Club when Murray was a freshman at St. Francis Xavier University in Antigonish. Murray wrote speeches for several Conservative candidates in the provincial election of 1956 and later, after spending a year in Montreal writing speeches for Donald Gordon, President of Canadian National Railways, he returned to Cape Breton to run in the provincial election of 1960 against the leader of the c.c.f. Murray lost, but made up his mind to stay in politics. In 1961, he went to Ottawa as executive assistant to Davie Fulton, then Minister of Justice in the Diefenbaker Government. He was Fulton's campaign manager in the leadership campaign and was instrumental in delivering Fulton's delegates to Stanfield on the final ballot. When the convention was over, Murray got on a plane, determined to see the world. He was in Tokyo, speculating more on the pretty girls of that city than on Canadian politics, when the new leader telephoned and asked him what his plans were. "I told him my plans were to continue what I was doing and take another month or two and come back by way of Europe," Murray says. " . . . He told me he would like it very much if I would come to work for him." Not prepared to commit himself, Murray said he would talk to Stanfield when he got back. The leader agreed – or so Murray thought. Two weeks later, in Saigon, he got another telephone call, this time from Davie Fulton. "Stanfield wants to know why you're not here or why you can't hurry up," Fulton said. Murray continued his leisurely travel, pausing in Thailand and Lebanon. His curiosity finally getting the better of him he flew back to Canada to find out what was on Stanfield's mind. "Now," said Stanfield when they met, "what role do you see for yourself in the organization?" "He didn't," recalls Murray, "say, 'I'd like you to be chief of staff,' or 'I'd like you to write my speeches or handle parliamentary strategy or look after relations with the party,' or anything specific." Murray told Stanfield that was up to him. "Well," Stanfield replied uncertainly, "I thought of you as being more along the creative side, speeches and that kind of thing, and I don't know, perhaps we can get someone else on the administrative side." Murray replied that was fine, but if he was not going to be in charge of the office, he wanted to know who was. "I didn't have anybody else in mind," admitted Stanfield.

Murray appointed himself to the senior spot on Stanfield's staff and set to work cleaning out the former Diefenbaker staffers who had stayed on after the leadership convention. The first people he got rid of were Diefenbaker's secretaries and stenographers; some of them had been there for years and their salaries had climbed to the $8,000-$10,000 range. "This was 1967, remember," says Murray. "I knew we could get young Ph.D.s for what we were paying them."

The males from Diefenbaker's staff proved harder to dislodge. Delegations of old Diefenbaker M.P.s waited on Stanfield to insist that he retain the men who had worked for the Chief. Exasperated, Murray told Stanfield: "Look, we've only got so many positions and it's easier to let people out now when you're coming in, rather than a month or two from now when it appears to be a reflection on their ability." Stanfield agreed to have a heart-to-heart talk with one of Diefenbaker's aides, Thomas Van Dusen. When he came back from talking to Van Dusen, Murray asked him: "Did you see Tommy?" "Yeah," replied Stanfield slowly. "Shall I go ahead and fill that position?" Murray asked. "Well," said Stanfield, "I don't think he got what I was driving at." "What do you mean?" demanded Murray. "Didn't you tell him?" "Well," Stanfield confessed, "I asked him what his plans were and I guess he indicated he'd like to stay on." Van Dusen stayed on for more than a year.

The most improbable character from the Diefenbaker retinue was the venerable Gilbert Champagne who, legend had it, had been working for the Conservative leader since the days of Sir Robert Borden. No one was quite sure what Champagne did or why he was on staff. "He would open the door for Diefenbaker," Murray recalls. "He would walk with Diefenbaker to the Parliamentary Restaurant when Dief went to lunch. Then he'd walk back down. An hour or two later, he'd go back up and collect Diefenbaker and walk back." Champagne had a private office next to Diefenbaker's and when the phone rang, the girl on the switchboard would get up, walk into Champagne's office and tell him the caller wanted to speak to Diefenbaker. Champagne would rise from his desk, walk into Diefenbaker's office, pick up the phone and hand it to the Chief. Finally, after much difficulty, Champagne was persuaded to take his pension and retire.

Bob Stanfield was elected to Parliament on November 6, 1967, with a 14,291-vote majority, and nine days later he arrived on Parliament Hill to take over officially as Leader of Her Majesty's Loyal Opposition. His first stop was the office of the Clerk of the House, Alistair Fraser, who administered the oath of office taken by all M.P.s and handed Stanfield the tools of his new trade – a copy of Beauchesne's *Parliamentary Rules and Forms* (Fourth Edition, 1958), a set of the Standing Orders of the House of Commons, a free railway pass, and a key to the leader's Centre Block office. While Mary Stanfield was being entertained by the Parliamentary Wives' Association, Stanfield lunched in the Parliamentary Restaurant. Then he walked downstairs for his first appearance in the House of Commons.

The only sour note of the happy day was a snub from John Diefenbaker. Rather than have to introduce his successor to the Commons, Diefenbaker stayed away from the sitting, and his new seat on the front bench, two seats removed from Stanfield's, sat embarrassingly empty all afternoon. In Diefenbaker's absence, Starr and Théogène Ricard, a Conservative M.P. from Quebec, ushered Stanfield into the imposing green chamber, marched him up the centre aisle and introduced him to Speaker Lucien Lamoureux. For the occasion, the new leader and all the members of his caucus sported white carnations dyed Tory blue – "the result of Conservative research into horticulture," explained gardener Stanfield. There was a full minute of applause as members of all party's banged their desks in approval of the new member. Stanfield left the chamber, walked around behind the curtains and re-entered mid-way down the east side to take Diefenbaker's old seat, directly opposite the Prime Minister. Pearson jumped up, crossed the floor and pumped Stanfield's hand. One by one, after Pearson, the other party leaders rose to welcome and to praise the new leader of the Opposition. "It was quite a friendly occasion," Stanfield said happily afterward.

The following week Stanfield made his maiden speech and in it he moved his first non-confidence motion, in the form of an amendment to a government supply resolution. The amendment stated: "This House regrets that the mismanagement of this government had endangered the rate of economic growth, the prospects of satisfactory levels of employment, and the ability of individual Canadians to meet their own commitments." That was pretty standard rhetoric for an opposition motion, but it was Stanfield's first big moment in Parliament.

The next day, however, Lester Pearson told Stanfield he had to be away on government business and inquired whether Stanfield would "pair" with him when the amendment was put to a vote that night. "Pairing" is an informal convention of Parliament. A government or opposition member who finds he has to be absent for a vote, arranges with a member of the other side to abstain from voting. In this way an absent M.P. does not affect the voting balance in the House. Of course, a member never "pairs" if his own motion is being voted on. But, still ignorant of the ways of Parliament, Stanfield readily agreed to Pearson's request.

Lowell Murray was horrified when he heard what Stanfield had done. "You're crazy," he told the person who brought him the news. "Stanfield wouldn't do that. He's got more sense than that." A little later, Murray went up to Stanfield in the Opposition lobby: "By the way, somebody says that you've paired." "I did," said Stanfield sheepishly. That night he had to sit in his seat in doleful embarrassment as his first non-confidence motion went down to defeat on a vote of 119 to 105. The Liberals were delighted. They had, they congratulated themselves, found an easy mark.

The Conservatives did not know what to make of their new leader. He was friendly, but he discouraged intimacy. They did not know what to call him. They could not very well call him the "Chief" as long as Diefenbaker was still around. Heath Macquarrie tried to persuade his colleagues to address Stanfield as "Skipper" – in honour of his Maritime connection – but Stanfield firmly discouraged that. Some of the other Easterners liked "Old

Hickory," for no apparent reason. In the press gallery, they called him "Big Thunder" presumably because the reporters could come up with no nickname that was less appropriate to the Stanfield style. None of the nicknames stuck. Those in the caucus who felt they knew him called him Bob; to others he remained "Mr Stanfield." He seemed like a decent enough fellow, but many Tory M.P.s concluded that he lacked political acumen. He was unclear in his view, ineffectual in Parliament, and innocent of any sense of political timing or tactics. Tories who had been raised to despise Grits could not fathom a leader who prefaced his attacks on the Government with an apology: "I don't want to be offensive, but. . . . "

His staff, sensing that he was drifting aimlessly, felt at a loss to help him. Says one of his aides: "You got up in the morning feeling 'My God, I've really got to do something. If I don't, everything is going to fall down.' He sometimes gave the impression of being almost helpless. He has that way about him."

Stanfield worked long hours in those early months, often twelve hours a day, but he seemed unable to accomplish anything. Sticking to the custom of his days in the Nova Scotia Legislature, he spent hour after hour sitting in the nearly-deserted Commons chamber listening to inconsequential debates. His aides decided he did not have enough to occupy his time. "We'll arrange meetings for you with businessmen, labour leaders, anybody," Lowell Murray proposed one day. "You're wasting your time down there in the House. How about it?" But Stanfield kept going down to the House.

He gradually made himself familiar with the arcane workings of Parliament, but his familiarity did not increase his confidence. One Monday night in February, 1968, the Conservative whips succeeded in engineering a snap vote on third reading on an important tax bill. Lester Pearson, who had announced his retirement from politics, was vacationing in the Caribbean, a Liberal leadership convention had been called for April, and half his cabinet ministers, or so it seemed, were out campaigning. Thus weakened, the Government lost that tax vote by two votes – eighty-four to eighty-two – and it appeared fleetingly as though Stanfield had brought down the Government. But the Conservative leader was bewildered by this sudden change in his fortunes and unsure of his next step. He failed to press his advantage. He gave the Government time to regather its scattered wits.

Pearson flew home, assembled his wandering ministers and plotted his next move. That next move was to send Louis Rasminsky, the governor of the Bank of Canada, to see Stanfield. There was a world monetary crisis at the time and the Government had been struggling to protect the Canadian dollar. To Stanfield, Rasminsky spelled out some of the implications to the dollar if the Government fell. He warned that the international financial community might lose whatever confidence it had in Canada's ability to manage her economic affairs if the tax measure were not passed. Pearson's use of Rasminsky under the circumstances was questionable. On the one hand, Stanfield was entitled to have – and probably needed to have – a report from the central bank on the international monetary situation in the light of the domestic political crisis. On the other hand, the Bank of Canada is held to be above partisan politics. Its function is to advise the Government on policy and problems involving economic and monetary matters. When Pearson asked Rasminsky to talk to Stanfield, he was sending him on an errand that, inevitably, was as much political as it was anything else. Under the circumstances, Stanfield could scarcely have refused to see Rasminsky, but he could have rejected Rasminsky's assessment. Instead, Stanfield persuaded himself that the monetary crisis was more grave than it was, and that the defeat of the Government would be more of a threat to the stability of the dollar than it probably would have been.

Many Conservatives were furious about Rasminsky's intervention; they could not see how an election in Canada would appreciably worsen the world's monetary woes; they were anguished by Stanfield's failure to give them crisp, decisive leadership; they railed at him for not going for Pearson's jugular. They dubbed him "the jelly fish." Over the objections of a majority of his caucus, Stanfield agreed to give Pearson twenty-four hours of grace before facing Parliament. Pearson, to the dismay of the Conservatives, used the time to go on national television to present his arguments as to why the Liberals should not resign. The Government drafted a motion stating that the tax bill defeat had not constituted an expression of non-confidence in the Government. With the Ralliement des Créditistes, which held the balance of power in the minority Parliament, supporting the motion, the Government won its vote of confidence easily. The hardliners in the Tory caucus railed furiously at Stanfield. One Diefenbaker stalwart, Gordon Churchill, resigned from the caucus in protest.

In retrospect, however, Stanfield made the right decisions. The only way the Conservatives could have brought the Government down was by obstructing Parliament, by refusing to permit a vote on Pearson's confidence motion, and by blockading all other government business. It would have required an extended blockade and Stanfield, to his credit, was not about to play obstructionist politics. The country had suffered enough of that when Diefenbaker was leading the Opposition.

The country, in any event, was less interested in the tax bill crisis than it was in the Liberals' April leadership convention. Who would the Liberals choose? Would it be Paul Hellyer, the former defence minister who had unified the armed forces over the protests of the military? Would it be handsome, ever-smiling Robert Winters, the big businessman who had returned to politics as Minister of Trade and Commerce? Would it be the rising young star, John Turner; or Eric Kierans, the Irish Quebecker and former provincial cabinet minister; or shy Allan MacEachen; or wily old Paul Martin; or folksy Joe Greene, the best stump speaker in the Liberal cabinet? Would it be – could it possibly be – Pierre Elliott Trudeau, the glamorous new Minister of Justice who had reformed the country's Victorian divorce laws and had proposed a bold renovation of the Criminal Code? Was the Liberal Party ready for this shy, charismatic intellectual, this swinging bachelor who loved beautiful women, fast cars, and unconventional dress? Was Canada ready for such a Prime Minister? Conservatives who were wise enough to comprehend Trudeau's appeal to a restive nation were very much afraid the answer would be Yes.

Just before the Liberal convention opened, Dalton Camp went to Ottawa again. He and Stanfield met in the dreary apartment that the leader had rented until repairs were completed at "Stornoway." They discussed the Liberal race and agreed that Trudeau would probably win. "It is going to be Trudeau and it is going to be bad for us," said Camp. "That's right," Stanfield agreed. "Both of us accepted the fact that if Trudeau was going to win we were going to be defeated," says Camp, bitterly. "It was because of you people in the media, making him into a god. He was so beautiful, he was so lovely, he was so gorgeous, he was so intellectual, and he could quote from Descartes and Socrates. And everybody was having orgasms every time he opened his mouth."

On April 6, 1968, Pierre Trudeau was elected leader of the Liberal Party. The atmosphere the next day was felicitously described by Christina Newman in *Saturday Night:* "Political Ottawa woke up on the morning after Pierre Elliott Trudeau was elected leader of the Liberal Party feeling a little like a sober maiden who'd unexpectedly found herself on a wild party the night before, and was now asking, if not in horror, at least in delicious trepidation, 'What have I done?' It was as though, having always been wooed and won by upright men in blazers, she'd suddenly succumbed to Belmondo in a Cardin suit."

On April 20, 1968, Trudeau was sworn in as Canada's fifteenth Prime Minister. Three days later, Parliament was dissolved and a general election called for June 25. Bob Stanfield had already lost that election. He had lost it the day Trudeau became leader, and if there were any doubt of that, the Conservatives had their own opinion poll to confirm it. As the election campaign began, the Tories' poll showed them trailing the Liberals by a staggering twenty-two percentage points.

Although it seemed that way as the campaign unfolded, the Conservatives did not set out deliberately to lose the election of 1968. They nominated their finest crop of candidates in years. In Quebec, where the Tories always had difficulty finding respectable candidates, financier Marcel Faribault, who was constitutional adviser to Premier Daniel Johnson, resigned as President of Montreal's Trust Général to run as a Stanfield candidate. He was followed by André Gagnon, President of the Montreal Catholic School Board; Yves Ryan, brother of the editor of *Le Devoir;* Julien Chouinard, Quebec's Deputy Minister of Justice; and Paul O. Trepanier, the controversial president of the Conservative organization in Quebec. In Ontario, Dalton Camp offered himself in Don Valley; Wallace McCutcheon resigned from the Senate to run in York-Simcoe; and Earl Brownridge quit his job as President of American Motors (Canada) Ltd. to be a candidate in Peel South. In Manitoba, Duff Roblin had resigned as premier and ran in Winnipeg South Centre, something he had refused to do for Diefenbaker in 1965. In Saskatchewan, Alvin Hamilton, redistributed out of his old riding moved into the new riding of Regina East. In British Columbia, Davie Fulton, the kingmaker of the Conservative convention, ran in Kamloops-Cariboo. All these men had two things in common. All were supposed to be stars of the Stanfield team, and all were destined to be defeated, many badly, as Trudeaumania swept the nation.

Pierre Trudeau – or "Pierre de la Plaza" as they called him in the back of his plane – jetted jauntily across the country, touching down here and there to accept the kisses of moonstruck adolescent girls and the adulation of their parents, and to proclaim his indistinct but compelling vision of a Just Society. The mood of the young was mirrored in a sign held by a girl in Kapuskasing, Ontario, when Trudeau arrived there – "Don't Just Stand There. Kiss Me, Pierre." A well-dressed matron in Vernon, B.C., spoke for the older generation when she confessed: "I like him because the kids like him. Our generation has made a mess of things, hasn't it? Maybe the next generation can do things better." Lester Pearson put his finger on the essence of Trudeau's appeal. "This man," said Pearson, "is truly an outstanding person. He is a man for all seasons, but especially a man for the season of tomorrow."

In comparison with Trudeau, Bob Stanfield seemed like a man for the season of yesterday. His candidates were as good as Trudeau's, but he lacked the organization, and he appeared at times to lack the will to win. Stanfield lumbered from city to city in a decaying old DC-7C that had spent its best years lugging American tourists to Japan and Canadian Legionnaires to London. Leased from Transair, the plane was christened "The Misajumax" (after the Stanfield children, Mimi, Sarah, Judy, and Max), but everyone called it the "Flying Banana." It had a cruising speed of three hundred miles per hour – barely half the speed of Trudeau's DC-9 – and Stanfield always seemed to be an hour or more behind schedule. He scheduled an open-air rally in Victoria Park in London, but no one thought to approach the city fathers. A municipal bylaw forbade political rallies in public parks, and the city enforced the bylaw. The organizers showed more foresight one memorable day in Quebec City. Knowing there was no passenger ramp that would fit the DC-7C, they ordered one built. But no one thought to measure the plane and the hastily-built wooden ramp was three feet too high for the plane door. The passengers had to hoist themselves up onto the ramp and scramble out on all fours. In Rivière-du-Loup, the streets were teeming with people an hour before Stanfield arrived, but when his motorcade passed through, they were deserted. It was as though the people had fled the city in terror. That night, they took Stanfield into Matane, a community of eleven thousand people in the Gaspé, to campaign for one of his star candidates, Julien Chouinard. Though the arena held fifteen hundred people (not an impossible number of seats for any half-competent organization to fill), only two hundred turned out for Stanfield, despite the added attractions of a free dinner of lethal-looking baked beans and the "music" of quite possibly the worst rock-and-roll band the country had ever produced. Not that it mattered. The sound system failed and no one could hear a word Stanfield said. A local Tory worker, much pleased with the night's work, kindly offered to drive two reporters back to the airport to catch the Stanfield plane. "How many people do you think were there to hear M'sieu Stanfield?" he asked. "No more than two hundred," the reporters replied. A heated auction ensued, with the organizer refusing to accept any estimate below fifteen hundred and the newsmen refusing to go above three hundred. The organizer resolved the dispute by the simple expedient of driving in the opposite direction from the airport and dumping his passengers on the road on the far side of Matane. It was that kind of campaign.

"The 1968 campaign was a disaster," concedes Lowell Murray. "When you're losing you can't do anything right. When you're winning you can't do anything wrong."

It began to go wrong for the Conservatives as early as the official campaign kickoff in Winnipeg. Stanfield surrounded himself with an impressive array of Tory power for the opener – premiers Robarts of Ontario, Smith of Nova Scotia, and Weir of Manitoba, plus Alvin Hamilton, Duff Roblin, and Marcel Faribault. The four thousand assembled Tories should have given Stanfield a rousing sendoff, but they sat resolutely on their hands. The preliminary speakers dragged on so long that the meeting had gone off national television before Stanfield got a chance to speak.

215

It was even worse later in Toronto. That night Pierre Trudeau was out in Victoria, a city of sixty thousand, addressing a crowd of ten thousand people gathered about his feet on the sunny slopes overlooking the Strait of Juan de Fuca. In Toronto, they took Bob Stanfield into the Coliseum at the Canadian National Exhibition grounds, a dirt-floored building that still stank of the cows that had been moved out to make way for the Conservatives. It was his only major campaign rally in the Ontario capital; the Coliseum was easy to reach by car or public transit, and it had only fifty-five hundred seats to fill. Yet one thousand of those seats remained empty. John Robarts, who should have been there to introduce Stanfield, arrived two hours late, mumbling apologies. While they waited for Stanfield to tell them about his plans to provide tax relief for homeowners, the audience was subjected to a troupe of ethnic dancers (passable if your taste runs to ethnic dancing), an acid rock group (loud and not much more), and a chorus of girl singers in formal gowns (looking as though they had stopped off at the cow barn on their way to the firemen's ball, circa 1940). "It looked somehow," wrote Peter Newman in the *Toronto Daily Star,* "like a spiritless tryout in some distant provincial town for the Ed Sullivan Show, with none of the contestants likely to bag a spot on his program." No one could argue with Newman's assessment of the evening: "Surely most thoughtful Conservatives coming out of Robert Stanfield's unlikely rally here last night must have been asking themselves some tough questions, beginning with the clincher: What the hell has happened to my party in the last nine months? Could the bungling amateurs who planned and executed that evening of political misfortune have been the same group that excited the nation last fall by staging the best leadership convention in Canadian political history? Yes, the very same."

The "bungling amateurs" could not be held responsible for everything that went wrong in that election campaign. Stanfield did not help things any. Early in the campaign, he announced that if he formed a government he would introduce what sounded like a guaranteed annual income program for all Canadians. The guaranteed-income approach to alleviating poverty and redistributing wealth was an issue well worth debating in the campaign, but having raised it, Stanfield debated it ineptly. He was unable to communicate to the voters exactly what he was proposing. "Experts concerned with overcoming poverty have discussed a number of concepts," he told an audience in London, "One is the idea of a guaranteed annual income. Another is the concept of the negative income tax. Each of these ideas has weaknesses if applied universally. But the larger concept we have to concern ourselves with is the realization of the goal that every Canadian, whether or not he is a member of the labour force, must have available to him a

216

minimum level of income." He seemed to be proposing, as a goal, a guaranteed annual income for every Canadian, although he did not hold out much hope for attaining that goal until the national economy had expanded enough to absorb the cost.

But then he went on firmly to suggest he was thinking in rather more concrete terms: "There are certain steps that it makes sense to take as a start. For instance, it is sensible and just to pay a guaranteed annual income to that group of Canadians which needs help and is unable to earn an income of its own. . . . We should therefore establish as an essential part of that [social assistance] program a guaranteed annual income for all those Canadians who cannot earn for themselves, and who live today below the poverty line." It sounded as though Stanfield was proposing two things: an eventual guaranteed income for all Canadians, and an early start in that direction by introducing a guaranteed income for the unemployable poor. But then Stanfield backed off. Referring to the latter group, he said: "This is our firm objective, although it cannot be accomplished immediately."

No one, least of all Stanfield, was able to explain with any clarity exactly what the leader *was* trying to say. His advisers were unable to say how many people might be covered, what the minimum income level would be or how much it would cost the treasury. As the campaign went on, Stanfield even backed away from the phrase "guaranteed annual income" – which seemed to have an unpleasant Socialist ring to it. He had never proposed a guaranteed annual income, he insisted: he was talking about a negative income tax. Confused enough at the outset, the policy became unintelligible as the campaign wore on. Meanwhile, the Liberals had considered and rejected making a guaranteed annual income program a part of their election platform. They sensed that, following the heavy welfare spending of the Pearson years, the public was in no mood for, as they put it, "any more of that free stuff." Pierre Trudeau dismissed Stanfield's vague policy in one crisp sentence: "I would not buy a set of long underwear if I didn't know how much it cost."

The guaranteed annual income-negative income tax confusion was typical of the essential weakness of Stanfield's campaign in 1968. In a futile attempt to stem the tide of Trudeaumania, he hurried about the country propounding hastily-conceived policies. He talked about a tunnel to Newfoundland (and later denied he had said he would build one), wheat subsidies, aid for the gas and oil industries, tariffs and quotas to protect the fruit and vegetable growers, an Income Tax Act amendment to permit homeowners to deduct ninety per cent of mortgage interest above seven per cent. His aides dutifully cranked out his promises on a duplicating machine in the back of the plane, but they could not explain them. Neither, it sometimes seemed, could Stanfield. While the calmly assured Trudeau was criss-crossing the country promising to make no promises (though, in fact, he made quite a few), Stanfield was stumbling from town to town giving the impression of a man reduced to reading pronouncements he did not understand.

All these problems, however, paled beside the problem of *deux nations.* The "Montmorency Resolution" as it was known, containing the reference to "two founding peoples" or, in French, *deux nations,* had seemed harmless enough. It likely would have been consigned to an obscure place on the dusty shelves reserved for long-forgotten political resolutions had it not been for Marcel Faribault and John Diefenbaker. Faribault had attended the "Thinkers Conference" at Montmorency Falls where he had made a too-spirited defence of the "deux nations" approach. He told the Conservative thinkers that he started from the premise that all provinces were equal and that there should be particular status for none. But Faribault went on to say that although he had not changed in his opposition to particular status, the people of Quebec had changed. "The question of two nations," he declared, "is no longer debatable in the province of Quebec." Taken out of context, as it later was, that pronouncement sounded menacing. To Conservatives from Western Canada and small-town Ontario it sounded like a prescription for separation. But there was nothing particularly threatening about it when it was read in the context of Faribault's full remarks. He continued in that speech to say: "Admit that you will put, you must put, at the preamble of a new Constitution, something that will be the recognition that there are in this country two founding peoples. You put that down. We might translate it in French 'two nations.' You will translate it 'two founding races, or people,' if you want. We cannot say 'people' because 'people' in our case doesn't mean 'nation,' the same way as 'nation' in English does not mean *nation* [in French]."

Was there really anything so terribly frightening about a political party that thought the preamble to a ·new constitution should recognize the indisputable fact that Canada is composed of "two founding peoples (or, in French, *deux nations*) with historic rights who have been joined by people from many lands"? It was a statement of the obvious. Anyone who thought the *deux nations* theory was radical had only to look at the other constitutional proposals made by the Montmorency Conference and to compare them with the policy of the Liberal Government. The Tory thinkers favoured the adoption of a formula for amending the Canadian constitution in Canada. That was the policy of the Trudeau Government, the Pearson Government and, before them, the Diefenbaker Government. The Tory thinkers favoured establishment of a constitutional tribunal to insure impartiality in disputes, something Quebec did not feel it got from the Supreme Court of Canada. The Trudeau Government established the Federal Court of Canada to arbitrate, among other things, inter-provincial and federal-provincial disputes. The Tory thinkers favoured affirmation of the right of French Canadians to use their own language in the courts and legislatures throughout Canada. The Trudeau Government affirmed that right, to the extent possible within federal jurisdiction, with passage of the Official Languages Act. The Tory thinkers favoured entrenchment of the Bill of Rights in the Constitution. The Trudeau Government proposed entrenching political and legal rights, but encountered opposition from some of the provinces.

The Montmorency proposals ceased to be a straightforward statement of common sense and became a lethal political issue when John Diefenbaker seized on the "two nations" policy to support his decision to seek re-election at the leadership convention. His cry was shrill, but his message was nonsense. There was no such thing as a Conservative "two nations" or *deux nations* policy. The thinkers at Montmorency Falls had passed a resolution, but that resolution never became party policy. It was never passed by the full party, nor was it ever considered by the full party.

Stanfield did not campaign on a *deux nations* platform in the election of 1968. He did have a poorly defined Quebec strategy that involved maintaining a strong federal government while offering Quebec certain additional powers – as long as the same powers were offered to all the provinces. It was not much of a strategy and it was lost sight of in the "two nations" controversy. Any chance that the "two nations" dispute might be allowed to die a natural death was eliminated when Faribault became a candidate in the Montreal riding of Gamelin. As the leading Conservative candidate in Quebec and, unofficially at least, Stanfield's Quebec lieutenant, he set the tone of the debate.

Faribault went to Winnipeg for the campaign kickoff where he made a determined defence of his constitutional views. He was cordially received and the part the Western crowd liked the best was where he declared: "There is no square inch of this land that I shall ever renounce." But when he returned home, Faribault's ideas seemed considerably less clear. One day he would say, "I don't want any particular powers for the province of Quebec which are not given the other provinces." The next day he would be talking about the need to recognize Quebec as the homeland of French Canadians and how Quebec needed the powers of a nation, in "the psychological sense." So unclear were Faribault's explanations that no one knew precisely where he stood.

Stanfield was hemmed in. Every time Faribault opened his mouth in Montreal he said something that Stanfield was called on to respond to at his next press conference or next public meeting. Meanwhile, John Diefenbaker was stumping around Saskatchewan, ignoring Stanfield and declaiming against the "two nations" heresy. It was far too good an opportunity for the Liberals to pass up. They wrung every possible drop of political advantage out of the English backlash to the Conservatives' constitutional confusion. Who, they demanded, spoke for the Conservative Party – Stanfield or Faribault or Diefenbaker? Or was it perhaps Daniel Johnson, the nationalist Premier of Quebec? What exactly was the Conservative position on Quebec? If they had a position other than "two nations," why did they not say what it was? If Stanfield did not agree with Faribault, why did he not disown him?

The issue came to a boil in Calgary in mid-June when the Liberals took a full-page newspaper advertisement that read, in part: "The Honourable Robert Stanfield says Two Nations – Special Status. So does Monsieur Faribault of the Conservative Party." Robert Stanfield was in Saskatoon that night and he lost his temper in a speech to two thousand Tory supporters. "This is a deliberate lie," he charged. "I have never advocated two nations. I believe in one Canada. I have never advanced special status." Stanfield told the audience, "No province should be offered authority that is not offered to all the provinces. Furthermore, Mr. Faribault has never advocated two nations in the English sense of the word. . . . Canada is and should be one country – one federal state, that is, it is composed of the original inhabitants and the two founding peoples with historic rights to maintain their language and culture, who have been joined by people from many lands who have a right to play a full part in Canadian life. We have stated this many times. Mr. Trudeau knows our position, this party knows our position. If he believes that lies and distortions are dangerous to our society, let him repudiate these distortions that were published by his party in Calgary."

Trudeau subsequently apologized for that particular excess by his party, but the damage had long since been done. In the eyes of English Canadian voters, Trudeau's Liberals stood for one Canada and Stanfield's Conservatives stood for two nations. An election campaign is the worst possible setting in which to convince the public that it is wrong about something as involved and as sensitive as constitutional policy, and Stanfield could not convince them. It was ironic and, if it had not been so serious, it might even have been funny. The Conservative Party was the party that had hung Louis Riel; it was the party of conscription. For most of the twentieth century it had had to bear the cross of being considered hostile to French Canada. Yet, in the election of 1968, it was accused of being soft on Quebec. Stanfield saw the irony of the situation, but he could not be expected to find it amusing.

The entire election was like that. It was an election in which the roles of the government and opposition were strangely reversed. The Conservatives had gone into the campaign assuming that the record of the Liberal Government from 1965 to 1968 would be an issue and that Stanfield could score politically by attacking the government's record on everything from inflation to medicare. But it did not work that way. Trudeau was a new prime minister. The public did not hold him responsible for the shortcomings of the Pearson administration.

To the voter, Trudeau was the prophet of the new politics. With no record to defend, he was able to draw about his shoulders the mantle of an apostle of reform. He was the man who would free Canada from the shackles of medievalism, who would reform the criminal law, who would find a new place for Canada in the world community. It was Stanfield who was on the defensive, constantly forced to justify his policies. Though he was new to the leadership and had never held a federal office, the voters perceived him as standing for everything they disliked about the politics and government of the past decade. With his painful little Nova Scotia jokes ("Have you heard the one about the Lunenburger and the cornpone?"), his uninspiring speeches, and his indistinct promises, he seemed to stand for everything that was outmoded and tiresome in Canadian public life. Anthony Westell, writing in *The Globe and Mail* during the campaign, was struck by the incongruity of the "Sock It To 'Em, Bob" signs that popped up along the Stanfield tour. "Mr. Stanfield has many qualities," Westell wrote, "but socking-it-to-'em isn't one of them. He's solid, sincere, respectable – and the kids say: 'Would you vote for a man who wears long underwear in the summer?' Unfair? Of course it is. What has long underwear got to do with the making of a prime minister? Subject . . . to correction, it seems to have everything to do with it, if we're going to be honest about campaign impressions. Image, personality, style, call it what you will, is terribly important in Expo-plus-one. The Canadian style changed in 1967. The Quiet Canadian became the Confident Canadian during the Centennial – or I think he did."

Westell had a good point. Trudeau seemed to be the incarnation of the Second Century Canadian – or, at least, the incarnation of what every Second Century Canadian dreamed of himself as being. He was brilliant, perfectly bilingual, master of the media, unfettered by convention, and unsullied by the old politics. A judo brown belt around his waist, a flower behind his ear, a beautiful girl by his side – what more could a Canadian hope to have? By comparison, Stanfield was a man from a prehistoric age, a parochial provincial politician who had not yet learned how to play to a national audience. How could a tired, stooped, droopy-eyed middle-aged man from Truro, Nova Scotia hope to understand the Canadian Dream?

Both leaders concluded their campaigning on June 24, the day before the election. It was St. Jean Baptiste Day, the day on which French Canada celebrates her patron saint. Trudeau went to Montreal that day and, after campaigning in the Montreal area during the afternoon, in the evening joined other dignitaries, including Premier Johnson and Mayor Jean Drapeau, in reviewing the annual St. Jean Baptiste Day parade. It was a dramatic night. Before Trudeau had even arrived at the reviewing stand, a thousand separatists from the Rassemblement pour l'indépendence nationale (R.I.N.) had begun to riot. "Tru-deau-au-pot-eau!" (Trudeau to the gallows!) they chanted. Pop bottles – some filled with paint or kerosene or, some said, acid – started to fly through the night air. Plainclothes police waded in, their truncheons cutting a swift arc before they landed with a satisfying "crunch" on demonstrators' heads. They bundled their dazed and bleeding captives into black police vans and returned to the riot for more. Suddenly, a Coke bottle sailed out of the crowd toward the Prime Minister, smashing into a thousand pieces on a marble portico six feet behind him. Two Mounties jumped on Trudeau, shielding him with their bodies. Most of the other dignitaries darted to safety, but Trudeau stood his ground. Brushing himself off, he told his aides: "I'm not leaving. I must stay." It was a memorable scene and, although the pre-election blackout would normally have precluded political broadcasting so soon before the polls were to open, the riot was carried by television into every home in the country. The sight of his Prime Minister standing up to the separatist thugs was etched on every voter's memory when he went to the polls the next day. The box score: 123 injured (including 43 policemen); 292 arrested; and, as a delighted Liberal organizer put it, 40,000 additional votes for the Liberals in Toronto alone. "When you are lucky in politics," Dalton Camp wrote a few days later, "even your enemies oblige you."

Bob Stanfield had no such luck. He left Ottawa on the morning of St. Jean Baptiste Day on a final swing through Southern Ontario before flying back to Halifax to await the election results. He was exhausted and the fatigue showed in the greyness of his pallor and the lifelessness of his voice. It was all he could do to muster a smile as he climbed aboard the "Flying Banana." There were not many faces left to smile at. The thirty-three reporters who had started the campaign with him had drifted away, one by one. Now there were only twelve left to keep the death watch. As the plane climbed above the Rideau River, Lowell Murray and Eddie Goodman, the national campaign chairman, joined Stanfield in the front compartment to give him the news he had been expecting. Although their polls showed that Stanfield had done moderately well in the campaign, narrowing the gap separating the

Tories from the Liberals from 22 percentage points at the beginning to 14 points at the end, there was no hope. The Quebec strategy had failed. The Conservatives would lose seats in both English and French Canada. There was no way Stanfield could win more than 80 of the country's 264 seats. The leader just nodded.

He campaigned across Ontario from west to east that last day, stopping briefly in London, Stratford, Ajax, Oshawa, Port Hope, Peterborough and Lindsay. His last appearance was in Belleville where he spoke at a picnic on the shores of Lake Ontario. Then, while the reporters went to file their final stories, he headed back to the plane to wait and to unwind. He had travelled 40,000 miles by air and land in 51 days. He had made close to 150 speeches, 6 national television appearances and 18 local television appearances. He had spent 100 hours aloft in his lumbering crate of a plane. He was worn out and there was no hope. It had all been for nothing. He settled into his compartment with a glass and a bottle of Scotch, and by the time the last reporter straggled back to the plane, he had had more than one drink.

After the plane took off, Stanfield came back to the press section and dropped into a seat in the front row beside a reporter from *The Globe and Mail.* Eyes flashing, he launched into his most remarkable performance of the long campaign. "Let me tell you something about the press," he said. "Let me tell you about *The Globe and Mail.*" Bitterly, he attacked *The Globe's* coverage of the election and the paper's editorial policy (it had endorsed Trudeau). Although *The Montreal Star* had not supported him either, he did not object – "At least they didn't distort my position as *The Globe and Mail* did."

Lowell Murray came back and sat down beside Stanfield. "Wouldn't you like your dinner now, sir?" Murray asked tactfully. "No, I don't want my dinner," Stanfield snapped. "Your're just trying to shut me up." He waved his half-empty glass and started again, this time on Trudeau. Trudeau's "One Canada" policy, he insisted, was "simplistic, unrealistic, and dangerously inflexible." The Prime Minister's stand on Quebec was "phony," and while Trudeau was a logical man, logic could be dangerous. A politician has to understand human relationships and he has to be flexible. "For Christ's sake," Stanfield roared, "doesn't he know that Quebec isn't going to let the federal government get into education?" There was a stunned silence on the plane. "God-damn it, doesn't he know that Ontario has carried on relations for years with London? You know what he's done in this campaign? He's legitimized prejudice. Quebec is too dangerous a matter to fool with. By playing it the way he did, he inflamed prejudice in such places as Calgary."

223

His tiny audience of newsmen was enthralled; none of them had ever seen the passionate side of Stanfield before. Accepting a fresh drink, he started to talk about his reading habits. Lest anyone think Trudeau was the only politician who could quote from great writers, Stanfield reeled off huge swatches of direct quotation from Alexis de Tocqueville, the nineteenth century French Liberal. He talked of Jane Austen and C.S. Forester, about classical music and the theatre. When he finished, Marsh Clark of *Time,* reached over from the seat behind and shook Stanfield's hand. "It was very nice to have made your acquaintance, Mr. Stanfield," he said.

Stanfield's final stop before Halifax was Moncton, where the Tories thought they had an outside chance of upsetting the incumbent Liberal the next day. Stanfield lurched across the tarmac to a passenger ramp that had been wheeled to the edge of a parking lot. An honour guard of pretty girls lined the steps of the ramp and Stanfield climbed past them and, illuminated by car lights, turned at the top to address the small crowd of well-wishers. "So I come home," he said, "with a feeling of pride, with a recognition of what Canada means and what Canada means to the world. . . . I entered federal politics because I felt I might help make it possible for Canada to grow, to help build a country of which we would all be proud." He looked down at the girls on the steps in their tight white blouses and short Tory blue skirts and, if the man standing there at the top of the ramp had been anyone other than Robert Stanfield, a close observer would have interpreted that peculiar expression on his face to be a leer.

His little speech was perfect, but for one unfortunate omission – he forgot to mention the local Tory candidate, Charlie Thomas. Someone whispered in Stanfield's ear and he moved through the crowd shaking hands. "Charlie Thomas," he said. "Charlie Thomas." "Charlie Thomas." (Charlie Thomas won that seat the next day, and there must be a moral in there somewhere.)

Back in Halifax, Stanfield was driven home to "The Oaks" and his waiting wife. The next day, as the Stanfields entered a church basement to cast their ballots, Mary Stanfield turned to *The Globe and Mail* reporter whom she judged to have been the cause of her husband's outburst the night before. "What did you do to my Bob last night?" she asked sternly.

There was something in her eye. It might have been a twinkle.

12

A Man for the Long Haul (1968-1972)

The Tory Party nationally is a grand piano, not a nickelodeon.
You've got to know how to play by touch and you've got to know how
to read the music.

– Dalton Camp.

The rebuilding of the Progressive Conservative Party began at noon on the day after the general election of 1968 on the flagstone patio at the rear of "The Oaks," the Stanfields' gracious old home in Halifax. It had rained overnight and the grass glistened in the mid-day sun. Birds flitted among the trees and shrubs shielding "The Oaks" from its neighbours on Gorsebrook Avenue, and in the distance could be heard the voices of children at play: "Tattle tale. Tattle tale. Tattle tale."

Newsmen who had covered the Stanfield campaign were finishing their post-election press conference and downing the last of their Bloody Marys when the trio from Ottawa slunk in, looking like recalcitrant schoolboys about to get a caning from their headmaster. Eddie Goodman, the normally effervescent lawyer who had run the Tories' national campaign, forced a feeble grin. Malcolm Wickson, the party's national director, looked as though he wished he were back on his sailboat in Vancouver. Gene Rheaume, the executive secretary from party headquarters, brushed imaginary lint from his suit. They joined Lowell Murray, Finlay MacDonald, and Flora MacDonald to start the post-mortem and to begin planning for the future.

Stanfield was wan, but not dispirited, though he was hard-pressed to find any encouragement in the election results. His Conservatives had won only seventy-two seats, their worst showing since 1953 and twenty-five seats fewer than they had won under John Diefenbaker in 1965. Pierre Trudeau's Liberals had elected one hundred and fifty-five members, twenty-four more than the Liberals had managed under Lester Pearson three years earlier. The new Parliament would have twenty-two New Democrats, fourteen

Creditistes, and one independent (the Speaker). For the first time in four consecutive elections, the Canadian people had returned a majority government.

Only the Atlantic Provinces had remained true to the Tories; Stanfield won twenty-five of the region's thirty-two seats – seven better than Diefenbaker had managed in 1965. But in Quebec, the Conservatives dropped from a meager eight seats to a near-invisible four (out of seventy-four). Their performance in Ontario was the party's worst since Confederation; Stanfield managed to retain only seventeen of the province's eighty-eight seats. He had lost seventeen seats on the Prairies, plus all three seats the party had held in British Columbia.

Out in Prince Albert, John Diefenbaker was interpreting the election results as proof positive of the party's folly in stripping him of his leadership. "The Conservative Party," the old Chief intoned, "has suffered a calamitous disaster." Many Conservatives agreed with Diefenbaker, but Stanfield was not one of them. "I don't accept that for a minute," he snapped.

The popular vote was almost the only ray of sunlight. Despite Trudeaumania, the Conservatives had retained 31.4 per cent of the popular vote. That was just one percentage point less than they had polled in 1965. But that one point, plus the effect of redistribution of the Commons' seats before the election, had done Stanfield in. In 1965, 32.4 per cent of the popular vote had been good for ninety-seven seats – or 36.6 per cent of the seats in the Commons. In 1968, 31.4 per cent was good for only seventy-two seats, or 27.3 per cent of the two hundred and sixty-four seats. Trudeau, meanwhile, won 45.5 per cent of the popular vote yet collected 58.7 per cent of the seats. It did not seem fair somehow.

The big names of the Conservative Party had fallen like ten-pins: Faribault, Chouinard, Ryan, and Gagnon in Quebec; Dick Bell, Jean Wadds, Mike Starr, Wallace McCutcheon, Earl Brownridge, and Dalton Camp in Ontario; Roblin in Manitoba; Hamilton in Saskatchewan; and Fulton in British Columbia. Only three of the candidates who had sought the party's leadership just ten months earlier had survived – Stanfield, Diefenbaker, and George Hees. Most of the old Diefenbaker members, however, had weathered the storm and their names read like a litany from dog-eared back issues of the Parliamentary Guide: Walter Dinsdale, Waldo Monteith, Hugh John Flemming, Angus Maclean, Théogène Ricard, Martial Asselin, P. B. Rynard, Wallace Nesbitt, Jack Horner, Jack Bigg, Robert Thompson (the former Social Credit leader), Marvin Howe, Jack McIntosh, Percy Noble. The list went on and on. "Stanfield told me afterwards," remembers Senator Grattan O'Leary, "that it was his misfortune in 1968 that all the 'bonks' got elected while all the good members were defeated."

Equally as ominous, outside of Alberta and the Atlantic Provinces, Stanfield had struck out in urban Canada. He had managed to elect just one member (out of twenty-six) in Metropolitan Montreal and one in Hamilton. He elected none at all in Toronto, Vancouver, Winnipeg, Ottawa, Quebec City, Windsor, London, Regina, Saskatoon, Sudbury, Sault Ste. Marie, Trois-Rivières, Sherbrooke, Kingston, Kitchener, St. Catharines, Niagara Falls, Oshawa, and Thunder Bay.

As Stanfield and his advisers reviewed the results, they saw that the election had accelerated a trend that if unchecked, would surely destroy their party. It was saddled with a diminishing constituency. Broadly speaking, the Conservative supporters in 1968 were older, rural, less affluent, and less well-educated than Liberal supporters in an age where the voting population was increasingly younger, urban, affluent, and educated. Queen's University political scientist John Meisel analyzed the 1968 results and voting trends in a book entitled *Working Papers on Canadian Politics.* "On virtually every one of our relevant indicators," Meisel wrote, "we saw that the Liberals obtained a larger proportion of the vote from those who had been favoured in life, whether in terms of the prestige of their occupation, their educational background, the degree of satisfaction displayed about how life has treated them or of any other of our dimensions. With the exception only of its appeal in the Atlantic Provinces . . . the Liberal Party has appeared as the prestige party, drawing to itself the votes of the more privileged segments on the population. . . . The party's appeal was greater to young voters than to old ones, to urban dwellers rather than to rural settlers, to Canadians with a high as distinct from a low sense of political efficacy, to people displaying relatively little cynicism about politics. In short, Liberal voters, more than those of the other parties, included what might be termed the most industrialized, urbanized, technocratic, and managerial Canadians. In terms of its supporters, therefore, the Liberal Party can be thought of as being most progressive or modern. . . . " And what about the Conservatives? Wrote Meisel: "It is generally safe to assume that for practically every statement made above about the Liberal Party, the reverse holds true for Conservative voters." If all that could be boiled down to a single, unacademic sentence, it would be this: The Conservative Party of 1968 was marching to a different drummer than the majority of the Canadian people.

Robert Stanfield sensed the dimensions of his problems as he talked to his advisers the day following the 1968 election. He was in much the same position that he had been in when he took over the battered Conservative Party of Nova Scotia two decades earlier. A long, slow process of rebuilding lay ahead and it would take all the patience and determination that this patient, determined leader possessed. Furthermore, he knew he would have to build with whatever secondhand material the uncaring electorate had left him in his caucus. Those who knew Stanfield best did not doubt that he would persevere. As one of them put it that day at "The Oaks": "Bob Stanfield is a man for the long haul."

Two challenges faced Stanfield as he set about to rebuild. First he had to re-unite his party that still bore deep wounds from the execution of John Diefenbaker. Second, he had somehow to turn his ragged collection of right-wingers, reactionaries, populists, unfocussed progressives, and political has-beens into a contemporary party that would be effective in opposition in Parliament and attractive to the modern Canadian voter. Of the two, his first priority had to be to unite the party – or, in the terminology of Grattan O'Leary, to woo the "bonks."

"His problems were immense," says Heath Macquarrie, the ardently pro-Stanfield M.P. from Prince Edward Island. "The caucus was not his caucus, really. He put his own Nova Scotians in a separate category and even they didn't always stay in that category. He had, say, a dozen to twenty supporters in caucus, plus the Nova Scotians – less than thirty altogether. It was not a tremendous cheering section for a man who needs a bit of cheering. If he were a normal man prone to getting discouraged, he would have needed more support than that. God, I was impressed by him as those years went by. He endured much. I would put him up against Job in terms of patience."

To Dalton Camp, Stanfield's relentless pursuit of party unity from 1968 to 1972 underscored his essential genius as a politician; he never loses sight of the possibility of reconciliation. "His concept of politics is that you must not alienate people," says Camp. "Although there are people who disagree with you, you mustn't polarize it. You must keep it flexible and fluid and loose enough that you never deliberately make people against you. . . . He never threw anything or anybody away, if he could help it. I think he really believes – and it's kind of a liberal view – that if everybody had the same information they'd come to the same conclusion that he did. And it would be the right one."

Stanfield's relations with Diefenbaker were typical of his approach to reconciliation. Though he was frequently outraged when Diefenbaker upstaged him in Parliament, Stanfield never let on. He never said anything about Diefenbaker that would have given the former leader cause for complaint or excuse to attack his successor. While the two men could not be friends, their relations were cordial. Stanfield consulted Diefenbaker occasionally and treated him at all times with respect, even deference. It was the same with the men who had stuck with Diefenbaker through the years of infighting over the leadership. Stanfield consulted them, took them into his confidence, and assigned them positions of responsibility in the caucus and in the House of Commons – positions from which their lack of ability, shortness of vision, and hostility to the leader would normally have excluded them. "I'll tell you," says Camp, "it takes a lot of nights sitting by yourself to think that through. Stanfield had a certain sense of resolve, of dedication, of discipline to do it. . . . To get to 1972 took sheer dogged determination. He never stopped trying to reconcile himself to the West. He endured a lot of injury, but he never stopped. People, you know, began to say 'He is going to be here for the next election, like it or not and we'd better make the best of it.' "

Characteristically, Stanfield declines to give himself any credit for pulling the party together. "I proceeded in the only way I knew how to proceed," he says, "and that was to deal with people and to work with them and to try to get their confidence. And not to try to keep people on too short a rein." That rein was often far too long, though, in the years following the 1968 election.

Disenchantment with Stanfield's leadership grew deeper, particularly among the Western M.P.s – men such as Jack Horner, Robert Thompson, Jack McIntosh, Robert Simpson, Stan Korchinski, and Stan Schumacher. They blamed Stanfield for the party's humiliation in the election and believed the Conservatives could never return to power under his leadership. Given the chance, they would have opted for a new leader, a leader of the sort Stanfield could never be, a chief more in the Diefenbaker style who would play politics the way they thought it should be played – by opposing the Government at every turn and in every endeavour. Because they thought him weak, they interpreted his attempts at reconciliation as proof of his weakness.

The issue came to a head in the spring of 1969 during debate on the Official Languages Act. It was the most important single piece of legislation brought down by the Trudeau Government. A landmark bill, it was every bit as important – and perhaps more so – than Diefenbaker's cherished Bill of Rights. The Official Languages Act recognized the equality of French and English in Canada; it provided for the use of both languages in federal courts, and it required that federal services be provided in both languages in areas where there were significantly large French or English-speaking minorities. Not least, it provided for the appointment of a languages ombudsman, the Commissioner of Official Languages, responsible to Parliament, to investigate cases of discrimination involving language. Progressive legislation, it deserved the support of every Canadian.

It was not, however, popular legislation in much of English Canada. A Gallup Poll showed that only 56 per cent of Canadians supported its principles. In the West, 70 per cent was opposed. Stanfield began to worry about the Official Languages Act the moment it was mentioned in Trudeau's first throne speech. He was determined personally to support the bill because he believed in its aims and because he knew the party would forfeit any claim to support in French Canada if it opposed it. His problem was to carry his party with him and, realizing he could not persuade all his M.P.s, he worried about the effect the vote would have on the party and on his leadership. "He communicated his concern months ahead," recalls Lowell Murray. "He'd say, 'The big problem I have to face is this official languages business.' He'd say this to Ged Baldwin [Tory House Leader] or Tom Bell [the Tory Whip]: 'We have to start thinking seriously about this.' A couple of days later, it would come up again. He'd keep coming back to it. What he was really saying was that he wanted us to give him some ideas, to discuss it, to put something forward. . . . None of us could see any way out of it. We knew we were going to take a beating on it."

Stanfield sent Tom Bell to talk to some of the Western members, and he talked to others himself. Lowell Murray asked Fred Blois, the senator from Nova Scotia, to talk to Robert Coates, a Nova Scotia M.P. who was dead-set against the bill. Blois called Murray back to report: "That son of a bitch won't budge." While Stanfield and his supporters were trying to cajole the unhappy caucus into backing the legislation, Jack Horner, an Alberta rancher and the self-styled leader of the "Prairie cavalry" was openly organizing opposition to the bill and to his leader. One day Stanfield reported to his staff what another M.P. had been told by Horner: "Well, this fellow [Stanfield] is finished anyway and a little push won't do him any harm. We might as well give him one push." "Stanfield," says one of his aides, "was under the impression that Horner was after his neck at that point."

Though it meant nothing of the sort, the rebel M.P.s interpreted the bill as meaning compulsory bilingualism; their sentiments were only too evident from their arguments during the Commons debate. It was a debate that brought to the surface all the latent bigotry in English-Canadians who, had they been asked under less emotional circumstances, would have insisted they were the best friends French Canada ever had. From Harry Moore, an obscure right-wing Albertan: "If the spokesmen for the Province of Quebec are to be believed, their aim is to have a unilingual province or separate state where the non-French will have to conform in every aspect of life or go under. Their cry is 'Masters in our own house.' I believe it may now have gone beyond that and could be 'Masters in yours, too.' " From

Manitoba's Robert Simpson: "If this program were not being demanded by the Government at this time, the cost of it for five years would possibly provide all the required housing for our native people in Canada." From Bob Coates: "We accomplish nothing by trying to impose the French language upon Canadians by compulsion. It is my belief that the schism in evidence today in this nation between the two major groups could become an unbridgable gap if we continue the debate on this bill." From Jack Horner: "West of the Great Lakes the people will find themselves having to fill out forms to determine what kind of Canadians they are." It was all nonsense.

Diefenbaker was not one of the instigators of the revolt, but he cast his lot with the rebels in a particularly odious speech in the debate. He treated himself to one of his patented attacks on a French-speaking cabinet minister. This time his target was Trudeau's Secretary of State, Gerard Pelletier whom Diefenbaker accused of making "abrasive, provocative" comments during visits to Western Canada that were of the sort "one has heard through the years from those who have opposed everything about English Canada." Diefenbaker dismissed the proposed languages commissioner as a "commissar." "What dictator," he demanded, "could ask for more than these powers?" Three times, Diefenbaker turned to the Conservative benches, glared at the Stanfield supporters and reminded them: "You are all asked to vote for this." One pro-Stanfield M.P. was amused. "That's the first time he's looked at me in the eye for years," said Patrick Nowlan. It took Dalton Camp, though, to put Diefenbaker into proper perspective. In a column in *The Telegram,* Camp noted that in the past Diefenbaker had always preached the supreme importance of loyalty to the party leader. "We now know the limitations of that doctrine," wrote Camp. "It extended only to Mr. Diefenbaker, not to his democratically elected successor." Conservatives who remembered how hard Stanfield had worked in Nova Scotia for Diefenbaker agreed fervently.

The Official Languages Bill passed second reading – approval in principle – in the Commons on a vote of one hundred and ninety-one to seventeen. All seventeen dissenters were Conservatives, sixteen of them, including Diefenbaker, from Western Canada and one, Bob Coates, from the Maritimes. Forty other Tories followed their leader in voting for the bill and the remaining fourteen, who decided they could not support the legislation, had enough respect for the leader to stay away. *The Globe and Mail's* George Bain was impressed by Stanfield's success in producing forty-one Yes votes out of his divided caucus. Referring to the Gallup Poll, Bain wrote: "It is easy to say that the 44 per cent over-all who didn't and don't like the bill reflect mainly yahoo ignorance, closed-mindedness, baseless fears, prejudice, reaction, and just plain mulishness. But there they are. And there are a hell of a lot more of them than were represented by those seventeen no votes on second reading; on this issue, Parliament was substantially ahead of the country, and the Conservative Party substantially ahead of its own followers. . . . What is more remarkable than that Mr. Stanfield suffered seventeen desertions is that he suffered *only* seventeen desertions. . . . Things could have been very much different, and, for the fact that they weren't, Mr. Stanfield deserves considerable credit."

The Official Languages uproar taught Stanfield an important lesson. He learned that, although gentle persuasion was a valuable weapon in a leader's arsenal, it also paid to carry a heavy club. He had reconciled himself to the party's splitting on the bill and he could have forgiven the seventeen M.P.s for defying him, but he could not forgive them for what they did during that vote. Many votes in the House of Commons are taken on a simple voice vote. The Speaker calls for the "yeas" and the "nays" and if he judges the "yeas" to be louder, he declares the bill carried "on division" – meaning it was not unanimous. Formal recorded votes are taken only if five or more members stand up to demand one. Then the division bells are rung, the members are herded in by the whips, and the members supporting and opposing the measure are identified by name and counted. Second reading of the languages bill would have been carried "on division" had not five of the Tory rebels – Jack Horner, William Skoreyko, Harry Moore, and Clifford Downey, all from Alberta, and Jack McIntosh from Saskatchewan – stood to force a recorded vote. Stanfield was upset and angry. "It was not so much that people had voted against the bill," says Lowell Murray, "but that they had embarrassed him and the party by standing and forcing a recorded vote. There were a lot of other guys with constituencies where the bill was very unpopular, but who voted for the bill because of the leader. That sort of thing only hurt them."

After the vote, Pat Nowlan and Steve Paproski, an M.P. from Edmonton who had supported Stanfield, joined the leader in his office for a drink and to discuss Stanfield's next move. It was clear that the time had come to use the club. Stanfield decided to sleep on it overnight; when he arrived in his office in the morning it was obvious he had done more thinking than sleeping. He had notes ready for a speech to the Tory caucus that morning and he rehearsed it in front of his staff. "It was a sulphurous speech," Murray remembers. "It was really sizzling." Stanfield walked over to the West Block to beard the rebels behind the closed doors of the caucus room. Conservative M.P.s had never heard their leader so angry. He told them he understood there were times when, on matters of principle, members had to break ranks. But by forcing a recorded vote when none was necessary, the rebels had tried deliberately to hurt their party and their colleagues. "Their stupidity," he said of the rebels, his voice dripping with sarcasm, "was exceeded only by their malice. There are some things in a political party one simply does not do to one's colleagues." Stanfield told the caucus he had supported the bill because he was working for the very survival of the party, in Quebec and all across Canada. The credibility of the party was at stake and he "god-damned well" was not going to see it undermined. Furthermore, he intended to lead the party into the next election, "and you'd better get used to that idea, too." To prevent further trouble, he said that a caucus committee, headed by Melvin McQuaid from Prince Edward Island, would be established to screen all Conservative amendments to the languages bill in the next stage of the debate, that no other amendments would be permitted, and that anyone who disobeyed these rules would face the consequences. He left the consequences to the imaginations of his members.

It was a remarkable performance from the mild-mannered Stanfield. The revolt dissolved in a sea of abject apologies. The unenviable task of replying to Stanfield fell to Jack Horner, the ring-leader. Apologizing profusely, Horner told the caucus he had had no intention of embarrassing his leader or his fellow M.P.s and that he had done what he had done solely as a matter of principle – the principle being his concern for his part of the country if the languages bill became law.

The Stanfield forces were exultant in victory and they waxed enthusiastic at the new, tough look of their leader. "It was vital for Stanfield to have spoken out," said a Maritime M.P. gleefully. "The whole process was like having an enema. After it's over, you feel weak, but much better." In a revealing, unpublished interview a few days later with Robert Lewis of *Time,* Stanfield conceded that the party split was bound to be regarded by the public as reflection on his leadership. He said he was determined to move the party into a position where it would truly be a national party and not just a spokesman for a variety of regional interests. "I feel the party's got to move," he told Lewis. "We've got to have positions that suit the country – on constitutional matters, on measures such as the languages bill – ones that are compatible with us remaining a national party, a party that can look forward to governing the country effectively. This inevitably means having some strength in Quebec, as well as in other parts of the country. There are other matters upon which we've got to be prepared to move. I don't think we can allow a minority to prevent the party as a whole from taking a position. . . .

"We have to risk a certain amount of dissension in the party to move. To put it quite bluntly, I'd sooner run the risk of a certain amount of splintering, than see the simple disintegration of the party over a period of time because we maintained antediluvian positions for fear of causing a little splintering." To Stanfield, the stakes on the languages bill had been high: "If we had opposed the languages bill as a party we would have run a grave risk of being reduced to just a regional group. I think it would have been very doubtful whether we could have remained a national party."

The intra-party battle over the languages bill was the most serious threat to Stanfield's leadership. He had survived the test, though his opponents were not quite ready to acknowledge their defeat. They tried once more. On April 13, 1970, a federal by-election was held in the Manitoba riding of Selkirk to fill a vacancy left by the resignation of Edward Schreyer, the new N.D.P. premier of Manitoba. The Conservatives fared badly in that by-election, polling slightly more than half the number of votes they had received in the 1968 general election. Without Stanfield's knowledge, Jack Horner wrote letters in June to the Conservative M.P.s from the Prairies and to defeated Tory candidates, inviting them to a "Prairie caucus" in Saskatoon at the end of August. Ostensibly, the meeting was to discuss the party's agricultural policies and to consider the possibility of appointing a campaign organizer for the West. "We felt we had fallen down badly in Selkirk," said Horner later, "that maybe there was too much interference from national headquarters and that we didn't want that to happen again. A lot of us sat around in Ottawa waiting to be called to go help in Selkirk and the call never came. We didn't get a candidate there until far too late and we made a very bad showing."

Inevitably, the meeting turned into a discussion of the leadership and the consensus of the fifteen-odd Tories who attended was unmistakable – the best way to prevent a repetition of the Selkirk rout was to get a leader who understood the West and could appeal to the Prairie voter. It was a vigorous meeting. "This thing is going to blow wide open," a man who was there said later. "The Diefenbaker assassination wound is still open. The only way it can be closed is through the election of a Western leader, and the East better get used to the idea. There will be no P.C. unity until that is done."

The Saskatoon meeting, however, quickly turned into the political farce of the year. No sooner had the first stories appeared in the newspapers, than the conspirators began to beat a disorganized retreat, stumbling over each other in their anxiety to dissociate themselves from any challenge to Stanfield's leadership. "A number of people did bring up the question of leadership," Horner admitted. "But this discussion has mushroomed out of all proportion. I think if you got ten Liberals together in Western Canada they might discuss Trudeau in the same way. I hope they would." As an afterthought, he added: "I don't think he [Stanfield] will be exactly happy with me."

Stanfield was furious. He knew nothing about the Saskatoon meeting until he heard a news report on the radio in Halifax. But he viewed the incident less as a threat to his job than as an opportunity to assert his leadership. "Frankly," he says, "I think it gave me a chance to take charge, to deal with things in the open." Handed the chance, he made use of it.

By coincidence, he was scheduled to spend the next week in Alberta, visiting his daughter Sarah in Edmonton and inspecting the state of the province's agricultural industry. On his way to a beef barbecue at a nearby farm, Stanfield stopped in Camrose to hold a press conference at which he described Horner and his followers as "very stupid" to have held the Saskatoon caucus. The next day, Stanfield visited a 10,000-acre cattle ranch near Calgary owned by Clarence Copithorne. While Stanfield, his wife, and members of his staff were looking over the ranch, Horner arrived to escort the Stanfield party to the next stop on their itinerary, a wheat farm at Arrowwood in Horner's constituency. Inviting himself into Horner's car, Stanfield talked to Horner for nearly two hours as they drove through the gathering dusk of southern Alberta. Stanfield demanded an explanation of the Saskatoon meeting and told Horner how stupid he had been to have organized it. Horner explained his concern that Western attitudes were not being properly represented in the party and in Parliament. Horner told Stanfield of the importance he attached to the preservation of the Western way of life – a lifestyle in which individual initiative and private enterprise are allowed to flower while government interference is held to a bare minimum. Then he told Stanfield he considered him to be a Socialist. "He expressed to me concern about my attitude toward welfare, for example," says Stanfield. "And I think he doubted whether I really understood the West or the Western point of view." The two men did not resolve their differences during that drive, but for the first time they understood each other.

Back in Ottawa, Conservative M.P.s and senators held a full regular caucus on September 9 to prepare for the resumption of Parliament following the summer recess. That caucus went on for four-and-a-half hours and there was a quiet fierceness in Stanfield's voice as he told his followers there must never be a repetition of the Prairie meeting. Henceforth, all regional meetings would have to be cleared in advance with party headquarters and with the leader's office. Such incidents only harmed the party, he warned, at a time when the Conservatives were in a position to exploit the increasing unpopularity of the Trudeau Government. "For God's sake, don't blow it," he said. Again, it was Horner who had to reply and again he was forced to apologize – "My God, I had no intention of splitting the party." "Horner was in sack-cloth and ashes," chuckles Grattan O'Leary and although the

Western members were often restless, in later months, they did not attempt to mount another challenge. "They discovered," says Senator O'Leary, "that they didn't have anyone but themselves."

It was one thing, however, for Stanfield to bring his unruly caucus under control, and quite another thing for him to establish the party in the public's eye as an attractive alternative to the powerful Liberals and himself as a realistic replacement for the charismatic Trudeau. That was not something Stanfield could do alone. He needed the cooperation of Trudeau and the Liberals. The more rapidly the Liberals dispelled the aura of excitement and goodwill that surrounded them following the election of 1968, the sooner the country would turn to the Conservatives. No one, not even the Liberals, expected the euphoria of 1968 to last forever. In an article published four days after the 1968 election, Dalton Camp had assessed the problem Trudeau would face: "What is known about the new Prime Minister is that he is, indeed, articulate, charismatic, and intelligent. It is impossible that he will fulfil all the expectations he has aroused, if for no other reason than that he has aroused them among Canadians with opposite views and conflicting interests." A senior Conservative official made much the same point when he told a reporter: "Canadians are having an affair right now, but they know they have someone reliable to whom they can turn after the affair is over. Stanfield will be the same Stanfield in three years as he is today."

One of Stanfield's strengths as a politician is his grasp of political strategy. Knowing that he could not make inroads into the Liberals' popularity until the public began to fall out of love with Trudeau, he developed a strategy in the summer of 1968 aimed at abbreviating the affair. By the time the seventy-two Conservative survivors assembled in Ottawa in mid-August for their first post-election caucus, Stanfield had his battle-plan ready.

Clutching a six-page outline, Stanfield spelled out the steps the party would have to take to rebuild its fortunes. It would not be good enough, he said, for the Conservatives simply to reinforce their strength in areas where they had elected members. Rather they had to concentrate on their areas of greatest weakness – among the young, in Quebec, and in the cities. "In the party generally," he continued, "we have to work in these areas with a planned and sustained effort in both organization and publicity." He reported on his post-election trips to Vancouver, Winnipeg, and Montreal and said he had found good spirit in the party and an eagerness to begin rebuilding. Though the Tory caucus was only one part of the party, it was essential to the rebuilding process because it was "the tip of the spear. . . . In developing our strategy and our attack, it is of the utmost importance that we remember that although we were elected from seventy-two constituencies, we have to speak for the whole party here – including, and perhaps especially including, those parts of the party where we did not elect members. And we have to develop our strategy and shape our attack bearing in mind that we are trying to develop a movement toward us and away from the Grits on a national basis."

The Conservatives, he told the caucus, could throw the Liberals offstride by concentrating on ridings won by the Liberals in the election. He warned that progress would be slow, because Liberal popularity among the public and the media was certain to keep rising for a short period. "The honeymoon is bound to last for a while longer," he said.

Stanfield warned his M.P.s not to get depressed or impatient; he told them to attack carefully selected targets only. "If we lash out incoherently and in obvious frustration because they are doing well in the first few months, we will make fools of ourselves." The Conservatives, he said, must undermine the Government "relentlessly and intelligently"; call it to account when it stumbles; insist that the great expectations created in the country be fulfilled; press for decisions on issues where the Cabinet is divided or where there is controversy in the country; insist on concrete proof that the "Just Society" is being created: expose areas where Government carelessness or incompetence is creating problems or hardship; be alert for signs of arrogance, for "evidence that the Liberals in a majority position are resuming their dictatorial habits"; watch for signs the Government is trying to circumvent Parliament; watch for evidence that the administration is more legalistic than compassionate in its concern for the individual and his rights. "This attack," Stanfield concluded, "has to be built brick by brick, not in one massive assault, or it will not be credible. It must be based on fact."

It was an exceptional speech for the leader of a badly beaten party. Stanfield indulged in no recriminations, in no second guessing of what might have happened had the election campaign been conducted differently. The speech revealed Stanfield's infinite patience, his willingness to wait, as he had waited for eight years in opposition in Nova Scotia, for the Government to expose its weaknesses. And every one of those potential soft spots – lack of compassion, arrogance, circumvention of Parliament, divisions in the cabinet – that Stanfield identified as early as August, 1968, eventually showed up on the soft underbelly of the Liberal Government.

Stanfield knew that it would not be enough merely to undermine the Government. At the same time, the Conservatives had to promote themselves as the only real alternative to the Liberals. He promised that meeting of the caucus that he would "sharpen" his own leadership image in Parliament and in the country by being more active in the daily question period and in selected debates. "I can't afford, however, to give the impression that I'm dedicated to spending a lifetime as Leader of the Opposition," he said.

"Every time we succeed in knocking the Government down a peg, we have to be in a position to raise our own stock another notch."

Central to Stanfield's strategy was the development of policies that would move his party well away from the curious blend of Prairie populism and traditional conservatism that it had embraced under Diefenbaker. He gradually nudged the party into adopting contemporary policies that would be attractive to the young and to the city dweller. The Official Languages Act was one example of the sort of progressive stance he favoured and he did not hesitate to vote with the Government on other occasions when its measures corresponded with his own thinking. Shortly after the election, the Government re-introduced the controversial omnibus Criminal Code amendments that Trudeau had originally unveiled when he was justice minister. Stanfield allowed his caucus a free vote on that bill – on the ground that many of its clauses, including abortion and the legalization of private homosexual acts between consenting adults, involved matters of conscience. He voted for the entire bill, himself, except for the homosexual clause.

Abandoning the Conservatives' customary "cold war" thinking in external affairs and defence, Stanfield pushed the party into a moderate stand on Canadian involvement in NATO. He adopted a humanitarian position on Biafra at a time when the Trudeau Government seemed more legalistic than compassionate in its approach to the civil war in Nigeria. While the Government was raising one obstacle after another, Stanfield endorsed radio and television broadcasting of the proceedings of Parliament. He sent Heward Grafftey, who had lost his seat in Quebec in the 1968 election, across the country to bird-dog the Government's task force on housing; every time the task force stopped, Grafftey was there to hold a counter press conference and give his opinion on housing problems. It did not produce much in the way of a Tory policy on housing, but it served to remind the public that there was a party called the Progressive Conservative Party, and that it, too, was concerned about the problems of the cities.

At times, Trudeau seemed to be intent on playing into Stanfield's hands. His night-clubbing, banister-sliding performance at his first Commonwealth Heads of Government conference in London at the beginning of 1969 gave Stanfield ammunition for his first biting (and effective) personal attack on the Prime Minister. Perhaps because of the mediocre quality of the Conservative opposition in previous years, Trudeau's Liberals consistently underestimated the Conservatives; Trudeau in particular underestimated Stanfield. Stanfield treated Trudeau with respect, if not cordiality; the Prime Minister responded, at times, with bored indifference and, at others, with amused contempt. While Stanfield maintained an even temper, Trudeau was often moody and occasionally petulant. The Prime Minister's use of four letter words and his contemptuous description of Opposition M.P.s as "nobodies" helped to reinforce the public's perception of Stanfield as a man of dignity and restraint. The contrast between the two leaders was heightened by their attitudes toward the public. Trudeau seemed bent on insulating himself from the public behind layers of advisers and bureaucrats, building a personal staff that eventually numbered close to one hundred with an annual payroll of almost one million dollars. Stanfield, by comparision, was always available. If he was not in St. John's, he was probably in Victoria, flying in with just one or two assistants and, in all probability, carrying his own suit-bag off the plane. No one found him remotely as exciting or interesting as Trudeau, but the people who met him could not help admiring his approachability and his lack of pretention.

Stanfield's major initiative in recasting his party's image was the creation of a policy committee under the chairmanship of Thomas H. B. Symons, a genial historian who was president of Trent University at the time. "The policy-committee idea," wrote Peter Newman in the fall of 1968, "accurately reflects Stanfield's philosophy of opposition. He's well aware that the mood of the country is to give the new government a chance and that any political opponent who attempts to colour it black at this point does so at his peril. The Conservative leader's chief aim at the moment is simply to be there, presenting attractive policy proposals as the head of a credible alternative government. He knows that he has to win the electorate away from a more dashing suitor and he's going about it in a characteristic, sober-sided, long-headed, slow-and-steady's best manner."

Tom Symons organized the Conservative Party's Policy Conference in Niagara Falls in October, 1969. Attended by about four hundred Conservatives, including M.P.s, constituency workers, and sixty invited academics, the conference was a showcase for the progressive thinkers of the party. It nailed together a party platform that, if not daring, at least brought the Conservative Party into the mainstream of Canadian opinion. The delegates approved a capital gains tax as being not only inevitable but (to the horror of old-line Tories) actually desirable. They came within a single vote of calling for more liberal laws on marijuana. In an inconclusive attempt to find the middle ground between the anti-Americanism of the New Democrats and the continentalism of the Liberals, they debated proposals to restrict foreign ownership of Canadian resources and industry. Stanfield began to flesh out the broken bones of hs guaranteed annual income scheme as his researchers came up with a proposal to assure every Canadian family of four a basic income of at least $2,030 a year. That was too much for those Conservatives who worried more about the preservation of the work ethic

239

than the wellbeing of the poor. Stanfield, however, managed to come out of the conference with a compromise of sorts – a basic income for those who could not work and job incentives for those who could. The Niagara Falls Conference was by no means a total victory for the reformers, but it was a major move toward modernizing the party's image and overcoming the anti-intellectualism in the party that had long blocked attempts at reform.

Rebuilding the party was a dreadfully slow process and it seemed suddenly in the fall of 1970 that all the work had been for nothing. In October, separatist terrorists of the Front de Libération du Québec kidnapped British diplomat James Cross and Quebec Labour Minister Pierre Laporte, eventually murdering Laporte and freeing Cross. After ten days of futile manoeuvring, the army was sent into Quebec, and the Trudeau Government followed that by declaring a state of "apprehended insurrection" in Quebec and invoking the War Measures Act, a draconian piece of legislation that had never before been employed in peacetime. It gave the police sweeping powers to enter premises without a warrant, to seize suspects, and to hold them indefinitely without charge or trial. With the advantage of hindsight, the Government can be accused of having over-reacted, but in those confused, traumatic days in October, 1970, it was hard for most people in Ottawa to see what else the Government might have done.

The crisis could not have come at a worse time politically for the Conservatives. After slumping badly in public esteem in the summer of 1970 (a Gallup Poll in August had shown the Conservatives down to 27 per cent compared to the Liberals' 47 per cent), the Tories seemed to be on the rebound. In fact, another Gallup Poll taken before the kidnappings but not released until after the imposition of the War Measures Act would show the Conservatives up to 31 per cent and the Liberals down to 42 per cent. But Trudeau's dramatic display of forceful leadership in a time of crisis was bound to reverse the Conservatives' upward movement. The evening following the proclamation of the War Measures Act, Trudeau was to go on national television to explain his course of action to the country. Stanfield was to follow him on television. But what to say? Stanfield was in a quandary. He recognized that the Government had had to act. But he did not know what information had been available to the Cabinet. Was there in fact an "apprehended insurrection"? Or were the kidnappings nothing more than two, possibly only tenuously related, criminal acts wrapped in a guise of separatist politics? As yet, Stanfield had no way of knowing. He dared not follow the Government blindly by giving a blanket endorsation of its use of the War Measures Act. On the other hand, he knew it was important to the country and crucial to his party's future that he not appear in any way to be tolerant of terrorism. It was the sort of dilemma politicians dread.

Stanfield conferred with his two new senior staff members to work out a statement for television. Both men had been hired following the departures earlier in the year of Lowell Murray, Stanfield's first chief of staff, and Joe Clark, an Albertan who had been his speech writer. One was Tom Sloan, a friendly, absent-minded native of Hamilton, who had been director of journalism at Laval University when Stanfield recruited him as his senior assistant. Sloan was so far to the left of most Conservatives that the Prairie wing was convinced he was either a Socialist or, worse, an intellectual. The other was Stanfield's new executive assistant, Graham Scott, a young Nova Scotian who had been practising law in Toronto and was president of the Young Progressive Conservative Association of Canada when Stanfield hired him. They discussed the approach Stanfield should take. Sloan argued that Stanfield should take a strong pro-civil rights stance and denounce the excessive powers given the police under the War Measures Act. Scott favoured a middle-of-the-road approach (a "balanced position," as they called it) in which Stanfield would support strong measures to deal with terrorists while tempering his support slightly with a concern for the civil rights of those detained. Stanfield agreed to a middle-of-the-road position and went on television to say he would support the Government's use of the War Measures Act for the time being until the Government could bring in new legislation that would give the authorities adequate powers to control the F.L.Q. without the wholesale suspension of civil rights. Under the circumstances, it was the only realistic position Stanfield could have taken for his party, but it made him seem dreadfully wishy-washy. Most people in the country fell into line behind the Government; the civil libertarians flocked to the N.D.P. Stanfield accepted the inevitability of that. "This is going to cause us a great deal of difficulty in the country," Stanfield told Sloan and Scott before he went on television that night. "It may hurt the party seriously, but it is something I've got to say." "Oh, bullshit!" Scott exclaimed. But Stanfield knew better. "He was right," Scott conceded later. "The civil liberties people denounced us for not endorsing their cause and the rest denounced us for being weak-kneed on law and order."

The Conservatives' dilemma worsened later when the Government introduced its new legislation, the Public Order (Temporary Measures) Act. Having demanded such legislation, Stanfield felt committed to supporting it, although he was coming to the conclusion that the Government had over-reacted in October, that the crisis was a good deal less serious than it had seemed at the time, and that the new legislation gave the authorities more power then they needed. He felt trapped.

Two Gallup Polls published in December confirmed his worst fears. The first showed that 87 per cent of the Canadian public endorsed the Government's use of the War Measures Act; only 6 per cent disapproved and 7 per cent was undecided. Within a week, the second poll – the first party popularity poll taken since the crisis – showed that the Liberals, who had sunk to 42 per cent before the crisis, had soared all the way to 59 per cent. The Tories meanwhile fell from 31 per cent before the crisis to a wretched 22 per cent after it.

Six weeks after the kidnapping of James Cross two federal by-elections were held in Quebec and Brian Mulroney, the Conservative organizer in Montreal, realized that there was no way, in the wake of the crisis, that the Conservatives could make a respectable showing. Telling Stanfield it would cost the party $20,000 to fight each by-election, Mulroney recommended the Conservatives not field candidates. "The hell you're not," Stanfield snapped. "You are going to run candidates." Mulroney found a pair of candidates and, as expected, both lost their deposits.

Stanfield seemed dispirited in the months following the October crisis. His friends found him listless and they confided to one another that the leader seemed to have lost his will to continue the fight. He seemed content to drift with events. Gradually, however, Stanfield pulled out of his depression and went back to work.

Much of that work was travel. No Canadian political leader ever travelled farther or harder than Stanfield did from 1968 to 1972. He averaged 7,300 miles of travel a month in those years and made a monthly average of eight major speeches outside of Ottawa. His activity increased each year: 59,000 miles in 1969; 87,000 in 1970; 109,000 in 1971; and, including the election campaign, close to 135,000 miles in 1972. It became a standing joke around the office: Where's Bob? Oh, he's in Vancouver (or Toronto or Montreal or Yellowknife). What, not again? Yes, afraid so.

The travel was part of his strategy to establish his image as the leader of an alternative government. In pursuit of that objective, he made two extended trips overseas to visit foreign capitals, to see and be seen on the international stage. In 1970, he set off on a tour of France, Belgium, West Germany, Yugoslavia, the Soviet Union, and Great Britain. Accompanying him were his wife and Tom Sloan, his senior assistant. His former aide, Lowell Murray, who was vacationing in Greece, joined them on the continent. As they travelled, Sloan ghosted a series of articles that *The Telegram* dutifully published and syndicated under the Stanfield byline. They spent a weekend in Leningrad where they toured the Arctic Institute, then went on to Moscow where Stanfield conferred with the first deputy premier, Kirill Mazurov, a member of the ruling Politburo.

The highlight of the trip, though, was Belgium where Stanfield talked to officials of the European Economic Community. He was intrigued with the operation of the Common Market, but he was less than entranced by the officials' answers when he asked them what role they saw for Canada in the world. "Look at the Swiss," they told him. "The Swiss specialize in things like watches. You fellows in Canada really ought to get into something like watches." When Stanfield protested that they did not understand the nature of the Canadian economy, they levelled with him: "Look, we don't know what has kept you fellows from joining the Americans long ago. It's obviously your place, just as Britain's place is with the continent, with Europe. Your place is with the Americans. What other place is there for you?" Stanfield shrugged his shoulders and moved on.

Though he had no great interest in NATO, he went through a set of meetings with officials of the alliance. The denouement came when Manlio Brosio, the secretary-general of NATO, threw a luncheon for Stanfield. A group of delegates from the NATO member nations assembled for the occasion and all went well as the several elegant courses were served and the various wines poured. Then the champagne arrived and, remaining seated (it being the diplomatic version of an informal lunch), Brosio made a warm little speech of welcome, praising Stanfield as a great friend of NATO, the Conservative Party as a great friend of NATO and Canada as a great friend of NATO. He lifted his glass, said "Welcome" and took a sip of champagne. Everyone followed suit. There was a deathly silence in the room. Stanfield smiled. The silence continued. At their places below the salt Murray and Sloan hunted for something to throw at Stanfield to wake him up to the fact that he was expected to respond to the toast. Everyone stared at him, waiting. Finally, it dawned on Stanfield. Picking up his glass he gave a four-word reply: "Good luck to NATO." The other guests sat in amazed silence. At last, it was broken by a British delegate who had partaken generously of the earlier wines. "Well," he said, a trifle too heartily, "I guess we can all drink to that."

In the summer of 1971, Stanfield went to Japan and China. After meetings with the acting foreign minister and the vice-chairman of the National Peoples' Congress in Peking, he, Mrs. Stanfield, Sloan, and Graham Scott flew to Shanghai where the Stanfields went on a shopping spree in the city's Friendship Store, and toured an industrial exhibition. They visited a primary school where they saw children wave paper sabres and pledge death to the American imperialist aggressors, and stopped at a Chinese home where the mother told him of the good life under the Communist regime (compared to the miseries of the pre-liberation period). Though it was not the sort of thing Stanfield had ever encountered in Truro or Toronto, the woman concluded her account by singing a song from a revolutionary opera.

243

That night the Stanfields were guests of honour at a civic banquet in Shanghai – nine courses washed down by toasts of fiery *maotai*. Although he seldom drinks much, Stanfield has an impressive capacity for liquor. But Graham Scott was feeling the effects. Finally, he leaned over to his employer to tell him he thought he would pass out if there were another toast. With a grin, Stanfield told him to keep drinking: "The integrity of Canada demands it. You can't let your side down."

From Shanghai, they travelled to Canton where the Stanfields, to their distress, were ushered into a hospital operating room to witness a demonstration of acupuncture used as an anaesthetic on a twenty-year-old boy undergoing a thyroidectomy. Afterwards, Stanfield and Sloan made the mistake of challenging their hosts to a few friendly games of table tennis. Sloan upheld the integrity of Canada by splitting his two games, but Stanfield dropped both games to an opponent who was trying desperately to lose to the distinguished visitor from Canada.

When he got back to Canada, Stanfield briefly enjoyed modest celebrity status as an expert on China. One day External Affairs Minister Mitchell Sharp invited Stanfield to attend a luncheon for ambassadors. The guest speaker was retired Canadian diplomat Chester Ronning, an old China hand, who talked at great length about China. Stanfield was bored to distraction. When Ronning finished, he asked whether anyone had a question and Stanfield broke up the assembled ambassadors with a puckish inquiry: "Mr. Ronning, how would you equate the Great Leap Forward with the last three years of [Finance Minister Edgar] Benson economics?"

Aside from those two major trips abroad – and a quick visit to Alaska to inspect the Trans-Alaska Pipeline route – Stanfield restricted his travel to Canada. In early 1971, he made a national unemployment tour, stopping in seven cities to talk to jobless youths, wives of unemployed workers, labour leaders, and welfare and social workers. Partly, the tour was to give Stanfield a little first-hand insight into the miseries of unemployment, partly it was to dramatize the Government's failure to relieve unemployment; mostly it was to bring Stanfield, the alternative Prime Minister, within range of local television cameras. Although it was mostly for show, it did produce a few spontaneous incidents. In Toronto, Stanfield dropped into the Pam Pam Coffee Shop to chat with the owner, Peggy Bragg, a lady of unusual kindness who every day supplied free coffee to the jobless men lined up in the snowy street to collect their cheques from a nearby welfare office. Stanfield forgot all about Mrs. Bragg, but she remembered his visit and when the 1972 election was called she mailed him a cheque for $200 to help get rid of Prime Minister Trudeau. "I resent Mr. Trudeau's careless spending," she wrote. "I don't want to discuss him because he is an ass." It was the sort of letter that is guaranteed to cheer the days of an opposition leader.

There were few towns that Stanfield did not visit at least once between 1968 and 1972. Everywhere he went he pointed out the weaknesses (as he saw them) in the Liberal Government and explained his own party's policies. He moved into a high-rise apartment in Toronto for a few days to find out how the "swingles" do it, inspected Indian schools in the Northwest Territories, drank coffee in a low-rental housing development in Vancouver, and beamed happily when they introduced him in Weyburn, Saskatchewan as the next Prime Minister of Canada. He suffered gamely, without even a hint of a grimace, as the Forest (Ontario) Excelsior Band serenaded him with what was quite possibly the most execrable rendition ever heard of Beethoven's *Ninth Symphony.* He went to Whitehorse and met Lipstick Lou who initiated him into the Grand Exalted Order (of what, no one was sure) and proclaimed him the "best darned garter watcher in the Yukon." He kissed a widow in Toronto (only Trudeau seemed to get the teen-aged girls), was christened "Bluenoser Bob" in Ancaster, and went on an open-line program in St. Catharines where he made such an impression that a little old lady called in to urge him to run for Parliament (as a Conservative, fortunately). He auctioned off a bicycle in Essex, Ontario, joined a tug-o'-war in Oakville, and slipped behind the wheel of a racing car in Toronto. He toured a paper mill in Cornwall, then turned around and made a speech denouncing people like paper mill operators who pollute the environment. In Toronto, he attended a performance of the rock musical *Hair,* and, with only a little prompting, jumped up on the stage to dance with the cast – for the "pure joy" of it, as Stanfield put it: it nearly sent countless staid Tories into cardiac arrest. "This Hairy thing is the final straw," grumped a Western Conservative.

Back in Ottawa, he made his stage debut as a stretcher-bearer in the National Ballet of Canada's production of *The Nutcracker Suite* before a packed house at the National Arts Centre. Stanfield's role called for him merely to carry off the Gingerbread Man after he had been done in by a gang of giant mice, but the Sugarplum Fairy turned stool pigeon and confided to the press that stretcher-bearer Stanfield had overplayed his part by taking a bite out of the Gingerbread Man in the belief he was Pierre Trudeau in cunning disguise. Much of it was fun in those four years, but most of it was hard work. Occasionally it was downright discouraging. The worst day must have been when he went on a hot-line radio program in Simcoe, Ontario, and the phone did not ring once during the hour.

He stepped up his pace as rumours mounted in 1972 that Trudeau was preparing to call an election. A summary of Stanfield's activities for one week in small towns in Southern Ontario that summer gives an idea of his pace: Monday – community breakfast, television interview, lunch with party workers, news conference, visit to old folks' home, tour glass plant, curling club reception, visit shopping centre, beef barbecue; Tuesday – community breakfast, visit old folks' home, visit Opportunities for Youth project, lunch with community leaders, question-and-answer session with students, tour factory, reception and Old Tyme picnic, coffee at roadhouse; Wednesday – public breakfast and reception, open-line show, visit hockey school, tour factory, visit historic site, visit social services centre for senior citizens, tour factory, open regatta, visit recycling centre, attend lacrosse match, wine and cheese party; Thursday – coffee with citizens in parking lot, news conference, open-line show, tour paper mill, visit fruit farm, visit old folks home, dance with Young Conservatives; Friday – open-line show, visit old folks home, visit Opportunities for Youth project, mainstreet to meet locals, open stock-car race, attend beerfest; Saturday – lunch with civic leaders, lead children's parade, attend pork barbecue. On Sunday, he was allowed to go home to see his wife.

It was a schedule that, week after week, demanded the stamina of a mountain climber and the stomach of a goat. Stanfield was well equipped for that sort of pre-election campaigning. "If you take all the qualities of physical strength, emotional strength, and political savvy, he would come out on top of the other leaders," observed Liam O'Brian, the Tories' national director. "When you come right down to it, he's a tough, fit guy. He's the old Chinese water torture – water on rocks."

There were days, however, when Stanfield doubted whether he could possibly wear the rock away in time. His mood varied from mild optimism to mild despair, depending on the response of the crowds along his route. There were some days when he wondered whether he could defeat the powerful Liberals. There were other days when he thought it might be possible in the not-too-distant future. The more astute Liberals started to worry a little as they watched Stanfield slowly and patiently getting to know the voters. "Stanfield," said one of Trudeau's politically alert ministers in the summer of 1972, "has a high quotient of trust among the people. That's a very valuable commodity."

But most Liberals scoffed. They were patronizing toward Stanfield, seeing him as an honest but uninspiring politician who had an uncanny ability to reduce voters to a state of ennui. They knew their man, Pierre Trudeau, could draw a larger crowd by walking across the street in the dead of a rainy night than Stanfield could attract with a band, dancing girls, and a free bar at high-noon in downtown Toronto. Everyone agreed with Jack Webster, the razor-tongued king of the radio hot-line artists, who pronounced his judgment after having Stanfield on his Vancouver program: "He's one of the nicest, dullest subjects in the country. It's impossible to be rude to him."

Everyone who could understand Marshall McLuhan agreed with the guru: "There's nothing for Stanfield to do as long as he's Stanfield."

13

And Now,
Bob Stanfield (1972)

If we couldn't be defeated, it wouldn't be a democracy. . . . I'll tell
you right now, we can lose this election, but we don't intend to.

> – Pierre Trudeau, announcing the 1972
> general election.

At one minute and thirty seconds after six o'clock (according to the script
in the TV producer's hand) on the evening of September 1, 1972, Pierre
Elliott Trudeau straightened his shoulders and lifted his head to stare
unsmilingly into the eyes of the TV cameras in Ottawa's National Press
Building. Reading quickly from a prepared statement, he announced that
he had just returned from Government House where Governor General
Roland Michener had agreed to dissolve the Twenty-Eighth Parliament. A
federal general election would be held on Monday, October 30. As Trudeau
spoke, Robert Stanfield slipped unnoticed into a dressing room a few feet
away where he watched the Prime Minister on TV as a girl applied the
makeup for his appearance following Trudeau's.

There was something wrong with Trudeau that day, though Stanfield,
like the reporters covering the press conference, could not put his finger on
it. Trudeau's performance was flat; he seemed almost bored. Although he
spoke of the challenges to be faced in the fifty-nine days of the campaign,
his voice betrayed no enthusiasm, no excitement, no sense that he was about
to embark on a voyage of political discovery. "The challenge," he said
obscurely, "is nothing less than the integrity of Canada – the homeland of
persons so dedicated to the social advantages of tolerance and moderation,
so convinced of the value of a single, strong economic unit, so proud of our
accomplishments and our image that we are committed to Canada." What
did it mean? Had someone – the Conservatives or the New Democrats,
perhaps – suggested that Canadians were not committed to Canada? Had
anyone implied that tolerance, moderation, and a strong economy were less
than national virtues? Trudeau provided no clarification. "The challenge to

Canada, the challenge of this election," he continued, "is to ensure that Canadians continue to exhibit the self-confidence and the assurance that will permit Canada to pursue its own policies and demonstrate the advantages of its value system." Had something happened in his four-plus years as Prime Minister to render fragile the self-confidence of Canadians? Was the nation seized with self-doubt? Trudeau did not say. He gave the impression of a man who had called an election not because he felt he needed one, not because there were issues to be resolved, but simply because the Constitution told him that he would have to have one soon. The claque of troubled Liberals gathered at the back of the press conference theatre breathed a sigh of relief when Trudeau finished and Stanfield moved in front of the cameras.

Over on Bank Street, in the well carpeted national headquarters of the Liberal Party of Canada, a confident, almost eerie, calm prevailed. Torrance Wylie, the party's national organizer, was unperturbed about the campaign. "The traditional way is to view elections as a competition between parties," Wylie explained. "I don't see it that way. I see an election as an opportunity to establish a relationship with the voter. That's what we will try to do. We will tell him what we have done, why we have done it, what we are planning for the future, and invite him to share in it." And what about the opposition parties? "I hate to admit it," said Wylie, "but I spend no time thinking about the opposition parties, because I don't believe in elections as competitions."

That was what was wrong with the Liberal election campaign of 1972. Although Trudeau admitted the possibility of defeat, neither he nor his party regarded it as a real possibility. The Liberals were going to run in the election as though they were running alone. Their theme would be a vaguely defined concept of Canadian integrity, which, as nearly as anyone was ever able to figure out, was a sort of Everyman's stew, consisting of left-over scraps of the Just Society, a few teaspoonfuls of national unity, and a pinch of mild nationalism. The Liberals would go on the hustings; they would reassure the public that the country was in good hands. Then they would sit back while the electors faithfully returned another majority Liberal government. The government was not about to go into tiresome explanations or defences of its record of the previous four years. Trudeau himself had made that clear in a speech six months earlier to the Liberal Party of Ontario. "People," Trudeau said on that occasion, "don't want to hear you enumerate a long list of accomplishments that you have on your record, or a long list of excuses for things that you've failed to do. They want to know how you're going to face the years to come."

The Liberals strolled complacently into the campaign, blinded by their belief that in 1972, as in 1968, the election was won the moment they called it.

They should have known better. Originally they had planned to call an election in the spring of 1972, but had been deterred by the public opinion polls. A Gallup Poll in March, for example, had shown that a stunning 43 per cent of the electorate did not know how it would vote. In June, Liberal popularity stood at only 39 per cent; that was 6.5 percentage points below the actual Liberal vote in the 1968 election. By late August, however, the Liberals had climbed to 42 per cent – a clear ten points ahead of the Conservatives. Assuming the trend to be upward, the Liberals called the election; they were sure they were within easy campaigning reach of the 43 to 44 per cent they needed to retain a majority in the Commons.

The Liberals acknowledged that the election would be different from the campaign of four years earlier, if only because the Prime Minister could no longer pass himself off as the dashing newcomer to politics. But they made two fatal assumptions: that the voters would not be much interested in their record; and that the public's perception of Trudeau had not altered significantly since 1968. They were sure the old magic was still there. They assumed that when Trudeau turned on the charisma, the voters would respond as they had in 1968.

Had they been more inclined to critical self-scrutiny, the Liberals might have worried. They would have seen what others saw – that there was little in the Government's past performance to inspire confidence in its ability to meet the problems of the future. Although he had had a majority in the House of Commons to do his bidding for four years, Trudeau had failed to make his mark on the country. At times it had seemed as though he was barely trying. He had, it was true, given the country the Official Languages Act and the forceful leadership the nation had needed during the F.L.Q. crisis. He had been moderately innovative in foreign affairs, staking out for Canada a place that was both intelligent and realistic. But his domestic record had, on balance, been lamentable. He had brought in a new, progressive, and generous system of unemployment insurance; he had transformed the white paper on Tax Reform into a new Income Tax Act that, although it was too diluted to be called a reform, did at least move some of the burden of taxation from the poor to the well-to-do.

But in most other areas, the dream of 1968 had turned to dust. The process of constitutional review that had begun so promisingly under Lester Pearson had ground to a halt under Trudeau. He had toyed half-heartedly with one of the growing problems of Canadian nationhood: the foreign domination of the country's resources and means of production. Finally, he produced a foreign-takeovers bill that touched on only one small corner of the problem. It was not passed. He introduced only one important piece of social welfare legislation: known as the Family Income Security Plan (FISP), it was intended to replace the universal family allowance system with allowances based on income. It, too, failed to pass, and the Government abandoned the concept. He promised in 1968 to give top priority to legislation to control election spending, then waited for four years before bringing in a bill that did not deal with the most serious abuses. It did not pass, either. He proposed a new Competition Act to deal with corporate monopolies and combines, only to withdraw it in the face of opposition from the business community. He promised a new deal for Canada's native peoples and published a white paper setting out the Government's policy. When the natives objected, he dropped it and did not replace it. He brought in legislation to assist middle-income families to obtain home mortgages, and amendments to the National Housing Act to pump money into urban renewal. The two measures constituted almost his entire housing policy, yet he gave neither bill sufficient priority to enable it to pass before the election.

Worse, Trudeau mismanaged the economy. Determined to curb inflation, even at the cost of higher unemployment, he adopted a ploy of fiscal restraint. Unemployment certainly increased – and inflation continued unabated. Then, to create jobs, he tried increasing government spending, even though he had said during the 1968 campaign, "One promise we are going to make, and we are going to keep, is that of making sure we keep the economy sound by spending no more than we earn as a government." The Government budgeted for a two billion dollar deficit for 1972-1973, but unemployment continued to rise so that by election-time it was nearing 7 per cent. NDP leader David Lewis set out the opposition line a few days before the election was called. "In pretty nearly every domestic issue of any importance," he said, "the Government has failed. Because Mr. Trudeau raised such high expectations in 1968, the anger and the frustration is so much greater."

The expectations of 1968 notwithstanding, the Liberals would have won easily in 1972 if the Pierre Trudeau of 1972 had been the Trudeau of 1968. But something had happened to Trudeau in those four years. The exciting reformer of 1968 had been overtaken by his image. He set out to modernize the process of government, yet his administration took more time to do less than almost any administration in the country's history. The swinging suitor of 1968 who had replied to a girl's request for a kiss with a jaunty, "Why not? It's spring," turned into a prime minister with a coarse tongue that he applied to strikers picketing Parliament Hill and opposition Members of Parliament. He was impatient with those he considered his intellectual inferiors. He surrounded himself with people who feared to disagree with him. The goodwill that had surrounded his ascension four years earlier turned to disenchantment and anger. The challenge facing him when he came to office was to demonstrate, in the words of Dalhousie University political scientist J. Murray Beck, "his ability to satisfy the demands of rational exponents of Trudeauism for a new kind of politics." He failed that test.

Ironically, Trudeau's major shortcoming as Prime Minister was his inability to do what he had done best in 1968 – communicate with the public. As Bruce Hutchison, the author and editor, put it in an open letter to Trudeau: "With all your genius for communication – the eloquent shrug, the corroding reply in "basic" English, the sly *mot juste,* the bilingual insult – you have not communicated the central truths of Canadian life; not clearly enough, anyhow, to reach the common mind."

Trudeau lost touch with his constituency. And the people, who had expected so much of him, felt alienated not only from the Prime Minister but from the whole process of government. There was a sense among the electors that *the* government in Ottawa was not *their* government. The public felt rather as Alden Nowlan, the New Brunswick poet, felt when he looked on the nation's capital.

> The first thing that you learn here
> Is that the country
> Bears the same relationship
> To the government
> That outer space
> Bears to the earth.

Twenty-four hours before the election was called, Robert Stanfield sat in his House of Commons office talking about Pierre Trudeau, the man he would have to defeat. "In 1968, Mr. Trudeau was accepted as the new spirit, above politics in the ordinary sense of the term," Stanfield said. "Now the people have seen him as Prime Minister for over four years. Some have seen him as a playboy who takes too many holidays. A great many doubt whether there is any warmth in his concern. . . . I think he has difficulty in listening to people, difficulty in spending enough time with his caucus, keeping in touch with them and, through them, with the people of the country. I've always believed that a party leader has to spend a lot of time with people. He has to spend a lot of time with members of his caucus and listen to things, listen to their arguments, some of which he frequently may not think much of. . . . I have the impression Mr. Trudeau is pretty largely making the main decisions himself and relying mainly for advice on people he chooses. I don't think he suffers fools gladly. I don't want to sound patronizing to the Canadian people when I say this, but the Prime Minister has to be prepared to listen and to understand all kinds of people."

The cooling of the love affair between the Canadian public and Pierre Trudeau did not mean the voters were ready to embrace Robert Stanfield. Far from it. Most of the people were still puzzled by him. Many were totally unimpressed. Those who had come to know Stanfield judged him to be Trudeau's equal in intelligence, if not in articulation. Although he lacked Trudeau's hard-edged brilliance, he seemed to many people to have more common sense. He was less doctrinaire than Trudeau, more flexible in his approach to the cornerstone issues of the country, particularly English-French relations, and more receptive to the opinions of others. "There was no way that people disliked or distrusted Stanfield," says Heath Macquarrie. "Unexcited by him, yes, but turned off by him, no."

Stanfield's problem was his inability to create a lasting impression. People met him, liked him, and promptly forgot him. His advisers begged him to be more dynamic, more aggressive, more positive. Stanfield would agree with their arguments, but he would not change. He did not intend, as he kept saying, to be someone he wasn't.

The Conservative election strategy recognized that the party would have to win or lose with Stanfield as he was, not as others thought he should be or might be. The campaign planners sought to exploit Stanfield's strengths – his stability, his reliability, his maturity, his good sense, his willingness to listen, his understanding of economics and financial issues, and his quiet good humour. They tried to extend to the voter their own perception of Stanfield, the man they watched around the office and joked with up front in the campaign plane.

The Conservatives were better prepared for the campaign of 1972 than they had ever been for an election before. They had begun planning in earnest in June, 1970 when the then national director of the party, Malcolm Wickson, had presented a candid report to the Conservative national executive. The report reached the same conclusions as had the studies being made at Queen's University by John Meisel. The picture painted by Wickson was not an encouraging one. "Our present base of support is characterized by two things," Wickson reported. "It is elderly and it is rural. This is obviously a diminishing base. The average age of the voting population is going down and we will soon see the minimum voting age lowered to eighteen. Demographic studies tell us that our country is becoming more and more urbanized. In twenty years, 90 per cent of all Canadians will live in large urban centres. Successive redistributions will inevitably reflect this trend, making rural seats fewer and therefore less important in the terms of overall electoral strategy."

Wickson told the executive that, to survive, the party had no alternative but to build a new coalition, both in French and English-speaking Canada, based on the young, educated, urban voter. "In order to reach this new constituency we must be perceived as a young progressive party with a modern approach to government." He said the party would have to adopt new tools of political technology and communications and "push boldly ahead" with the formulation of an attractive, contemporary platform. "Above all," he stressed, "we will have to achieve the cooperation and commitment of all levels of the party." Wickson did not need to spell out this last point. To win in 1972, Stanfield would need the whole-hearted support of the provincial Conservative governments – something he had not received in 1968. "While some of these initiatives might have seemed vaguely desirable before," Wickson concluded, "the [party's] surveys have shown us that they are absolutely necessary to ensure our survival, let alone our success."

The national director proposed that a program for Stanfield be developed and implemented over the succeeding two years. It would be aimed at "increasing his public exposure and improving his public perception as a solid, decisive, statesmanlike leader and potential prime minister." From that came a decision to accelerate Stanfield's travel in Canada and abroad. The party also commissioned a survey to determine Stanfield's marketability – the same sort of market survey that a soap company would order before introducing a new dishwasher detergent. The survey found that Stanfield had almost no strength, in the public's mind, in dealing with international affairs, and that he trailed Trudeau dismally in "public personality" (meaning the ability to excite and involve the voter). But they were encouraged to find him running "slightly but significantly" ahead of Trudeau in the public's perception of his ability to cope with economic problems. That dictated a strategy: Stanfield should concentrate on such issues as inflation, unemployment, taxation, and housing. Because the party was desperately weak in three sections of the country, Stanfield should devote his primary attention to them: Ontario, Quebec, and British Columbia.

The Wickson report also identified the voters that the party would have to concentrate on. These were what Wickson called the "switchers," the one voter in five who had no commitment to any party and who was apt to vote for any of them. Wickson listed five characteristics of the "switcher": Grade XIII or better education, often with a university degree; slightly above average income; young to middle aged; employed in business or in a professional or managerial occupation; resident in an urban or suburban community. "It is this group of people who will decide the outcome of the next election," Wickson said. "In 1968 Trudeau got almost all of them. Our immediate task is to win them back."

On December 28, 1970, Wickson presented an interim planning paper on election arrangements. In it, he recommended the creation of a nine-member campaign planning committee with himself as chairman and including as members his successor as national director, Liam O'Brian, Claude Dupras, the chairman of the Tory organization in Quebec, and Robert Teeter of Market Opinion Research, an American pollster who worked for the Tories as "Voter Research Consultant" when he was not occupied with Republican candidates in the United States. The interim paper also listed a staff of 147 people who would be required for the campaign, and outlined a headquarters budget of $3.245 million (later raised to $3.8 million). The budget allocated $140,000 for the leader's tour (the bulk of it to go for the lease of a DC-9 jet), $750,000 for national advertising, and $50,000 for Teeter's polling.

The plans were fine, but they did not help Stanfield in meeting his most urgent problem: establishing a political base in Quebec. He needed better organization in the province and new candidates, preferably including a few who were known outside of Quebec. In the summer of 1971, Graham Scott, Stanfield's executive assistant, went to Montreal to spend a weekend with Michel Cogger, a young Tory who had worked for Davie Fulton in the leadership campaign. As they discussed the party's dilemma in Quebec with Brian Mulroney, the labour lawyer and Conservative organizer who had also worked for Fulton, they agreed that they needed at least one "star" candidate. They made a list of names, and one of the names on the list was Claude Wagner, a judge and former provincial Liberal justice minister who had been defeated by Robert Bourassa for the leadership of the Quebec Liberal Party.

They were worried about Wagner's reputation as a hardline law-and-order man; they wondered whether he would fit the new moderate image Stanfield was trying to create for the party. They were concerned about his political credentials; although he had a reputation for being a strong federalist, he still carried the Liberal label, and he had been wooed as a prospective leader by both the provincial Créditiste Party and the Union Nationale. Still, Wagner was undoubtedly a popular figure in Quebec, and Mulroney decided he would be worth approaching. He telephoned Wagner, made an appointment to see him, then called Stanfield to tell him what he was up to. Stanfield told him to go ahead. "I knew we couldn't win across the country," Mulroney says, "unless the English voter knew we had a strong federalist voice in Quebec."

In September, 1971, Mulroney arranged a meeting at his apartment between Stanfield and Wagner. The two men had a long talk. Wagner probed Stanfield's views on Quebec, on constitutional reform, and on welfare. He was impressed that Stanfield, following the collapse of the federal-provincial constitutional talks at the Victoria conference in June of that year, had gone to see Premier Bourassa and Quebec's Minister of Social Affairs, Claude Castonguay, to discuss Quebec's objections to the Victoria Charter. "I'm not a separatist," says Wagner, "but I found his federalism flexible. He sought to avoid the confrontation of the Trudeau style. . . . I found him understanding." Wagner and Stanfield also found that they liked each other. Stanfield told him he would be delighted to have him as a candidate; Wagner said he would give the idea serious thought.

They kept in touch after that meeting with Stanfield phoning periodically to inquire, without pressure, how the judge was coming in his thinking. Much of the time, Brian Mulroney acted as intermediary. "I hate to think how much money I spent buying lunches for that guy [Wagner]," laughs Mulroney.

Although he knew Wagner was popular in Quebec, Mulroney did not know *how* popular he was, or in what parts of the province and among what sort of voters. In January, 1972, he had Robert Teeter do a survey. The poll, with a sample of 475 people and a price tag of more than ten thousand dollars, asked a broad range of questions on voter attitudes. But the question that interested Mulroney was one that asked the respondents which person on a list of names was "best qualified to represent the interests of Quebec in Parliament." The purpose – to compare the popularities of Wagner and Trudeau – was disguised by listing other names, including Réal Caouette, Lucien Saulnier, Jean Drapeau, and Marcel Masse. To the Tories' delight, Wagner led the poll with 26 per cent, two points ahead of Trudeau. (In view of the election results, the survey was unquestionably misleading; the important thing was that the Conservatives believed it and acted on it.) Mulroney showed the poll to Stanfield. "I'm interested," the leader said. "Go ahead."

The courtship of Claude Wagner began in earnest. Wagner, however, presented a host of obstacles that had to be overcome. What sort of constituency would the Conservatives provide him with? They offered him Saint-Hyacinthe, east of Montreal, because it was the closest thing to a "safe" Tory seat in the province (Théogène Ricard having held it with a majority of 788 votes in 1968). Could they get him elected? They assured him they could, promising whatever money he needed for his campaign. (They wound up giving him twelve thousand dollars.) Was Stanfield, Wagner asked, talking only for himself when he urged him to run? Or was he speaking for the full party? Would the Western Conservatives accept him? They assured him his candidacy would be welcomed throughout the party; to help to convince him of that, they arranged to have others telephone him.

One of the callers was William Davis, the new premier of Ontario, who told Wagner: "We'd be proud to have you run for us, Claude, and I hope you will." "That," says Wagner, "helped a lot."

Wagner had still not made up his mind by the summer of 1972 when he took his family away for their annual vacation at Cape Cod. When he returned in August, he again met Mulroney who, knowing an election was imminent, was getting extremely worried. "Look," he told Wagner, "this bus only passes once. If you want to get on, this is the time." "I agree," replied Wagner. "I'm going to get on." The decision became final on the night of August 30 – forty-eight hours before the election was called – when Wagner and his wife went to Ottawa for dinner with Robert and Mary Stanfield at "Stornoway." The next night, Thursday, Finlay MacDonald, the Tory campaign chairman, went to Montreal to meet Wagner and Mulroney and, in Mulroney's words, "to put the baby to bed." The election was called on Friday, and Saturday was the night of the first Canada-Soviet hockey game in Montreal. Stanfield attended the game, stayed overnight, and went to Wagner's home on Sunday to confirm the campaign arrangements worked out by MacDonald. Stanfield was determined not to allow a repetition of the situation that occurred in 1968 when Marcel Faribault, his Quebec leader, ran an independent and at times embarrassing campaign. Stanfield insisted that it had to be a team approach this time. The "Stanfield-Wagner" campaign in Quebec reflected his desire. Wagner was to be the first among the Quebec candidates, but Stanfield was the leader. At Stanfield's insistence, the party pumped a disproportionately large (in view of the results) share of its campaign funds into Quebec – $1.2 million. (They won only two seats, Wagner's and Heward Grafftey's, surely making them the most costly pair of seats in Canadian political history.)

No sooner had Wagner announced his candidacy than rumours began to spread. According to these rumours, the Conservatives had "bought" the judge by guaranteeing him a huge cash settlement if he failed to win a seat or if the Conservatives failed to win the election. The rumours varied, but the most persistent one in Ottawa was that the Tories had agreed to pay Wagner three hundred thousand dollars over ten years. There was, and is, no evidence to suggest the rumours were anything more than rumours; everyone who might have been in a position to know about a deal denies there was one. "I would that it were so," says Wagner with a laugh. But the rumours, coupled with Wagner's change in political allegiance from Liberal to Conservative, hurt both him and the party. "People," says Wagner, "said of me, 'Well, he's been a Liberal and a judge and now he's a Conservative. He must be doing it because there is something in it for him.' We didn't have time to convince them that wasn't the case."

Wagner seriously overestimated his own popularity in the province; he also made the basic error of taking it for granted that people who had liked him as a Liberal would still like him as a Conservative. Thinking he could mount a swing no matter when he entered, he left his entry far too late. By the time he became a candidate, the Tories' Quebec campaign organization, such as it was, was in place. Wagner had to live with it and with the candidates it had nominated.

Although Claude Wagner did not enable the Conservatives to establish the base they needed in Quebec – they declined both in terms of seats and popular vote – he did help make the party more creditable in other parts of the country by creating an illusion of strength in Quebec where, in fact, no strength existed. Brian Mulroney grins at the memory: "Wagner helped us a lot in the West because no one knew how weak we really were here until the votes were counted. He scared the shit out of the Liberals for the first four weeks."

Stanfield had less luck with one of the big-name Conservatives of Ontario than he had with Wagner, the big-name Liberal in Quebec. Before the election was called, Stanfield and Finlay MacDonald went to Toronto where they invited former Premier John Robarts to join them for breakfast in Stanfield's hotel suite. They asked Robarts to serve as chairman of a small committee to find outstanding candidates for ridings in the Toronto area. Robarts agreed, the committee was established, and an official was designated to co-ordinate the committee's work, arrange lunches with prospective candidates, and look after other practical details (including picking up the lunch tabs). The committee collapsed, however, because the others could never reach Robarts to notify him of meetings. One disappointed Conservative estimates that as many as six prominent persons in the Toronto area could have been persuaded to run for the Tories with a bit of a push from a man of Robarts' stature.

Robarts also agreed tentatively to make a number of appearances on Stanfield's behalf, both in Ontario and elsewhere. He showed up only once, and that by accident. Robarts was in Thunder Bay on business when he heard Stanfield was in town campaigning; he dropped in at a Tory reception to offer one of the most laconic endorsations on record: "Ontario needs Bob Stanfield." "I'm afraid," says a man close to the situation, "that John Robarts is a spent force."

Although Robarts would have been useful to Stanfield, particularly in candidate recruitment, the loss was more than offset by the discovery of a new, more potent ally. That ally was William Davis, the former education minister who had succeeded Robarts as provincial leader and premier in 1971. Although their styles are very different, Davis and Stanfield are alike in one important way: both are party men. They both take the view that a Conservative in provincial politics must also be a Conservative at the federal level, and *vice versa,* and that a good Conservative works for his party in elections at both levels. In the federal election of 1972, Davis worked as hard for Stanfield as Stanfield, in his days as Premier of Nova Scotia, used to work for John Diefenbaker. Davis appeared at Stanfield's side at rallies in points as far scattered as Oakville, Calgary, and Saint John.

Davis' landslide victory in the provincial election of October, 1971 was quite possibly the most important development in the Conservative Party between the federal elections of 1968 and 1972. Following that victory, Malcolm Wickson – who had worked for Davis in the campaign – revised his federal campaign plans to incorporate lessons learned in the Ontario election. There were three key man in Stanfield's campaign organization: his own man, Finlay MacDonald, as chairman; the national director, Liam O'Brian, also a Stanfield man, as chairman of organization; and Wickson, now both a Stanfield and a Davis man, as chairman of operations. Wickson established his operations headquarters in Toronto and filled it with veterans of the Davis organization. One Davis man was put in charge of the Stanfield tour; another travelled with Stanfield as on-tour manager; a third acted as a press officer to Stanfield. Several Davis men ran Stanfield's advertising and a Davis girl took charge of the "Stanfield Girls" – the red-jacketed, blue-skirted, local girls who materialized at each stop on the Stanfield itinerary. Davis even loaned Stanfield the six-member band that he had used in the provincial campaign. Called "Jalopy," the band flew with Stanfield throughout the campaign and warmed up the crowds at his rallies. Whenever he went mainstreeting, "Jalopy" marched ahead of him drawing people into the streets with the Stanfield song: "There's a New Way Coming."

Although Stanfield's success in the 1972 campaign was popularly attributed to Davis' "Big Blue Machine," it is a moot question whether Stanfield was using Davis' organization or whether Davis was simply returning, with interest, the organization he had borrowed from Stanfield for use in the 1971 Ontario election. Most of the key personnel in the provincial campaign, from Dalton Camp and his brother-in-law, Norman Atkins, on down, had been long-time members of the Stanfield machine.

Either way, the infusion of talent from the Ontario machine enabled Stanfield to run every bit as slick and crisp a federal campaign as the Liberals. Using a DC-9 identical to Trudeau's, Stanfield arrived at places on time, entered meetings on cue, made his short speeches, then waded into the crowd to shake hands. Good organization alone does not win elections, but it gave the Stanfield campaign an aura of confidence and professionalism, something it had sadly lacked in 1968.

The improvements in the campaign organization rubbed off on Stanfield. He appeared to be a different man, more relaxed, more confident of his ability to hold an audience's interest, and harder hitting. Although he was still not an exciting politician, he found that if he worked at it he could generate a measure of enthusiasm in his crowds.

His strategy was carefully thought out and developed. Until the final two weeks of the campaign, he concentrated on attacking the Government and exposing its weaknesses. His aim was to force Trudeau to go on the defensive, to make him try to justify his government's record, particulary on economic questions. Then, in the last two weeks, Stanfield switched his emphasis to talk more about the sort of alternative policies the Conservatives would offer. But he made the switch too late. Although he succeeded in making the public question the performance of the Liberal Government, he ran out of time before he could convince the voters that he would make a better prime minister than Trudeau.

Stanfield received a substantial assist in undermining the Government's credibility from David Lewis, the leader of the NDP. Lewis waged the most effective campaign of all the party leaders by concentrating almost exclusively on a single issue. It was what he called the "corporate rip-off." Lewis challenged the Liberals' tax policies that, he argued, benefitted big business through tax concessions and incentive grants at the expense of the individual taxpayer. His assault on these so-called "corporate welfare bums" was the most telling attack of the election campaign. Ironically, the Conservatives probably benefitted more from Lewis' campaign than did the NDP. Lewis "loosened" thousands of government votes by causing Liberal supporters to question seriously the Government's policies. Once loosened, these votes were swept up by the Conservatives who, the public realized, were the only party that had a chance to replace the Liberals.

The Liberal campaign was a mystery. It seemed to lack direction, focus, and content. The Prime Minister moved about the country at a stately pace, pausing frequently to tend to what his itinerary called "government business," although in most cases that was merely a euphemism for a rest break. Although he had said at the beginning that the Liberals would have no election slogan, one soon appeared. "The Land is Strong" was the Liberal rallying cry. (Somehow it seemed more appropriate to a fertilizer company than to a political party.) Trudeau still drew large crowds almost everywhere he went, even packing seventeen thousand people into Toronto's Maple Leaf Gardens late in the campaign. But the mood was different. Whereas crowds had turned out in 1968 to demonstrate their approval of Trudeau, they turned out in 1972, uncommitted and unconvinced, to hear what he had to say and to speculate on whether the old magic had vanished or was simply under wraps. In many ways, the voter of 1972 was a different voter than the voter of 1968. He was worried about the problems of his country, about unemployment, inflation, taxation, and the seemingly limitless spending on welfare and unemployment insurance. He feared that somehow the country had gone awry in the preceding four years; nothing the Liberals could say in defence of their record could assuage that fear. Trudeau harmed his own cause when he announced the Government would have "goodies" or "candies" for everyone, then proceeded to trot out an array of promises that smelled more of pork than of candy. There would be a new wharf for Yarmouth, N.S. (where the Liberals thought they could win a seat), improved harbour facilities for Halifax, a massive federal subsidy for the short take-off and landing (STOL) aircraft project, and even a thirty-million-dollar eighty-acre national park for downtown Toronto (where the Liberals were fighting to hold their eighteen seats). "So blatant was the distribution of goodies," commented *Time,* "that they raised the possibility of Canada's first pork-barrel backlash." The Trudeau who had appealed to Canadians four years earlier as the apostle of the New Politics seemed to have become the cynical practitioner of the old.

Trudeau's troubles played into Stanfield's hands because it meant that Stanfield could fight the campaign on the issues. He promised to reduce income taxes to stimulate employment, to remove the capital gains tax on family farms so that farmers would be able to leave their property to their sons, and to impose temporary wage and price controls, if necessary, to curb inflation. In another anti-inflation proposal, he reiterated his intention to introduce a "Constant Dollar" tax scheme – under which the taxpayer would be taxed only on the real increase in his income, not on the portion attributable to inflation. He promised a three hundred million dollar "Canadian Investment Credit Incentive" plan to give tax credits for investments in small, Canadian-owned businesses. He proposed to create a ministry of state to co-ordinate the economic planning of all government departments – so that, for example, one department would not be closing an airbase in a town while another department was trying to create jobs in the same town by subsidizing the establishment of a plastics factory. He said he would turn over to the provinces 100 per cent of the proceeds of offshore mineral rights, recognize the aboriginal claims and treaty rights of the native peoples, declare "unqualified Canadian sovereignty" over the waters of the Arctic, and require his cabinet ministers to disclose their personal holdings. The fiercely Liberal *Toronto Daily Star* was sufficiently impressed by the new look of the Conservative Party – and distressed by Trudeau – that it gave its editorial blessing to the Tories for the first time in its history. Meanwhile, *The Globe and Mail* rejected Stanfield in favour of Trudeau, as it had in 1968, although it was kinder to Stanfield personally in disowning him than the *Star* was in embracing him.

The Stanfield style changed as the campaign unfolded. He stopped worrying about being fair to the Liberals; he hammered away at the flaws in their performance. Stanfield sensed the mood of conservatism that seemed to grip the nation in the autumn of 1972. If the Quiet Canadian of the pre-Centennial years had become the Confident Canadian in 1968, by 1972 he had become the Concerned Canadian. Everywhere Stanfield went in the campaign, he came across people who were worried that the country was drifting aimlessly. They were disturbed about people who would not work, people who preferred to live on welfare or on unemployment insurance rather than do a day's work. Everyone, it seemed, knew someone who could not find people to work in his factory, pump gas in his filling station or help on his farm. The work ethic seemed to be eroding and the Government appeared to be unconcerned. Stanfield went to great lengths to draw a distinction between the attitude of his party and that of the Liberal Party toward the work ethic. "In our party," he told a rally in Medicine Hat, "we believe a job is a social need, not just an economic proposition. A job is more important than that to the individual. Just ask an individual who has lost one."

He was still no orator, but he did manage the occasional flight of near-eloquence. He was at his best one day in September when he addressed an open-air meeting of fifteen hundred people, mostly elderly, in Centennial Square in Victoria, the geriatric capital of Canada. Although his words seem almost trite on paper, they had a moving quality when he delivered them, from notes, that sunny noon-hour in Victoria. "Let me tell you something about the kind of Canada I would like to live in, the kind of Canada I would like to see my children inherit, and their children after them," he said slowly. "It would be a country in which the accident of birth did not mark a child for life, where the very fact of life will be sanctified, celebrated. It will be a country in which the very fact of birth will bring with it the right to acceptance and love, the right of a child to grow at his own pace, the right of an opportunity to satisfy his curiosity about the things around him, the right to live up to the full capacity of his understanding. It will be a country in which freedom of thought, freedom of expression, freedom of movement, freedom of determination will be available to all our citizens. It will be a country whose people are governed responsibly and gently by men and women who truly wish to serve the common weal, a country in which to fulfil man's most profound aspirations and to live his finest dreams, a country in which people can grow old without fear."

His remarks were perfectly pitched to his audience. When he finished, a crowd followed him down the street, clustering about him whenever he stopped. A group of excited old ladies surrounded him in the middle of a busy intersection and they would not move until Stanfield chided them lightly: "Come ladies. Get off the street or you'll get run over. We wouldn't want that to happen just before the election."

Stanfield was in no danger of becoming a humourist, but he at least abandoned the tired collection of Nova Scotia jokes that he had clung to in the 1968 campaign. Perhaps his best line in 1972 was one he used several times: "I truly believe the time has come in this country for us to have a truly charismatic leader of the opposition. I've brought myself to accept the switch and I don't see why either I or Prime Minister Trudeau should stand in the way of the desires of the people." He was funniest in spontaneous situations. Main-streeting in Kenora in Northern Ontario, he was stopped by a drunk who shook his hand, then stuck out his palm for money. Stanfield turned to avoid that encounter, only to bump into a woman who looked him up and down and announced: "I hear Stanfield's in town." Not at all taken aback, Stanfield replied dryly: "I'm afraid I'm here, ma'am." In another Northern Ontario town, Espanola, the mayor told him proudly: "If you fired a gun down the main street here, you could hit a person of any nationality." "I want to assure you that I have no intention of shooting a gun down the street and hitting anyone," Stanfield said. "The fellow I'm after doesn't live here!"

The fellow he was after, Pierre Trudeau, had cause for concern as the campaign raced into its final weeks. In dramatic contrast to the half-empty halls that had yawned at him in 1968, Stanfield was drawing overflow crowds almost everywhere he went. That was partly the result of better organization and partly because the public seemed to want to get a look at him, to take his measure. In Calgary on a Sunday night, he drew forty-five hundred to an auditorium that seated only twenty-six hundred. One thousand wedged into a six-hundred-seat hall in Moose Jaw; there were five thousand in Saint John and seventeen hundred in little Penticton, B.C.

As the campaign neared election day, Trudeau, his hopes of a great triumph fading, began to warn the people of the danger of electing a minority government. It was a sure sign that the Liberals knew they were in trouble; the Tories were ecstatic. Their spirits soared even higher a week and a half before the election when Robert Teeter delivered a new Conservative poll that showed that the gap between the Liberals and the Conservatives – ten points at the outset of the campaign – had narrowed to just four points. Because of distribution of voters between rural and urban ridings, the Conservatives calculated that they could run three percentage points below the Liberals and match them in seats. All at once, a minority Conservative Government seemed to be within reach.

Stanfield started to sound as though he really believed what he had been predicting for several weeks: that the election would return a Tory Government. "I'm encouraged as I've never been encouraged before," he said in Moose Jaw. "There is a tide running here that indicates victory for us next Monday. One Government is on the way out this week and a new government, a Progressive Conservative Government, is on the way in next week."

Relaxing on his DC-9 a few days before election day, he assessed his campaign. "I think it was very important that we succeed in identifying Mr. Trudeau with the problems of the country, and I think we've done that," he said. "We have done that thanks to the problems in the unemployment insurance system, and to the unemployment and cost of living statistics. People are looking at us more and more." He said he recognized that the mood of the public, though restive, was not yet clear. The people were dissatisfied with the Government, but it was by no means certain that they would decide to trade the Liberals for the Conservatives. "In Nova Scotia in 1956, there were about ten seats that no honest man could say who would win," said Stanfield. "I feel something is going on in the country. I don't know how far it will go."

He still did not know when he flew back to Halifax to cast his ballot on election day and to wait for the verdict. It was sixteen years to the day since he had come to power in Nova Scotia.

The voters did not know either, and in their uncertainty they rendered one of the most confused judgments in the history of national politics.

Robert Stanfield watched, perplexed, as the results came in on election night. As expected, the Conservatives held the Atlantic Provinces, although they dropped two seats in Newfoundland and one in Prince Edward Island. But Quebec was a disaster. The Tories had prayed for eight to ten of the province's seventy-four seats; they barely won two, and they slipped behind the Social Credit Party into third place in popular vote. The rest of the country exceeded Stanfield's wildest hopes as the Conservatives registered dramatic gains across the Prairies and in British Columbia. Ontario was the key. Just four years earlier, the Conservatives had given their worst display in history, winning only seventeen of Ontario's eighty-eight seats. This time, with an assist from the Davis machine, they won forty seats. The Liberals tumbled from sixty-four seats to thirty-six. Pierre Trudeau's hopes of returning with a majority government, or even with a fairly safe minority government, died in the bustling cities, the sleepy towns, and the gentle countryside of Ontario.

264

Stanfield did not know what to make of the results. The lead changed hands repeatedly in the course of the long evening. At times, the Liberals were one or two seats ahead; at others, the Tories had a lead of a seat or two. The Conservatives pulled close to the Liberals in popular vote – 35.1 per cent to the Grits' 38.5 per cent; they proved they could win in the cities and among the young. They defeated the Liberals both in seats and popular vote in every province except Quebec. In English Canada, Stanfield had a clear mandate to form a government. He had no mandate at all in French Canada. Finally, he went home to bed, telling his supporters on the way that he was prepared to form a government. Characteristically, he attached a note of caution. "I think," he said, "we should wait and see what the morning brings."

The morning brought no clarity. The Conservatives appeared to have won the election by a seat or two. The counts, however, were still unofficial, and the results in some ridings were so close that they would have to be decided by judicial recounts. Stanfield was disappointed, but not surprised or disheartened when Trudeau announced that he would remain in office. When the election tabulations were complete, they supported Trudeau's decision; the Twenty-Ninth Parliament would have 109 Liberals, 107 Conservatives, 31 New Democrats, 15 Social Crediters, and 2 Independents.

"I'm tired," Stanfield admitted to members of his staff. He went home to "Stornoway" to rest, to plan and to think about the next election, and to write letters of gratitude to people who had campaigned for him and who had brought him to the very threshold of power. One of those letters was to Finlay MacDonald, the member of his Maritime Mafia who had worked for him in Nova Scotia, had helped convince him to seek the federal leadership, and had come to Ottawa to run the 1972 election campaign. Now Stanfield wanted to persuade MacDonald to remain in Ottawa as his chief of staff and to help him start building for the new election that could not be far in the future.

"You may consider this a little formal," Stanfield wrote, "but I was brought up properly and in any event I do wish to thank you profusely for all your help during the past year, and especially during the campaign, although I am not sure when it began or when it will end. Of course, I recognize that since you talked me into my present insane course some five years ago, it is only just that you should share some of the delirium, but you have probably had more than your share during 1972. My own capacity for accepting madness is now virtually unlimited – after five years – and I may soon be ready for the ultimate – trying to run this country – which you have almost achieved for me.

"In any case you have brightened, lightened, and heightened a very difficult and exciting challenge for me. I thank you for all you have done, and in particular for your friendship. No dog ever needed it more. I should be ashamed to ask more of you, but after all this country is worth saving.

                                          Sincerely,
                                          Bob."

Index

Blake, Edward 14
Blois, Fred 19, 21-22, 23, 24, 113, 184
Bloomingdale's 142
Board of Trade (Halifax) 139
Borden, Sir Robert 4, 18, 19, 209
Bosky, Bennett 36
Boston, Massachusetts 36, 118, 202
Bourassa, Robert 255, 256
Bracken, John 47
Bracken House 77
Bradford, England 15
Bridgetown, N.S. 96
Bridgewater, N.S. 109
British Army 23
British Columbia 3, 214, 226, 254, 264
British Labour Party 79, 139
British North America Act 14
Brockville, Ontario 187
Brookfield, N.S. 131
Browning, Robert 141
Brownridge, Earl 214, 226
Bruce, Harry 25
Burns and Roe 151, 152, 153

Calgary 220, 223, 259, 263
Cambridge, Massachusetts 35
Cambridge University 31
Camp, Dalton Kingsley 8, 25, 27, 40, 54, 55-59, 67, 72, 73, 74, 75, 76, 77, 78, 79, 81, 82, 87, 91, 92, 99, 100, 101, 114, 119, 123, 134, 139, 144, 156, 159, 160, 161, 163, 164, 165, 166, 167, 168, 169, 170, 171, 173, 174, 176, 177, 178, 179, 180, 181, 182, 183, 184, 185, 187, 188, 191, 193, 195, 196, 206, 207, 213, 214, 222, 225, 226, 228, 229, 231, 236, 259

Camp, Linda 176
Canada Cement 131
Canada Games 75
Canada Packers 129
Canadian Club (Montreal) 159
Canadian General Electric 150, 153, 156
Canadian Institute of International Affairs 185
Canadian Junior College (Lausanne) 204
Canadian Motor Industries Ltd. (C.M.I.) 131, 143, 147
Canadian National Exhibition 216
Caouette, Réal 3, 256
Cape Breton, N.S. 45, 62, 67, 68, 72, 76, 83, 94, 98, 100, 103, 107, 109, 115, 124, 134, 141, 143, 150, 151, 155
Cape Breton North 99, 149
Cape Breton Post 149
Cape Breton South 72, 76
Castonguay, Claude 256
C.C.F.
   (*See* New Democratic Party)
Cemp Investments 153
Chamberlain, Neville 36
Champagne, Gilbert 209
Chancery Club 36
Charles River, Massachusetts 36
Chateau Laurier Hotel (Ottawa) 55, 79, 81, 168, 174, 207
Chesapeake, The 109
Chester, N.S. 46, 64, 131
Chicoutimi 187
China 243
CHNS 72
Chouinard, Julien 214, 215, 226
Christie, Lou 24
Chronicle-Herald, The 72, 107, 133, 134, 149, 167, 184

186, 209, 218, 219, 220, 223, 226, 233, 236, 240, 254, 255, 264, 265
Quebec City 9, 227

Ralliement des Créditistes (*See* Social Credit Party)
Rankin, R.J. "Bob" 48
Rasminsky, Louis 211, 212
Rassemblement pour l'indépendence nationale (R.I.N). 222
Reardon, Henry 99, 123, 124
Regan, Gerald 62, 66, 85, 106, 110, 114, 119, 124, 135, 137, 138, 156
Regina 227
Regina East 214
Regional disparity 6, 8
Reid, Alfred 98
Reilly, Peter 2
Rheaume, Gene 82, 207, 225
Ricard, Théogène 209, 226, 256
Riel, Louis 220
Ritchie, Roland 48
Rivière-du-Loup 215
Robarts, John 79, 158, 161, 170, 171, 173, 215, 216, 258
Robertson's Point, N.B. 55, 173, 176, 177, 180, 181, 182
Robichaud, Louis 136
Roblin, Duff 58, 78, 79, 158, 161, 171, 172, 173, 175, 178, 180, 182, 186, 187, 188, 191, 192, 193, 194, 195, 214, 215, 226
Rockcliffe Park (Ottawa) 28
Roman Catholics 63, 72, 83, 84, 92, 94, 99, 107
Roosevelt, Franklin 29, 36
Royal Bank of Canada 41
Royal York Hotel (Toronto) 187, 188, 189
Ryan, Claude 190, 226

276

Ryan, Yves 214
Rynard, P.B. 226

Sackville, N.S. 96
St. Catharines 227, 245
St. Croix 15
St. Croix Woollen Mills 15
St. Francis Xavier University 72, 183, 207
Saint-Hyacinthe 256
St. Jean Baptiste Day 222
Saint John, N.B. 259, 263
St. John's, Nfld. 239
St. John's Anglican Church 16, 22
St. Laurent, Louis 55
Salmon River, N.S. 15
Saskatchewan 148, 150, 214, 220, 226, 232
Saskatoon 220, 234
Saturday Night 213
Saulnier, Lucien 256
Sault Ste. Marie 227
Sawka, Mary Walker 187, 192
School of Library Science (Toronto) 202
Schreyer, Edward 234
Schumacher, Stan 229
Scott, Graham 241, 243, 255
Selkirk riding 234
Shanghai 243
Shannon, H.M.S. 109
Sharp, Mitchell 58
Shaw, Ralph 68, 86, 87-88
Shaw, Walter 58, 78, 81, 158
Shelburne, N.S. 166; 167
Shell Oil Company 88
Sherbrooke, N.S. 227
Sherwood, Cyril 180
Simcoe, Ontario 245
Simenon, Georges 205
Simpson, Robert 229, 231

278